Finding the Right Place
on the Map
Central and Eastern European Media
Change in a Global Perspective

Finding the Right Place on the Map
Central and Eastern European Media Change in a Global Perspective

Edited by Karol Jakubowicz and Miklós Sükösd

This publication is supported by COST.

intellect Bristol, UK / Chicago, USA

First Published in the UK in 2008 by
Intellect Books, The Mill, Parnall Road, Fishponds, Bristol, BS16 3JG, UK

First published in the USA in 2008 by
Intellect Books, The University of Chicago Press, 1427 E. 60th Street, Chicago,
IL 60637, USA

A catalogue record for this book is available from the British Library.

Cover Design: Gabriel Solomons
Copy Editor: Holly Spradling
Typesetting: Mac Style, Beverley, E. Yorkshire

ISBN 978-1-84150-193-2

Printed and bound by Gutenberg Press, Malta.

Neither the COST Office nor any person acting on its behalf is responsible
for the use which might be made of the information contained in this
publication. The COST Office is not responsible for the external websites
referred to in this publication.

European Communication Research and Education Association (ECREA)

This series consists of books arising from the intellectual work of ECREA members. Books address themes relevant to the ECREA's interests; make a major contribution to the theory, research, practice and/or policy literature; are European in scope; and represent a diversity of perspectives. Book proposals are refereed.

Series Editors
Nico Carpentier
François Heinderyckx

Series Advisory Board
Denis McQuail
Robert Picard
Jan Servaes

The aims of the ECREA are

a) To provide a forum where researchers and others involved in communication and information research can meet and exchange information and documentation about their work. Its disciplinary focus will include media, (tele)communications and informatics research, including relevant approaches of human and social sciences;
b) To encourage the development of research and systematic study, especially on subjects and areas where such work is not well developed;
c) To stimulate academic and intellectual interest in media and communication research, and to promote communication and cooperation between members of the Association;
d) To co-ordinate the circulation of information on communications research in Europe, with a view to establishing a database of ongoing research;
e) To encourage, support and, where possible, publish the work of young researchers in Europe;
f) To take into account the desirability of different languages and cultures in Europe;
g) To develop links with relevant national and international communication organizations and with professional communication researchers working for commercial organizations and regulatory institutions, both public and private;
h) To promote the interests of communication research within and among the Member States of the Council of Europe and the European Union;
i) To collect and disseminate information concerning the professional position of communication researchers in the European region; and
j) To develop, improve and promote communication and media education.

CONTENTS

TWELVE CONCEPTS REGARDING MEDIA SYSTEM EVOLUTION AND DEMOCRATIZATION IN POST-COMMUNIST SOCIETIES

Karol Jakubowicz and Miklós Sükösd

The present book is a contribution to the effort to take stock of changes in media systems in post-communist society, as well as of the scholarly debate on the subject. Of course, it is not yet possible to formulate final and definitive views on either topic, given both the enormous scope of the process of change after 1989, and the fact that that process is far from finished. Nevertheless, several strong themes concerning the nature and effects of the process emerge from the papers included in the book. What sets the present book apart from much of the literature on the subject is its comparative perspective, placing developments in post-communist countries in a much broader context. Perhaps for the first time, Central and Eastern European media scholars are willing to take a cold, critical look at other media systems and assess what is happening in their own region also by reference to processes unfolding elsewhere.

Since the collapse of the communist system in 1989 to 1991, Central and Eastern European societies[1] have been overtaken by a process of change that is perhaps of unprecedented magnitude and complexity in modern world history. This has involved "triple"[2] or "quadruple"[3] post-communist transformation, as well as (in addition to, but also in tandem with, or as a result of, transformation), modernization, globalization and international integration, including particularly (for selected post-communist countries) accession into the European Union. In this introductory essay,[4] we try to outline twelve conceptual frames that may help to capture the key features of this deep and many-sided transformation, with a special focus on changing media systems in the post-communist world. As Sparks notes in his contribution to this volume, traditional "transitology" is in crisis. No coherent theory of the process unfolding in post-communist countries has emerged to replace it, nor indeed is expected to emerge. Therefore, our intention here is quite modest: to point to key aspects of the process in the hope that this will contribute to better understanding of its complexity.

1. Media as a key area of systemic change: spillover effects

Media system change is, of course, part and parcel of the general process of what may be called systemic social transformation. McQuail (2005) describes the media system as the actual set of mass media in a given national society, characterized by such main dimensions as scale and centralization, degree of politicization, diversity profile, sources of finance and degree of public regulation and control. Each system is also characterized by certain organizing principles expressed in what Merrill and Lowenstein (1979) call a "philosophy" of the press system as well as in a set of normative goals the system is intended to pursue. These, in turn, reflect the given society's general circumstances and its view of the media, resulting in its media policy. Media system change results from changes in both these cultural (cognitive, conceptual) and structural (policy, economic, institutional etc.) factors.

According to liberal theories of democratic state, such as those of John Stuart Mill, democracy is unthinkable without freedom of speech, freedom of press and freedom of association. Accordingly, media freedom is generally seen today as a necessary precondition of democracy – and vice versa. This volume confirms that the media are both an independent and a dependent variable in democratic development. Much is made in the literature of the need for an "enabling environment" for media freedom and contribution to democracy. What, however, if the social, political and economic environment is less than favourable and "enabling"? In the present volume, Bajomi-Lazar looks at the prerequisites for consolidation of media freedom, while Sparks, Mungiu-Pippidi, Jakubowicz and Gross analyse the reasons why in post-communist countries the media often operate in a "disabling environment".

To perform its functions, the media have to fulfill a number of expectations and provide a number of services for democracy. Gurevitch and Blumler (1990) list eight key expectations regarding the democratic performance of the media:

- Surveillance of the socio-political environment, reporting developments likely to impinge, positively or negatively, on the development of citizens;
- Meaningful agenda setting, identifying the key issues of the day, including the forces that have formed and may resolve them;
- Platforms for an intelligible and illuminating advocacy by politicians and spokespersons of other causes and interest groups;
- Dialogue across a diverse range of views, as well as between power holders (actual and prospective) and mass publics;
- Mechanisms for holding officials to account for how they have exercised power;
- Incentives for citizens to learn, choose and become involved, rather than merely followed and kibitz over the political process;
- A principled resistance to the efforts of forces outside the media to subvert their independence, integrity and ability to serve the audience;
- A sense of respect for the audience member as potentially concerned and able to make sense of his or her political environment.

We should remember, however, that at the beginning of the post-communist transformation, mass publics did not have much or, indeed any, experience of democracy. Democratic change in 1989 to 91 started after 40 to 45 years, or over 70 years of communist rule (in Central Europe, Soviet domination began between 1945 to 1949, and in the Soviet Union the communists took over in 1917). One should add that most countries in Central and South-Eastern Europe had *never* experienced fully developed democracies, as they had been run by authoritarian or semi-democratic regimes also in the pre-World War II period (the only exception probably being Czechoslovakia).

In this historical context, the media also performed particular roles that characterized the specific post-communist situation. As the political agenda of the early transformation period was dominated by democracy building (and also by nation-building in several countries), democratic expectations of the media included roles in related processes. In partial overlap with, but also adding specific demands to the list above, the media had to perform several specific roles in the post-communist media systems, as indeed in any young democracy. These included (Sükösd 1997/98, 2000):

- Introduction and legitimization of the concepts of democracy, rule of law and constitutionalism;
- Introduction and legitimization of the concepts of political pluralism, competition; and new political parties and candidates as legitimate competitors;
- Developing civil society by introducing NGOs and other civic groups as legitimate public actors;
- Democratic agenda setting and framing of current issues along the concepts above;
- Challenging the space and degree of transformation for further democratization;
- Safeguarding new democratic institutions;
- Exploring wrongdoing by old as well as new elites (e.g., investigative journalism) and covering socio-political scandals to define boundaries of acceptable conduct
- Developing accountability to citizens/viewers;
- Personalization of politics: introducing candidates and parties before the first democratic elections by applying criteria regarding democratic programs and personal skills;
- Democratic education regarding elections and voting procedures;
- Offer a space for democratic evaluation of national past (including the communist period and its leaders) and the discussion of historical justice;
- Contribution to national integration along democratic lines (in many newly formed countries, contribution to nation building);
- Democratic performance of the media as a contribution to the democratization of other sectors (media communication as a facilitator).

In the process of nurturing young democratic institutions and democratic citizenship, democratic performance of the media had an important impact on democratization in general, but also on its specific sectors. By covering issues of the day as well as longer term trends, media democratization often had *spillover effects* (or *trickle-down effects*) regarding democratization of particular institutions.

By framing stories and building agendas according to democratic criteria, media performance had the opportunity of shaping public opinion about concretes cases reinforcing rule of law both in politics and the economy. By uncovering wrongdoing and abuse of power, investigative reporters and political scandals in the media helped to set the norms of acceptable vs non-acceptable behaviour in new pluralist democracies (on the role of political and media scandals in defining socially acceptable norms of conduct, see Lull and Hinerman 1997; Markovits and Silverstein 1988). Insofar the media performed their democratic roles, they also contributed to the process of consolidation of democracy in all its five dimensions listed by Linz and Stepan (1996, 7–15).

2. The ontogenesis of democratic media institutions

Besides spillover effects, another relationship between democratization of media and systemic democratization may be captured by the metaphor of *ontogenesis*, introduced by Jakubowicz in his paper. The concept of ontogenesis in developmental biology captures "individual development of a living thing, all sequence of its transformations".[5] In other words, it means that every specimen of the species repeats in the course of its development all the stages of evolution that the entire species had gone through in the process of its philogenesis.

As the starting point of the transformation, the official Central and Eastern European media systems up to 1990 were characterized by a wide-ranging system of censorship overseen by Communist Party agencies, the monopoly of state broadcasting and exclusive state/party ownership of the press, party *nomenklatura* as media executives, and hegemonic propaganda content (Sükösd 2000).

Given this historical context, as Jakubowicz notes in his paper about public service media in the emerging democracies,

> Central and Eastern European countries are thus discovering that when they transplant an institution copied on Western patterns, they are in reality launching a process that will retrace the developments that ultimately led to its successful development elsewhere. They must therefore repeat – albeit probably in an accelerated form – the experience (and all the mistakes) that Western European countries went through before they were able to achieve something close to the desired results (PSB is strong and truly independent only in a few Western countries). It is almost like the process of ontogenesis in biology.

In a historical view of systemic transformation, the concept of ontogenesis may refer to the development of particular institutions of democracy, replicating (in whole or in part) the historical sequence of their earlier development in other societies. The institutional pattern of newly established and transplanted democratic media institutions may be seen as one in which democratic potentials are encoded. However, whether such potentials can be realized and the institutions can be utilized according to their basic principles remains subject to conflicts and particular conditions of their social, cultural and institutional embeddedness.

In Central and Eastern Europe, repeated media wars, i.e., continued struggle for media independence, have been characterizing media system transformation. In media wars, journalists, editors, their unions, media managers and civic groups fought in various coalitions with governments, oppositions, political and as well as business clans. Media wars and other similar developments can be seen as subsequent periods through which the ontogenesis of democratic media institutions proceeds.

Such media wars included fights by various clan media and several phases of struggle against central control and for independence in Russia and Ukraine from the 1990s; Hungarian media wars around public service broadcasting that became focal conflicts of political struggles (during the 1990s); a famous strike of public television personnel against government intervention in the Czech Republic (2000); similar recent developments in Slovakia; street protests against the persecution of the Rustavi-2 TV station in Georgia (October 2001); street protests in Moscow against the elimination of NTV, an independent TV station (2001); a campaign against changes in PSB law, threatening its political subordination in Slovenia (2005); protests in Poland against pressure being put on public and independent media and against ultimately unsuccessful attempts to vet journalists for possible history of collaboration with communist-time secret police, with the threat that they would be banned from the journalistic profession for ten years if they refused to submit to this (2005–2007).

All this has had the effect of qualifying the role and impact of the media on the democratization process, as they were caught up in a struggle against what we have called "the disabling environment".

As Hungarian sociologist Elemér Hankiss, first president of Hungarian television in the post-communist period, notes about resistance to repeated attempts by authoritarian leaders in his country's media war,

> In their stubborn fight for autonomy, Hungarian Television and Radio became the major actors of a society protesting against and authoritarian efforts of the government.... [We] had to learn that democracy cannot be... established overnight by a first and free election. It may be generated only in the course of a long and tedious process in which everybody has to take part and has to take up his or her responsibilities...The facts that two fragile public institutions, which could rely only on the letter and spirit of the law, were able to protect their newly won autonomy against extremely strong pressures and attacks from the government and the governing parties proves that all the main political actors observed, at least until the last act, the rule of law, and have accepted the basic rules of the democratic game.

In this sense, ontogenesis refers to a long societal learning process, with all the attendant crises and conflicts, in which democratic rules ultimately become accepted "as the only game in town" and respect for media independence finally wins the day. The legal and institutional framework for that may exist on paper, but political and cultural preconditions needed to safeguard it take a long time to develop.

Media institutions are exceptional organizations as they are very visible and by nature occupy central positions in their respective countries' communication system. When media executives openly resist prime ministers' and presidents' attempts to exert control over national television and radio, their resistance, supported by journalists, editors, civic groups and public intellectuals, becomes not only well known, but also sets an example and sends a message about legality and professional norms to audiences in all segments of society.

> It was an interesting exercise in learning about democracy. It was almost moving to see how governing party deputies, or at least some of them, struggled with their consciences—to see how they tried to squeeze their party interests (and their antipathies for this meddlesome television president) into the forms and straitjacket of legal rules. By that time, the whole country was watching. (Hankiss 275)

Eventually, Hankiss and many other media executives like him were removed in heavily disputed procedures, authoritarian actions of post-communist governments. Nevertheless, the ontogenesis of democratic media system continues through acts of professional and political resistance like his.

3. Political, market and social demands in post-communist media policy

In an empirical sense, the media in Central and Eastern European transformation only partially fulfilled the normative expectations listed above. The democratic performance of the media was largely up to media policies crafted by post-communist elites.

Raboy, Proulx and Dahlgren (2003) differentiate between "market demand" and "social demand" legitimation for media policy – in addition to official public policy, oriented to serve the public interest. While "market demand" conceptualizes public interest as "what the public is interested in", i.e. what the public is prepared to consume, "social demand" would allow for legitimation of types media/cultural policy which incorporate a fuller understanding of the public interest and its ties to the exercise of democratic cultural citizenship.

Media policy in all countries in Central and Eastern Europe has been a mix of the three types of approaches. The "public policy" orientation – though often serving political, rather than public interest objectives – predominated in the early period of most regimes, and in later periods of non-competitive, war-torn and authoritarian regimes. The "market demand" orientation strongly impacted media systems in competitive as well as concentrated political regimes. Several papers in this volume, e.g., those by Peruško and Popović, Hozic, Lauk and Baltyciene, illustrate the resulting commercialization of the media and impact of the market on media and journalism evolution. The "social demand" orientation made itself felt primarily in the competitive regimes.

However, we should highlight that all three logics have been continuously present in all countries and it is their relative strength that characterized specific systems in specific periods. Perhaps what differentiates the historical dynamics of post-communist regimes from other regimes types is the heavy impact of political demands in the early period, and then the emergence and relative strengthening of "market demands" and "social demands" in later parts of the transition, especially in competitive regimes.

A framework for analysis of communication policy-making should, at a minimum, encompass the various actors and their goals and objectives; the level at which policy is made (supra-national, national, regional etc.); the issues which preoccupy policy-makers most at any given time (resulting from general processes in the media and the challenges they pose); and the process by which policy is made (see Siune et al. 1986). Formulation of media policy involves several stages: identification of issues requiring action or resolution, policy analysis and choice of appropriate policy instruments, development of regulatory instruments (if required), usually involving consultation (at least in a democratic process of policy-making), implementation and evaluation.

We may distinguish several types of media or, more broadly, communication policy:

- Systemic media policy – formulated with a view to creating, maintaining or changing the overall shape of the media system;
- Sectoral media policy, oriented towards some sector of the media (e.g., broadcasting policy);
- Operational media policy, involving the resolution of issues arising within an already existing media system.

The task that all early post-communist societies faced was the formulation and implementation of systemic media policy, i.e., the development of a media system that differs fundamentally from media systems under communist rule. Within this overall systemic transformation (and usually only after the primary system had been set up), sectoral media policies were crafted. In that sense, several sectoral policies were hammered out or fine-tuned in what may be called a "second wave of media reform" that targeted specific tasks (e.g., the formation of community media policy or minority media policy) (Sükösd and Bajomi-Lázár 2002). Finally, operational media policy has been performed by the institutions that were set newly set up and started to function in a gradually consolidating fashion.

Of course, in democratic societies the aims of media regulation combine political and democratic with both cultural and economic objectives. Many of the former are public policy objectives and they may potentially clash with economic ones, including the encouragement of free choice and competition, facilitating exports and free trade, stimulating domestic and independent production and encouraging international competitiveness. The opposition between public policy and economic objectives may indeed be seen as the key dilemma of media policy. Accordingly, one of the fundamental choices to make in developing policy is between different forms of intervention into the media market, as types of regulation may range from minimal regulation through market-opening, industry-based (i.e., self- and co-regulation), market-correcting and up to market-overruling regulation (Thomas 1999). That, in turn, depends on the nature of the objectives being pursued and on the socio-ideological context within which policy is formulated.

4. The challenges: compressed waves of media change

Above, we used the metaphor of *ontogenesis* to describe a key aspect of media development in post-communist countries. This process also encompasses replication of the broader process of media system change in Europe and elsewhere in former communist countries where the media system was largely frozen for several decades in a form needed by the political system for its command and control purposes.

Kopper (2000) lists the following "spheres of change" in European media: technological change and convergence; progressive fusion of public and private spheres and of information and entertainment; commodification; changing structures and functions of the media; economics and financing; visuality, interactivity etc.

Another way of approaching analysis of the process of change in the history European media (and, to a degree, the history of democratic media systems in general) could be to list its particular elements and manifestations. The following list, seeking to arrange them in an approximate chronological order, is one attempt to identify those elements:

- "Media differentiation", or separation from government and/or political structures, began with the formation of the public sphere (i.e., Enlightenment journals) in the eighteenth century, continued with the gradual separation of independent press from party newspapers during the nineteenth century and the establishment of public service radio after WW I. Media differentiation was given a boost after WW II, but continued in the 1960s and 1970s in those Western European countries which still had state- or government-controlled broadcasting systems that were then transformed into public service ones.
- Professionalization of journalists involved a gradual shift from partisan roles to embracing objectivity and non-partisanship as central professional norms (during the twentieth century, in Western Europe particularly after WW II).
- Democratization promoted by a powerful movement in western media oriented to satisfying what was perceived as a general need to communicate and realize the right to communicate, to provide opportunities for social access to, and participation in running the media in Europe (in the 1960s and 1970s).
- Media decentralization, specialization and diversification, promoted by both a public-service- and a market-driven desire to identify and cater for social and interest groups, as

well as minorities inadequately served by mass-audience national media (from the 1960 to 70s).

■ Demonopolization, "deregulation" and liberalization of the broadcast media in the western world, resulting from the triumph of neo-liberalism (as exemplified by Thatcherism or Reaganomics) and involving a reduction of public interventionism into the media and abolition of state broadcasting monopoly, setting the stage for the emergence of a private sector of broadcasting in Western Europe (in the 1980s).

■ Commercialization of private and partly also public broadcast media as a result of subjecting them to liberalization and market laws as well as the increasing role of market realities in financing them (advertising, sponsorship, product placement) and in organizing them (e.g., market segmentation) in the 1980s.

■ Europeanization, i.e., the formation of a common European media market as a result of EU trade and media policies, the harmonization of some key aspects of television policy (EU regulation (Directive) and the emergence of major European media companies (from the late 1980s).

■ Concentration of media ownership at national and international scale, to be followed by the formation of dominant multinational media and telecommunication/digital media companies that control the whole value chain from production to distribution and merchandizing (especially from the 1990s).

■ Internationalization, transnationalization and globalization, both of content (especially of television, film and music) and in many cases of ownership and scale of operation, which in means globalization of some media conglomerates (from the 1990s).

■ Commercialization of content, including political news and other current affairs programmes (tabloidization, infotainment, human interest stories, new genres fusing popular culture and public affairs).

■ The emergence of and massive access to digital, interactive new media (the Internet and mobile communication technology) from the 1990s.

■ Digitalization and convergence with all their wide-ranging ramifications for the entire media system, economy and society (from 2000 onwards).

The dramatic feature of post-communist societies' media systems is that they faced, and partly performed or became subjected to, all these historical processes in an extremely compressed, short period of time. Many of these waves of change hit them immediately after communism fell, while others had deep impacts in the late 1990s and the early twenty-first century. If one were to list the main tendencies in media system evolution in post-communist countries, one could identify the following processes or clusters of complementary or contradictory processes:

■ Demonopolization and (partial) remonopolization
■ Commercialization and marketization of media systems (along with the rise of infotainment and tabloidization of political content)
■ Change as regards media freedom and independence
■ Democratization of media
■ Pluralization and diversity in the media
■ Professionalization of journalists
■ Development of public service broadcasting from state media
■ Internationalization, Europeanization and globalization of content and ownership

- ICT development and impact on the media
- Digitalization and convergence of media systems

Indeed, the two lists are very similar. The major changes in European (and, to a certain degree, global) media also later characterized media system evolution in post-communist countries. The challenges are the same; however, one may discern certain limited exceptionalism of post-communism in the speed (the historical time frame) of the process, and certain specific factors characteristic of post-communist regions (e.g., the relative lack of domestic capital, professional skills and democratic political culture).

The fact that commercialization and marketization are placed so high on the list of processes transforming media systems in post-communist countries may seem surprising. That they should play such a role certainly was not the intention either of the idealistic dissidents before the collapse of the communist system, nor of the policy-makers immediately after its demise. Nevertheless, as pointed out by a number of authors in this volume, it is the market forces which now provide most of the impetus for media evolution and change in post-communist countries, especially those where democracy is the strongest and societal conflicts (that always intensify political pressure on the media) have, to an extent, been contained and channelled in the political process.

5. The responses: idealistic, mimetic and atavistic orientations in media policy

How did post-communist societies, particularly media policy-makers, react to the compressed (and, at the same time, pressing) challenges that are listed above? One may identify three media policy orientations that contributed to shaping views on the new media order.

The first was the *"idealistic"* orientation. In line with the tendency of dissidents, underground democracy activists and democratic oppositions to think in terms antithetical to the communist system itself, this orientation assumed the introduction of a direct communicative democracy as part of a change of social power relations. This was promoted by the intellectual, cultural and later political opposition to the communist system, fascinated with western concepts of "access", "participation" and "social management" of the media. The idea was to implement the democratic participant press theory and create a media system based on the values of equality/justice and solidarity (McQuail 1992: 66–67), with a facilitative and dialectical/critical role for journalists (Nordenstreng 1997). While the concept of "public service broadcasting" may have appeared in this thinking, the real plan was to turn "state" into "social" broadcasting (i.e., directly managed and controlled by society).

Another strand within the idealistic orientation grew out of theorizing *samizdat*,[6] the self-published, underground literature that broke censorship and the official communication monopoly of the Communist Party. This independent communication network involved participation in an emerging public sphere in which authors and activists freely discussed matters of the public (Habermas 1989). The creation of a *samizdat* culture originated from the Soviet Union (Hollander 1972, 1975; Feldbrugge 1975; Meerson-Aksenov and Shragin 1977; Rubinstein 1980; Cohen 1982) with acts of exercising free personal and public expression and artistic freedom as human rights, and a desire to avoid censorship. Later, *samizdat* related to the socio-political idea of "self-limiting revolution", i.e., the strategy "civil society against the state" of the Polish opposition (Arato 1981), the idea of "parallel polis" by the Charta 77 movement in Czechoslovakia (Skilling 1989) and the idea of "second public" and "second society" in Hungary. Central concepts in this stream of thought included freedom of artistic and political expression (Haraszti 1988), freedom, independence and peacefulness of communication while the importance of institutions, markets and the state was downplayed. In terms of general political theory, this orientation related to a vision of non-authoritarian, self-managed civil society, particularly to the syndicalist features in the philosophy of the Solidarity trade union (Staniszkis 1984) and self-managing workers councils during the 1956 revolution in Hungary (Lomax 1976, 1990).

The strengths and, indeed, historical achievement of the "idealistic" orientation of media policy was the emphasis on freedom in general and freedom of speech and press in particular. The value of freedom helped to defy censorship, publish freely and to use independent social and political communication to organize democratic resistance against the party-state. *Samizdat* communication also introduced democratic discourses (most important, that of human rights), agendas and frames. However, the weakness of both strands of the "idealistic orientation" is their lack of institutional models, let alone a blueprint for the democratic transformation of "the official" media systems. This may be explained by the fact that basically up to 1989, nobody expected the sudden crash of Soviet type communism and the whole Yalta system (i.e., the end of communism in Central and Eastern Europe), so it seemed there was no need for such blueprints.

After the democratic breakthrough in 1989 to 91, the "mimetic" orientation in media policy was conceived as a way of achieving realistic and practical approximation to "the West", including full liberalization of the print media would and creation of a dual system of broadcasting. On the one hand, the "mimetic" orientation was dedicated to the pursuit of the goals of the public service phase of media policy development in Western Europe. Accordingly, influences on the "mimetic orientation" included the social responsibility press theory, a guardianship/stewardship role for the media, an administrative paradigm, service and democratic surveillance functions for journalists.

However, on the other hand, neo-liberal economists' arguments for a free market in general and for a free media market in particular prepared liberalization of the media market and the introduction of commercial broadcasting. Under the umbrella of the key terms of "westernization" and "Europeanization," public service enthusiasts and neo-liberal free market advocates forged an alliance in the "mimetic" orientation.

The third impact on the formation of the "mimetic" orientation was that of the European Union. Several societies and governments in the Central and Eastern European lands looked at EU membership as one of the major goals of post-communist transformation. During the long 1990s, when the EU conducted decade-long accession talks with national governments, "harmonization" with European standards became the key jargon, and the full transplantation of the *acquis communitaire* (the body of EU regulation) to national legislation became the key policy goal in several new democracies. Joining the EU meant that these countries had to comply with EU regulations (though in the media field as related to society and democracy the EU admits to relying primarily on Council of Europe standards), thus, "mimetic" could be understood literally in this sense. It is remarked by some analysts of normative media theories that no "post-communist media theory" has been developed. In these circumstances, it never had a chance to develop, as thinking outside the "EU box" was actively discouraged. It is only now that new, original thinking can emerge (though, of course, there is no certainty that it will, indeed, produce a new normative media theory).

In the typical political scene of the post-communist world, elites representing "westernization" and "Europeanization" discourses fought with nationalist and other counter-elites for domination. In the Central European and the Baltic States, "westernization" and "Europeanization" became dominant discourses (often, with some variation of democratic nationalism) right from the fall of communism, and then hegemonic discourses during the 1990s. In several former Yugoslav republics, post-communist elites adopted nationalist discourses that recently gave way to "westernization" and "Europeanization" discourses after years of ethnic wars and international marginalization.

The mimetic orientation focused on transplanting – in some aspects importing without any change – Western European media institutions and policy models assuming that they would work (in line with the institutional focus of transition and consolidation studies in mainstream political science). Few understood at the beginning of the transformation that social, political, cultural (and, in some cases, economic) prerequisites for the proper operation of independent and impartial media, including public service broadcasting organizations, did not really exist. During the last one and a half decades, however, that transplantation of the legal and institutional frameworks of PSB (and in a sense other democratic media as well) would have to be followed by a long period of development of the kind of political and journalistic culture required for PSB to be able to flourish.

One of the very clear messages of several papers in this volume (see those by Sparks, Jakubowicz, Gross, Hozic, Lauk, Balčytienė) is that of disappointment with "western models" and their applicability to post-communist countries, as well as with the ability of those countries successfully to adopt such models and breathe life into them. The strong impression is that the international community and organizations, as well as all the other western players involved in the process, presented to post-communist societies an unrealistic, idealized and wart-free image of "free and democratic" media and journalism to emulate, while the reality in their own countries may have been different. Jakubowicz shows that public service broadcasting in Mediterranean European countries is as distant from the ideal of independent public service media, as it is in post-communist countries.

The third orientation could be called "atavistic". What really emerged in post-communist countries after transition was not civil society but a political society, "partitocratic" systems of political and public life dominated, indeed, "colonized" by political parties. There is no doubt that the new power elites, while ostensibly accepting the "mimetic" orientation, in many cases sought to cling to any elements of the old command system they could still maintain. This, then, was a plan for a media system based, in different proportions, on social responsibility, paternal, development communication and authoritarian press theories, infused with different versions of nationalist discourse. All this served the pursuit of the value of "order" imposed from above, performing the functions of hegemony or guardianship.

In this model, journalists are expected to be "cooperative", i.e., guided by a sense of responsibility for the process of transformation and assist the government as the leader of the process, rather than exercise an independent, impartial and critical watchdog role. The same applied to public service broadcasting, if its introduction was proposed at all instead of the continued old state television and radio stations. In Russia, post-communist political and business clans used "westernization" and "Europeanization" discourses again communists and right-wing populists during the 1990s, to be replaced by a strong development state and nationalism discourse under President Putin whose administrations refused the mimetic orientation and implemented authoritarian media policies.

Since the "idealistic" orientation was immediately discontinued and rejected everywhere after the demise of the communist system, only the use of the other two orientations – usually some combination of both – remained a possibility for Central and Eastern European countries. One could say that in more democratic post-communist countries, mimetic elements dominate over atavistic ones, while in the less democratic ones, the reverse is true. We may observe several versions of this, a typical regional blend being political elites using "mimetic" discourses, while engaging in "atavistic" actions of behaviour.

Nevertheless, the contribution of Kaposi and Mátay in the present volume suggests that there may yet be hope for the "idealistic" media policy orientation which proposed a system of direct communicative democracy as a remedy for the ills of the command-and-control media system of the communist times. They show how Hungarian radicals were able to use the Internet and mobile phones at a time of violent street protests against the government in September-October 2006, completely bypassing the traditional media system, to express their views on social and political issues, to create an alternative public sphere and participate in ongoing political action. Formally, this was "semiotic democracy" in action, showing that new technologies offer grass-roots organizations and individuals a chance to practice direct communicative democracy. This may be a portent of future changes in the system of social communication and media policy.

Ironically, the radicals described by Kaposi and Mátay represented extreme right-wing populism, mystical monarchist nationalism, xenophobia and violent mobilization which was the opposite of "self-constrained revolution" strategy of civil society in the 1980s, or deliberative online democracy today (cf. Dahlgren 2002, 2003). Moreover, the contexts also differed completely: radical mobilization in 2006 took place against a constitutional state and a democratically elected government that enjoyed formal legitimation. Nevertheless, the concept of direct communicative democracy is a valuable contribution by the "idealistic" media policy orientation to the study of media democracy, civic cultures and interactive digital media networks today. Blogging represents the *samizdat* of the twenty-first century.

6. Factors of change: domestic vs international, structural vs cultural

Having outlined the international environment and orientations of post-communist media policy, we may want to locate systemic media transformation within the wider context of social transformation in Central and Eastern European societies. An attempt to create a model of systemic change in post-communist countries has yielded the following result (see Figure 1).

This model would need to be significantly developed in order fully to render the complexity of the process of post-communist transformation (see Jakubowicz 2007 for its further development). However, it will suffice as a starting point for our purposes.

Systemic social transformation encompasses a wide variety of processes, involved in the elimination of the communist legacy and in "triple" or "quadruple" transformation. Moreover, as post-communist countries are integrated into the European and global community, they are overtaken by global processes of political and economic change and come under ever stronger impact of external forces. Thus, developments in post-communist countries must be studied as resulting from the interplay of transformation, integration and globalization.

To this, we could add technological and economic change resulting from the onset of the Information Society. In this sense, transformation in Central and Eastern European countries comprises at least three sub-processes, adding up to accelerated social change (Figure 2).

As we try to identify enabling and limiting factors as far as media transformation is concerned, we may have to look at the set of interrelationships between processes of media change and key sectors of social change. The scheme below offers an outline of such an analysis, focusing on the role of political, economic and cultural conditions (Figure 3).

Figure 1: Institutionalization of Systemic Change

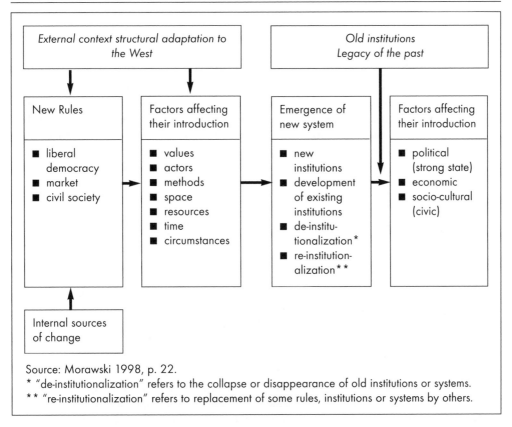

Source: Morawski 1998, p. 22.
* "de-institutionalization" refers to the collapse or disappearance of old institutions or systems.
** "re-institutionalization" refers to replacement of some rules, institutions or systems by others.

Looking at the historical dynamics of media change, it may also be important to explore the interplay of *cultural* vs *structural* factors. In the beginning of the transition period from 1989 to 1991, one may witness the key importance of cultural factors: cognitive patterns and value orientations of political and cultural elites (including democracy activists, public intellectuals,

Figure 2: Sub-processes of Social Change in Post-Communist Societies

Sub-process	Description
Elimination of communist legacy	Programme of managed (or partly managed) change serving to eliminate the communist legacy
"Triple" or "quadruple" transformation	State- and (where necessary) nation-building, economic and political reform and the consequences of these processes (e.g., operation of democracy, changes of government and policy; effects of economic growth etc.)
Response to global and European change	Involvement in processes of global and European integration, efforts to pursue informatization/digitalization, response to globalization etc.

Figure 3. Processes of Media Change as Influenced Key Areas of Society in Post-Communist Countries

I. Depending on political factors, the media can:	II. Politics, economy determine whether the media can:	III. Economy, market mechanism, techno-logical development favour or hinder:	IV. Cultural conditions and "cultural change" are required for:
Be deregulated and demonopolized Become pluralistic and open Be covered by a democratic legal framework Enjoy an enabling and effective policy for digitalization	Gain autonomy Decentralize Diversify in content Address minority groups Internationalize Promote professionalization of journalists	True removal of media monopoly Commercialization Concentration Globalization Tabloidization Development of ICTs and convergence	Non-existence or resolution of national and ethnic conflicts Depoliticization of media Rule of law Ability to define and serve the public interest Role for public opinion The media to serve as impartial watchdogs

reform-communists etc.) contributed greatly to the conceptualization of post-communist order, including its constitutional system and the formation of key political institutions (Bozóki 1999; Glenn 2001). This was a period of democratic planning, thus, patterns of thought and visions about democratic models by the key architects of post-communist societies as well as their foreign advisers played important roles (Glenn 1999). Such cultural capital was mobilized by in the face-to-face round-table negotiations between democracy activists and late communist elites (Bozóki 2001) and, even more importantly, the first democratically elected governments that passed "founding legislation" and policies that defined the patterns of post-communism. For a few years such cultural "framing power" could utilize structural opportunities (McAdam et al. 1996) that resulted from the unique historical environment, the fall of Soviet-type socialism.

However, once the major constitutional models were decided upon and the building of a new institutional system in all sectors was underway, the dynamics of change shifted from active cultural "framing", "planning" and "design" to institutional and structural factors. In all sectors of social life – legal, political, economic – the newly created institutional system and capitalist market economy introduced a new social order with structural constraints. In the area of media, "mimetic" media laws and regulations institutionalized changes of and defined new roles for all actors. In commercial media markets, profit-oriented media investors, domestic owners and western companies positioned themselves as hegemonic actors. The transformation of state media to western type public service began by the transplantation of public service broadcasting institutions. The new institutional order and new structural factors significantly weakened the relevance of creative "framing power".

However, after media laws and institutions had been transplanted from Western to Eastern and Central European contexts, the danger became apparent that democratic laws would not be implemented, or implemented only partially, and democratic institutions would serve as a façade for non-democratic practices. Without the supporting environment of democratic political culture, democratic institutions remain empty, and the implementation of democratic norms as well as their proper operation and performance is missing (Gross 2004). Moreover, such empty institutions often turn into a Potemkin village: they satisfy merely formal criteria while their essence is misinterpreted and misused in the interest of political and economic elites.

This brings the issue of culture, particularly political culture, back to centre stage. Democratic political culture, which is necessary for substantial consolidation of democracy, would rest to a large degree on a supportive civil society, including networks of trust and social capital that developed in long historical trajectories (Seligman 1992, 2000; Putnam 1993). However, civil society is historically weaker (and acts of civic and journalistic courage remain less forceful) in the East and Central European region than in Western Europe (Bibó 1991; Szűcs 1983). Of course, it may be a mistake to engage in cultural essentialism as political culture itself is also changing as a result of institutional and structural factors. However, its change is slower – one can thus witness a discrepancy between the pace of systemic and cultural change.

7. Is post-communism over?

What it is that is actually happening in post-communist societies is, of course, the object of a heated debate. In the present volume, this issue is taken up by Sparks who believes that of the two approaches that he considers – "transitology" (positing revolutionary transition from communism to liberal democracy and market economy) and "elite continuity" – that of elite continuity has superior explanatory power. (Ironically, this thesis in Eastern and Central Europe is much touted by right-wing forces, such as the Law and Justice Party in Poland, that challenge the post-1989 arrangements as a sell-out to former communists and – as if reliving the Chinese cultural revolution – seek to remove the post-1989 elite from power and to replace it with their own power elite.)

Here, we will proceed from the assumption that there is more to what has taken place in post-communist countries than just elite continuity: multiple transformations *and*, within them, a certain degree of elite continuity, together characterize these societies.

Taken literally, neither social, nor media transformation can ever be "over", of course. Change never stops, though it may be faster or slower, depending on the circumstances. Also in a *normative* sense, media democratization is an open-ended process. Communicative participation and public deliberation based on access to information are processes where it would be wrong to suggest that an endpoint of evolution may be reached. Communicative democracy remains a normative ideal that may serve as a guiding principle and that may be approached by certain communities in certain empirical contexts – but, perhaps, never fully realized.

Generally speaking, in the context of Central and Eastern Europe today, the question refers to a specific historical process of post-communist transformation. Determining when this form of transformation is over depends on whether or not it is seen as a *teleological* process, implying a preconceived or normatively defined end result, or a certain pre-determined set of outcomes. If so, the question becomes whether that result should be defined in a *negative* or *positive* way. If, on the one hand, post-communism is defined as abolition of communism (negative result), then transformation was over once that had been done in the great majority of countries in the early 1990s (some Central Asian republics may be seen as continuing the old system, in a different form), irrespective of what followed that process.

If, on the other hand, transformation is seen as serving the creation of a different and sustained institutional order (positive result), then transformation will be over when that has happened. This was the mainstream transition studies or "transitology" tradition in American political science that focused on institutional variables (Stepan and Linz 1996). This approach may be illustrated by the questions put by Philip G. Roeder (1999, 747–749) as he sought to ascertain the progress of transformation by the end of the 1990s:

- First, at the end of this decade, did the country constitute a consolidated nation-state?
- Second, at the end of this decade, did a democratic regime rule this country? Following Robert Dahl's definition, democratic states both guarantee political liberties for unfettered public contestation and extend the franchise to the entire permanent resident adult population.
- Third, at the end of this decade, were economic decisions concerning production, pricing, and distribution made in the private sphere and marketplace rather than in governmental agencies? Countries may be divided into two categories based on the extent to which the government continued to play a commanding role in the economy.

Of course, a fine-tuned assessment of the quality of democracy (differences between competitive, majoritarian, liberal and other forms of democracy) is missing here. Also, there exist a number of democratic capitalisms with multiple roles of the state and state-economy relations, so the simple alternative between the free market vs government agency is not tenable. However, assuming for a moment such a teleological understanding of transformation we may distinguish a number of principal criteria for assessing its progress:

- The first criterion concerns the reversibility of change: when change (of whatever nature and proceeding in whatever direction) has reached the point of no return, partial transformation has already taken place (i.e., the old order no longer exists as a functioning system and cannot return, even though no coherent new order has yet emerged). We may call this transformation <u>out of the old order.</u>
- The second relates to the achievement of critical mass of transformation <u>into a new order</u>. This is an interim stage when enough features of a new, internally consistent system have crystallized for this system to function, whatever shortcomings or legacies of the past still remain.
- And the third principal criterion concerns the <u>consolidation</u> of the new order, coalescing into a new integrated whole. In this phase, the process of fundamental systemic change is replaced by "business as usual" of change and procedure of reforms.

In terms of media policies, Lukosiunas (1998, p. 3) combines the first and the second criterion in assessing the situation in the Lithuanian media system:

> One may probably say that the first phase of the transition - which included the disruption of Soviet media system and emergence of the new structure of the media which is capable of integrating Western journalistic practices and is ready to be integrated into the structures of Western media businesses — is over, and the next stage — which is to find its place and voice in united Europe — has just started.

In the teleological paradigm, we may also consider different criteria for assessing whether transformation is "over" or not. They are:

- Systemic criteria, e.g., the transition is over when the problems and the policy issues confronted by today's 'transition countries' resemble those faced by other countries at similar levels of development.

- Concentrating on formal outcomes, as in the view that transition is over for the post-communist countries when they become members of the EU.
- And institutional, i.e., whether the old institutions have been dismantled and new ones created and sustained for a historically longer period.

In the teleological tradition, transformation can be also said to be over when the media of a post-communist country resemble those of western democracies rather than those of a communist state (once again, the criteria would be typically institutional). Using a longer term perspective, another conceptual benchmark could be when processes of continued change no longer have anything to do with overcoming the legacy of the communist past (although indirect causal relations may be very hard to evaluate empirically).

So is post-communism over? On the one hand, if we accept that social change in post-communist countries encompasses the three sub-processes listed in figure 2: a) elimination of communist legacy, b) "triple" or "quadruple" transformation and c) response to global and European change, then not one of these sub-processes has been accomplished fully. If we define communism not so much in an ideological sense, but as a period of national development which was radically different from what older democracies went through at the same time, then its legacy continues to weigh heavily over everything else. Such a legacy cannot be removed or forgotten in just one generation. At the very least, all Central and Eastern European countries are still "post-communist" in this general sense of social path-dependency.

On the other hand, however, some believe that the label "post-communist" should no longer be used, as the transformation is "over" and Central and Eastern European societies have entered a qualitatively new stage of their history. One may also argue that groups of countries in Central and Eastern European in the last twenty years became so different in terms of democratic performance, capitalist transformation and economic integration with global markets (e.g., some are liberal democracies in the European Union, others are authoritarian states or even dictatorships) that the common denominator "post-communist" has lost most its explanatory power.

In the area of media systems, this position could be supported by comparative perspectives suggesting that commonalities between certain Central and Eastern European countries and media systems elsewhere (e.g., southern Europe) could be already more significant than structural similarities within the post-communist world. Another comparative approach could offer the concept of "multiple post-communisms", i.e., typologies pointing to differences between groups of countries (e.g., Central Europe, South-Eastern Europe, the Baltics and other groups of post-Soviet states).

8. Comparative approaches

Comparative approaches to systemic media change may offer alternatives to the teleological paradigm. Instead of focusing on a trajectory from a point of departure (the communist media system) to an endpoint (a normatively defined end result, or a certain pre-determined set of outcomes), perhaps more can be learned about substantive issues via comparative methods.

The archetype of comparative media systems theory, *Four Theories of the Press* (Siebert et al. 1956), is seldom quoted recently. However, its concepts made a deep and sometimes unconscious impact on generations of media scholarship. Although the four models (the authoritarian, the libertarian, the Soviet and the social responsibility theories of the press) suggest a comparative perspective, they also imply deeply normative discourses in two senses. On the one hand, they present a description of all four models in an ideal typical way, i.e., how the four models should be (and not how they, in fact, empirically are). On the other hand, positive characteristics are grouped on one side (the libertarian and the social responsibility theories), while negative traits characterize the other side (the authoritarian and the Soviet theories of the press). These two related processes of normativization result in a polarized classification. Instead of exploring how media systems function in different parts of the globe and what accounts for their differences, we are presented a bipolar opposition that reflects a Cold War dichotomy.[7]

The *Four Theories of the Press* remained influential in media research as well as journalism education up to the end of the Cold War and even beyond that, and we suggest it also made its impact on the teleological understanding of the transformation of East and Central European media systems. The *Four Theories of the Press* matched well with the logic of "transitology" in political science: in their polarized opposition a transition from the communist political system (and the Soviet media model) took place targeting an idealized, "western" democratic system and free market (and the libertarian, or social responsibility, media model).

As empirical evidence and cases regarding media change in Central and Eastern Europe became available during the 1990s, the need for less ideological comparative approaches became obvious. In *Democracy and the Media: A Comparative Perspective*, Gunther and Mughan presented a systematic framework for the analysis of ten single-country cases in different regime types: consolidated democracies, cases of democratization after WW2, as well as emerging democracies of the third wave of democratization (Gunther and Mughan 2000a, 2000b). Their approach transcended the Cold War logic in several ways. First, they broke with the idealization of any western models and introduced critical and historical aspects regarding their change (in the United States, the United Kingdom and the Netherlands).

> To be sure, this association of democracy with a free press and authoritarianism/ totalitarianism with a media enslaved is overdrawn and has never been fully convincing. The media in non-democratic regimes, for example, never enjoyed the pervasiveness penetration, or omniscience popularized in George Orwell's *1984*. In the same vein, the media in democratic societies have never been fully free of government control.... [T]he traditional stereotype of the uniformly positive contribution to democracy by free, unregulated communications has come under increased scrutiny and criticism. (Gunther and Mughan 2000a: 5, 7)

In contrast to an idealized view of the performance of western media, they call attention to trivialization and personalization of politics, the spread of infotainment instead of substantive political issues, a focus on ephemeral matters, unsubstantiated rumours and personal insults (e.g., in US talk radio), and negative advertising that supposedly gives birth and cynicism and disillusionment with politics (2000a: 7–8).

Second, Gunther and Mughan compared post-communist transitions (Russia and Hungary) with post-World War II waves of democratization (Germany, Italy, Japan) as well as post-authoritarian democratization in southern Europe (Spain) and Latin America (Chile). This had some parallels in political science (e.g., Linz and Stepan 1996).

Third, they synthesized micro- and macro-level perspectives. By considering both media impacts on audiences (especially agenda setting, priming, framing, and media effects in election campaigns) as well as its media impact on systemic change, they argued that "what accounts for change in the relationship between media and politics of democracy and democratization is the *interplay* between macro- and micro-level developments" (2000a: 15, italics in original). Using a political communication perspective, they focused mostly on media as an independent variable, asking how the media impacted democratization, "government-initiated liberalization of political communications helped to undermine support for authoritarian or post-totalitarian regimes, as well as the contribution of the media to the transition to, and consolidation of, political democracy" (2000a: 2).

Finally, they also synthesized major political science concepts (like voter de-alignment) with a media communication perspective and developed a framework of variables that conditioned specific media impacts. These variables included "political culture, electoral law, historical legacy, type of social structure and party system, style of executive leadership" [...] "be they in the area of democratic transitions from authoritarianism or in influencing popular attitudes and behaviours in established democracies" (2000a: 9) .

In the process of the emergence of empirical comparative perspectives on media systems, Hallin and Mancini's *Comparing Media Systems: Three Models of Media and Politics* (2004) represents a milestone. On the one hand, they offer a systematic comparative study of eighteen West European and North American democracies, by empirically testing hypotheses concerning the relationship of media system and political system variables. These variables include development of media markets, the degree of parallelism between political and media systems, journalism cultures and the nature and degree of state intervention into the media system. They identify variation in media systems and the political variables which have contributed to their formation.

On the other hand, based on those empirical patterns in these variables, Hallin and Mancini identify three main models of media systems. The *Mediterranean* or *Polarized Pluralist* model characterizes countries of relatively late democratization in southern Europe with political systems of polarized democracy where state dirigisme relates to a strong role of the state in media affairs. The parallelism between state and media is high, with strong political instrumentalization of broadcasting, a partisan press and weak journalistic professionalism.

In turn, the *North/Central European* or *Democratic Corporatist* model usually represents earlier democratization that resulted in consensus democracy with a strong welfare state (e.g., Germany). The media system is characterized by a tradition of state intervention ensuring external pluralism, a balance the role of the state and freedom of media and media markets and strong journalistic professionalization.

Finally, the *North Atlantic* or *Liberal* model (e.g., the US, UK, Ireland) features majoritarian political systems of early democratization, a liberal role of the state, internal pluralism of the media and market-dominated media systems (except strong public service broadcasting in the UK and Ireland).

Although Hallin and Mancini emphasize that their models emerge from empirical evidence from a limited and relatively homogeneous group of countries (2004: 6), they also suggest that their models could be used for developing more comprehensive, comparative perspectives. Given this opportunity, we need to determine if and how these models are useful for understanding media systems in Eastern and Central Europe.

9. Mediterraneanization of post-communist media systems

The title of this book refers to "finding the right place on the map". It is actually less surprising than it might appear that post-communist countries may experience difficulties with finding where they are on the map. First of all, they all emerged out of World War II with different borders than before. Secondly, after the collapse of the communist system, post-Soviet countries regained national sovereignty and borders, while other post-communist countries fell apart (to mention only Czechoslovakia and Yugoslavia).

Another dimension of this issue is, of course, geopolitical: most post-communist countries sought to shed their "Eastern European" identity and to "return to Europe". One of the "theories" which have been developed to explain why different post-communist countries have fared differently after 1989 is the "proximity theory", according to which those with cultural and physical proximity to Western Europe, and greater receptivity to historical waves of western influences resulting from that, have been more successful. The Baltic States have always identified more with Scandinavia than with the Soviet Union and that has been an important factor in their ability to resist the Soviet influence and to find their bearings after 1989 more easily than some of the countries that had been more isolated.

And, then, there has been the question of "media models". Central and Eastern Europe have provided a venue for "a battle of the models", where the American and Western European concepts of media system organization fought for dominance (see the article by Hozic in this volume). The "Western European model" finally won — not least because it was supported by the European Union which left candidate countries in no doubt as to what was expected of them in terms of "systemic media policy". In any case, post-communist countries themselves wanted to build their new media systems by "testing the best of the West" (Kleinwächter 1995), i.e., by putting together a patchwork of ideas and solutions for democratizing the media from various sources. They soon realized, however, that there is no one single Western European model, but a variety of systemic arrangements, not all of them necessarily very democratic or in keeping with what we have described as the idealized, wart-free image that they were supposed to emulate.

Hallin and Mancini's (2004) book on media systems offer a framework, also in geographical terms, for defining the parameters of this search for models. Policy-makers and researchers in post-communist countries have to answer the question where on this mental map of media systems their countries were (i.e., whether in the liberal system of northern Europe, or the democratic-corporatist system of Central Europe, or finally in the polarized pluralist model of the Mediterranean), and on what model and area of Europe to set their sights in planning the future development of their media system.

This issue is taken up most explicitly by Jakubowicz who uses the Hallin-Mancini framework for conducting a comparative analysis of PSB in post-communist and polarized pluralist media systems and concludes: "Thus, we may have found a place on the map for post-communist media systems. Contrary to what an encyclopaedia may tell you, post-communist countries appear to be located — figuratively at least — around the Mediterranean, and on both its sides, too, as some of them are politically closer to North African regimes than to any Southern European country." This confirms Slavko Splichal's (1994) diagnosis that post-communist countries have been witness to the "Italianization" of their media.

Jakubowicz points out that if countries like Spain, Portugal and Italy have not yet been able create conditions for truly public-spirited and independent public service media, than it is unrealistic to expect that post-communist countries could have done it in less than twenty years.

10. Multiple post-communisms

Hallin and Mancini emphasize that their three models are crystallized from eighteen countries in Europe and North America that are all democracies. They also call attention to how limited and homogeneous the group of case selection was (2004: 6). This presents a challenge to students of post-communist media systems as the democratic character of many countries in the post-communist lands is questionable and some countries are clearly not democracies. It also poses limits on the applicability of the Hallin and Mancini typology (including the Mediterranean model).

However, the great variation of post-communist societies calls for the development of typologies in which political as well as media system characteristics are pinpointed on the basis of empirical evidence. Such a typology could also combine normative (if not teleological) and comparative approaches.

In terms of political systems, the World Bank (2002) has developed a typology of four types of post-communist states as they were at the end of the 1990s, based on the extent of political contestability and consequently in strategies of economic reform, if any. "Competitive democracies" have maintained both a high level of political rights to compete in multiparty democratic elections and an extensive range of civil liberties, as well as advanced economic reform.

"Concentrated political regimes" conduct multiparty elections, but have either curtailed full rights to participate in those elections or otherwise constrained civil liberties. They comprise both political systems which have a high degree of political contestability, but with power concentrated (usually) in the executive branch of government, to those where oligarchs and insiders capture the state. Partial economic reforms mostly fail to support effectively functioning markets. These countries exhibit high levels of corruption.

"Non-competitive political regimes" constrain entry of potential opposition parties into the electoral process and sharply restrict political participation through the exercise of civil liberties. They have been most likely to reject key elements of market transition and to maintain greater continuity with the previous command system.

"War-torn political regimes" have engaged in prolonged wars or civil conflicts, generally rooted in ethnic or territorial divisions. Such conflicts have placed severe strains on the capacity of the state, resulting in some of the countries in a prolonged loss of political order and control and serious weaknesses in the provision of basic public goods. War-torn countries have been characterized by weak state capacity and a zigzag pattern of economic reform, creating an environment that is not conducive to entry and investment.

Comparative aspects become especially complex when we take into consideration Russia and other post-Soviet countries where the democratic nature of the state may be questioned and media freedom faces major limitations. Regarding Ukrainian media, Dyczok (2006) suggests that censorship intensified under President Kuchma and this may be seen indicator of the country's democratic backlash before the Orange revolution as recently as 2004. Becker defines contemporary Russian media as a "neo-authoritarian media system" (2004). Simons and Strovsky focus on "censorship" (2006), and several authors point out recent authoritarian tendencies in media control under President Putin (Lipman and McFaul 2003; Ryabov 2004).

As table 1 indicates, there exist dramatic differences between groups of post-communist countries in the level of media freedom that they enjoy. Media freedom is not respected in several post-Soviet states while other groups of countries like the Baltic or Central European states became, according to Freedom House data, comparable to consolidated democracies.

How could one develop a typology for the large post-communist and post-Soviet spaces that include semi-authoritarian, authoritarian, dictatorial as well as democratic states? This task would involve the consideration of different (including non-democratic) roles of the state, based on normative concepts (but not teleological transitology) and empirical variables that may be operationalized and supported by qualitaive and quantifiable data.

Freedom of the Press in Central and Eastern Europe and the Former Soviet Union 1989–2006[8]

Each year cell below gives, where available, the *Score* and *Status* (F = Free, PF = Partly Free, NF = Not Free, N/A = not available). For 1989–1993 only *Status* is given; from 1994 onward both *Score* and *Status* are given.

	1989	1990	1991	1992	1993	1994	1995	1996	1997	1998	1999	2000	2001	2002	2003	2004	2005	2006
Albania	NF	NF	NF	PF	PF	53 PF	67 NF	71 NF	75 NF	56 PF	56 PF	56 PF	56 PF	48 PF	50 PF	49 PF	51 PF	50 PF
Armenia	N/A	N/A	N/A	F	PF	52 PF	57 PF	56 PF	56 PF	56 NF	56 PF	57 PF	59 PF	60 PF	65 PF	64 NF	64 NF	64 NF
Azerbaijan	N/A	N/A	N/A	N/A	NF	70 NF	69 NF	69 NF	74 NF	74 NF	73 NF	70 NF	76 NF	77 NF	73 NF	71 NF	72 NF	73 NF
Belarus	N/A	N/A	N/A	N/A	PF	66 NF	67 NF	70 NF	85 NF	90 NF	80 NF	80 NF	80 NF	82 NF	82 NF	84 NF	86 NF	88 NF
Bosnia & Herzegovina	N/A	N/A	N/A	N/A	N/A	70 NF	72 NF	76 PF	71 NF	74 NF	56 PF	56 PF	54 PF	53 PF	49 PF	48 PF	45 PF	45 PF
Bulgaria	NF	NF	PF	PF	PF	43 PF	39 PF	46 PF	44 PF	36 PF	39 PF	30 F	26 F	29 F	30 F	35 PF	35 PF	34 PF
Croatia	N/A	N/A	N/A	N/A	NF	56 PF	56 PF	58 PF	63 NF	63 NF	63 NF	63 NF	50 PF	33 PF	33 PF	37 PF	37 PF	39 PF
Czech Republic	N/A	N/A	N/A	N/A	N/A	20 F	21 F	19 F	19 F	19 F	20 F	20 F	24 F	25 F	23 F	23 F	22 F	20 F
Czecho-slovakia	NF	PF	F	F	F	N/A	N/A	N/A	N/A	N/A	N/A	N/A	N/A	N/A	N/A	N/A	N/A	N/A
Estonia	NF	PF	F	F	PF	28 F	25 F	24 F	22 F	20 F	20 F	20 F	20 F	18 F	17 F	17 F	17 F	16 F
Georgia	N/A	N/A	N/A	N/A	PF	73 NF	70 NF	68 NF	55 PF	56 PF	57 PF	47 PF	53 PF	53 PF	54 PF	54 PF	56 PF	57 PF
German Democratic Republic	NF	PF	N/A	N/A	N/A	N/A	N/A	N/A	N/A	N/A	N/A	N/A	N/A	N/A	N/A	N/A	N/A	N/A
Hungary	NF	PF	F	F	N/A	30 F	38 PF	34 PF	31 PF	28 F	28 F	30 F	28 F	23 F	23 F	20 F	21 F	21 F
Kazakhstan	N/A	N/A	N/A	N/A	PF	60 PF	61 PF	62 NF	64 NF	66 NF	68 NF	68 NF	70 NF	69 NF	73 NF	74 NF	75 NF	75 NF
Kyrgyzstan	N/A	N/A	N/A	N/A	PF	49 PF	52 PF	60 PF	61 NF	64 NF	64 NF	61 NF	61 NF	68 NF	71 NF	71 NF	71 NF	64 NF
Latvia	N/A	N/A	N/A	N/A	PF	29 F	29 F	21 F	21 F	21 F	21 F	24 F	24 F	19 F	18 F	17 F	17 F	19 F
Lithuania	N/A	N/A	N/A	F	PF	30 F	29 F	25 F	20 F	17 F	18 F	20 F	20 F	19 F	18 F	18 F	18 F	18 F
Macedonia	N/A	N/A	N/A	N/A	PF	N/A	34 PF	36 PF	33 PF	44 PF	42 PF	42 PF	44 PF	46 PF	50 PF	53 PF	51 PF	49 F
Poland	NF	PF	F	F	F	30 F	29 F	21 F	27 F	25 F	25 F	19 F	19 F	18 F	18 F	19 F	20 F	21 F
Republic of Moldova	N/A	N/A	N/A	N/A	PF	41 PF	47 PF	62 NF	57 PF	58 PF	56 PF	58 PF	59 PF	59 PF	59 PF	63 NF	65 NF	65 NF
Romania	NF	NF	N/A	PF	F	55 PF	50 PF	49 PF	47 PF	39 PF	44 PF	44 PF	44 PF	35 PF	38 PF	47 PF	47 PF	44 PF
Russian Federation	N/A	N/A	N/A	N/A	PF	40 PF	55 PF	58 PF	53 PF	53 PF	59 PF	60 PF	60 PF	60 PF	66 NF	67 NF	68 NF	72 NF
Serbia & Montenegro	N/A	N/A	N/A	N/A	N/A	86 NF	87 NF	77 NF	75 NF	75 NF	81 NF	81 NF	56 PF	45 PF	40 PF	40 PF	40 PF	40 PF
Slovakia	N/A	N/A	N/A	N/A	N/A	47 PF	55 NF	41 PF	49 PF	47 PF	30 F	30 F	26 F	22 F	21 F	21 F	21 F	20 F
Slovenia	N/A	N/A	N/A	N/A	N/A	40 PF	37 PF	27 F	28 F	27 F	27 F	27 F	21 F	20 F	19 F	19 F	19 F	20 F
Tajikistan	N/A	N/A	N/A	N/A	N/A	93 NF	93 NF	96 NF	95 NF	94 NF	85 NF	94 NF	79 NF	80 NF	76 NF	73 NF	74 NF	76 NF
Turkmenistan	N/A	N/A	N/A	N/A	N/A	89 NF	84 NF	84 NF	84 NF	84 NF	85 NF	86 NF	89 NF	91 NF	92 NF	95 NF	96 NF	96 NF
Ukraine	NF	N/A	N/A	N/A	PF	44 PF	42 PF	39 PF	49 PF	49 NF	50 PF	60 PF	60 PF	60 PF	67 NF	68 NF	59 PF	53 PF
USSR	NF	NF	PF	N/A	N/A	N/A	N/A	N/A	N/A	N/A	N/A	N/A	N/A	N/A	N/A	N/A	N/A	N/A
Uzbekistan	N/A	N/A	N/A	N/A	NF	85 NF	79 NF	75 NF	76 NF	76 NF	79 NF	83 NF	84 NF	84 NF	86 NF	84 NF	85 NF	90 NF
Yugoslavia	NF	NF	NF	NF	PF	N/A	N/A	N/A	N/A	N/A	N/A	N/A	N/A	N/A	N/A	N/A	N/A	N/A

* CEE/FSU = Central and Eastern Europe and the Former Soviet Union

Sükösd (2007) has suggested twelve variables for empirical comparisons of media democratization in East-Central Europe and Eurasia:

- State violence against journalists
- Structural censorship: from general limitations on human rights (freedom of speech, press freedom) to softer measures (penalty taxes, blacklists, t'emniki, monopoly of printing etc.)
- Government control of state/public service media
- Media laws and their implementation (rule of law)
- Independent media structures (national, regional, local) and their audiences
- Freedom of information regulation and implementation
- Access to media by minorities and ethnic minority media
- Nationalist hegemony in the media
- Journalism cultures (partisanship)
- Media ownership (pluralism, problems of western vs local ownership)
- Commercialization of media (tabloidization)
- Internet control/freedom and access/participation

These variables can be operationalized by comparative, open-ended indicators, and allow for the use of both quantitative (cf. Freedom House, Reporters Sans Frontieres etc.) and qualitative data. Based on the variables above, one may break "post-communism" into "multiple post-communisms", i.e., classify groups of political and media systems:

- Dictatorial (e.g., Belarus)
- Authoritarian (etatist: e.g., Russia; paternalistic: e.g, Kazakhstan; depressed: e.g., Moldova, southern Caucasus)[9]
- Democratic (e.g., East-Central Europe, Baltic)

The comparative variables above (potentially with other analytical angles) may also contribute to the comparative analysis of late communist media systems of China and other South-East Asian state socialist countries, as well as Cuba, that are still mostly before post-communist transformation. Such comparative work can also help to see if and how the Central and Eastern European experiences may be relevant for later waves of the exit from communism.

In a sense that would be a comparative exercise that relates to the past of Central and Eastern European societies. However, in light of recent trends of media change one may also attempt to update the list of democratic expectations of the media to make it more relevant in the twenty-first century. In the context of widespread commercialization, the emergence of interactive media, digital convergence and related user segmentation, the democratic expectations of media performance could also include these demands:

- Encourage democratic citizenship and participation in a stimulating and easy to access fashion;
- Provide opportunities for interactivity and feedback;
- Create publics for community-building;
- Representation and self-representation of minorities;
- Multicultural and intercultural communication, reducing negative stereotypes and hatred in society;

■ Coverage and analysis of trends related to globalization;
■ Offer a space for public information campaigns.

11. Media and nationalism

No matter where they are located on the cognitive map of media systems, the real contours of national borders and substantive national identities within them remain contested subjects in the post-communist world. As mentioned above, three multinational, federal states –Yugoslavia, Czechoslovakia and the Soviet Union – dissolved after the collapse of the communism system and gave birth to many new nation states. More than a dozen post-Soviet countries in Eastern Europe, the Baltic region, the southern Caucasus and Central Asia regained national sovereignty. Czechoslovakia transformed into two separate states. Yugoslavia disintegrated into several countries, and the process still continues, as Montenegro and potentially Kosovo secede from Serbia.

In this context, media and nationalism scholars should join forces to analyze the interaction of the mass media with different types of nationalism, nation-state formation and contemporary nationalist political practice, and consider the impact of media on national and regional identities. Such research could take several approaches.

First, historical approaches to earlier forms and waves of nationalism may offer useful tools to understand the interplay of nationalism and media systems in the development in contemporary post-communist nation states. As new nations are being born in front of our eyes, Anderson's (1991 [1983]) concept of "imagined communities" about the role of media communications in creating national publics (originally, the historical role of the print press in the birth of modern nationalism) could be as timely and relevant as ever. This calls attention to the ubiquitous nature of "banal nationalism" (Billig 1995) which is played out by innocent and unrecognized ways by the mass media: weather reports on national media always use maps of *our* nation, sports programmes always put *our* team to the forefront (and eventually cover the national anthem and show the flag), and political coverage also usually offers implicit national frames of reference. All this serves unintentionally national integration which is so high on the agenda in new nation states (and which is also an explicit task for public service media in many systems).

Second, structural and institutional approaches explore media policies that contribute or hinder national integration, democratic patriotism, but also aggressive forms of nationalism. According to concordant analysis of several authors, the decentralized media system played a major role in "the disintegration and ethnic division in former Yugoslavia" (Sofos 1999) as well as "forging war" (Thompson 1999) along ethnic lines (Slapsak et al. 1997). The media of conflict curbed war reporting and representations of gendered ethnic violence (Zarkov 2001), as "killing screens" identified mythical national heroes of the past with present-day warriors by their ability of compressing space and time (Reljić 2001 [1998], 2001). But after "prime time crime" (Kurspahic 2003), how could the media contribute to "forging peace" (Price and Thompson 2002), i.e., how could foreign intervention and domestic policies contribute to post-conflict peacemaking and ensure media freedom and peaceful national integration at the same time? (See the chapter by Hozic about Bosnia and Herzegovina in this book.)

Third, war propaganda is efficient if it is supported by silencing opposition to the war. "War on terrorism", e.g., in Russia, "has provided the authorities with ample excuses to curtail media reporting, such as protecting the work of the security forces in combating terrorist activity, stopping the spread of terrorist propaganda" and others (Simons and Strovsky 2006: 189).

Security concerns are used as legitimating different forms of communications control in several post-communist countries as well as other parts of the world: a "security state" tends to restrict media freedom by nature.

Fourth, regarding media content, media anthropological approaches (Dayan and Katz 1992; Alexander and Jacobs 1998; Marvin and Ingle 1999) could give special attention to nationalist rituals (including flag ceremonies, public commemorations, reburials (Verdery 1999), symbols and myths, their construction and representation as media events by mass media and their use in political communication; gendered images in nationalist media; the media construction of Us, the Other and the Enemy; and the structure and discourses of media propaganda.

Fifth, journalistic practices are important as they produce nationalist vs responsible (diversity oriented, sensitive) media coverage. Difference and diversity are conceptualized here as 'otherness', be it ethnicity, religion, race (but also other diversity issues such as age, physical abilities, gender or non-traditional sexual orientation) in different multicultural communities of post-communist societies.[10]

Finally, other important questions concern nationalism vs. the creation of transnational identities by media structures. Are 'cool' or 'civic' forms of nationalism qualitatively different from 'hot' nationalism in terms of the role of the media production of ethnic loyalties? Should national identities indeed be perceived as a barrier to European integration? This seems to be the unspoken assumption of EU policy as well as scholarship, but is this assumption justified? How should and could transnational European publics be created in an environment that does not feature any significant pan-European commercial or public service media as we know these institutions from the experience of nation states? How can media contribute to the creation of the culture of Europeanness and European citizenship?

12. Traumas of transformation, globalization, and democratic backlash

Taking a historical perspective, we may suggest that a few more decades may be needed in Central and Eastern Europe for the development of supportive political culture and democratic media institutions, including public service media. At least that is the time span that comparable and still unfolding media change in southern Europe indicates as realistic. This is small comfort, however, as there is a price to pay for disappointed expectations. Society's patience is limited and the existence of flawed institutions, failing to fulfil the promise that attended their creation, soon turns into a race against time and potentially rage against the regime.

What will come sooner: full observance of the law (e.g., the broadcasting law that introduced, on paper, independent public service broadcasting) as a result of successful consolidation of democracy or public disillusionment and cynicism in a situation when parts of the law constituting a democratic institution may be honoured more in the breach than in the observance?

Such frustration and disillusionment may prove dangerous, as public opinion may not be prepared to wait forever. This may contribute to a more general backlash, as people realize that democracy and societal change are failing to bring the expected benefits. Such a backlash may lead to a change of political course, for example, in the direction of populism, authoritarianism or managed democracy.

Recent general elections in a number of countries in Central and Eastern Europe have changed the political situation and brought to power very different coalitions than previous ones. A coalition government of right-wing populist and extreme right-wing parties took over in Poland in 2005 and sought to impose highly centralized government, dismantle the checks and balances of liberal democracy (e.g., to weaken and control the courts) and engage in media capture (by taking direct control of public media and exerting pressure on private media). In Slovakia, the formation of an unusual government coalition, that includes the Slovak National Party (an extreme right-wing, nationalist and anti-minorities party led by Ján Slota), has been creating concerns internally and internationally since 2006. A series of violent riots by the extreme right rocked the democratic system in 2006 on the 50th anniversary of the 1956 revolution in Hungary. In Russia, under President Putin, in addition to censorship and government media control, state security is used against political opponents and leading journalists, threatening not only democratic pluralism and competition, but also the lives of those in the way of the regime.

Related to this regional backlash, there is evidence in these as well as other countries that new governments and parliaments have succeeded in changing broadcasting laws or have actively pursued negative policies with other means vis-à-vis the media, including particular public service broadcasting organizations.

The question is if the nature of the political process will change significantly and how it is impacting on the situation of the media, their freedom and independence, and their role in democracy in the longer run.

The answer will depend in each country on the political evolution since the fall of the communist system; the level of consolidation of democracy; the nature of political actors, the political process unfolding in the past few years; the background and the factors leading to any significant change of political orientation and culture; and, consequently, to changes in official media policy. Any such changes, whether of a formal nature (changes of legislation etc.) or of an informal one, should be analysed and assessed in terms of their impact on the democratic performance of the media. Where appropriate, this analysis should be conducted against the background of the general process of consolidation of democracy, noting any positive or negative impact on this process. In the case of EU member states, the interrelationship between the political process and membership should also be considered.

How deep and relevant this backlash remains to be seen. There are many signs of tension and exhaustion (and also of maturation, progress and hope) as a result multiple shocks or traumas that post-communist societies suffered during the transformation:

> The first was the anticlimax of the early post-1989 years when it was discovered that the removal of the Communist system not only did not solve all problems, but in fact created a host of new ones; when the leaders of the opposition were found to be squabbling politicians, no necessarily averse to corruption and arrogance.... The second came when the ideas and ideals that had kept the opposition alive and serve as an inspiration to rise up against the Communist system had to be discarded overnight as impractical and useless. The third was when the true nature of the capitalist system became apparent. The fourth was when European unification turned into a tedious process, often seen as humiliating, instead of the joyful embrace of long-lost brothers. And the fifth came when the realization sank in that "Westernization" and "Westification" are the best that can be hoped for and that Western Europe appears to think that Central and Eastern Europe has nothing of value to contribute except its markets. (Jakubowicz 2007: 370)

Several new items must be added to this list of traumas, such as the realities of twenty-first-century capitalism, globalization and its discontents: rocketing social inequalities, job insecurity, and the threat of unemployment in daily capitalist competition (and under politically motivated public administrations), deep reform of security systems (health, pension), and privatization of risk in societies where basic material security and full employment had been the norm for decades. Another set of traumas comes with decreasing sovereignty and increasing weakness of national governments in the global competition for transnational investments, and globalization of everyday culture, in a region where nationalism remained a source of pride, inspiration and resistance during decades of illegitimate rule or foreign occupation. What also has to be considered are ambiguities with consumer society as a hegemonistic ideal that puts pressures on every family and individual, but that also contributes to visible environmental degradation and new risks to present and future generations.

All this comes on top of earlier traumas such as the Holocaust that have not yet been worked through (the subject of the Holocaust was basically under taboo during the decades of communism, and debates like the German *historikerstreit* hardly begun in Eastern and Central Europe). Further, constituencies in these societies are deeply divided over issues like moral responsibility for the crimes under communism, and in the case of post-war societies, moral responsibility for the war and war-related genocide and the political solutions.

The list also includes tensions around fundamental issues of the political community and national identity, such as the republican vs monarchic (or, in Russia, even communist) foundations of the state, or state-church relations. As a result, fundamental constitutional questions (and related issues like symbols of the nation, the flag and the anthem) remain highly contested and unresolved in many countries, resulting in socio-political stress. Finally, add ethnic tensions and related issues of territorial claims and citizenship between numerous ethnic minorities and majorities.

Will these traumas and challenges overwhelm our societies' collective ability to cope and integrate tensions related to these experiences (cf. Alexander 2004)? Will the sense of being overwhelmed give birth to anomie, resentment, hostility and frustration, and reason to blame others for one's frustration?[11] Will Eastern and Central European societies continue to create enemies, to protect themselves from culpability? Will jealousy, inferiority complex and the rejection of the democratic system emerge from emotional stress, triggered by collective shocks? Or will disenchantment lead to a collective learning process, maturity, self-awareness, self-assurance and confident action?

*   *   *

No human being, no medium and no media system is an island unto itself, but embedded in social and ecological networks, "the web life" (Capra 1997). Accordingly, in media research a socio-centric approach to the media is by far preferable to a media-centric approach. In this introduction we have tried to adopt precisely such a socio-centric approach to aid our understanding of why media system evolution and democratization in post-communist countries is the complex, multidimensional and prolonged process it is. Contributors to this book explain this further and in more detail.

Notes

1. In this essay, we use the term as interchangeably with "post-communist countries" (except in section 10 where we also present data re post-Soviet states in Southern Caucasus and Central Asia).

2. According to Offe (1999), "triple transformation" comprises (i) the issues of nationality and territoriality involved in the delineation of borders and the national or ethnic composition of particular countries; (ii) constitutional issues involved in determining the system of government; (iii) and issues of the economic order, property and management of the process of production and distribution. Ekiert (1999), too, speaks of "triple transition", but in the sense of the simultaneous transformation of political, economic and social structures.

3. Kuzio (2002) says that unlike other Central and Eastern European countries, which are undergoing "post-authoritarian transformation", former Soviet countries are in the process of "post-colonial transformation", comprising the quadruple processes of democratization, marketization as well as state- and nation-building.

4. It draws, in part, on Jakubowicz, 2007.

5. www.endeav.org/evolut/age/sntut/sntut.htm. Last accessed on 18 Sept. 2007.

6. *Samizdat* (самиздат, the Russian term for "self-published") was the clandestine copying and distribution of government-suppressed literature and other media in Soviet-bloc countries. In the history of the Polish underground press, the term used in the 1980s was *drugi obieg* or "second circulation" of publications, the "first circulation" referring to legal (censored) publications. (http://en.wikipedia.org/wiki/Samizdat Last accessed 18 Sept. 2007.) In the first period of *samizdat*, a few handwritten copies were made, and those who got a copy were requested to make more copies. With more advanced copying and printing technology, however, *samizdat* reached larger audiences. In the 1980s in Poland, the independent Solidarity trade union reached millions of readers directly with independent newspapers. Foreign radio stations (especially Radio Free Europe and Radio Liberty) used *samizdat* as a news source and rebroadcast their content, reaching large audiences in all countries behind the Iron Curtain.

7. This Cold War dichotomy represents structural sameness with the superpower rivalry of the United States and the Soviet Union and the ideological construct of "Free World vs Evil Empire".

8. Source: Freedom of the Press Historical Data, http://www.freedomhouse.org/template.cfm?page=274. From 1980 to 1993, Freedom House rated countries by category, e.g., "Free", "Partly Free", or "Not Free", but did not provide numerical scores. From 1994 onwards, data regarding both category designations (F, PF, NF) and the more nuanced numerical scores are available. In the numerical scores, smaller values indicate higher observance of freedom of press.

9. Vartanova (2007) differentiates Eurasian etatist (Russia), paternalistic (Central Asia), depressive (Moldova, trans-Caucasian countries) media systems without using generic terms like authoritarianism.

10. Cf. Media Diversity Institute (MDI) "Overview and summary of the project Training the media, empowering minorities: a project for improved media coverage of ethnic and minority issues in the South Caucasus" 2005. http://www.media-diversity.org/about%20MDI.htm (last accessed 12 September 2007). The MDI teaches best practices of media coverage of diversity by analyzing examples of irresponsible reporting as well as successful cross-cultural and intercultural conflict resolution and collaboration. Their "Reporting Diversity" programme offers responsible journalism methods and curricula to journalism schools. They also explore the main obstacles, focusing on stereotypes and prejudices in media discourses. Presentations and demonstrations are accompanied by role-playing and developing story ideas. See also the Society of Professional Journalists'. Guidelines for Countering Racial, Ethnic and Religious Profiling, 2005. http://www.spj.org/divguidelines.asp. (Last accessed 12 September 2007.)

11. Cf. "Psychological trauma", http://en.wikipedia.org/wiki/Psychological_trauma.

References

Alexander, Jeffrey C. et al. 2004. *Cultural trauma and collective identity*. Berkeley: University of California Press.

Alexander, Jeffrey C. and Ronald N. Jacobs 1998. Mass Communication, Ritual and Civil Society. In: Liebes, Tamar and James Curran (eds.) *Media, Ritual and Identity*, London: Routledge, 23–41.

Anderson, Benedict 1991 [1983]. *Imagined Communities: reflections on the origin and spread of nationalism*. London: Verso.

Arato, Andrew 1981. Civil Society Against the State. *Telos 47* (Spring): 23–47.

Becker, Jonathan. 2004. Lessons from Russia: A Neo-Authoritarian Media System. *European Journal of Communication*, volume 19, number 2 (June), 139–163.

Bibó, Istvan 1991. *Democracy, revolution, self-determination: selected writings*. Edited by Károly Nagy. Boulder, Co.: Social Science Monographs.

Billig, Michael 1995. *Banal nationalism*. London: Sage.

Bozóki, András (ed.) 1999. *Intellectuals and politics in Central Europe*. Budapest: CEU Press.

Bozóki, András (ed.) 2001. *The roundtable talks of 1989: the genesis of Hungarian democracy. Analysis and documents*. Budapest: CEU Press.

Calhoun, Craig 1992. *Habermas and the Public Sphere*. Cambridge, MA and London: The MIT Press.

Capra, Fritjof 2007. *The web of life: a new scientific understanding of living systems*. London: HarperCollins.

Cohen, Jean 1996. The Public Sphere, the Media and Civil Society. In András Sajó (ed.) *Rights of Access to the Media*. The Hague: Kluwer Law International, 19–50.

Cohen, Stephen F. 1982. *An End to Silence. Uncensored Opinion in the Soviet Union. From Roy Medvedev's Underground Magazine, Political Diary*. New York, London: W.W. Norton.

Curran, James 1991. Rethinking the Media as a Public Sphere. In Peter Dahlgren and

Colin Sparks (eds.) *Communication and Citizenship: Journalism and the Public Sphere*. London and New York: Routledge, 27–57.

Curran, James 1992 [1991]. Mass Media and Democracy: A Reappraisal. In James Curran and Michael Gurevitch (eds.), *Mass Media and Society*. London: E. Arnold, 82–117.

Dahlgren, Peter 2002. In search of the talkative public: media, deliberative democracy and civic culture. *Javnost/The Public* vol. 9, no. 3, 5–26.

Dahlgren, Peter 2003. Reconfiguring civic culture in the new media milieu. In John Corner and Dick Pels, eds, *Media and Political Style: Essays on Representation and Civic Culture*. London: Sage, 151–170.

Dayan, Daniel and Elihu Katz 1992. *Media events: the live broadcasting of history*. Cambridge, Mass.: Harvard University Press.

Dyczok, Marta 2006. Was Kuchma's censorship effective? Mass media in Ukraine before 2004. *Europe-Asia Studies*, volume 58, number 2, 215–238

Feldbrugge, F. J. M. 1975. *Samizdat and political dissent in the Soviet Union*. Leyden: A. W. Sijthoff.

Glenn, John K. 1999. *International actors and democratization: US assistance to new political parties in Czech Republic and Slovakia*. Florence: European University Institute.

Glenn, John K. III 2001. *Framing democracy: civil society and civic movements in Eastern Europe*. Stanford, Calif.: Stanford University Press.

Gross, Peter 2004. Between Reality and Dream: Eastern European Media Transition, Transformation, Consolidation, and Integration. *East European Politics and Societies*, volume 18, number 1, 110–131.

Gunther, Richard and Anthony Moughan 2000a. The Media and Democratic and Nondemocratic Regimes: A Multilevel Perspective. In: Gunther, Richard and Anthony Moughan. (eds.) *Democracy and the Media: A Comparative Perspective*. Cambridge, Cambridge University Press, 1–28.

Gunther, Richard and Anthony Moughan 2000b. The Political Impact of the Media: A Reassessment. In: Gunther, Richard and Anthony Moughan. (eds.). *Democracy and the Media: A Comparative Perspective*. Cambridge, Cambridge University Press, 402–447.

Gurevitch, Michael and Blumler, Jay G. 1990. Political Communication Systems and Democratic Values. In Lichtenberg, Judith (ed.) *Democracy and the Mass Media*. Cambridge: Cambridge University Press, 269–289.

Habermas, Jürgen 1989. *The Structural Change of the Public Sphere*. Cambridge, MA: MIT Press.

Hankiss, Elemér 1996. The Hungarian Media War of Independence. In András Sajó (ed.) *Rights of Access to the Media*. The Hague: Kluwer Law International. 243–258.

Hallin, Daniel C. and Paolo Mancini 2004. *Comparing media systems: three models of media and politics*. Cambridge, UK; New York: Cambridge University Press.

Haraszti, Miklos 1988. *The velvet prison: artists under state socialism*. London; New York: I.B. Tauris: New Republic.

Hiebert, Ray Eldon (ed.) 1999 [1998]. *Impact of mass media: current issues*. New York: Longman.

Hollander, Gayle Durham 1972. Soviet Political Indoctrination: Developments in Mass Media and Propaganda Since Stalin. New York: Praeger.

Hollander, Gayle Durham 1975. Political Communication and Dissent in the Soviet Union. In: Tokes, Rudolf L. *Dissent in the USSR: Politics, Ideology and People*. Baltimore: The Johns Hopkins University Press.

Hroch, Miroslav 2000 [1993]. Nationalism and national movements: comparing the past and the present of Central and Eastern Europe. In Hutchinson, John and Anthony D. Smith (eds.) *Nationalism: critical concepts in political science*. London: Routledge, 607–617.

Jakubowicz, Karol 2001. Virtuous vs. Vicious Circles: Systemic Transformation and Media Change in Central and Eastern Europe. Paper presented at the *Democratization and the Media* conference, Bellaggio, Italy, April 9–13, 2001.

Jakubowicz, Karol 2007. *Rude awakening: social and media change in Central and Eastern Europe*. Cresskill, N.J.: Hampton Press.

Kaminski, T. 1987. Underground Publishing in Poland. *Orbis*, vol. 31, no. 3. (Fall), 313–330.

Kleinwächter, Wolfgang 1995. From the Mountains of Visions to the Valleys of Reality – New Legal Frameworks for Broadcasting in Eastern and Central Europe. *Canadian Journal of Communication* 20(1) www.wlu.ca/~wwwpress/jrls/cjc/BackIssues/20.1/kleinw.html).

Kopper, Gerd G. 2000. *Changing Media. Spheres of Change and Steps of Research*. Paper presented to a meeting of Working Group No 3, European Science Foundation Programme "Changing Media – Changing Europe, Seville, 22–23 June 2000.

Kurspahic, Kemal 2003. *Prime time crime: Balkan media in war and peace*. Washington, D.C.: United States Institute of Peace Press.

Linz, Juan J. and Alfred Stepan 1996. *Problems of democratic transition and consolidation: southern Europe, South America, and post-communist Europe*. Baltimore: Johns Hopkins University Press.

Lipman, Masha and Michael McFaul 2003. Putin and the media. In: Dale R. Herspring (ed.) *Putin's Russia: past imperfect, future uncertain*. Lanham, Md.: Rowman & Littlefield.

Lomax, Bill. 1976. *Hungary 1956*. London: Allen and Busby.

Lomax, Bill (ed.) 1990. *Hungarian workers' councils in 1956*. Boulder, Colo.: Social Science Monographs.

Lukosiunas, M. 1998. Is the Transition Over? Mass Media Law and Practice. Latvia Lithuania Estonia (Baltic Edition of *Mass Media Law and Practice Bulletin*, Moscow). Issue 6, July (http://www.medialaw.ru/e_pages/publications/zip/baltic/vil106-1.html).

Lull, James and Stephen Hinerman 1997. The Search for Scandal. In Lull and Hinerman (eds.) *Media Scandals. Morality and Desire in the Popular Culture Marketplace*. New York: Columbia University Press, 1–33.

Markovits, Andrei S. and Mark Silverstein (eds.) 1988. *The Politics of Scandal: Power and Process in Liberal Democracies*, New York and London: Holmes and Meier, 1–12.

Marvin, Carolyn and David W. Ingle 1999. *Blood sacrifice and the nation: totem rituals and the American flag*. Cambridge: Cambridge University Press.

Mazzoleni, Gianpietro, Julianne Stewart, and Bruce Horsfield (eds.) 2003. *The media and neo-populism: a contemporary comparative analysis*. Westport, Conn. Praeger.

McAdam, D., McCarthy, J. D. and Zald, M. N. (eds.) 1996. Opportunities, mobilizing structures and framing processes – toward a synthetic, comparative perspectiveon social movements. In: McAdam, D., McCarthy, J. D. and Zald, M. N. (eds.) *Comparative Perspectives on Social Movements*. Cambridge: Cambridge University Press, 1–20.

McQuail, Denis 1992. *Media Performance. Mass Communication and the Public Interest*. London: Sage Publications.

McQuail, Denis 2005. *McQuail's Mass Communication Theory*. London: Sage Publications.

Meerson-Aksenov, Michael and Boris Shragin (eds.) 1977. *The political, social, and religious thought of Russian "samizdat": an anthology*. Belmont, Mass.: Nordland Publishing Company.

Merrill, J. C., and Lowenstein, R. L. 1979. *Media, Messages and Men: New Perspectives in Communication*. New York, London: Longman.

Nordenstreng, Kaarle 1997. Beyond the Four Theories of the Press. In J. Koivisto, and E. Lauk, eds. *Journalism at the Crossroads. Perspectives on Research* (pp. 47–64). Tartu: Tartu University Press.

Offe, Claus 1999. *Drogi transformacji. Doswiadczenia wschodnioeuropejskie i wschodnioniemieckie*. Warsaw-Krakow: Wydawnictwo Naukowe PWN.

Paletz, David and Karol Jakubowicz (eds.) 2003. *Business as usual. Continuity and change in East Central European media*. Cresskill, New Jersey: Hampton Press.

Price, Monroe E. and Mark Thompson 2002. *Forging peace: intervention, human rights and the management of media space*. Edinburgh: Edinburgh University Press.

Putnam, Robert D. with Robert Leonardi and Raffaella Y. Nanetti 1993. *Making democracy work: civic traditions in modern Italy*. Princeton, N.J.: Princeton University Press.

Raboy, Marc, Serge Proulx and Peter Dahlgren 2003. The Dilemma of Social Demand. Shaping Policy in New Civic Contexts. *Gazette*, 65(4–5): 323–329.

Reljić, Dušan 2001 [1998]. *Killing Screens: Media in Times of Conflict*. London: Central Europe Review.

Reljić, Dušan 2001. *The News Media and the Transformation of Ethnopolitical Conflicts*. Berghof Handbook for Conflict Transformation. Berlin: Berghof Research Center for Constructive Conflict Management.

Roeder, P. G. 1999. Peoples and States after 1989: The Political Costs of Incomplete National Revolutions. *Slavic Review*, 58(4), 854–882.

Rothenbuhler, Eric W. 1998. *Ritual communication: from everyday conversation to mediated ceremony*. Thousand Oaks: Sage.

Rubinstein, Joshua 1980. *Soviet Dissidents: Their Struggle for Human Rights*. Boston: Beacon Press.

Ryabov, Andrei 2004. The mass media. In: McFaul, Michael, Nikolai Petrov and Andrei Ryabov (eds.). *Between dictatorship and democracy: Russian post-communist political reform*. Washington, D.C.: Carnegie Endowment for International Peace, 174–194.

Seligman, Adam B. 1992. *The idea of civil society*. York: Maxwell Macmillan International.

Seligman, Adam B. 2000. *The problem of trust*. Princeton, N.J.: Princeton University Press.

Siebert, Fred S., Theodore Peterson, Wilbur Schramm 1956. *Four theories of the press: the authoritarian, libertarian, social responsibility, and Soviet communist concepts of what the press should be and do.* Urbana: University of Illinois Press.

Simons, Greg and Dmitry Strovsky 2006. Censorship in Contemporary Russian Journalism in the Age of the War Against Terrorism: A Historical Perspective . *European Journal of Communication*, volume 21, number 2, 189–211.

Siune, Karen et al. 1986. A Framework for Comparative Analysis of European media Policy-Making. In: McQuail, D., and K. Siune, eds., *New Media Politics. Comparative Perspectives in Western Europe* (pp. 12–26). London, Beverly Hills: Sage Publications.

Skilling, Gordon H. 1989. *Samizdat and an Independent Society in Eastern and Central Europe.* Houndmills: MacMillan Press, 3–18.

Slapsak, Svetlana [et al.] 1997. *The war started at Maksimir. Hate speech in the media: content analyses of Politika and Borba newpapers, 1987–1991.* Belgrade: Media Center.

Sofos, Spyros A. 1999. Culture, Media and the Politics of Disintegration and Ethnic Division in Former Yugoslavia. In: Allen, Tim and Jean Seaton (eds.) *The media of conflict: war reporting and representations of ethnic violence.* London: Zed Books, 162–174.

Splichal, Slavko 1994. *Media Beyond Socialism: Theory and Practice in East-Central Europe.* Boulder: Westview Press.

Staniszkis, Jadwiga 1984. *Poland's self-limiting revolution.* Princeton, N.J.: Princeton University Press.

Sükösd, Miklós 1990. From Propaganda to Oeffentlichkeit: Four Models of the Public Sphere Under State Socialism. *Praxis International*, X(1–2): 39–63.

Sükösd, Miklós 1997/98. Media and Democratic Transition in Hungary. *Oxford International Review*, VIII(3): 11–21.

Sükösd, Miklós 2000. Democratic Transformation and the Mass Media: from Stalinism to Democratic Consolidation in Hungary". In Richard Gunther and Anthony Moughan (eds.), *Democracy and the Media: A Comparative Perspective.* Cambridge, Cambridge University Press, 122–164.

Sükösd, Miklós 2007. Media democratization, hegemony and social movements: views from East/Central Europe and Eurasia. Paper presented at the Social Science Research Council/ Warsaw University workshop *Justice, Hegemony and Social Movements: Views from East/Central Europe and Eurasia,* Center for East European Studies, Warsaw University. 13–15 April 2007.

Sükösd, Miklós and Péter Bajomi-Lázár (eds.) 2003. *Reinventing media: media policy reform in East Central Europe.* Budapest: CEU Press.

Szűcs, Jenő 1983. The three historical regions of Europe: an outline. Budapest: Hungarian Academy of Sciences. *Acta Historica Academiae Scientiarum Hungariae 29*, 131–184.

Thomas, A. 1999. *Regulation of Broadcasting in the Digital Age.* London: DCMS, www.culture.gov.uk.

Thompson, Mark 1999. *Forging war: the media in Serbia, Croatia, Bosnia and Hercegovina.* Luton: University of Luton Press.

Vartanova, Elena 2007. Russian media model: a Eurasian dimension. Paper presented at the workshop *Comparing Media Systems Beyond the Western World,* City University of Perugia, March 23–24, 2007.

Verdery, Katherine 1999. *The political lives of dead bodies: reburial and postsocialist change.* New York: Columbia University Press.

World Bank 2002. *Transition. The First Ten Years. Analysis and Lessons for Eastern Europe and the Former Soviet Union.* Washington, D.C.

Zarkov, Dubravka 2001. The Body of the Other Man: Sexual Violence and the Construction of Masculinity, Sexuality and Ethnicity in Croatian Media. In: Moser, Caroline O. N. and Fiona C. Clark (eds.), *Victims, Perpetrators or Actors? Gender, Armed Conflict and Political Violence.* London: Zed Books, 69–82.

PART ONE: DIMENSIONS OF CHANGE

After Transition: The Media in Poland, Russia and China

Colin Sparks

Introduction

It is now nearly twenty years since the great crisis of Communism that led to the struggles, revolts and revolutions of 1989–92. The outcomes of those events have differed widely from place to place. Probably only North Korea survives today as a museum of a fully functioning Stalinist state. Elsewhere, even where the Communist parties continue to hold monopolies of political power, for example, in China, there have been changes, more or less extensive, to the nature of social and economic life. At the other extreme, eight of the European former Communist countries have changed sufficiently as to join the European Union, and two others are preparing for accession. Between the extremes, there are different types of political and economic systems established with a greater or lesser degree of stability.

The variety of different patterns of social organization is mirrored by the different patterns of media system. The rankings of 'Global Press Freedom' produced annually by Freedom House score Estonia and Latvia as "Free" at 17 points (equal 24th with the USA and Canada and one point better than the UK). Poland is "Free" at 20 points (equal 37th with France and two points ahead of Spain). Russia is "Not Free" at 68 points (equal 145th with Afghanistan, Egypt and Ethiopia and one point ahead of Malaysia). China is "Not Free" with 82 points (equal 177th with Vietnam, one point better than Syria and two points better than the Israeli-Occupied Territories/Palestinian Authority). Right down the bottom, number 194 in rank order, definitely "Not Free" and scoring 97 points is North Korea, one point below Burma, Cuba and Turkmenistan (Freedom House 2005). Whatever one makes of the value of the methodology employed to construct these rankings, and it strikes the current author as crude and frankly ideological, there is no doubt that the overall order does illuminate important differences. Other, equally limited, surveys, for example, that produced by *Reporters Without Frontiers*, differ in detail but produce similar rank orders, although everyone seems to agree that the Nordic countries are tops (*Reporters Without Frontiers* 2005).

Given that there were some strong similarities in the political and economic systems of all of these states at the start of the process of change, explaining the different outcomes, for the media no less than for the societies as a whole, is a major theoretical and empirical challenge. This paper suggests that the dominant political science tradition of understanding post-communist social change, which is usually, and inelegantly, called 'transitology,' is mistaken in its fundamental approach. Since most studies of the mass media rest, either implicitly or explicitly, upon the same assumptions, it is also the case that much of the writing about media in post-Communist societies has proved unable to theorise the very interesting empirical material it has generated. An alternative approach, that of 'elite continuity,' developed to account for changes on the western fringe of the former Warsaw Pact, is presented as an alternative to explain media change in three major cases: Poland, Russia and China. It is argued that this way of theorizing the processes at stake provides a more satisfactory account of the evidence, and also provides a possible basis for extension to other instances of transition.

The crisis of 'transitology'

The collapse of European communism in 1989–1991 was widely seen as part of the 'third wave' of democratization whose most famous proponent was the US political scientist Samuel Huntington (1991). Scholarly thinking about the events has largely been conducted within the intellectual current often known as 'transitology.' This had been developed a decade or so previously, and had focused most of its attention on the end of European fascism and the military dictatorships that dominated South American politics up to the mid 1980s. The concepts and methods developed to address those processes were extended to try to analyse the new wave of changes. The aim of transitology is to explain explicitly political change from dictatorial to democratic regimes and for them; 'What we refer to as the "transition" is the interval between one political regime and another' (O'Donnnell and Schmitter 1986, 2). With this intellectual background, it is hardly surprising that there has been an underlying assumption that post-Communist change was a process of which led from totalitarian communism to democratization. The bulk of this writing can fairly be termed 'teleological' since it assumes that there was a definite end, democracy as practiced in the 'originator' countries of north-west Europe and North America, towards which countries in transition are inevitably tending. The processes of change can therefore be understood, and judged, by measuring how far along the trajectory towards democracy the countries in question were. Despite the fierce theoretical debates that the term 'democracy' continues to provoke, the consensus amongst authors working in this tradition, however much they disagree about other things, is to follow Schumpeter and to stress a 'minimalist' conception of democracy (O'Donnell 2000, 6–11). As one author put it: 'a transition to democracy is complete when: (1) there is a real possibility of partisan alternation in office, (2) reversible policy changes can result from alternation in office, and (3) effective civilian control has been established over the military.' (Przeworski 1992, 105). In the purer forms of transitology, issues of social structure are an obstacle to a proper understanding of political transition: as one writer proudly proclaimed, transitology 'deliberately excludes from [the] basic denotation of democratic government, as a tactic of inquiry, any references to social structures and socioeconomic relations, believing that their inclusion is likely to obscure rather than facilitate the scientific comparative probing of political regimes' (Shain 1995, 47). Even rather more critical writers, who do acknowledge that democratization has the potential of profound social implications, distinguish these issues from the consideration of democratization *per se* (O'Donnell and Schmitter 1986, 11–14).

This bold intellectual project immediately confronted an obvious and distinctive feature of post-Communist transition, which is that alongside the political changes consequent on the collapse of the Communist Party's monopoly of power, there were also thorough-going economic changes. The political changes were characterized as democratization and the economic changes as marketization. It was, thus, necessary to modify the absolute insistence on isolating the political level from any other kinds of factors, and to argue that these two processes are interdependent. With some honourable exceptions, the project of democratization was, in most cases, held to be theoretically impossible without the concurrent introduction of a market economy (Przeworksi 1991; Linz and Stepan 1996, 11). The bulk of writing may be fairly characterized as "teleological" in this second aspect, too, in that it assumes that end of the process is already set and determined as a market economy and that these societies can be studied from the point of view how far they have progressed upon the path leading towards the economic relations that exist in the 'originator' countries, or more specifically the United States of America. The pure teleology of the original formulation of transitology was modified into a 'twin teleology' of democratization and marketization. Social change in post-Communist countries has thus been scrutinized for evidence of the fact that the societies in question are both becoming more democratic and more market-oriented, with the two processes dependent, one upon the other.

Discussions of the mass media play a surprisingly small part in political science accounts of transition or, indeed, of democracy. Logically, a theory derived from the view of democracy advanced by Schumpeter fits well with Lippmann's view of public opinion. But this connection is seldom or never explicitly drawn, although, of course, however unpalatable in theory and objectionable on normative grounds, in practice it provides a good working account of the situation in the originator countries. In general, it is stated that a free and independent media is a necessary condition for democracy, but the discussion remains innocent of any of the issues concerning such a statement that have been raised by research into media and communication. There are one or two honourable exceptions (Pei 1994; O'Neil 1998) but: 'Students of democratization often assert that a free press is one of the key 'pillars of democracy', but this idea is rarely developed any further' (O'Neil 1996, 3).

Communication scholars have naturally been more attentive to the problems of the media in transition, although it is fair to say that in the West the topic has received far less attention than other media phenomena, like the avatars of *Big Brother*, which are perhaps of lesser world-historical importance. They have, however, generally been more or less directly influenced by the twin teleologies of democracy and marketization developed by the transitologists. Again, there are important exceptions (Splichal 1994; Downing 1996; Zhao 1998; Reading 2003; Koltsova 2006) but the mainstream, while differing substantially over the pace of progress, more or less wrote the history of transition in terms of the struggles for media freedom and market economics (Lee 1994; Mickiewicz 1999; Gross 2002; Jakubowicz 2003a).

Nearly two decades later, this account of the trajectory of both society and the media no longer seems at all convincing. As one of the key critics of the 'transition paradigm' pointed out, only some of the societies that had begun a process of political change in 1989 had, by 2002, established what political scientists recognize as stable democracies (Carothers 2002). If the foundation of the paradigm had placed a very strong emphasis upon elections as the defining feature of a democracy, later scholars had wished to qualify that by adducing other factors. The end state was redefined as a 'liberal democracy', which was differentiated from a variety of other states, variously classified by different authors as 'electoral democracy', 'feckless pluralism', 'dominant power politics', 'sultanism' and so on. The seemingly endless proliferation of different intermediate stages between democracy and dictatorship not only reduces the elegance of the paradigm but also calls into question its explanatory power. In place of the belief in a straightforward and more or less linear transition to democracy as the ideal type of transition, with all instances of imperfection being regarded as anomalies, Carothers argued that theory and practice should: 'start by assuming that what is often thought of as an uneasy, precarious, middle ground between full-fledged democracy and outright dictatorship is actually the most common political condition today of countries in the developing world and the post-communist world' (2002, 17–18).

There are some signs that a similar conclusion is being drawn within studies of media in transitional societies even by some of those writers earlier associated with the transition school. Thus, Jakubowicz writes after a detailed account of the failure to establish public service broadcasting in the region that: 'It could be said, as with post-Communist transformation in general, that from one point view, media system change will be achieved once what is happening in Central and Eastern European media no longer has anything to do with overcoming the legacy of the Communist system – and that is quite some time away' (2004, 68). Similarly, recent studies of the press in China have tended to stress the extent to which the supposed contradictions between journalists and state have been resolved in the construction of 'Chinese Party Publicity Inc.' (Zhou 2000; Lee, Zhou and Huang 2006). In the case of Russia, of course, the consolidation of the Putin presidency is seen as establishing a new form of authoritarian control over the media (Belin 2002).

The evident failure of the 'transition paradigm' to provide a satisfactory account of political and economic development, either at the general level of political science or in the narrow but central field of the media, necessitates a reconsideration of our theoretical orientation. One option is to attempt to modify the paradigm, à la Tycho Brahe, in order to account for the observational anomalies. An alternative is to re-examine the problem and seek to discover whether there might be a better paradigm to explain it. It is the latter course that is adopted here.

The theory of elite continuity

As an alternative explanation of the dynamics of post-Communist media systems we may consider the theory of elite continuity. When studying the complex and protracted evolution of the media in Poland, Hungary, the Czech Republic and Slovakia in the first years after the fall of Communism, it quickly became apparent that the course of events was not following the programmes outlined either by the former dissidents who were now in power nor by the legion of consultants from Western Europe and the USA who were offering them advice as to how to restructure broadcasting and the press. The very worthy aim shared by almost everyone involved in the early years of transition might be summarized not too inaccurately as an attempt to create newspapers like the New York Times and broadcasters like the BBC (Sparks 2001). In fact, what emerged were newspapers that were highly partisan in their orientation and broadcasters that remained closely aligned with the state rather than the public (Sparks 1998).

In an attempt to offer a theoretical explanation for these realities, seven major components were identified:

■ The events in Central and Eastern Europe were genuine revolutions. In many cases these revolutions were negotiated between a section of the dissident opposition and the reform wing of the Communist Party, and very fortunately few of these revolutions involved any violence, but even in those cases they represented a clean break in the organization of political life. The monopoly of political power held by the Communist Party was broken both formally and substantially and new political parties were formed and contested for power.

■ There was considerable continuity in both institutions and personnel between the old regime and the new. Institutions like the civil service, the army and the broadcasters remained substantially intact, both in their social position and in terms of their internal structure. In broadcasting, for example, the old state broadcasters were nowhere broken up or privatized. They remained central to the media systems, and they retained a very high proportion of their existing personnel.

■ The shift towards a market economy was a highly political process, with the award of favourable opportunities being very closely connected to political power. The licensing of the new commercial broadcasters was a case in point, where political connections were essential to the winning of franchises.

■ The media institutions that emerged from the process of transition were everywhere strongly influenced by the political elite. This was particularly obvious in the case of the broadcasters, where regulatory bodies were recomposed to follow the shifting results of elections. The media had changed from being one locus of power to being one of the stakes of power.

■ The revolutions were, following this logic, certainly political revolutions, in that they transformed very rapidly the ways in which the countries in question were governed, but they were not social revolutions in that they did not pose any fundamental challenge to the social order in industry or the state machine.

■ The main dynamic of the revolutions was that it permitted the old elite (roughly, the *nomenklatura*) to transform itself from one that rested upon the collective ownership of state property, which it guaranteed through its political monopoly, to one that rests on private property, acquired formally or informally through the exercise of political power, but sustained economically in the manner familiar from western capitalist societies.

■ Democratization, still less the degree of democratization, is not a necessary part of this model. While the shift to individualised private capital certainly implies a pluralization of power in the society compared with the concentration of power in the old order, it does not automatically follow that this pluralism will be articulated through a democratic framework. In the cases studied during the 1990s, there was indeed a considerable degree of democratization, notably in elections, in establishing rights to free expression and political association, but theoretically this remained a contingent feature of the new order, not its essence.

This theoretical model, which lays its primary stress upon the social continuity in societies in transition, rather than assuming that the process was essentially one of democratization, provided a good fit to the events in the first decade after the fall of Communism in the western-most of the European Communist states. The weakest parts of the model were, first, that there was then little sociological evidence as to the personnel shifts in the elite; and, secondly, that the examples studied did not provide any evidence to test the hypothesis that democratic rule was a contingent factor rather than an integral part of the process. In all four cases considered, the outcomes were sufficiently close to at least the Western European model of democracy as to permit the countries successfully to apply for members of the EC.

In addition, it was not clear whether the model was specific to its particular time frame and geographical focus, or whether it could be extended to explain the features of transitions away from established dictatorships more generally, for example, in East Asia or in other comparable transitions in Europe itself. Given the unique economic and political structures which lent credibility to the description of these regimes as "totalitarian", it was not at all clear that similar tendencies would be observable in societies with an "authoritarian" structure: that is, where economic power was more widely dispersed in private hands and the ruling elite did not have the same degree of control of every form of social organization. In such cases the expectation would be that the process would exhibit a different dynamic since the nature of any change would necessarily have a different scope.

Poland, Russia, China

One cause of the problems facing the transition paradigm is the heroic scope of its ambitions. It seeks, at least, to attempt to offer an explanation of events as distinct as the fall of the Franco regime in Spain in the 1970s, the replacement of the military dictatorships of Latin America in the 1980s, the aftermath of the fall of Communism, the end of the Apartheid regime in southern Africa, and so on. In its grander form, it would stretch back to include decolonization, the reconstruction of the former Axis powers after 1945, possibly the fall of the Kaiser, or even the 1832 Reform Act. We cannot here attempt anything so ambitious. Indeed, we cannot even hope to cover the huge variety of experiences arising out of the crisis of 1989–1992. Rather, we restrict ourselves to an attempt cautiously to extend the range of the theory through the consideration of three national cases: Poland, Russia and China. This at least reduces the scope to something more manageable, but such a drastic restriction does demand some justification.[1] We need first to consider the extent to which these societies can be considered comparable, and secondly to ask how far they can be considered as representative of wider trends in the post-Communist world. If we can construct a case for the comparability of the three countries, then it remains to specify exactly what aspects of the media systems we intend to examine in order to make the comparison.

The countries chosen are widely separated geographically and culturally, but there are sufficient similarities in the starting point of their transition for them to be considered together. They were, 30 years ago, all variations of a recognizable 'communist' (or, if you prefer, 'Stalinist') type of society. They were marked by state control of the major leavers of the economy, and Communist Party control of the state machine. Further, in none of the cases was the rule of the Communist Party subject to any kind of democratic sanction, whether formal or informal. The leadership of the Party exercised complete control over the senior levels of all aspects of society, including the mass media. The existence of independent organizations, or the establishment of independent organizations, even pursuing very innocuous ends, was very strictly regulated where it was not completely forbidden. In short, the leading elements of the Party, through the 'nomenklatura' system, controlled all areas of economic, political, social and cultural life in the societies they presided over, for which they handsomely rewarded themselves with goods and services that were not available to the mass of the population. Their exact status and the central dynamics of the societies which they ruled have been the subject of intense and protracted debates, to which we will return later.

Having identified sufficient similarities in the initial system states to warrant comparison, we should also note important differences. The first of these was that while neither Poland nor Russia was 'totalitarian' in the original sense, since they were no longer characterized by constant social mobilization, nor did they possess an elite with markedly utopian historical goals. China in the 1970s was just emerging from the Cultural Revolution and, thus, did have recent experience of mass top-down mobilization and of a leadership with grandiose ambitions to transform the world.

Secondly, the societies differed greatly in their level of development. All three had large agricultural sectors, it is true, but Poland and Russia were significantly more urbanised and industrialized than was China. Similarly, and largely as a result of these demographic factors, Poland and Russia, while not wealthy by world standards, were qualitatively richer than China.

Thirdly, the regimes had come to power in different ways. The regimes in Russia and China had come to power through autochthonous revolutions and struggles against foreign invaders. The Polish regime, on the other hand, had come to power essentially as an extension of the Soviet military victory of 1945 and the subsequent political settlement. While the Communist Party did enjoy some popular support, there can be no doubt that the regime was imposed by foreigners rather than resulting from resistance to invaders. As a result of these different paths to power, the regimes enjoyed different degrees of legitimacy. The Russian and Chinese Communist Parties could claim the mantle of national defence alongside any other claims they might make, while the Polish Party was widely perceived as an alien imposition lacking in any national mandate. Partly as a consequence of this, the nature and scale of popular discontent with the system varied widely, being by far the most explicit and militant in Poland.

Fourthly, Poland was (and remains) a remarkably homogeneous country, ethnically, linguistically and religiously, largely as a result of horrible barbarisms of the Second World War and its aftermath, including most notably the Holocaust. China, while predominantly homogeneous in ethnic terms, contained (and continues to contain) important ethnic, religious, linguistic and national minorities, some of which, in Tibet and in north-western China, are politically sensitive. Russia, on the other hand, was then embedded in the Soviet Union, in which ethnic Russians were the dominant national grouping. The population of the USSR was enormously diverse, ethnically, religiously, linguistically and nationally, and politics in the successor states remain very strongly marked by the working through of those divisions.

If there are grounds for careful comparison between the countries, it is important to ask whether the cases we have chosen are at all representative of broader trends, or whether they are unique and the results, therefore, ungeneralizable. We began by noting the differences between the degree of media freedom in different countries, and it is important to recognise that all cases have unique features that defy the theorist's desire to abstract and categorize. However, at a certain level of abstraction it is possible to undertake some tentative categorizations which allow us to consider our chosen cases as more or less representative of different classes of countries. There are no agreed standards by which we might undertake this classification, and we are not in a position in this paper to offer a rigorous typology of post-communism, but one study, which reviewed a range of indicators for European countries, including the rankings produced by Freedom House and *Reporters Without Frontiers* mentioned above, came to the conclusion that although they individually lacked any genuine scientific basis, the extent to which their judgements tended to converge lent some confidence to attempts to categorize (Berg-Schlosser 2004). His categories, which are interestingly reminiscent of a professor grading students, and certainly suggest an underlying teleological model, run through A (Full Democracy), B (Almost Liberal Democracy) C (Electoral Democracy) to D (Not Democratic). Poland, rated at A-, is in the top tier of formerly Communist countries, along with the Czech Republic, Hungary, Slovenia and Slovakia, and Italy. Russia, rated at C, along with Turkey, is near the bottom, which is populated by places like Belarus with a score of D (Berg-Schlosser 2004, table one). The geographical scope of this article does not include China, but it would presumably rate a D, or perhaps a new special category of E (Exceptionally Not Democratic). The countries we have chosen, we can therefore reasonably claim, can be taken to stand for at least some of the different social and economic media arrangements in actually existing post-Communism. We might also add that these three countries happen to be the largest in each of the groups to which they are assigned and, thus, we can discount some of the differences that arise from disparities of scale. (Even within Group A, where issues of 'democracy' are not really at stake, differences of scale obviously result in significant differences in the media systems, as a comparison of RTE in Ireland with the BBC, for example, would undoubtedly illuminate).

Comparing Russia and Poland would be accepted more or less without demur by the proponents of the 'transition paradigm', however, they might balk at China, since this has not yet made any noticeable progress towards democracy. That objection is valid if, and only if, we accept the view that there is a democratic teleology at work in the world that will produce similar outcomes in China to those elsewhere. But this is precisely the assumption that is now in crisis. As is common knowledge, China has for the last quarter century been undergoing a transformation of enormous scale and depth, and including China in the comparison allows us to consider what the mechanisms of transition actually are, rather than prejudging the question by assuming that we already know the answer. There are therefore adequate grounds for a cautious attempt to compare the three cases, while making all due allowances for the inevitable differences that history, geography and culture will necessarily introduce into the analysis.

If we accept that examining these three countries will yield at least some insights into the nature of post-Communist transitions, it is necessary to identify those aspects of the media systems that we intend to compare. Contemporary discussions of comparative media systems are heavily indebted to Hallin and Mancini's work, which was developed in order to consider the media systems of Western Europe and North America. Their book has provoked considerable interest and debate, and it is impossible to accept their views without reservation, particularly with regard to its functionalist theoretical dimensions. It is, however, worth attempting to make use of as much of their framework as possible as a useful starting point for considering how to operationalize our own, geographically and historically distinct, concerns, partly at least because such an effort will illuminate parallels and differences between the media systems they survey and the ones which lie at the centre of our interests.

Hallin and Mancini identify four key dimensions of media systems along which they may be compared:

> (1) the development of media markets, with particular emphasis on the strong or weak development of a mass circulation press; (2) political parallelism; that is, the degree and nature of the links between the media and political parties or, more broadly, the extent to which the media system reflects the major political divisions in society; (3) the development of journalistic professionalism; and (4) the degree and nature of state intervention in the media system. (Hallin and Mancini 2004, 21)

These four categories provide a useful starting point for a comparison of post-Communist societies, although they cannot be adopted without reservation, and we consider them in turn.

Political parallelism is a way of thinking about the extent and manner of the links between media and political forces that are central to our concerns, but it rests on the assumption that there are both a plurality of media and of political forces between which there might be a greater or lesser degree of parallelism. We do not wish to make this assumption, either on theoretical grounds or for reasons of simple empirical observation: there are cases in which since well-established alternative political positions are not able to establish their own links with media and while there is a plurality of media they are all closely linked to one political force. In practice it is better to term the phenomenon we are examining political alignment, of which parallelism is one distinctive version.

Journalistic professionalism, in the sense of journalists being a distinct occupational group able to act 'autonomously', free from direct intervention from outside the newsroom, is again a valuable consideration in our three cases, but it obscures some very important features of the cases we are considering. As we shall see, in the Russian case, journalists 'autonomously' took a range of decisions to align themselves with various economic forces without any external coercion. Again, in the Chinese case, some of the key negotiations over professional autonomy we will note are conducted within the newsroom itself between journalists.

The utility of considering state intervention is, we think, self-evident in this context since none of the evidence we are examining can be understood without reference to the state. The concept of state intervention, however, can cover a huge range of different activities, and it is, of course, essential to distinguish, at least in theory, between 'state' and 'government' (Sparks 1986). Some aspects of state intervention can have benign effects for the media, for example, the decision to exempt newspapers from value added tax, and others, obviously including sending the police to close down newspapers, can be very detrimental, so it is always essential to specify the kinds of state intervention under discussion rather carefully.

The issue of the development of a media market, and particularly a mass circulation press, seems problematic even in their own account and does not provide much insight for our purposes. The issue of the development of the media market further needs to be clearly distinguished from issues of press circulation. The development of a media market is logically independent of the existence of a mass press: the USSR was famously home to a mass circulation press that was, as we shall see, decimated by the introduction of the 'market'. Press circulation has been subject to such rapid changes, in different directions, in all three of our cases, that it is difficult to see how it might be taken as a distinctive, or even a stable, feature for comparison. The rise of press circulation in China, and the change in its composition, stands in such sharp contrast to the collapse of press circulation in Russia and Poland, and is the result of such different economic and political factors that it makes no sense whatsoever to make it a key comparator.

The term 'market' itself is central both to Hallin and Mancini and to transitology, and it is thus a central question for our investigation. It is used by almost all writers to cover three quite distinct processes, leading to three quite distinct end states, which may not occur together in any given instance, and it is important to distinguish between them. While in the case of the Western European and North American cases considered by Hallin and Mancini, discussion is mostly about the nature of the end states; in our cases most of the discussion is around the processes whereby these end states are brought in to being. The first process is commercialization, which consists of the subjecting of part or all of the media system to revenue-raising goals, whether through subsidy, sponsorship, circulation or advertising. This subordination of media to commercial imperatives can occur in any system and is independent of ownership or market: RTVE, which for a long time held a monopoly on television broadcasting in Spain, and Channel 4 in the UK, for example, while both clearly state-owned, have always raised their revenues primarily from the sale of advertising space. The second is privatization, which in our case concerns the transfer of ownership from the state to companies or individuals, which is independent of commercialization or market: the French state, for example, sold off the channel TF1 in 1986. The third is marketization proper, which involves media entering into competitive relations for revenue, which can exist independently of ownership but not of commercialization: an example is that of commercial terrestrial broadcasting in the UK which, from the inception of Channel 4 in 1982 to the implementation of the 1990 Broadcasting Act, had two competitive channels financed by advertising, but only one group of companies selling advertising, the revenue for which was divided between the two, one privately and the other state owned, on a basis determined by a political decision. It is the interplay of these three processes, rather than an abstract judgement of the "market" that is the important feature of the media in the countries we are examining.

In using all four of these categories, we are not attempting to apply them in exactly the same way, or with exactly the same content, as do Hallin and Mancini. On the contrary, we think there are significant ways in which their categories are, no doubt unconsciously, dependent upon a teleological conception of the media very close to that of the transitologists, and they seem expressly to believe that there is a process of evolution towards one of their models underway. But it makes sense, in the interests of developing a common body of knowledge, to follow them as far as is practicable in the very different environment that we wish to consider, to which we now turn.

Poland

The distinctive feature of Poland during the Communist epoch, which distinguished it from all of the other cases under consideration, is that there was open, protracted and intense opposition to the regime. The opposition was widespread, often erupting in mass movements, and was primarily working class in social character. While opposition never reached the pitch of intensity of Hungary in 1956, resistance in Poland was a relatively frequent phenomenon, culminating in the Solidarity period in 1980 and 1981. According to one authoritative account, this opposition succeeded in constructing an alternative public sphere from at least 1976. The Catholic Church had enjoyed, since 1956, the right to publish its own newspapers, and from the mid-1970s onwards there was an increasing tide of illegal publications, rising from around 15 in 1977 to 50 in 1979 (Jakubowicz 1990, 339). It has been argued that there were, in effect, three public spheres in Poland by the end of the 1970s: the "official" run by the party-state; the alternative run predominantly by the Roman Catholic Church; and the opposition in the underground periodicals and books (Jakubowicz 1991, 158–61).

The great popular mobilization during the Solidarity period gave rise to very radical proposals for restructuring the principal mass media (Jakubowicz 1990, 341–42; Goban-Klas 1994, 165–82; Jakubowicz 1995b, 130–33)). The intention was to establish a media system in which a whole range of social groups would both participate in the management of the mass media and in directly expressing their ideas and beliefs in and through the mass media. The number of illegal, although now quite open, publications rose to around 1,500 in 1981 (Jakubowicz 1990, 339). There was a genuine and wide-ranging debate about the media and media freedom. The participants included journalists and broadcasters but also involved huge numbers of newly aware people from outside the media industries. In an intense debate taking place over a compressed time span in rapidly changing social conditions, these plans were far from complete and systematic, different sections of the movement clearly had different interests, and the shape of the desired outcomes shifted over time, but the common desire was for a radical break with the existing structures of media power.

In December 1981, martial law was declared in Poland, allegedly as the price for preventing a Soviet invasion, and Solidarity was driven underground. Excluded from the electronic media and the press, from which more than 1,200 journalists were purged, it established a wide range of underground news-sheets. According to one estimate a total of 2,077 underground periodicals were produced during the martial law period (Jakubowicz 1991, 159–60). The Party, or at least its reform wing, recognized that they would need to strike a deal with their intransigent opponents and by 1988 they were engaged in direct negotiations with Solidarity representatives. These were formalized in the next year into Round Table discussions that included the mass media (Goban-Klas 1990; Jakubowicz 1990, 345–46).

The Solidarity stance in these negotiations represented a more moderate approach than that developed in the preceding period. The proposals called for Solidarity to gain representation in broadcasting and for a degree of empowerment of civil society in broadcasting in the longer term (Jakubowicz 1991, 169–70). In the event, both the proposals of the reform Communists and the suggestions from Solidarity proved unworkable when the result of the first reasonably free elections resulted in a massive popular mandate for the latter. By 1990, they had the power and the support to remake the media according to their own prescriptions.

Ideas about the media inside Solidarity were developing very quickly away from theories of 'direct communicative democracy' towards theories of 'representative communicative democracy' (Jakubowicz 1993, 44–50). In practice, this quickly came to mean the representation of political forces in the media. In the press, some of the old underground papers survived and prospered, notably *Gazeta Wyborcza*, and dozens of new titles were launched by parties and social groups alike. The existing party press was rapidly privatized. In some cases (71 out of 170) titles were handed over to their staff, thus at least going some way towards empowering civil society, although in the longer term most of these were so undercapitalized that they were sold on to private interests. In others, they were sold according to political rather than commercial criteria (Jakubowicz 1995b).

In broadcasting, however, there were no proposals for civil society to have a role in running radio or television. Faced with a choice between a 'German' and a 'French' system of governance, politicians of all stripes opted to empower themselves through choosing the latter. The National Broadcasting Council (KRRiT) was set up to reflect the will of the President, the Lower House and the Senate. The clear aim of government, then and later, was to dominate broadcasting in order to dominate the national political debate (Jakubowicz 1995a, 40). Private broadcasting, which might potentially challenge this, was only introduced very slowly.

The media system that emerged from these changes was, by the mid-1990s, one that was thoroughly politicized. The media were certainly plural, but they could not in any real sense be classified as 'independent'. Rather, in the printed press, they reflected a wide range of ownership, both Polish and foreign, but they were overwhelmingly 'political' rather than 'commercial' in orientation (Goban-Klas 1996, 26–28). Many journalists, too, were far from seeing themselves as neutral reporters and observers on a situation: rather, they considered themselves to be representing a particular point of view. The result, according to Jakubowicz, is that the press: '...helps air diverse views and opinions, but usually of party elites, rather than their rank-and-file members or of groups in society in general.' (2003b, 237).

Broadcasting was, and is, even more clearly politicized. The KRRiT, which appoints the supervisory boards of public broadcasters, which in turn appoint the boards of management, has been the subject of continual battles between political parties keen to ensure that their views have been represented in the overall control of broadcasting, and through that into the management of the dominant, state-owned radio and television broadcasters. One detailed study of the regulation and operation of Polish broadcasting concluded that: 'The composition of the KRRiT has been systematically politicized, not only in the sense of who appoints its members, but, more importantly, in the fact that members have been more or less clearly affiliated to political parties (Krajewski 2005, 1144).

This politically determined media landscape does not appear to be a temporary phenomenon related to the immediate aftermath of Communism. Whether it constitutes the 'stable state' of subordination to the power structure, and to particular political forces inside it, that Jakubowicz identifies is a matter of debate (2003b, 241). The evidence from recent events appears to show that politicization is, if anything increasing as a result of the actions of the new Law and Justice (PiS)-dominated government following the elections of 2005. This passed a new media act in December 2005 that reconstituted the KRRiT, again on the basis of political appointment, and promptly filled the new board with its own supporters. After a number of legal challenges, the new board went on to appoint a Supervisory Board for Polish Television that reflected the parties of the governing coalition (PISS 19 May 2006). Subsequently, members of one of the coalition parties (Sambroona or SD) sought a distribution of management posts in both radio and television to reward its members. The third member of the coalition, the League of Polish Families (LPR), appointed one of their leaders to the management board and defended him (successfully) when it was revealed that he had edited an anti-Semitic newspaper in the 1990s.

This, one of the most successful examples of the 'democratic teleology', has therefore not seen the emergence of an independent media as called for by the transitional paradigm. What exists in Poland today is certainly a plural media, but it is hardly one that can claim to stand for society rather than interest groups. The other dimension of the transition paradigm, however, can be dealt with much more simply: the 'market teleology' was substantively realized from very early on. The press was cut loose from subsidies very early on, and with a declining circulation was forced to rely on developing advertiser support from the beginning, although this was far from fully developed. Broadcasting, for its part, also depends very heavily on advertising. Even the state broadcasters gain the vast majority of their revenues from the sale of advertising space, and the commercial broadcasters are completely dependent upon this revenue stream. There is no question that Polish media have been subject to a process of marketization. This is not, of course, unproblematic, and it is a matter of debate what effect it has had on the conduct of the media, but there is no doubt that it has taken place. Large sections of the media, in both press and broadcasting, have been privatized, although public broadcasters remain central to the system. Both the state-owned and the privatized media have become thoroughly commercialized. Finally, they have been subject to a process of marketization proper, in that they have entered competitive economic relations with each other. In terms of the other categories adapted from Hallin and Mancini, the Polish media today are marked by a high degree of political parallelism, by a low degree of journalistic professional autonomy and high, direct and frequent state intervention into the media.

Russia

The Communist Party in the USSR certainly faced discontent and dissidence, but unlike Poland this does not seem to have taken a mass form in the recent past. The initiative for social change came from within the Party itself and it was this that drove media changes (White, Gill and Slyder 1993; Ryabov 2004, 175). While there was an interchange between the Gorbachev section of the Party and some dissidents during the 1990s, there is little evidence that this was on the scale of Poland (Horvath 2005, 50–80). Rather, a wing of the Party attempted to restructure the system and later to open it to more debate. This was immediately reflected in the media, which was effectively divided between three groups of the nomenklatura: the radical Yeltsin wing, who wished to make substantial changes; a conservative wing opposed to change, grouped around Ligachev, and the Gorbachev centre that oscillated between perspectives (Gibbs 1999, 60–61 and 66ff). The situation that developed by 1989 was, according to many observers, one of relative freedom, indeed, a 'golden age', in which the media were free to pursue self-determined journalistic objective, while at the same time enjoying subsidies that made them free from financial constraints (Hagstrom 2000, 200–206; Ryabov 2004, 178).

In the press, employees started to take over their papers as the crisis of the regime intensified after 1990, and the failed coup of 1991 accelerated this process (Zassoursky 2004, 15–16). The press now enjoyed a substantial degree of journalistic freedom, but its economic position was much weakened. Politically, however, the new Yeltsin regime, which came to power after the 1991 coup, faced a hard struggle against the defenders of the old regime, who constituted a large bloc in the parliament. They threatened to seize back control of their party's alienated assets, so the press found itself, in self-defence, aligned politically with Yeltsin's side in an increasingly tense conflict rather than acting as a neutral reporter.

Privatization had its economic price as well. Costs of production and distribution rose rapidly while circulation fell dramatically, and the new revenues from advertising were very slow to develop. As a consequence, most of the newly-independent newspapers found themselves in severe financial difficulties and in need of subsidy in one form or another. state subsidies, however, were dependent upon political support for the Kremlin and not adequate to cover rising costs. The only other source of financial support was the newly-rich business class (the 'oligarchs') and it was to them that the press was forced in the main to turn (Belin 2002a, 140–41). During the first years, there developed a "market for influence" as one independent newspaper after another was bought up by one of the oligarchs. (Zassoursky 1999, 162–63). The oligarchs used their new properties to promote their own causes and interests (Fadin 2002).

The process in television, on the other hand, was much more controlled, with different groups of politicians holding on to parts of the old broadcasting apparatus. One observer argues that 'the process of commercialization and restructuring of television in Russia were orchestrated in the early 1990s by senior state officials' (Rozanova 2006).When private television and radio did develop, it was from the start in the hands of the same oligarchs as had come to control the press. In the early part of the 1990s, these were almost all very closely allied with the Kremlin, to whose influence many of them owed their fortunes (Klebnikov 2000; Hoffman 2002; Freeland 2005). State television was also altered to a more commercially driven model concerned with audiences and advertising. In addition, the strength of the conservative opposition, who controlled the Duma and attempted a counter-coup in 1993, posed a constant threat of re-appropriation of the oligarchs' dubious fortunes and the private broadcasters, as much as the state broadcaster and the press, welcomed the bloody defeat of the parliamentarians (with more than 100 killed). It is, thus, a mistake to see the private broadcasters as having fundamentally different orientations than the state-controlled broadcasters. It is true that the Gusinsky-owned NTV did engage in reporting that was independent and critical of the Kremlin during the first Chechen war, beginning in 1994, but by the time of the 1996 presidential election all of the oligarchs had struck a deal with Yeltsin and gave him systematic and enthusiastic support that helped him to win an election which he had entered very much as an outsider (Lipman and McFaul 2005).

What occurred in the first five years after the fall of Communism in the USSR was thus a process whereby a highly politicized media system evolved. Alongside the national broadcasters who remained directly controlled by the Kremlin, the large national private media had fallen in to the hands of big businesses. These businesses had differing interests, and used their media to pursue them, but they were all allied in one way or another with the Kremlin. In the provinces, the links between business and the local political leadership were even tighter (Hagstrom 2000, 231). Thus, while there was a limited plurality of views present, the media functioned not to represent the diversity of society but the interests of their paymasters. As Koltsova put it: 'what differentiates this situation from the previous Soviet regime is that various power groups compete in their struggle for resources, thus providing some pluralism of interpretations that sometimes grows into fierce 'information wars' (2001, 322–23). With very few exceptions, the mass media were all highly politicized, even though most of the leading national print media and radio had been privatized. Compared with the last years of Communism, things seemed to some observers have got worse. Ryabov argues that, taken together, the influence of the Kremlin and the oligarchs meant that 'The replacement of the media's democratizing mission with the more narrow goal of supporting Yeltsin, compounded by their economic dependence in the new market economy, explain the notable decline from the early transition period' (Ryabov 2004, 182–83).

This, however, is not the end of the story. The collapse of Communism had seen a collapse of the Russian economy (worse than the Great Depression in the USA according to most accounts) and a severe crisis of the Russian state. Although there was a bargain between the Kremlin and the new oligarchs, the terms of that deal were not equal. If anything, in the years up to Yeltsin's re-election in 1996, the terms were very favourable to the oligarchs who obtained, or seized, former state assets at remarkably reduced prices. As the state machine began to recover from these reverses, it attempted to reign in the worst excesses of the oligarchs and to reassert its definition of the public, national, interest as against the private interests of businesses. Yelstin and his chosen successor Putin launched a campaign aimed at bringing significant sections of the media, and in particular television back under their own close control (Belin 2002b). Through complex manoeuvres, Putin was able to seize NTV in 2000, effectively re-nationalize Channel 1 and force ST-6 to wind up in 2002 (Lipman and McFaul 2005, 62–64).

Although private ownership of the media has grown in Russia in recent years, the range of owners of large-scale media politically independent of the Kremlin has certainly been reduced since the mid-1990s, and their degree of operational freedom has certainly shrunk since the beginning of that decade. The media in private hands are either dedicated to non-political entertainment or, if they continue to have a political dimension, are very closely linked to the Kremlin. The second Chechen war, despite its horrors, has seen little critical reporting of the kind that NTV conducted in 1994. On the other hand, it is wrong to see this as a structural change from the first Yeltsin presidency. It is a change and a retreat from the years around 1991, but the realities of privatization forced the media into the hands of oligarchs long before Putin came to prominence, and the bargaining between the Kremlin and business is a common theme of the whole period. The media are, therefore, more plural today, but they are no more responsible to the interests of society as a whole than they were in 1996.

Again, we have a situation in which the democratic teleology has not worked through as required by the transition paradigm. The media are plural, but they are even less free and independent than those in Poland. The market teleology, on the other hand, appears to have been rather thoroughly implemented, at least at the formal level. If we unpack the category, however, we discover that while much of the media has been privatized, although some of it has remained in state hands and some has been purchased back by the sate or state companies, both in the press and in broadcasting. The media have been thoroughly commercialized but it is much more problematic to say that they have been marketized. One of the major factors that drove the press into the hands of the oligarchs was that when they were forced to turn to the market it proved impossible to generate the revenue needed to sustain the press, and they had to look to politically motivated subsidy in order to survive. It is, more generally, very questionable as to whether we can claim that there is yet a developed media market in Russia. The concept of political parallelism is also difficult to apply directly, since although the media have been politically engaged, the large national media have since the early 1990s been overwhelmingly on the side of the Kremlin, even when political opinion in the elite was deeply divided. It is better in cases like this to say that the media in Russia display strong political alignment with the dominant power rather than they have paralleled political divisions. Very low journalistic independence, however, and marked state intervention are clearly strongly present in this case.

China

The obviously distinctive feature of China is that the Communist Party there is in rude health (with more than 70 million members) and continues to enjoy a monopoly of power. There has been no transition, however problematic, at the political level. What there has been, however, is a rapid and very successful movement towards a market economy. In terms of the twin teleologies, there is no doubt that there has been no interrupted march to democracy but there does seem to have been a very successful implementation of the market teleology. The same paradox is visible at the level of the mass media: the Party, through the Central Propaganda Department and its local equivalents at every level of society, continues to control the mass media, not simply negatively in terms of censorship but much more positively through issuing instructions about what to cover and how to cover it (Brady 2006). At the same time, as all serious observers would agree, the overwhelming majority of Chinese media have become increasingly market oriented along with the rest of the economy (see, for example: Polumbaum 1994 Zhao 1998; Wu 2000, 57–60; Lee, He and Huang 2006, 582–84).

The route to this state of affairs began with the defeat of the survivors of the Cultural Revolution and the 1978 decision by the Deng Xiaoping leadership to start opening the Chinese economy to elements of the market, apparently impressed by the success of 'market socialism' in Hungary and Yugoslavia (Meisner 1999, 451). The 1980s saw a steady opening of the economy, the ending of the commune system and start of private enterprises in the countryside together with the ending of many of the social guarantees provided by the state, notably the erosion of lifetime employment for workers in state industries (Leung 1988; Weil 1996; Hart-Landsberg and Burkett 2005, 34–61).

These economic and social changes produced an intellectual ferment, particularly amongst journalists. Some sections of the Party encouraged a more critical and investigative reporting, partly perhaps from conviction and partly to strengthen their hands in factional battles with the opponents of reform (Pei 1994, 179–204; Polumbaum 1990). Not only do journalists working in the official media look back on this period as a golden age when there was a degree of freedom both from political control and from market pressures, but there was also the establishment of a number of titles, notably the *World Economic Herald* (Hsiao and Wang 1990). Even sections of the leadership argued for serious media reform in the direction of press freedom (Lee 1994, 7–9).

The effect of economic reform and political liberalization was the social discontent that triggered the Tiananmen events of 1989. Beginning as an unofficial memorial service for one of the leading reform Communists, Hu Yaobang, who was closely associated with the argument for greater press freedom, this initially student-led event quickly broadened to include a wide range of supporters, including journalists. On 4th May, an important political anniversary in China, journalists marched with banners saying things like 'Don't force me to spread rumours, news must speak the truth' (Gittings 2006, 233). A total of 500 journalists from the official central party newspaper, *People's Daily*, marched behind a banner demanding 'Freedom of the Press'. Two days later, the official press began to report the demonstrations (Goldman 1994, 33). The December 1989 strike by Czech TV workers that forced the state channel to broadcast the events in Wenceslas Square is an obvious parallel, albeit with a different and happier outcome.

Just like Poland and the other countries of Central and Eastern Europe, and like Russia two years later, China had its 1989. The horrible difference was that the hard-line faction in the CCP leadership defeated the reformers and, on 4th June, the opposition was crushed by the military. Alongside the many deaths at the hands of the military, and the executions that followed, thousands were arrested and beaten, many were jailed and others driven in to exile (Gittings 2006, 241–49). The media did not escape the general purge. The *World Economic Herald* and similar papers were closed down. The troublemakers on the staff of *People's Daily* (those who had demanded press freedom) were fired and replaced by loyal recruits from the provinces (Goldman 1994, 34). Zhao Ziyang, the reformist Prime Minister, was placed under house arrest, where he remained until his death in 2005.

On the face of it, it looks as though the outcome in China was the direct opposite of what occurred in Russia and Poland. The Communist Party had hung on to political power, and the process of economic reform was stopped in its tracks. In fact, in 1992, Deng Xiaoping went to Shenzhen Special Economic Zone in south China and announced the launch of a new phase of economic reform. The hardliners were defeated and marginalised. The consequence, as is well known, is that the Chinese economy launched into a new phase of marketization and export-led economic growth.

The media have been marked by the settlement of 1992 every bit as much those of Poland and Russia. The paradox of a market orientation combined with political control is a more or less direct reflection of the general situation in China. As the economy has expanded, so the media have grown along with it, catering to the varied tastes of their audiences in much the same way as any other newspapers and magazines that are driven by advertising and circulation income. Alongside the official Party-approved news, television stations show imported dramas (Korean, for preference) and game shows and talent contests derived from the West (Hunan TV's *Super Girl*, remotely derived from Thames TV's *Pop Idol*, has been the most successful to date). There is also, however, a well-developed tradition of investigative journalism that survived the crackdown and re-emerged with the renewal of economic development. This journalism, although always directed at abuses of the system rather than the system itself, is not merely tolerated by the Party but was and is actively encouraged by it. As Zhao put it: 'In contrast to Western media portrayal of maverick Chinese journalists challenging the Party line from below and from the outside by discussing hot social issues and exposing official corruption, the most significant step towards the rise of watchdog journalism was initiated at the top of the party's propaganda hierarchy' (2004, 55). It is, of course, functional for the Party leadership to allow the exposure of outrageous abuses, like CCTV's News Probe investigation into the local police murder of a worker in custody on the instigation of the factory manager (de Burgh 2006, 123).

The co-existence of market-driven media and political authoritarianism has lasted now for more than a decade, without any signs of a loosening of the Party's hold. On the contrary, the last two or three years have seen a tightening of control under Hu Jintao's regime as part of the effort to defuse the gathering social crisis of unequal development. Whether this constitutes a stable system is a matter of some controversy but Zhang was undoubtedly correct when she wrote recently that 'TV current affairs programmes in China have been exploited to play a key role in shaping public discourse and creating social or psychological climate favourable for political stability' (Zhang 2006, 734). Certainly, the current evidence seems to suggest that, at least so long as macroeconomic growth continues at the current pace the Party can find ways of staying in power in the country as a whole, but the longer term future is completely unpredictable. There is, for example, massive popular discontent amongst peasants and urban workers who have not benefited from the boom, and have lost their previous social safety net (Chan 2001). Within the field of the media, however, it is possible to identify a number of possible points of tension that have attracted the interest of researchers, although here again there is considerable controversy.

The first of these is the status and role of journalists. At one pole there are those who see Chinese journalists as influenced by western journalistic examples and attempting to find ways to reach an accommodation between their professional desires and the concrete reality of their situation. Younger journalists in particular 'interact with the commandist institution and "negotiate" the boundary of the official ideology by broadening the sources of symbolic resources and by diversifying social practices within the official ideology' (Pan 2000, 75). On the other hand there are researchers who argue that the Party has managed to reach an accommodation with journalists so that as they 'became economically privileged in the 1990s, they became increasingly apolitical and contented with the status quo' (Lee, Zhou and Huang 2006, 600). In between is a position that recognizes that while journalists as a group were in the 1990s and 2000s among the beneficiaries of increasing wealth, and that this has led many of them to conform, there remain many others who are prepared to risk punishment in order to carry out investigative reporting and push against the restrictions imposed by the party-state (Zhao 2004, 60–64). Strong evidence for this is the constant series of struggles between journalists and the party-state, which is particularly likely to intervene sharply, closing titles, moving critical journalists away and importing loyal substitutes, and even jailing people on trumped-up charges, if the reports go beyond criticizing individual abuses and expose the weaknesses of the system (Zhao 2005, 66–70). Certainly, that has been the fate of Chen Guidi and Wun Chuntao, who in December 2003 published a book detailing the terrible conditions of the Chinese peasantry in Anhui province. The book was an immediate success, but was banned by the Central Propaganda Department. It has circulated massively in clandestine editions, but the two authors have suffered threats, violence and official persecution, and Chen was told to resign from his job (Chen and Wu 2006). There are numerous other cases of similar repression directed against journalists and titles that have pushed the limits of acceptability just too far. The reality is likely very similar in structure, but certainly not in the severity of the outcomes, to the situation in western countries: many journalists are quite contented with the system that rewards them so well and see no reason to challenge it; some are discontented but conform to the norms for career reasons; some are either fortunate enough or brave enough to try to publish what they believe to be important truths in defiance of the threat of sanctions.

The second area of debate is the extent to which the Chinese market functions as a genuinely free market. There are two issues here. In the first place, there has been a conscious policy of constructing large media conglomerates in the press and broadcasting over the last decade, partly in anticipation of the effects of entry into the WTO (Hu 2003). According to some commentators, very far from marketization leading to an opening of China to foreign media we are approaching a stage when China will have the potential to become a major international exporter (Keane 2006). This concentration of economic power has not been as the result of an 'organic' process of merger and takeover but as a result of bureaucratic decision-making. The second issue concerns the degree to which there is genuine competition between media. The central party media (CCTV, *People's Daily*, Xinhua etc.) have a privileged position in the Chinese market: other TV stations must carry CCTV's main news bulletin and they are prevented from developing competing services with national coverage. Another example is the broadcasting of the 2006 World Cup (soccer World Cup, that is), the rights to which were held exclusively by CCTV, as the direct result of administrative fiat rather than market competition. The importance of these administrative restrictions continues down the state hierarchy (Chan 2003). These political conditions, which are sometimes compared to activities described by economists as "rent-seeking behaviour", are endemic to Chinese media (Feng 2003). They lead, however, to sharp conflicts both between media outlets and the different sections of the political apparatus to which they are responsible. Control over the media is a powerful asset, both politically and financially, for sections of the bureaucracy, and there are frequent struggles over who has the rights to a particular kind of delivery system reaching a particular kind of audience (Sun 2006). The evidence appears to suggest that a quite well-developed media market operates within strict political limits but that these are the subject of struggle and bargaining between different sections of the elite.

The media are unquestionably subject to frequent, often contradictory and arbitrary state intervention, the degree of journalistic autonomy is in theory very low although in practice there are areas which are open for negotiation, and there is very marked political alignment with the one party that has power. The media in China have not been privatized: they remain effectively the property of the Party. On the other hand, they have been thoroughly commercialized and, to a considerable degree, if not fully marketized, subject to very strong market disciplines.

Explaining the changes
The Chinese case is, thus, one that has many more parallels with Poland and Russia than strikes the casual observer. In all three cases we can observe something which may resemble the operation of a teleology of the market, but this has worked its way through the different societies in very uneven ways. Its presence is most strongly apparent in China, followed by Poland and, finally, Russia. On the other hand, there is no apparent teleology of democracy. Even in the 'best' case, Poland, the media remain intensely politicized and partisan, and there is little pretence at public service in either the press or broadcasting. In Russia, it is commonly argued that there has been a movement away from even the relatively limited democracy of the early 1990s, and those sections of the media that deal with public affairs are dependent either upon the political elite or upon its closest business associates and they use this control for factional purposes. In China, the Party retains control of the media and continues to use it for its own

ends. There is, it is evident, no easy fit between the type of media system and the nature of the economic system. These three examples clearly bear some resemblance to Hallin and Mancini's 'polarized political model' or what Splichal, extending earlier work by Mancini had a decade before, identified as the "Italian" model of media, and this raises fundamental questions of social theory to which we will briefly return in the conclusions (Splichal 1994, 145–48).

The transition paradigm is manifestly inadequate to explain this history. A full discussion of the reasons this failure would require as a starting point a detailed critique of the assumptions upon which the transition paradigm rests, for which we have no space here. If we examine the evidence presented above, it is difficult to sustain any of the three main claims of transitology:

■ There is no clear and unequivocal evidence of 'progress towards democracy'. If anything, the Chinese case demonstrates how enduring dictatorial regimes can be even in the face of rapid social change, and the Russian case suggests that there are circumstances in which the increased democratic role of the media can be halted or even reversed.
■ There is no clear and unequivocal evidence of 'progress towards market reform'. There has certainly been a great deal of movement in this direction in China, but in both other cases large sections of the mass media do not follow market logic in any serious sense. Again, the Russian case suggests that this process is a reversible one.
■ There is no evidence whatsoever of any correlation between marketization and democratization, at least with regard to the mass media. The Chinese case demonstrates that one can have rapid marketization, including the floating of important parts of the media system, although not those concerned with editorial content, on the stock market, without having any relaxation of authoritarian control. The evidence, indeed, is that in the last couple of years, alongside a continuation of marketization, there has been an increase in political control.

To note these realities is not to claim that in any case either the societies under review or their media system have reached any stable and enduring conclusion to the process of change. On the contrary, there is every sign that in all three cases there remain powerful, if contingent factors that could transform the situation. Particularly noteworthy in this respect is the evidence of mass discontent in China, particularly in the countryside and amongst laid-off workers, which regularly and frequently breaks out into demonstrations and rioting. According to one report: 'demonstrations of discontent are on the rise. In 2004, the Public Security Bureau reported that the number of "mass incidents" had risen to 74,000. In 2005, the number jumped another 13 percent' (Kwong 2006; Liu 2005). Similar upheavals are naturally also possible in the other two cases, although the new regimes there have been remarkably fortunate in avoiding mass opposition from the victims of market reform (Ost 2001; Crowley 2001).

Our proposed alternative theory of elite continuity, as outlined above, starts precisely from these social and economic factors, and consider the political arrangements as simply one mechanism for the exercise of social power amongst several. As discussed above, the current author earlier advanced the view that the events in Central and Eastern Europe in 1989 constituted political revolutions, but that they did not constitute social revolutions since the same institutions (police, army, broadcasting etc) continued in the new order, and there was a strong continuity in personnel. On this basis, it was argued that the events could best be seen in terms of elite continuity and that the political revolution was necessary in order to create the conditions that allowed the old collective bureaucratic elite to transform itself into a new, individually property-owning, elite (in other words, a classical capitalist class). The political revolution, by allowing a plurality of parties in all cases, and what is unquestionably an electoral democracy in many cases, permitted the use of political power to transform state property into individual property, either through legitimizing previous act of appropriation, granting exclusive and lucrative rights to individuals, or through privatization schemes that favoured the existing elite.

When this theory was first advanced, its key thesis about institutional continuity was easily supported. In the media, the state broadcasters remained central to the system and many of the old Communist press titles retained a substantial market share. The claims for social continuity amongst the elite, however, lacked a great deal of supporting evidence. In the last decade, however, empirical sociologists have been exploring the nature of the new elites emerging in all three of the countries under review. The main finding is precisely one of continuity.

In the case of Poland, one study based on data from 1999 found that 'the present elite has its roots in the former system'. (Wasilewski 2000, 214). The degree of continuity was particularly marked the case of the business elite, and least marked in the case of the political elite. True, most of the new elite had not held leading positions in the old order but, rather, had been junior figures who had already embarked on professional careers and had most often been associated with the Communist Party. (A similar picture can be painted of other "A-" countries, like the Czech Republic and Hungary – Klavňa 2004; Eyal, Szelényi and Townsley 1997).

In the case of Russia, the degree of elite continuity was apparently even higher than in the more westerly countries: 'In Russia, major segments of the previous elite were transplanted wholesale into the new regime so that, compared with other post-communist regimes, there has been a remarkable degree of continuity in the Russian elite' (Steen 2003, 8). We also have a very interesting account of how this process, which began during the last years of Gorbachev, took place. By the mid-1990s:

> The distribution of power on this basis appears to have been completed and with it the 'second Russian revolution' has come to an end. It was a revolution in which a younger generation of the nomenklatura ousted its older rivals. In effect it was a bourgeois revolution, in that it led to a change in the socio-political system in the direction of private property and political pluralism. And it involved a redistribution of political power, towards a group of younger, more pragmatic nomenklaturists, some of whom became politicians and some businessmen. In the economy there was a corresponding shift of power into property, based upon the privatisation of the key sectors of the infrastructure: finance, retail trade, international economic relations, and the most profitable sectors of industry (especially the energy and extracting complexes) (Kryshtanovskaya and White 1998).

In China, too, the evidence suggests that the nomenklatura has provided the bulk of the new capitalist class (Greenfield and Leong 1997). Party officials have systematically used their position of power to enrich themselves, their relatives and their friends (Lau 1999, 61–68). The mechanisms of privatization in the countryside, for example, were systematically organised to ensure that the local political chiefs and enterprise managers were the main beneficiaries (Ho, Bowles and Dong 2003). More generally, Pei (of all people) reports a survey taken after the Party agreed formally to recruit entrepreneurs, which found that

> A survey of 3,635 private entrepreneurs in 2002 showed that 35 percent were members of the CCP at various levels. Surprisingly, 30 percent were party members, about six times the percentage of the general population. This represented more than a doubling of the

percentage of private entrepreneurs who were CCP members in 1993. The rapid increase in the number of private entrepreneurs who were also CCP members, however, was not the result of a massive recruitment campaign.

Indeed, the survey revealed that only a tiny minority – 5.6 per cent of private entrepreneurs joined the CCP after they had set up their businesses. Jiang's famous speech on July 1, 2001, in which he implicitly called for the recruitment of private entrepreneurs, appeared to have had no immediate impact on admitting private businessmen into the party. Only 0.5 percent of the private entrepreneurs in the sample had joined the CCP after the speech. This showed that nearly all the private entrepreneurs were already CCP members before they became owners of private firms. The privatization of SOEs appeared to be more responsible for the growth of private entrepreneurs inside the CCP than the party's organizational recruitment. Indeed, of the 3,635 firms surveyed, 837 were former SOEs and collectively owned enterprises. Of these privatized firms, about half (422) were now owned by CCP members who were either party officials or well-connected CCP members who were able to gain control of these firms during the privatization process. The result of the survey implies that roughly half the privatized firms may have ended up in the control of CCP members (Pei 2006, 93–94).

If, perhaps, half of privatized firms ended up on the hands of Party members, we may assume that others were taken over by their relatives, friends and business associates who were not Party members. Liu reports that

A research report entitled "The Present Economic Situation of All Classes of Society" was recently produced jointly by the Central Research Office, State Council Research Office and Chinese Social Sciences Academy. The version for internal circulation reveals that at present China has 5 million people with assets of 10 million *yuan* or more. Of these, 20,000 people have assets of at least 100 million *yuan*. Among those with assets of at least 10 million *yuan*, the report's survey found that more than 90 percent were from the elite clans of the Chinese Communist Party. Only 5.5 percent were rich by virtue of being related to persons or operating businesses outside of China, and only 4.5 percent became rich from their own efforts. According to scholars who specialize in researching the highest levels of government, more than 200 "Princelings" currently hold positions in the upper levels of the government... (Liu 2003, 75)

The transformation of China appears to be changing almost everything about the country except for the identity of the people who run the country and benefit from its new prosperity.

The evidence for continuity, both institutional and social is, therefore, quite strong. Whatever else happened, the old Communist elite has in all three cases shifted the basis of its position from the collective control of the economy towards individual control. In political terms, the picture in Poland and Russia is more mixed, but even amongst the Polish political elite there is a surprisingly high degree of continuity: the successor to the Communist Party dominated the political scene for many years in the mid-90s and later. In the case of China, of course, there is no doubt about political continuity.

The second part of the continuity thesis was that a political revolution was necessary to effect the transition from a collective to an individual ownership of economic power. This proposition was clearly wrong. While it explains both Poland and Russia, it is demonstrably not the case that there has been a political revolution in China. The necessary modification to the theory, in fact, makes it much more elegant. It suggests rather that instead of their being sharp distinction between totalitarian and authoritarian rule (which tend to reflect a single social interest) and democracy (which necessarily reflects multiple interests), it is quite possible for a totalitarian regime to transform itself into an authoritarian regime, and that the latter is capable of representing a range of interests, albeit a carefully controlled range.

The third element of the continuity thesis is that political power and economic power, far from being opposed, are closely linked and that the political power of the state is a central element in the distributing economic power. This, again, seems well supported by the evidence from these three cases. Russia and China are very clear instances of this phenomenon. Koltsova says of Russia in the 1990s that

> ...nearly all media, including private ones, are owned externally [that is by corporations that have their main interests in other industries, whose interests they might be expected to promote}, and the majority of them are unprofitable. Because Russian business and political elites are extremely interdependent, both see media first of all as weapons to gain political capital – a vital resource that later can be converted into all other forms of capital outside the media domain. (Koltsova 2001, 322)

Subsequent developments in Russian media have led to increases in profitability, but the close relationship with political power remains central to their functioning. Similar statements about China's media can be multiplied at will. Meisner, for example, argues that: 'the fact of the matter is that the Communist state, far from being an obstacle to Chinese capitalism, has been its essential agent and promoter' (1999, xiii). Poland presents something more of a difficulty, but the analysis of the privatization of the Polish holding RSW Prasa-Ksiazka-Ruch, which owned the majority of Polish-printed media, was conducted according to political rather than strictly economic criteria. German capital, for example, was unwelcome, while French capital was (Jakubowicz 1995b, 139–40). The scandals surrounding the attempt to obtain a bribe from Adam Michnik, which he correctly exposed in the media, also suggest that the award of broadcasting licences is subject to similar sorts of power transactions (Krajewski 2005, 1097–98).

The final hypothesis, that democratization was only a contingent element in this process has, rather unfortunately, been confirmed. Even if we accept that Russia would meet the formal 'minimalist' definitions of democracy beloved of transitologists, this is certainly not the case with China. The social nature of transition, the shift from state control of productive property to private control of productive property, and the consequent direct introduction of market relations into the internal working of the economy, is clearly a political process in that it is the state that sets the rules for privatization (or neglects to notice wild privatization – a.k.a. theft). What is not the case, however, is that this requires the formal political processes that are entailed in democratic government: in fact, they can be achieved by a more or less informal bargaining process. In China, these have been conducted entirely under the auspices of the Communist Party, and in Russia they took place out of public view in the chaotic years around 1991. Poland, and by extension other Eastern European countries, emerges not as the normal pattern of post-Communism but as one particularly privileged variant of a process that can, and often does, take darker forms.

One criticism that might legitimately be levelled at the continuity thesis should be noted here. While the thesis is correct in emphasizing continuity both of institutions and of elites, it did not give due recognition to the degree to which there was also renewal. It is obvious from the figures above that the new elites, while heavily drawn from the old nomenklatura, also involve new forces who were previously outside of the circles of social power. Continuity has been strongest amongst the economic elites, while new entrants are more prominent in the political elite. Similarly, while the old broadcasters and newspapers remain central to the media landscape, we can point to new institutions – *Gazeta Wyborcza*, the former underground voice of Solidarity and now the flagship of an extensive media empire, for example, or the metropolitan dailies in China that dominate newspaper circulation and have pushed the old Party papers to the fringes – that have developed as a result of the process of transition. The theory of elite continuity therefore needs modifying to stress the extent to which there is also a subordinate process of elite renewal, which is stronger in some areas, notably politics, than in others.

Conclusions

The attempt to test the relative explanatory power of transitology and the continuity thesis with regard to post-Communist societies demonstrates the superiority of the latter. It is possible to extend the range of the continuity thesis to cover both a broader group of countries and a longer time span than were considered in the original formulations, and it appears to be predominantly successful in explaining important features of transition. It offers a way of understanding change in general, and change in the media in particular, which allows for the range of observable outcomes and provides an explanation as to why they have such strongly marked common features. To the extent that it must be modified to account for the evidence, it is in a direction that strengthens its explanatory power. The fact that the existence of a revolutionary end to Communist power, and the consequent installation of democratic procedures, is not a necessary element in the transitional process gives greater weight to the dimension of continuity. In contrast, the transitology model provides very little purchase on the cases under review, which do not appear to demonstrate the characteristics of steady progress towards a predetermined goal of democratization and fails particularly miserably in its assertion that there is a necessary link between democratization and marketization.

The theory of elite continuity, thus, seems right for extension. So far, it has only been applied to cases originating in Communism, but these are far from being the only examples of transition that require analysis. Indeed, as we saw, transitology was born from the consideration of quite different cases (notably in southern Europe and Latin America) and it is logical to examine whether elite continuity theory can successfully challenge transitology on its own ground, so to speak, or whether the processes are so distinct as to require different theoretical frameworks in order to explain them. At first glance, it is likely that in these cases the fact that there already was a separation of political and economic power before the fall of the dictatorships (i.e., they were, in the jargon of transitology, authoritarian rather than totalitarian regimes) means that evidence of elite continuity in the economic and social sphere would be more prominent than in the cases we have considered here. On the other hand, the end of racist rule in South Africa might pose a different challenge to the theory, in that the political elite in this "one-party democracy" has clearly undergone more or less complete renewal, while the issues of economic and social change are much more problematic.

Finally, the success of the theory of elite continuity raises a very general question of social theory. The majority of accounts, from Brzezinski on the Right to Mandel on the Left, have held that Communism and capitalism are fundamentally antagonistic social systems with nothing significant in common. One might expect to find within a stable, democratic capitalist society, the

USA, for example, that there would be considerable elite continuity over time, since there is no question of systemic change. But if transition means the shift between quite different systems, then findings of elite continuity should be puzzling as, indeed, many commentators have found it: 'To the surprise of most observers, the collapse of communist rule involved no comprehensive turnover of elites. The founding of democratic regimes has instead been accompanied by a marked continuity in elite composition' (Higley, Kullberg and Pakluski 2002/1996, 35).

If, as we have seen, the transition from one to another can be managed, not without great misery and too many deaths, but without fundamental social turmoil, then we have to ask whether the theorists who stressed the fundamental incompatibility between Communism and capitalism were, in fact, correct. Obviously, the systems have differences, but if the main common feature of the transition is that the new elite is derived so substantially from the old elite, then to what extent can it be maintained that the systems are antagonistic? If the Communist editor or producer can so easily become the capitalist editor or producer, if the same stations and the same papers can continue to thrive under both regimes, to what extent are we dealing with fundamentally different forms of society? If, as it transpires, we do not need to hypothesize a revolution for one system to be transformed into the other, perhaps it might be better to consider their similarities rather than their differences? If the media systems that have emerged from the end of Communism resemble so closely the 'polarized political model', which in its exemplary Italian case emerged so clearly from fifty years of militant anti-Communism, then, perhaps, the sharp distinction between these ways of organizing the media requires reconsideration. Answering these questions is far beyond the scope of this paper, but they go to the root of our understanding of the last century and the prospects for this century. Within our narrower field of concern with the media, they strongly suggest that a great deal of the debate over the relative merits of state and market in the provision of democratic information were, not so much mistaken, but certainly over-inflated. The search for a media system that does not, in one way or another, answer to the elites in society demands a different starting point.

Note

1. I should make it clear that I am not claiming to be an expert on all or any of these countries. On the contrary, I must confess that I have relied perforce very heavily on secondary sources in English and on the assistance provided by a wide range of colleagues and students who have much more expert knowledge of the countries in question. Most of my debts are acknowledged in the citations, but I am so greatly indebted to some colleagues, who can claim to be experts in their particular fields, and who gave generously of their time to comment on my drafts and to correct some of my more egregious errors, that I must thank them by name: Dr Karol Jakubowicz, Dr Olessia Koltsova, Professor Miklós Sükösd and Dr Xin Xin. They are not, of course, at all responsible for any remaining errors or for the judgements expressed in this paper.

References

Belin, Laura. 2002a. The Russian Media in the 1990s. Rick Fawn and Stephen White eds. *Russia after Communism*. London: Frank Cass. 139–60.

Belin, Laura. 2002b. The Kremlin strikes back: The re-assertion of state power over the Russian media. Monroe Price, Andrei Richter and Peter Yu eds. *Russian Media Law and Policy in the Yeltsin Decade*. The Hague: Kluwer International. 273–302.

Brady, Anne-Marie. 2006. Guiding Hand: The role of the CCP Central Propaganda Department in the current era. *Westminster Papers in Communication and Culture*, volume 3, number 1. 57–76.

Berg-Schlosser, Bart. 2004. The quality of democracies in Europe as measured by current indicators of democratization and good governance. *Journal of Communist Studies and Transition Politics*, volume 20, number 1. March 2004. 28–55.

Carothers, Thomas. 2002. The end of the transition paradigm. *Journal of Democracy*, volume 13, number 1. 5–21.

Chan, Anita. 2001. *China's workers under assault: The exploitation of labor in a globalizing economy.* Armonk, NY: M.E. Sharpe.

Chan, Joseph Man. 2003. Administrative boundaries and media marketization: A comparative analysis of the newspaper, TV and Internet markets in China. Chin-chuan Lee ed. *Chinese Media, Global Contexts.* London: RoutledgeCurzon. 159–76.

Chen, Guidi and Wu Chuntao. 2006. *Will the boat sink the water? The life of China's peasants,* translated by Zhu Hong. London: Public Affairs.

Crowley, Stephen. 2001. The social explosion that wasn't: Labor quiescence in postcommunist Russia. David Ost and Stephen Crowley eds. *Workers after workers' states: Labor and politics in postcommunist Eastern Europe.* Lanham, MA: Rowman and Littlefield. 199–218.

de Burgh, Hugo. 2006. *China: Friend or Foe?* London: Icon Books.

Downing, John. 1996. *Internationalising media theory: Transition, power, culture.* London: Sage.

Eyal, Gil, Iván Szelényi and Eleanor Townsley. 1997. The theory of post-communist managerialism. *New Left Review* No. 222. 60–92.

Fadin, Andrew. 2002. In Russia, Private does not mean Independent: Bankers and Oil Tycoons use the media as a business weapon. Monroe Price, Andrei Richter and Peter Yu eds. *Russian Media Law and Policy in the Yeltsin Decade.* The Hague: Kluwer International. 257–259.

Feng, Chien-san. 2003. The State, the Media and "Market Socialism" in China. *Javnost/The Public,* volume X, number 4. 37–52.

Freedom House. 2005. *Table of Global Press Freedom Rankings 2005.* Available at http://freedomhouse.org/template.cfm?page=204&year=2005. Accessed 22 August 2006.

Freeland, Chrystia. 2005. *Sale of the century: The inside story of the second Russian Revolution.* London: Abacus.

Gibbs, Joseph. 1999. *Gorbachev's Glasnost. The Soviet media in the first phase of perestroika.* College Station, TX: Texas A&M University Press.

Gittings, John. 2006. *The changing face of China: From Mao to the Market.* Oxford: Oxford University Press.

Goban-Klas, Tomasz. 1990. Making media policy in Poland. *Journal of Communication,* volume 40, number 4. 50–55.

Goban-Klas, Tomasz. 1994. *The orchestration of the media: The politics of mass communications in Communist Poland and the aftermath.* Boulder, Colo.: Westview.

Goban-Klas, Tomasz. 1996. Politics versus the Media in Poland: A Game without Rules. *The Journal of Communist Studies and Transition Politics,* volume 12, number 4, December 1996. 24–41.

Goldman, Merle. 1994. The role of the press in post-Mao political struggle. Chin-chuan Lee ed. *China's media, media's China.* Boulder, Colo.: Westview. 23–35.

Greenfield, Gerrard and Apo Leong. 1997. China's communist capitalism: The real world of market socialism. *Socialist Register 1997.* London: Merlin. 96–122.

Gross, Peter. 2002. *Entangled evolutions: Media and democratization in eastern Europe.* Baltimore, MD: Johns Hopkins University Press.

Hagstrom, Martin. 2000. Control over the media in Post-Soviet Russia. Jan Ekecrantz and Kerstin Olofsson eds. *Russia reports: Studies in the Post-Communist transformation of media and journalism.* Stockholm: Almqvist and Wiksell International. 197–246.

Hallin, Daniel and Paolo Mancini. 2004. Comparing Media Systems: Three Models of Media and Politics. Cambridge, UK: Cambridge University Press.

Hasrt-Landsberg, Martin and Paul Burkett. 2005. China and Socialism: Market reforms and class struggle. New York: Monthly Review Press.

Higley, John, Judith Kullberg and Jan Pakulski. 2002 (1996). The persistence of post-communist elites. Larry Diamond and Marc Plattner eds. Democracy after Communism. Baltimore, MD: Johns Hopkins University Press. 33–47.

Ho, Samuel, Paul Bowles and Xiaoyun Dong. 2003. "Letting go of the small": An analysis of the privatization of rural enterprises in Jiangsu and Shandong. Development Studies, volume 39, number 4. April 2003. 1–26.

Hoffman, David. 2002. The Oligarchs: Wealth and power in the new Russia. New York: Public Affairs.

Hu, Zhengrong. 2003. The post-WTO restructuring of the Chinese media industries and the consequences of capitalization. Javnost/The Public, volume X, number 4. 19–36.

Huntington, Samuel. 1991. The third wave: Democratization in the late twentieth century. Norman, OK: University of Oklahoma Press.

Hisao Ching-chang and Yang Mei-rong. 1990. "Don't' force us to Lie": The case of the World Economic Herald. Chin-chuan Lee ed. Voices of China: The interplay of politics and journalism. New York: The Guildford Press. 111–121.

Jakubowicz, Karol. 1990. Solidarity and media reform in Poland. European Journal of Communication, volume 5, number 2–3. 333–353.

Jakubowicz, Karol. 1991. Musical chairs? The three public spheres in Poland. Peter Dahlgren and Colin Sparks eds. Communication and Citizenship: Journalism and the public sphere in the new media age. London: Routledge. 155–75.

Jakubowicz, Karol. 1993. Stuck in a Groove: Why the 1960s approach to communication democratization will no longer do. Slavko Splichal and Janet Wasko eds. Communication and Democracy. Norwood, NJ: Ablex Publishing Corporation. 33–54.

Jakubowicz, Karol. 1995a. Media as agents of change. David Paletz, Karol Jakubowics and Pavao Novosel eds. Glasnost and After: Media Change in Central and Eastern Europe. Cresskill, NJ: Hampton Press. 19–47.

Jakubowicz, Karol. 1995b. Poland. David Paletz, Karol Jakubowics and Pavao Novosel eds. Glasnost and After: Media Change in Central and Eastern Europe. Cresskill, NJ: Hampton Press. 129–48.

Jakubowicz, Karol. 2003a. Social and media change in Central and Eastern Europe: Frameworks of analysis. David Paletz and Karol Jakubowicz eds. Business as Usual: Continuity and change in Central and Eastern Europe. Cresskill, NJ: Hampton Press. 3–42.

Jakubowicz, Karol. 2003b. Change in Polish media: How far to go yet? David Paletz and Karol Jakubowicz eds. Business as Usual: Continuity and change in Central and Eastern Europe. Cresskill, NJ: Hampton Press. 205–42.

Jakubowicz, Karol. 2004. Ideas in our heads: Introduction of PSB as part of media system change in Central and Eastern Europe. European Journal of Communication, volume 19, number 1. 53–74.

Keane, Michael. 2006. Once were peripheral: creating media capacity in East Asia. Media, Culture and Society, volume 28, number 6. 835–855.

Kelbnikov, Paul. 2000. Godfather of the Kremlin. New York: Harcourt Inc.

Klavňa, Tomaš. 2004. New Europe's civil society, democracy, and the media thirteen years after: The story of the Czech Republic. Harvard Journal of Press Politics, volume 9, number 3. 40–55.

Koltsova, Olessia. 2001. News production in contemporary Russia: Practices of power. European Journal of Communication, volume 16, number 3. 315–335.

Koltsova, Olessia. 2006. *News Media and Power in Russia*. London: RoutledgeCurzon.

Krajewski, Andrzej. 2005. Television across Europe: Regulation, policy and Independence – Poland. Open Society Institute ed. *Television across Europe: Regulation, policy and independence*, volume 2. Budapest: Open Society Institute.

Kryshtanovskaya, Olga and Stephen White. 1998. From power to property: The *Nomenklatura* in Post-Communist Russia. Graeme Gill ed. *Elites and leadership in Russian Politics*. Basingstoke: Macmillan.81–105.

Kwong, Peter. 2006. The Chinese face of neo-liberalism. *Counterpunch*, Weekend Edition, 7/8 October 2006. At http://www.counterpunch.org/kwong10072006.html. Accessed 25 October 2006.

Lau, W-K. 1999. The 15th Congress of the Chinese Communist Party: Milestones in China's Privatization. *Capital and Class*, number 68, Summer 1999. 51–87.

Lee, Chin-chuan. 1994. Ambiguities and contradictions. Issues in China's changing political communication. Chin-chuan Lee ed. *China's media, media's China*. Boulder, Colo.: Westview. 3–20.

Lee, Chin-chuan, Zhou He and Yu Huang. 2005. 'Chinese Party Publicity Inc' conglomerated: the case of the Shenzhen Press Group. *Media, Culture and Society*, volume 28, number 4, July 2006. 581–602.

Leung, Wing-yue. 1988. *Smashing the Iron Rice Bowl: Workers and Unions in China's Market Socialism*. Hong Kong: Asia Monitor Resource Center.

Linz, Juan and Alfred Stepan. 1996. *Problems of democratic transition and consolidation: Southern Europe, South America and Post-Communist Europe*. Baltimore MD: Johns Hopkins University Press.

Lipman, Masha and Michael McFaul. 2005. Putin and the Media. Dale Herspring (ed.) *Putin's Russia: Past imperfect, future uncertain*. Lanham, MA: Rowman and Littlefield. 55–74.

Liu Xiaobo. 2003. China's robber barons. *China Rights Forum*, #2 2003. 73–77.

Liu Xiaobo. 2005. Atop a volcano. *China Rights Forum*, #1 2005. 39–44.

Meisner, Maurice. 1999. *Mao's China and After: A History of the People's Republic*, Third Edition. New York: The Free Press.

Mickiewicz, Ellen. 1999. *Changing channels: Television and the struggle for power in Russia*, second edition. Durham, NC: Duke University Press.

O'Neil, Patrick. 1996. Introduction: Media Reform and Democratization in Eastern Europe. *The Journal of Communist Studies and Transition Politics*, volume 12, number 4, December 1996. 1–6.

O'Neil, Patrick H. ed. 1998a. *Communicating Democracy: The media and political transition*. Boulder, Co.: Lynne Reiner Publishers.

Ost, David. 2001. The weakness of symbolic strength: Labor and union identity in Poland, 1989–2000. David Ost and Stephen Crowley eds. *Workers after workers' states: Labor and politics in postcommunist Eastern Europe*. Lanham, MA: Rowman and Littlefield. 79–96.

Pan, Zhongdang. 2000. Improvising reform activities: The changing reality of journalistic practices in China. Chin-chuan Lee ed. *Power, Money and Media: Communication patterns and bureaucratic control in Cultural China*. Evanston, IL: Northwestern University Press. 68–111.

Pei, Minxin. 1994. *From Reform to Revolution: The demise of Communism in China and the Soviet Union*. Cambridge, Mass.: Harvard University Press.

Pei, Minxin. 2006. *China's trapped transition: The limits of developmental autocracy*. Cambridge, Mass.: Harvard University Press.

PISS. 2006. *Polish International Satellite Service Report*. As reported by BBC Monitoring on 19 May 2006.

Polumbaum, Judy. 1990. The Tribulations of China's Journalists after a Decade of Reform. Chin-chuan Lee ed. *Voices of China: The Interplay of Politics and Journalism* New York: The Guildford Press. 33–68.

Polumbaum, Judy. 1994. Striving for Predictability: The Bureaucratization of Media Management in China. Chin-chuan Lee ed. *China's Media, Media's China*. Boulder, Colo.: Westview. 113–28.

Przeworkski, Adam. 1991. *Democracy and the market: Political and economic reforms in Eastern Europe and Latin America*. Cambridge, England: Cambridge University Press.

Reading, Anna. 2003. Sale of the Century: Gender and media policies in Eastern Europe in the 1990s. David Paletz and Karol Jakubowicz eds. *Business as usual: Continuity and Change in Central and Eastern Europe*. Cresskill, NJ: Hampton Press. 385–411.

Reporters Without Frontiers. 2005. *Worldwide press freedom index 2005*. At http://www.rsf.org/rubrique.php3.id_rubrique=554. Accessed 22 August 2006.

Rozanova, Julia. 2006 Behind the screen: The role of state-TV relationships in Russia, 1990–2000. *Canadian Review of Sociology and Anthropology*, volume 43 number 2.

Ryabov, Andrei. 2004. The Mass Media. Michael McFaul, Nikolai Petrov and Andrei Ryabov eds. *Between dictatorship and democracy: Russian post-communist political reform*. Washington D.C.: Carnegie Endowment for International Peace. 174–94.

Sparks, Colin. 1988. The media and the state. James Curran, Jake Ecclestone, Giles Oakley and Alan Richardson eds. *Bending Reality*. London: Pluto Press. 76–86.

Sparks, Colin with Anna Reading. 1998. *Communism, Capitalism and the Mass Media*. London: Sage Publications.

Sparks, Colin. 2001. Media and Democratic Society: A survey of post-communist experience. Margaret Blunden and Patrick Burke eds. *Democratic Reconstruction in the Balkans*. London: Centre for the Study of Democracy.

Splichal, Slavko. 1994. *Media beyond socialism: Theory and practice in East-Central Europe*. Boulder, Colo.: Westview.

Steen, Anton. 2003. *Political Elites in the New Russia*. London: RoutledgeCurzon.

Sun Wusan. 2006. A small Chinese town television station's struggle for survival: How a new institutional arrangement came into being. *Westminster Papers in Communication and Culture*, volume three, number one. 42–56.

Wasilewski, Jacek. 2000. Polish post-transitional elite. Janina Frentzel-Zagórska and Jacek Wasilewski *The Second Generation of Democratic Elite in Central and Eastern Europe*. Warsaw: Institute of Political Studies, Polish Academy of Sciences. 197–215.

White, Stephen, Graeme Gill and Darrell Slider. 1993. *The politics of transition: shaping a post-Soviet future*. Cambridge, UK: Cambridge University Press.

Wu, Guoguang. 2000. One head, many mouths: Diversifying press structures in reform China. Chin-chuan Lee ed. *Power, money and media: Communication patterns and bureaucratic control in cultural China*. Evanston, Ill.: Northwestern University Press. 45–67.

Zassoursky, Ivan. 1999. Russian journalism and the open society. Yassen Zassoursky and Elena Vartanova eds. *Media, Communications and the Open Society*. Moscow: Moscow State University Faculty of Journalism/IKAR Publishing. 160–66.

Zassoursky, Ivan. 2004. *Media and Power in Post-Soviet Russia*. Armonk, NY: M.E. Sharp.

Zhang Xiaoling. 2006. Reading between the headlines: SARS, *Focus* and TV current affairs programmes in China. *Media, Culture and Society*, volume 28, number 5. 715–37.

Zhao Yuezhi. 1998. *Media, market and democracy in China: Between the party line and the bottom line*. Urbana, IL: University of Illinois Press.

Zhao Yuezhi. 2004. Underdogs, lapdogs and watchdogs: Journalists and public sphere problematic in China. Edward Gu and Merle Goldman eds. *Chinese intellectuals between the state and the market*. London: RoutledgeCurzon. 43–74.

Zhao, Yuezhi. 2005. Who wants democracy and does it deliver food? Communication and power in a globally integrated China. Robert Hackett and Zhao Yuezhi eds. *Democratizing global media: One world, many struggles.* Lanham, MA: Rowman and Littlefield. 57–80.

Zhou He. 2000. Chinese Communist Party Press in a tug-of-war: A political economy analysis of the *Shenzhen Special Zone Daily.* Chin-chuan Lee ed. *Power, money and media: Communication patterns and bureaucratic control in cultural China.* Evanston, IL: Northwestern University Press. 112–51.

THE CONSOLIDATION OF MEDIA FREEDOM IN POST-COMMUNIST COUNTRIES *

Péter Bajomi-Lázár

1. Introduction: Status of media freedom in the post-communist countries

In the late 1980s, the liberation of the mass media was an axiom of the political transformation in the countries of East Central and Eastern Europe. Yet, throughout the 1990s and the early 2000s, *media freedom*[1] was repeatedly challenged in all countries of the region. From Poland to Albania and from the Czech Republic to Russia, practically all of the new (sometimes old-new) political elites exerted pressure on the media in an attempt to propagate their policies and to suppress critical voices. Many of these attempts succeeded: now a wide range of sources describe, unanimously, *a deficit of media freedom*[2] in the countries of the region. Analysts agree that the performance of the news media has fallen short of both normative expectations and the standards set by the media in most advanced democracies (cf. Paletz et al., 1995; Giorgi, 1995; Gross, 2002; Gunther & Mugham, 2000; Paletz & Jakubowicz, 2003; Sükösd & Bajomi-Lázár, 2003).

Most analyses of the status of media freedom rely upon qualitative descriptions such as the annual reports released by the Committee to Protect Journalists (McGill Murphy, 2002; Elingwood, 2003; Sweeney, 2005). Quantitative data on the issue are sporadic. Currently, only the NGOs Freedom House (FH) and Reporters Sans Frontiers (RSF) provide such data; however, those by RSF cover but the last few years.[3] By contrast, the FH annual press freedom surveys cover a longer period of time and allow for a longitudinal comparative analysis of the status of media freedom in the various countries. The organization's quantitative data reveal that, from the early 1990s until the mid-2000s, the degree of media freedom varied across the countries of East Central and Eastern Europe. Table 1 below, based on the FH surveys, includes

---

* This paper is an updated summary of the author's Ph.D. thesis entitled "Media Freedom in Hungary, 1990–2002", supervised by Miklós Sükösd and László Bruszt, and defended at the Political Science Department of the Central European University, Budapest, Hungary. The full text of the thesis can be found at http://www.ceu.hu/polsci/dissertations/BajomiThesisEdited.doc (last accessed 7 June, 2007).

Table 1: Freedom House annual surveys of press freedom, 1994–2006 (selected countries)

	1994	1995	1996	1997	1998	1999	2000	2001	2002	2003	2004	2005	2006	Average
Norway	10	8	5	5	5	5	5	5	9	9	9	10	10	7.31
Belgium	7	7	10	10	10	9	9	9	9	9	9	11	11	9.23
Denmark	11	9	9	9	9	9	9	9	9	8	10	10	10	9.31
Sweden	11	10	10	10	10	10	11	10	8	8	8	9	10	9.62
Finland	17	15	15	15	15	15	15	14	10	9	9	9	9	12.85
Netherlands	14	18	14	14	14	14	14	15	15	15	12	11	11	13.92
USA	12	12	14	14	12	13	13	15	16	17	13	17	16	14.15
Germany	11	18	21	11	11	13	13	15	15	15	16	16	16	14.54
Austria	19	18	12	12	12	12	12	14	24	23	23	21	21	17.15
Malta	27	24	17	17	17	17	17	14	13	13	15	18	18	17.46
Cyprus	30	24	16	18	18	16	16	18	18	18	18	22	22	19.54
UK	24	22	22	22	21	20	20	17	18	18	19	18	19	20.00
Estonia	28	25	24	22	20	20	20	20	18	17	17	17	16	20.31
Lithuania	30	29	25	20	17	18	20	19	19	18	18	18	18	20.69
Czech Rep.	20	21	19	19	19	20	20	24	25	23	23	22	20	21.15
Latvia	29	29	21	21	21	21	24	24	19	18	17	17	19	21.54
Poland	30	29	21	27	25	25	19	19	18	18	19	20	21	22.38
France	19	27	30	26	26	27	24	21	17	17	19	20	21	22.62
Slovenia	40	37	27	28	27	27	27	21	20	19	19	19	20	25.46
Italy	25	30	30	27	27	28	27	27	27	28	33	35	35	29.15
Hungary	30	38	34	31	28	28	30	28	23	23	20	21	21	27.31
Slovakia	47	55	41	49	47	30	30	26	22	21	21	21	20	33.08
Bulgaria	43	39	46	44	36	39	30	26	29	30	35	35	34	35.85
Romania	55	50	49	47	39	44	44	44	35	38	47	47	44	44.85
Ukraine	44	42	42	39	49	50	60	60	60	67	68	59	53	53.30
Albania	53	67	71	75	56	56	56	56	48	50	49	51	50	56.77
Russia	40	55	58	53	53	59	60	60	60	66	67	68	72	59.31

Scores: 0–30 = free; 31–60 = partly free; 61–100 = not free
Source: http://www.freedomhouse.org/template.cfm?page=274
(last accessed June 2006.)

a selection of countries in Europe, as well as the United States of America, in the period 1994–2006. The higher the score, the more intense the pressure on the media. The nine-year average scores are added to the original table. The post-communist countries that joined the European Union (EU) in 2004 are marked in grey. The ratings under the subsequent years refer to the year when the data were released, i.e., for example, 10 under "Norway/1994", refers to the period 1 January–31 December 31, 1993.

As the Freedom House studies focus on political interference and pay much less attention to commercial pressure,[4] one can safely argue that a greater score equals a greater deal of *political* pressure. The average scores in the table thus reveal that from the early 1990s until the mid-2000s (except for the first three years of the 1990s, as there are no data on the Freedom House's website for the period 1990–1994), the media encountered, as a general rule, *more intense political pressure in the post-communist countries than in advanced Western western democracies.* Of the Western western countries listed in the table, the exceptions to this general rule are France and Italy.

The average scores in the table also show that, as a general rule, *political pressure on the media was less intense in the post-communist countries that joined the EU in 2004 than in the rest of them.* The first-wave accession countries of East Central and Eastern Europe, marked in grey in the table, are the Czech Republic, Estonia, Hungary, Latvia, Lithuania, Poland, Slovakia and Slovenia, while the other post-communist countries listed in the table are Albania, Bulgaria, Romania, Russia, and the Ukraine. Of these, Bulgaria and Romania, i.e., the post-communist countries that joined the European Union in early 2007, came right after the first-wave accession countries.

The table also reveals that, despite the greater intensity of political pressure on the media in the East compared to the West, the scores of the post-communist countries in the period 1994–2006 display a gradual improvement, i.e., *a gradual decrease in the intensity of political pressure on the media.* The status of media freedom as measured by Freedom House was approaching that of the advanced democracies toward the end of the period studied. In most of the EU-member post-communist countries, the media in the early 1990s were rated by the Freedom House as 'partly free', i.e., scores 31–60 as well as the upper 20s, whereas by the end of the decade most of them were described as 'free', i.e., scores 1–30 and especially the lower 20s. In particular, in the period 1994–2006, Estonia displayed a 12-score improvement (28 → 16 scores), Lithuania a 12-score improvement (30 → 18 scores), Latvia a ten-score improvement (29 → 19 scores), Poland a nine-score improvement (30 → 21 scores), Slovenia a 20-score improvement (40 → 20 scores), Hungary a nine-score improvement (30 → 21 scores), Bulgaria a nine-score improvement (43 → 34 scores), Slovakia a 27-score improvement (47 → 20 scores). Even in the countries in which the status of press freedom was qualified as 'partly free' or 'not free' in the early 1990s, there was a more or less significant improvement in the period under discussion (55 → 44 scores for Romania, and 53 → 50 scores for Albania). In all of these countries, the freedom of the media was improving throughout the 1990s and early 2000s. The exceptions to this general rule, i.e., the post-communist countries where the intensity of political pressure on the media increased, are the Ukraine (44 → 53 scores, a 9-point deterioration) and the Russian Federation (40 → 72 scores, a 32-score deterioration).

2. Key question: Why has political pressure on the media survived the declaration of media freedom?

Based on the data above, the question that has to be asked is why was media freedom repeatedly challenged after the formal declaration of media freedom in East Central and in Eastern Europe? Why have the various forms of hidden censorship survived the abolition of overt censorship?[5] And what explains the fact that, despite their largely identical historical and political heritage, the status of media freedom was better in some post-communist countries than others? In an effort to contribute to the study of these questions, this paper attempts to set up a theoretical framework that merges two related approaches, namely theories of media transformation and theories of democratic consolidation.

Most authors representing the first approach and focusing on *the transformation of the media* in the post-communist democracies describe the process in terms of Schramm et al.'s classic "four theories of the press" (e.g., Gijsbers, 1993; Kováts, 1995), or in the context of the development of civil society (e.g., Splichal, 1994; Sparks & Reading, 1998; Gross, 2002). They conceptualize the transformation of the media as a gradual and potentially never ending move from the 'totalitarian' or the 'authoritarian' toward the 'libertarian' or the 'socially responsible' models, that is, from complete or partial state control toward the full autonomy, or the full social control, of the media. Despite the growing number of studies devoted to the transformation of the media in East Central and Eastern Europe, however, no widely accepted theory has been elaborated to frame the systematic analysis of the process as yet. The media transformation literature has been criticized for failing to cover all aspects of the process and to explain regional differences (Downing, 1996). The degree and success of media transformation across the countries of East Central and Eastern Europe have been judged on the basis of fragmentary data and, mostly, qualitative descriptions of the various post-communist countries' media landscapes.

By contrast, those representing the second approach and focusing on *the transformation of the political system* have devoted several studies to the establishment of a theory that helps to analyze the various aspects of the political transformation, to assess the degree of democratization, and to explain regional differences (Linz & Stepan, 1996; Plasser et al., 1998; Hollis, 1999; Pridham & Ágh, 2001). However, most of these studies focus on changes in the party system, the economy, and civil society, while – despite the media's central role to democracy – devoting much less, if any, attention to the transformation of the media.

By merging these two approaches one may attempt to set up a theory that helps to explain the puzzles described at the beginning of this chapter. The introduction of a new concept, namely that of *the consolidation of media freedom*, may help to systematically explain the process of media transformation, the deficit of media freedom experienced in the 1990s and the early 2000s, as well as the differences in the status of media freedom across the post-communist countries. It may also help to identify the key factors hindering the stabilization of media freedom in some of the countries of East Central and Eastern Europe.

3. Measuring media freedom

Evident as it seems at a first sight, the concept of media freedom is not easy to operationalize. Whether and how citizens can actually exercise their right to impart and to gather information depends on a number of factors including overt or hidden political pressure on the media, the status of the economy in general and the size of the media market in particular, the development of communication technology, and the performance of journalists. Yet all the concept of media freedom as defined above (see endnote 1) implies is that the media are either free or not, depending on whether or not the base criteria for media freedom, i.e., the lack of censorship and the plurality of accessible sources of information, are met. The concept of media freedom can primarily be used as a two-value variable. It fails to reveal the actual extent of media freedom and obscures regional differences.

Some analysts overcome this problem by way of using the concept of media freedom as a three-value variable. For example, as mentioned in section 2, Freedom House uses the categories 'free', 'partly free' and 'not free' when describing the status of media freedom in various countries in its annual surveys. Having three categories allows for a more precise assessment of the status of media freedom, and is a great tool for cross-country comparison. The analysts of Freedom House grant scores ranging from 1 to 100 to each country on the basis of a preliminary determined checklist; scores 1–30 qualify a country as 'free', scores 31–60 as 'partly free', and scores 61–100 as 'not free'. However, the lines dividing the three categories are defined on an arbitrary basis: 30 scores qualify a country's media as 'free' whereas 31 scores qualify them as 'partly free'. The consequence is that a one-score difference on a 100-score scale may change the end result.

The Freedom House annual press freedom surveys are designed for the purposes of policy analysis, and their methodology is developed accordingly. However, for the purposes of academic research, a gradual variable seems more convenient. Such a variable can be created by the introduction of the concept of the *consolidation of media freedom*, by way of analogy to the concept of *democratic consolidation*, frequently used by transitologists. The introduction of this concept allows one to make a distinction between the establishment of media freedom on the one hand, and the degree to which citizens can actually enjoy that freedom on the other.

But how to define and operationalize the consolidation of media freedom? Before attempting to do this, I will first briefly recall theories of democratic consolidation.

4. Democratic consolidation and the consolidation of media freedom

Theories of democratic consolidation vary. Some researchers focus on structures or *institutions* (e.g., Hollis, 1999; Ágh, 2001), others on actors or *culture* (e.g., Schedler, 1998; Jones, 2002) as the key factor defining democratic consolidation. Whereas the former argue that democratic political culture is fostered by democratic institutions, the latter suggest that a pre-condition for the establishment of democratic institutions is the existence of some kind of a democratic culture (Gross, 2002). Yet others avoid this 'chicken or egg' problem by merging the two approaches, stressing the importance of both institutions and culture in enhancing the consolidation of democracy (Linz & Stepan, 1996; Diamond, 1997; Plasser et al., 1998). In this paper, I will rely on these more complex theories.

Most of these complex theories are rooted in an influential work by Juan J. Linz and Alfred Stepan. Linz and Stepan argue that democratic consolidation requires a wide-scale consensus about the basic norms of multi-party parliamentary democracy: no significant groups in society should challenge the whole system, and the citizenry, including the political elites, should be committed to the basic norms of democracy (Linz & Stepan, 1996). Following Linz and Stepan's notion of the development of wide-scale consensus among the actors of democracy, Lerry Diamond describes democratic consolidation as the process by which the rules, institutions, and constraints of democracy come to constitute "the only game in town", i.e., the only legitimate framework for seeking and exercising political power. The name of this game is the transfer of power from one political party or coalition to another through fair competition. This is not to say that this condition needs to be met all of the time in a consolidated democracy; it merely suggests that this must be the main rule, violations of which must be sanctioned (Diamond, 1997).

In a similar vein, Fritz Plasser et al. argue that political transformation consists of two phases: transition and consolidation. They define *transition* as the transformation of the basic political, legal and economic institutions into a democratic model, i.e., as the establishment of the formal and minimal criteria for a democratic regime, such as competition, participation as well as basic human rights and liberties. Then they define *democratic consolidation* as follows:

> Democratic consolidation [...] aims at completing regime change by stabilizing the behavioral and attitudinal foundations of democracy. Consolidation thus denotes the continuous marginalization or elimination of behavior patterns incompatible with the base line of democracy and the stabilizing of those in harmony with it (Plasser et al., 1998: 8).

Transition concerns the transformation of the basic institutions, while consolidation the development of institutions and political culture, the latter comprising both behaviour patterns and attitudes. Democratic consolidation thus has three interrelated and simultaneous dimensions, namely:

- the institutional dimension, i.e., the establishment of democratic institutions and procedures that stabilize social interactions,
- the behavioural dimension, i.e., the rise of consensus among the political elites that democratic institutions and values are legitimate, and
- the attitudinal dimension, i.e., the citizens' commitment to democratic values (Linz & Stepan, 1996; Plasser et al., 1998).

Based on the distinction (political) transition vs. democratic consolidation, one may make an analoagous distinction between media transition and the consolidation of media freedom. *Media transition* can be defined as the transformation of the basic media institutions into a democratic model (i.e., the abolition of the state's information, printing and broadcasting monopoly). It is further the establishment of the formal and minimal criteria for media freedom, such as the declaration of media freedom and the creation of a plural media landscape. The *consolidation of media freedom* can be defined as the process which aims at completing the behavioural and attitudinal foundations of media freedom. The consolidation of media freedom thus denotes the continuous marginalization of behaviour patterns incompatible with the base line of media freedom and the stabilization of those in harmony with it. This is not to suggest that there can be no deviations from media freedom in a democratic system, but to say that media freedom must be the main rule, while the institutions, behaviour patterns and attitudes that challenge the freedom of the media either need to be justified by reference to exceptional circumstances such as a war (cf. Sparks, 1998), or are considered undemocratic and are marginalized accordingly. The consolidation of media freedom may be temporally subsequent to media transition, but the two phases may overlap as well.

It is important to note that the consolidation of media freedom is not an irreversible process, i.e., it is an open-ended and potentially never ending one. Evidence from some of the most advanced democracies in the world demonstrates that challenges to media freedom may, at least temporarily, grow more significant even after periods marked with the almost total lack of such challenges. For example, the annual press freedom surveys by the Freedom House show that in the period 1994–2006, the status of media freedom declined even in countries like the United States and Austria (even though the decline was relatively small and the media in these countries were still qualified as "free").

5. Three dimensions

How to operationalize and assess the consolidation of media freedom? Based on the analogy of democratic consolidation, the consolidation of media freedom is considered to have three interrelated dimensions, namely:

- the institutional dimension, i.e., the legal establishment of the *institutions* (laws, regulatory authorities, and funds) that safeguard media freedom vis-à-vis political and commercial pressure,
- the behavioural dimension, i.e., the rise of consensus among *the political elites and the journalists* that freedom of the media is the "only game in town", so that no significant political group challenges the institutions safeguarding media freedom and the legitimacy of that freedom, and
- the attitudinal dimension, i.e., the commitment of *citizens* to media freedom as a legitimate value that is inseparable from a democratic system.

The more these institutional, behavioural and attitudinal requirements are met, the more consolidated, i.e., stable, media freedom is. The question is, of course, how to asses the extent to which these requirements are met.

5.1. The institutional dimension

Although those studying media transformation have not used the institutional, the behavioural and the attitudinal arguments as a complex theoretical framework to explain the deficit of media freedom in the post-communist countries, all three arguments can be found in the literature. For example, in an introduction to a comparative study on the status of the media in post-communist East Central and Eastern Europe, Andrew K. Milton uses the institutional argument, suggesting that

> ...institutional legacies, left by incomplete legal reform, in which the role and valuation of the news media as an institution are carried over from the state socialist period, constrain the complete democratic re-institutionalization of the news media. In consequence, their performance has fallen short of rhetorical expectations (Milton, 1997: 8).

The institutional argument thus suggests that institutional change does not happen overnight and, after the political transformation, the post-communist countries continued to live with a legacy of undemocratic institutions. Furthermore, the institutional argument suggests that the new institutions safeguarding the independence of the media in the post-communist countries were not established or were established the wrong way. In other words, the argument is that the institutional conditions for the consolidation of media freedom were lacking.

As Milton further observes, the democratic re-institutionalization of the media in the post-communist societies is a two-step process, comprising the deconstruction of the communist structure and the construction of new press and media laws and organizations (Milton, 1997). Various authors criticized different aspects of the re-institutionalization of the media in the spirit of this argument, pointing out that the reasons responsible for political and commercial pressure on the media lie either in the late deconstruction of communist institutions or the failure of the newly established institutions to guarantee the media's independence vis-à-vis the political and the business elites (Sükösd, 1993; Gálik, 1994; Gellért Kis, 1997; Vásárhelyi, 1998; Szente, 2001).

In an attempt to answer the questions formulated in section 2 of this chapter and on the basis of the institutional argument, the hypothesis can be formulated that *fast and well-designed institutional change in the media fosters the consolidation of media freedom in the post-communist democracies, whereas slow and poorly designed institutional change hinders it*. The existence and quality of the institutional requirements is best assessed in terms of a comparative analysis of media regulation in countries that performed well and poorly in the FH annual press freedom surveys. Regulation improves the predictability of interactions between the media, the political and the business elites, and limits the means that politicians and investors can use when attempting to influence media content. Media regulation aims at eliminating behaviour patterns incompatible with the base line of media freedom. In this respect, special attention should be devoted to the regulation of:

- the supervision and funding of public service broadcasters,
- the licensing of private broadcasters and
- press funds supporting quality newspapers and investigative journalism.

Evidence is consistent with the institutional hypothesis if media regulation in the post-communist countries was either passed late or does not comply with the standards of the advanced democracies. If it was passed early enough, or does comply with these standards, the hypothesis must be reconsidered.

5.2. The behavioural dimension

The behavioural argument can also be found in several studies on media transformation. For example, it is in this spirit that Richard A. Hall and Patrick O'Neil observe that

> ...because of the legacy of the Leninist political culture, post-Communist governments will attempt to subordinate the media to their wishes; they are not accustomed to the tolerance and freewheeling debate characteristic of a democracy (Hall & O'Neil, 1998: 143).

Barbara Trionfi also notes a certain continuity in the political elites' approach to the media:

> Many of the current leaders of the post-Communist countries were a part of the old party states and maintain the same attitudes toward the media, asking journalists to perform ideological and educational task" (Trionfi, 2001: 95).

This version of the behavioural argument suggests that political re-socialization does not happen overnight and, after the political transformation, the post-communist countries continued to live with a legacy of undemocratic political culture. The argument is that the persistence of undemocratic political culture, i.e., of totalitarian or authoritarian concepts regarding the media's role in society among the political elites, hindered the consolidation of media freedom. In other words, the behavioural requirements for the consolidation of media freedom were lacking.

Another version of the behavioural argument suggests that the currently experienced deficit of media freedom is in part explained by the behavioural legacy of journalists who are unable to fight for media freedom and to preserve that freedom. For example, Éva Vajda suggests that

> [t]hroughout the decades of [state] socialism, journalists were – with due respect to the exceptions – servants of those in office, loudspeakers of the official communiqués of the party. [...] In this situation, they have not learnt just the thing that would be their basic job in (and, by the way, the basic means of) a democratic society: to ask questions" (Vajda, 2001: 155).[6]

This version of the behavioural argument suggests that many journalists in East Central and Eastern Europe had been socialized in a 'Prussian' or 'Soviet' tradition of respect for authority and, even after the political transformation, they explicitly or implicitly define their professional role as being the "Party's soldiers" rather than "watchdogs of democracy".

In an attempt to answer the questions formulated in section 2 of this chapter and on the basis of the behavioural argument, the hypothesis can be formulated that *the fast rise of democratic political culture fosters the consolidation of media freedom, whereas the endurance of totalitarian/authoritarian political culture hinders it*. The existence and quality of the behavioural requirements is best assessed by means of (1) a comparative analysis of media policy rhetoric and media policy practice before and after the political transformation and (2) a comparative analysis of journalism standards and practice before and after the political transformation. In this respect, special attention should be devoted to:

- media policy declarations,
- political intervention into the privatization of the print press and the broadcast media,
- political intervention into the (re-)distribution of resources, and, in particular, information, advertisements by state-owned companies, and radio and television frequencies,[7]
- political intervention into the appointment and dismissal of leading personnel for the public service broadcasters,
- journalistic standards in journalism school books and codes of ethics.

Evidence is consistent with the behavioural hypothesis if significant uniformities are found between the two periods. If, however, differences dominate, the hypothesis must be reconsidered.

5.3. The attitudinal dimension

Last but not least, there are also examples of the attitudinal argument in the media transformation literature, although this approach seems to occur less frequently. For example, John Downing argues that

> [i]t is very doubtful [...] that legislation in a positive direction, in the direction of freedom for the entire public to create its own realm of mass communication, could actively generate these realms. Legislation would have to follow the public's demand in order to ratify and secure what already had been achieved. It could not initiate it. It is for these reasons that the focus on media laws has not so much been misplaced, but over-emphasized (Downing, 1996: 124).

Although Downing does not elaborate on his point any further, the argument can be made that the lack of public responsiveness has made intervention into media freedom a risk-free political and commercial venture: since the citizenry would not sanction such undemocratic measures, the political and the business elites were ready to infringe upon the media's freedom. Furthermore, the lack of such public reaction may re-enforce political intervention into the media. In other words, the attitudinal requirements for the consolidation of media freedom were lacking.

In an attempt to answer the questions formulated in section 2 of this chapter and on the basis of the attitudinal argument, the hypothesis can be formulated that *public commitment to the freedom of the media enhances the consolidation of media freedom, whereas public alienation hinders it*. The existence and quality of such public commitment can be assessed (1) by an analysis of the various forms of public reaction to the political and the business elites' attempts to challenge media freedom, such as street demonstrations, public petitions, hunger strikes, etc., and (2) by collecting survey data on how the public perceived the importance of media freedom as a core value to democracy.

Evidence is consistent with the attitudinal hypothesis if public outcry in reaction to political attempts to curtail media freedom is found to be lacking. If, however, the public holds media freedom to be a major democratic value, and reacted accordingly to instances of political or commercial pressure, yet the intensity of that pressure on the media did not diminish, the hypothesis must be reconsidered.

6. Conclusion: Perspectives for further research

Introducing the concept of the consolidation of media freedom allows one to re-phrase the first two questions described in section 2 of this chapter (why was media freedom repeatedly challenged after the formal declaration of media freedom in East Central and in Eastern Europe? Why have the various forms of hidden censorship survived the abolition of overt censorship?) like this: *what factors have hindered the consolidation of media freedom in the various post-communist countries?* Thus, the dependent variable is the consolidation of media freedom, whereas the independent variables are the institutional, the behavioural and the attitudinal requirements. A systematic cross-country comparison of these independent variables, based on the FH annual press freedom surveys, may also allow one to find an answer to the question of why, despite their largely identical historical and political heritage, the status of media freedom was better in some post-Communist communist countries than in others.

Notes

1. According to article 19 of the United Nations' Universal Declaration of Human Rights (1948), "[e]veryone has the right to freedom of opinion and expression; this right includes freedom to hold opinions without interference and to seek, receive and impart information through any media and regardless of frontiers". Furthermore, the European Court of Human Rights declared that "[f]reedom of expression constitutes one of the essential foundations of [a democratic] society for its progress and for the development of every man [...] it is applicable not only to 'information' or 'ideas' that are favorably received or regarded as inoffensive or as a matter of indifference, but also to those that offend, shock or disturb the State or any sector of the population" (Handyside v. United Kingdom, 7 December 1976, 1 EHRR 737, para. 49.). Based on these rulings, *media freedom* will be defined as the people's right to impart any fact and opinion, however unpopular, and to gather information on

matters of public interest through the media. Accordingly, the *base criteria* for the media to be free are the lack of censorship and the plurality of accessible sources of information.

2. The *deficit of media freedom* will be defined as the recurring prevention by political or business pressure of the publication of information detrimental to various interest groups, as a result of which the transparency of the activities of the political and the business elites and, by consequence, their control by the citizenry, is hindered.

3. For the quantitative descriptions released by RSF, see http://www.rsf.org/article.php3?id_article= 11715 (last accessed 7 June 7, 2007).

4. For a detailed description of the FH research methodology, see http://www.freedomhouse.org/ uploads/fop/2007/fopmethod2007.pdf (last accessed 7 June 7, 2007). For more on this methodology, see also chapter 3 of this paper.

5. Although the Communist communist regimes did not officially recognize the existence of censorship, the concept of *overt censorship* does apply to the state socialist period because, as a main rule, the state had a monopoly over information that was only occasionally challenged by, among other things, the *samizdat* press. By contrast, the concept of *hidden censorship* applies to the period following the political transformation because, as a main rule, the state has lost its information monopoly, and only occasionally managed to prevent the publication of unwanted information.

6. My translation — P.B.L.

7. What matters here is, of course, not the transparent and politically neutral (re-)distribution of resources, but (re–)distribution based on political considerations.

References

Ágh, Attila (2001). Early democratic consolidation in Hungary and the Europeanisation of the Hungarian polity. In Pridham, Geoffrey & Ágh, Attila (eds.) *Prospects for Democratic Consolidation in East Central Europe.* Manchester & New York: Manchester University Press.

Diamond, Lerry (1997). Introduction: In Search of Consolidation. In Diamond, Larry & Plattner, Marc F. & Chu, Yun-han & Tien, Hung-mao (eds.) *Consolidating the Third Wave Democracies. Regional Challenges.* Baltimore & London: The Johns Hopkins University Press.

Downing, Jones (1996). *Internationalizing Media Theory. Transition, Power, Culture. Reflections on the Media in Russia, Poland and Hungary, 1980–1995.* London & Thousand Oaks & New Delhi: Sage.

Elingwood, Susan, ed. (2003). *Attacks on the Press in 2002. A Worldwide Survey by the Committee to Protect Journalists.* New York: CPJ.

Gálik Mihály (1994). Törvényre várva. A magyar rádiózás és televíziózás szerkezetéről [Awaiting the broadcasting act. On the structure of radio and television in Hungary]. *Jel-Kép,* no. 2.

Gellért Kis Gábor (1997). Ékszer és játékszer. Másfél év után a médiatörvényről és egyebekről [Eighteen months later. On the broadcasting act and some other things]. *Jel-Kép,* no. 2.

Gijsbers, Bart (1993). Politikai televízió és televíziópolitika [Political television and television policy]. In Kurtán Sándor & Sándor Péter & Vass László (eds.) *Magyarország politikai évkönyve 1993* [Yearbook of Hungarian politics, 1993]. Budapest: AULA–OMIKK.

Giorgi, Liana, ed. (1995). *The Post-Socialist Media: What Power the West?* Aldershot, UK: Avebury.

Gross, Peter (2002). *Entangled Evolutions. Media and Democratization in Eastern Europe.* Baltimore & London: The Johns Hopkins University Press.

Gunther, Richard & Mugham, Anthony, eds. (2000). *Democracy and the Media. A Comparative Perspective.* Cambridge University Press.

Hollis, Wendy (1999). *Democratic Consolidation in Eastern Europe. The Influence of the Communist*

Legacy in Hungary, the Czech Republic, and Romania. New York: Columbia University Press.

Kováts, Ildikó (1995). Társadalmi rendszerváltás és tömegkommunikáció [Societal transition and mass communication]. *Info-Társadalomtudomány*, no. 35. (December).

Linz, Juan J. & Stepan, Alfred (1996). *Problems of Democratic Transition and Consolidation.* Baltimore: The Johns Hopkins University Press.

McGil Murphy, Richard, ed. (2002). *Attacks on the Press in 2001. A Worldwide Survey by the Committee to Protect Journalists.* New York: CPJ.

Milton, Andrew K. (1997). News Media Reform in Eastern Europe: A Cross-National Comparison. In O'Neil, Patrick (ed.) *Post-Communism and the Media in Eastern Europe.* London: Frank Cass.

Paletz, David & Jakubowicz, Karoel & Novosel, Pavao, eds. (1995). *Glasnost and After. Media and Change in Central and Eastern Europe.* Cresskill, New Jersey: Hampton Press.

Paletz, David & Jakubowicz, Karol, eds. (2003). *Business As Usual. Continuity and Change in East Central European Media.* Cresskill, New Jersey: Hampton Press, Inc.

Plasser, Fritz & Ulram, Peter A. & Waldrauch, Harald (1998). *Democratic Consolidation in East Central Europe.* Hampshire & London: MacMillan Press Ltd.

Pridham, Geoffrey & Ágh, Attila, eds. (2001). *Prospects for Democratic Consolidation in East Central Europe.* Manchester & New York: Manchester University Press.

Siebert, Fredrick S. & Peterson, Theodore & Wilbur Schramm (1956). *Four Theories of the Press.* University of Illinois Press.

Sparks, Colin with Anna Reading (1998). *Communism, Capitalism, and the Mass Media.* London: Sage.

Splichal, Slavko (1994). *Media Beyond Socialism. Theory and Practice in Central Europe.* Boulder, Colorado: Westview Press.

Sükösd, Miklós (1993). *Politika és média a mai Magyarországon* [Politics and media in contemporary Hungary]. In: Miszlivetz, Ferenc (ed.) *Kultúra és társadalom egy új korszakban* [Culture and society in a new era]. Budapest & Szombathely: Pesti Szalon Könyvkiadó & Savaria University Press.

Sükösd, Miklós & Bajomi-Lázár, Péter, eds. (2003). *Reinventing Media. Media Policy Reform in East Central Europe.* Budapest: CEU Press.

Sweeney, Bill, ed. (2005). *Attacks on the Press in 2004. A Worldwide Survey by the Committee to Protect Journalists.* New York: CPJ.

Szente, Péter (2001). Médiapolitikai vázlat [Media policy: A draft proposal]. *Médiakutató*, winterWinter.

Trionfi, Barbara (2001). Freedom of the media in Central and Eastern Europe. In Bajomi-Lázár, Péter & Hegedűs, István (eds.) *Media and Politics. Conference Papers on the Interplay of Media and Politics.* Budapest: Új Mandátum Publishing House.

Vajda, Éva (2001). Közeg és szakma [Context and profession]. In: Csermely, Ákos & Sükösd, Miklós (eds.) *A hír értékei. Etika és professzionalizmus a mai magyar médiában* [News values: professional ethics in contemporary Hungarian media]. Budapest: Média Hungária.

Vásárhelyi, Mária (1998). Törvénytől sújtva [Down by law]. In: Vásárhelyi, Mária & Halmai, Gábor (eds.) *A nyilvánosság rendszerváltása* [Regime change and the public sphere]. Budapest: Új Mandátum.

PART TWO: NORMATIVE AND POLICY APPROACHES TO MEDIA AND DEMOCRACY

How Media and Politics Shape Each Other in the New Europe

Alina Mungiu-Pippidi

Line of inquiry

How well do media theories from the developed West fit post-communist Europe? Surely since the late eighties of the twentieth century to nowadays the evolution of the media in Eastern Europe (EE) was spectacular and often unpredictable for media theorists. In their classic *Four Theories of the Press*, authors Siebert, Peterson and Schramm[1] famously claimed that 'the press has always taken on the form and coloration of the social and political structures within which it operates. Especially, it reflects the system of social control whereby the relations of individuals and institutions are adjusted'. How does this fit the role that media seems to play in prompting revolutions, insurrections and other forms of rapid political change, a role so obvious in Eastern Europe that it shaped the budgets of democracy promoters and donors everywhere for the last two decades? The ascension of Al-Jazeera, ignored for many years by the American government, also opened the door to fresh reflection on the influence of the media. Some believe that we have entered an age where electronic transnational media can be more influential than any government. It can mobilize or discourage government action, but can also play a role towards other politically influential groups: political oppositions, subversion movements and civil society. In American military academies media studies re-experience the flourishing of the Vietnam War days, the previous war lost by the US in newsrooms prior to being settled on the battlefield. Media researchers side either with classical theory, which denies much political influence to the media, or new, post-CNN theory, which credits them with great influence. It is only fair to say that history moved faster than theory and there is considerable catching up to do by scholars in this field.

The history of the media in post-communist Europe in the last two decades could find an equivalent in a history of the French media between 1788, with the invitation by the King to citizens to address pamphlets to the General States, and 1800, when Bonaparte's law re-established control. In between, one can find moments of triumph and moments of agony, journalists rising to be heads of legislatures as well as journalists sentenced by revolutionary tribunals. One needs a broad historical framework to examine the relationship between media and politics before, during and after times of upheaval, or, depending on the point on the time curve a study focuses (ascending-revolutionary or descending counter-revolutionary), results may seriously distort the general picture. Alexis de Tocqueville famously said that the Revolution which began in 1848 was not another one, but another chapter of the one which had started in 1789. This sheds some light on what could be a good time frame to study revolutionary times.

The new era of media influence we entered with the 1989 revolutions is certainly related to technological progress. The main newspaper of the Ukrainian Orange Revolution, Ukrayinska Pravda, was an Internet-based publication which had 1.5 million hits a day during the 2004 elections. When Serb authorities cracked down on Belgrade B92 radio station it could move to the Internet and continue to broadcast. Denying the huge influence of 'new' media over politics in our times would be foolish: and since politicians are no fools, the development of the new media seems to be accompanied by the development of new strategies to control media contents and influence. While it remains undeniable that the social control patterns of a given society have a considerable influence over how the media system is shaped, I believe that globalization has opened the door to outside influences on a scale undreamed at the times of Four Theories of the Press. Classic media consumption may depend on the national context:[2] however, it is the 'new' media which has a growing public, and the exchanges between the new and the old, as well as directly between new media and politics, allow a media system presently to develop more independently from the local circumstances. This gives the media higher potential for playing an influential role and makes it harder to control by traditional means.

To understand the relation between media and politics in post-communist Eastern Europe this paper builds on scholarship that presumes a two-way relationship[3] and discusses a circular model. It also looks at a broad time frame, to cover revolutionary aftermaths as well as revolutions themselves. I attempt initially to propose a historical explanation for the birth of free media in post-communist Europe, and the different paths that national media systems travel from a moment on, as well as the causes of this divergence and of change more generally. Once this framework is established, I discuss the direct influence of media over politics looking at two different periods. For revolutionary times, and the influence of media on changing governments, I review briefly the role of the media in the recent 'coloured' Revolutions in non-European Union accession countries Georgia and Ukraine. For aftermaths, and the role of media in 'normal' policy-making, I use a survey of cabinet members in ten (post-communist) new EU member countries.

Divergent Development Paths

The fall of communism triggered intense processes of change across Eastern Europe, especially the part geographically closer to the West and subjected to greater western influence. The transitions that followed were supposed to accomplish transformations from command economies to market economies and from authoritarian/totalitarian regimes to liberal democratic ones. In fact, even more complicated processes were initiated in order to accomplish these goals. These can be defined as nation-building (agreeing who belongs to the political community), state-building (moving from despotic to infrastructural power) and, last but not least, society-building. Out of the social standardization imposed by communism, new social categories were needed to emerge during transition, in order to build capitalism and democracy, the entrepreneurs, the politicians, the journalists. Politicians and journalists are, therefore, equally newcomers on the public scene of Eastern Europe, at least in the democratic framework, and both the political system and the media system had to be created from scratch.

To what end? Following the fall of communism, nearly all East European countries embarked on the building of a new, free media. Countries that have made the most rapid progress with the reforms did also privatize the state media, took it off the budgets of the national and regional authorities and pursued economic and regulatory policies aimed at creating an environment in

Table 1: Freedom House scores of media freedom in EE

Country	Status 1994	Score 1994	Status 1999	Score 1999	Status 2006	Score 2006
Albania	PF	53	PF	56	PF	50
Armenia	PF	52	PF	56	NF	64
Azerbaijan	NF	70	NF	73	NF	73
Belarus	NF	66	NF	80	NF	88
Bosnia & Herzegovina	NF	70	PF	56	PF	45
Bulgaria	PF	43	PF	39	PF	34
Croatia	PF	56	NF	63	PF	39
Czech Republic	F	20	F	20	F	20
Czechoslovakia	N/A	N/A	N/A	N/A	N/A	N/A
Estonia	F	28	F	20	F	16
Georgia	NF	73	PF	57	PF	57
Hungary	F	30	F	28	F	21
Kazakhstan	PF	60	NF	68	NF	75
Kyrgyzstan	PF	49	NF	64	NF	64
Latvia	F	29	F	21	F	19
Lithuania	F	30	F	18	F	18
Macedonia	N/A	N/A	PF	42	PF	49
Poland	F	30	F	25	F	21
Republic of Moldova	PF	41	PF	56	NF	65
Romania	PF	55	PF	44	PF	44
Russian Federation	PF	40	PF	59	NF	72
Serbia & Montenegro	NF	86	NF	81	PF	40
Slovakia	PF	47	F	30	F	20
Slovenia	PF	40	F	27	F	20
Tajikistan	NF	93	NF	94	NF	76
Turkmenistan	NF	89	NF	85	NF	96
Ukraine	PF	44	PF	50	PF	53
USSR	N/A	N/A	N/A	N/A	N/A	N/A
Uzbekistan	NF	85	NF	79	NF	90
Yugoslavia	N/A	N/A	N/A	N/A	N/A	N/A

Source: Freedom House 2004, www.freedomhouse.org
Legend: Greater scores mean less freedom.

which the media business could take hold. As in Western Europe, there was one great exception to this — state broadcasting. In the same time, an alternative, unauthorized and unregulated media erupted in many of these countries soon after the fall of the Wall, sometimes preceding the privatization of state media.

By 2006, the Freedom of the Press survey captured a mixed picture of post-communist Eastern Europe. Less than half of the former communist countries are free (EU new members plus a few Balkan countries), with the rest stranded between partly free and not free. If we look back in time, we find Poland, Hungary and the Czech Republic evolving from not free to free in the space of only two years (1989–1991), with a year of 'partly free' in between. This is 'revolution'. Countries that seceded from federal USSR (the Baltics especially) or Yugoslavia also record the greatest evolution for the media during the political upheaval. But later the trends become more mixed and even revert in some cases. Countries like Romania, Bulgaria, Belarus, Ukraine have known alternate periods of progress and regress. So trends do not only vary across countries, but also over time for some of them.

By and large, we can identify two first phases common to all the countries, liberalization, or the passage from total control to limited pluralism, with censorship and repression replaced by self-censorship and partial control. The second phase is of deregulation, mixing planned and spontaneous elements. From here on, national paths travel in different directions. The explanation of these divergent paths far exceeds the role of the media and falls within more general democratization theory. The trajectory of a country is greatly influenced by its proximity to the West and all that derives from it (western interest, influence of FDI), and of its own social pluralism (development of civil society, itself influenced by a range of other factors). However, it is fair to say, as Way does,[4] that a phase of *pluralism by default* of the early 90s (due mostly to *the inability of incumbents to enforce authoritarian rule*) is followed by a divergence of paths, post-communist countries becoming either more democratic or, indeed, more autocratic. I do not discuss more distant traditions here, as none of East European countries, with the exception of the Czech Republic, had a serious democratic tradition. And yet, the European Union and Freedom House now consider many of them to be accomplished democracies. Whatever it is at the source of path divergence in Eastern Europe, it is not *pre-communist* tradition.

Communist tradition seems to matter more, and, indeed, different types of communism operated in Eastern Europe. Censorship in Soviet Union, Romania and Albania was far harsher than in Poland or Yugoslavia, and this impacted on the formation of a class of real journalists with aspirations to be more than just propagandists for the Party. Otherwise, censorship was a general rule, broken only by Gorbachev's decision to replace outdated apparatchik-censors with professional editors with the task to urge self-censorship from journalists themselves.

The first two phases, from full control to partial control during glasnost, and then next to deregulation, either partial or total, were common to most post-communist societies, excepting some Central Asian countries. The fall of the Berlin Wall brought fast deregulation and anarchy, with underground newspapers surfacing without licence, pirate radio stations and a strong western pressure to liberalize the media. The state media is first de-monopolized, and then liberalization follows as state frequencies are offered for the bidding of the private sector. The deregulation went faster and deeper in Central Europe than in former Soviet Union, except for the Baltic States, where freedom of the media was inseparable from the nation-building process. In any event, more decisive steps were taken to protect the new nascent free media in countries where anti-communists won the first round of free and fair elections. As shown in figure 1, from deregulation following the demise of communism, three different paths were available, so as

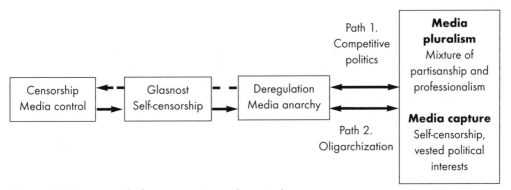

Figure 1: Divergent paths from communist media control

national political systems traveled different journeys so did the respective media systems. In some countries, politics became more and more competitive, and the media more and more pluralistic, although it has remained a complex mixture of professional with partisan media. In others, control of the media returned, as the media was captured again, either directly by governments or by vested interests networked with politics.

At the extreme end of path 2, in some FSU countries, the media, even after a promising beginning, ended up captured. On the other end, in countries with very competitive politics, the media landscape has become gradually more plural and mostly free, with considerable partisanship and only limited capture. The freedom of the media score computed by Freedom House and presented in table 1 correlates strongly with the corruption scores of post-communist countries also given by Freedom House within its *Nations in Transit* project.[5] This means that in an environment of systemic corruption we are likely to find a captured media alongside a captured state. By media capture, I mean a situation in which the media has not succeeded in becoming autonomous to manifest a will of its own and to exercise its main function, notably of informing people, but has persisted in an intermediate state, whereas various groups, not just the government, use it for other purposes. State capture in a post-communist context designates the situation in which the post-communist state has not succeeded in becoming an autonomous actor towards interest groups or vested interests. Media capture in post-communist Europe is, therefore, not necessarily captured by the state. As the groups which capture the media either have already captured the state or seek to do so, capture of the media (either public or private) should be seen as a companion of state capture, a complementary phenomenon. Among the features that make the landscape of media capture we can count concentrated, non-transparent ownership of media outlets, with important political actors controlling the media, a strong linkage between media and political elites, and important infiltration of the media by secret services. Indicators of media capture can give us important information on the trend the media is on, towards more freedom or more capture. We can find precise indicators to measure capture, although indirectly. For instance, a large sector of non-viable media living on covert sponsorship[6] indicates a captured, not an autonomous media. Media cannot operate in a democratic country if they are not economically viable.

Capture distorts the main role of the media: captured media outlets exist to trade influence and manipulate information rather than to inform the public, a phenomenon hard to fit into the classic government-perpetrator and media-victim paradigm. This also indicates that media influence does exist, although it could not be further from the influence of professional journalism, be it more or less framed, measured in laboratories of western universities. When media practices ranges from sheer disinformation to blackmail it can be remarkably influential in politics. An influential media mogul in Romania created a small party and, despite its never passing the electoral threshold, he managed to participate in both Left and Right government coalitions. He has even managed to prevent the first nominated Romanian politician to become an EU commissioner, claiming – without any foundation – that he was an informer of communist secret police. Disinformation wars raged in 'transitional' Russia and are frequent in other countries as well.

The extent of media capture varies across the spectrum of countries taking path 2. Scandals have surfaced even in the most advanced democracies in the region, bringing evidence to document 'capture' attempts. In the Polish Rywingate scandal, editor of *Gazeta Wyborcza*, Adam Michnik, who needed a change in legislation, so to buy TV network Polsat, was offered an informal 'deal' by a government intermediary. Such deals are actually carried out in other countries and nothing more is heard of them. Path 2 and Path 3 (simple regression to censorship) can go separately or can coexist, for instance, the private media takes path 2 and the public one returns to path 3. Ukraine and Russia are countries where the system has been 'mixed' during most of the transition. Prior to the 2004 Orange Revolution, the Ukrainian government had fallen back to 'temnyky', written guidance for the media on how to cover and interpret the news. In the leaked transcripts of the 2000–2004 Romanian government meetings, two major government characters compared the two types of control: capture (indirect control) and open censorship (direct), to find the latter much more effective. In their words: 'I keep wondering why do we continue to support the media with the old tax breaks, with sponsoring and advertising, while what we get in return is just some vague, individual reprieve'.[7]

Governments unable or unwilling to resort to direct media control contribute to media capture either directly or indirectly. State subsidies, bailouts in case of debt, preferential distribution of state advertising and tax breaks for media owners are traded in exchange for favorable treatment of the media. In the case of public broadcasting, anti-communists and post-communists alike showed remarkably firm beliefs in direct media effects.[8] Inheriting a system in which public broadcasting was legally and financially dependent upon government, they have slowly

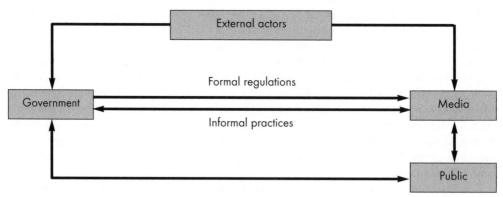

Figure 2: Context of the interaction media-government interaction

reformed it so to make it dependent of the political majority in Parliament, practically legalizing political control, a model also found in some EU countries. The tenure of top executives, for instance, general managers and news director was less than a year during transition, except for the Baltic States, and legislation has often been revised to provide fresh opportunities to dismiss executives who were not obedient enough.[9]

By and large, a model summarizing the complex relationship between press and government in transition accession countries is approximated in figure 2. The government regulates media through formal regulations, but as those are influenced strongly by international actors, it also uses less overt means to control the media. External influence of various types varies greatly across the countries. Unlike for other regions of the world, however, western influence mattered enormously in post-communist Europe. First, for providing an accessible cultural model to be followed by journalists and politicians alike; second, for the conditionality related to Council of Europe, NATO and EU accessions; third, through the permanent channels of communication between professions, contributing to the re-socialization of Easterners according to western standards. This third influence is mostly exercised directly on the media, through training and assistance programmes.

A mix of incentives and penalties, as well as conditionality, played the most direct and impressive role. President Francois Mitterand famously called Romania's President Ion Iliescu in the summer of 1990, when opposition newspapers were closed to argue for a softer handling of political opposition and the media. International influence turned Ion Iliescu into an EU-accession promoter and this conversion eventually changed the path of the country. No such call on record exists for Alexander Lukashenko, the Belarusian president, already elected four times (Mr Iliescu stepped down after a third mandate). International conditionality seems to be powered only by strong incentives, such as a prospect of EU accession, which converts captors into more or less convincing pro-Europeans. Most of the behaviour described here under 'media capture' falls in the realm of 'informal practices'. Practices can complement formal regulations, but can also be competitive or substitutive in others, where formal freedom (as enshrined in the Constitution) is effectively sabotaged by capture or direct control.

The public has an important feedback, to the media via audience and circulation, to the government through elections or opinion polls. The question is why should governments care about media, if they can buy or bully it at their will? The model suggests two important answers to this question. The first is on the role of the international community. As EU accession progresses or non-EU countries ask for foreign assistance (such as grants from Millennium Corporation) the cost of repressing the media grows and becomes unaffordable for any government but an isolated one, which either does not care for the opinion of the international community or is able to buy a good one by resources (such as oil or gas). Capture develops as a substitute, but Freedom House Nations in Transit or IREX Sustainability Index developed precisely in order to be able to look at media freedom more qualitatively. The second explanation refers to the direct feedback of the public to the government, as presented in the model. In electoral democracies or in times when revolutions occur as 'waves', only be popular governments can afford to defy the media. Some governments, such as Putin's or Lukashenko's, had enough resources to subsidize household energy and come up with a variety of perks for the public. These governments will not be brought down by the media, as they are genuinely popular. The largest share of the budget of the city of Rostov, in Southern Russian Federation, is used to cover utilities bills from private households: the majority of inhabitants are beneficiaries. A comparable city, Bucharest in Romania dedicates less than 3 per cent to the same purpose, at a comparable purchasing parity power of the population. But most countries cannot afford such strategies, as they do not have the natural resources. In those countries the voters' feedback is likely to work and the media can be very influential.

The three paths of the relations between media and government in figure 1 thus amount to three government strategies: 1. direct control through repression 2. indirect control through capture 3. accommodation. The third strategy might be inspired by genuine concern on how to sell policy acts to the media or incorporate the views of public opinion into policy, as well as by rational calculations of how to 'look good' to the media.

3. Media Strikes Back

The overriding concern of the first years, both in Eastern Europe itself and the West, was on securing media freedom in post-communist Europe and establishing it on a firm legal and economic basis. But even prior to setting up media as an autonomous actor – a process completed only partly in some countries – media had been at the center of political change in Eastern Europe, right from the very beginning. Starting with the 1989 Romanian Revolution, public television became not just a mouthpiece of government or the victim of abuse, but also a crucial actor. In 1989 Romania, public television extended what could have arguably been a manageable revolt in Bucharest only, into a national scale collapse of communism, by broadcasting the news that Ceausescu had fled. One year later in Bulgaria, a shift in the attitude of journalists working in public television led directly to the fall of communist PM Petr Mladenov and opened the door to radical political change. Seen as the main reason why the Milosevic regime was still popular in rural areas, Serb national TV was bombed by NATO in 1998, on charges of...disinformation.

Two more recent examples illustrate how media can help prompt decisively a breakthrough for radical political change. The Ukrainian Orange Revolution had its origins in the president of the country losing his patience with a journalist. A tape alleging that the president was involved in the killing of investigative journalist Georgy Gongadze, recorded by a former presidential bodyguard was posted on the site of his newspaper, *Ukrayinska Pravda*, turning this small Internet publication into number-one rated Ukrainian media website. This also made the support for the regime an 'immoral' option. During the electoral campaign the number of Internet users tripled in Ukraine, as official censorship pushed voters to Internet cafes in search of real news. Only three days before the first round of elections 40 journalists, representing five TV channels, publicly declared that they would not work under *"temnyky"*. Later, representatives of another eighteen TV channels and media companies joined the petition. The breaking point was 25 November, when the system of censorship and capture collapsed like a house of cards, in the words of a journalist.[10] On the day when official results were to be reported by the central election commission, the sign interpreter, Natalia Dmytruk, ignored the text of the main presenter about the outcome of the election. Instead, she gestured to her deaf viewers: "The official results by Central Election Committee are falsified. Do not trust them. Yushchenko is our president. I'm really sorry that I had to translate the lies before. I will not do this again. Not sure if I will see you then." Her statement triggered others as well.

Georgia's Rose Revolution was another bet won by donors who believed in the power of the media. The key actor was a provincial TV, Rustavi-2, founded in 1994 in the town of Rustavi, not far from Tbilisi. It was initially a tiny, private local TV station. Its main founder, with help and advice from the US media assistance organization Internews (USAID-backed), built it into a professionally sound media company, both in economic and journalistic terms. In the space of a mere two years, Rustavi-2 moved into Tbilisi, survived two attempts of the regime to close it, was made stronger by the assassination of one of its journalists and became a national model where other stations and journalists looked for inspiration. Current President Michael Saakashvili, then the challenger, later said that '*Most of the students who came out on the streets were brought out by Rustavi*'.[11] Its role became crucial on election day, as it ran a scrawl at the bottom of the screen 24 hours a day showing the official results compared to a credible NGO exit polling and parallel vote count.

The assembled evidence that democracy promotion of this kind can be more effective than embargos or military interventions has, by now, persuaded the donor community and endowed it with a strong argument when facing policy-makers.[12] In the ten years leading up to the Georgian revolution, the US government spent just over $154 million on democracy assistance projects in Georgia, most of it under the Freedom Support Act of 1992.[13] In Eastern Europe and the former Soviet Union as a whole, $350 million has been spent since 1991, specifically to develop independent media.[14] Some critical reservations were made that following the victory of opposition in electoral revolutions, media again did not show much autonomy, but instead became more partisan. This is in all likelihood true, and the concern is justified. Good media is autonomous media. Partisanship, however, is an indication that pluralism exists, and pluralism is superior to autocracy. There is another evolutionary cycle to go from pluralism to substantive democracy.

What about 'normal', non-revolutionary times, for instance, during and after EU accession? Does the media still matter? Seeing the public trust in media (television especially) and government, the likelihood is that media has a good position. It enjoys far more public trust than the government does. Around their accession date in 2004, even EE governments with a good record on EU accession were facing major popularity problems; after accession, a period of

Table 2: Trust in media and the government

Country	Print press (%)	Radio (%)	Television (%)	Trust in national government (%)
Bulgaria	35	51	70	19
Czech Republic	59	67	65	25
Estonia	52	75	75	45
Hungary	27	42	44	31
Latvia	52	67	68	28
Lithuania	55	65	68	31
Poland	50	59	54	7
Romania	57	69	73	36
Slovakia	57	71	68	17
Slovenia	54	64	62	27
ECE-10 (average)	50	63	65	27
EU-15 (average)	46	63	53	30

Source: Eurobarometer – Public Opinion in the Acceding and Candidate Countries, February–March 2004

political instability followed in Poland, Czech Republic and Hungary. Television has more than double the popularity of government in most countries, three or four times in some. Television is a strong actor, and TV owners a force to be reckoned with.

Influence on policy-making is, of course, much harder to prove than influence on revolutions. The study of the media's direct effects on politics generally looks at how media might influence who makes political decisions through the selection of political personnel; how media affects political styles and procedures, therefore, how it influences political actors behaviour; how media might co-determine about what decisions are taken due to their agenda-setting role; and, finally, how media might affect the actual content of political decisions, via their directional coverage or framing through bias or partisanship. *The role of the media in elevating issues to the systemic agenda and increasing their chances of receiving consideration on policy agendas is subject of considerable controversy nowadays, after being nearly orthodoxy in the 70s.*[15] In their influential overview of agenda-setting research, Dearing & Rogers state that "*The mass media often have a direct influence on the policy agenda-setting process*".[16] Reviewing a large body of research, Walgrave and Nuytemans[17] found that the media's impact on agenda setting depends on place, issues, political agendas, media agendas and time.

What does evidence from Eastern Europe tell us? In 2003 and 2004, I participated in the organization of a survey in the ten East European EU accession countries asking cabinet members on the role of media on policy-making. Ministers were asked to provide their subjective views on the amount of media influence during their tenure, specifically in reference to topics of cabinet discussions, amount of time given to media in cabinet discussions, presentation of decisions and, finally, substance of cabinet decisions. These questions should be judged together to get a complete picture of media's weight. If the media influence government topics and prompt discussion in the cabinet, this means it influences agenda-setting. The third question on presentation or wrapping up of cabinet decisions is more ambiguous, referring both to the communication skills of the government as well as to the media's influence.

Table 3: Media influence as acknowledged by cabinet ministers

Country	Topics	Time	Presentation	Substance	Specific newspaper/ TV channel
Bulgaria	44	24	44	44	16/16
Czech Republic	10	10	43	5	10/0
Estonia	56	53	66	33	33/33
Hungary	40	35	43	45	10/10
Latvia	53	48	48	43	25/23
Lithuania	70	59	65	56	41/27
Poland	56	53	56	27	22/7
Romania	49	73	27	24	46/33
Slovakia	23	64	9	14	0/0
Slovenia	33	57	24	19	38/24
ECE	47	49	45	33	25/18

Source: Project database. See note

The fourth question, on influence over substance of decisions, which should provide the clearest cut evidence of impact, depends strongly of awareness of politicians of being influenced and their readiness to admit this publicly. While politicians love to present themselves as oversensitive to media's policy warnings, they do not want to give the impression that they are ruled by the media.

The results of the survey suggest that media in east-central European countries influence both agenda-setting and substance of policy decisions. From our pooled sample of ministers, 47 per cent acknowledge influence over topics, 49 per cent over discussion time and 33 per cent over content of decisions. Variation is minimal across political ideology and type of cabinet and is significant by country only. The great exception seems to be the Czech Republic, whose ministers steadily denied influence of media, to the extent that none of them named an influential TV programme. The countries where ministers acknowledged that media influences the substance of decision to a greater extent are Bulgaria, Hungary and the Baltic States. Lithuanian ministers come on top with the greatest contribution of the media to their agenda, and Romanian ministers seem to lose considerable time discussing in cabinet meetings what they saw on TV the evening before.

Answers show some inconsistency of respondents. Slovak ministers allow discussing topics raised by media a lot in the cabinet, but claim their choice of topics and decisions are their own. This makes us suspect that ministers are reluctant to admit that they are influenced by public opinion as expressed through media. The Czech and Slovak ministers did not indicate any specific programmes and newspapers as more influential than others, although it is hard to believe that those do not exist. In other countries, with Romania on top, ministers acknowledge the particular influence of some newspapers or TV programmes. Some governments seem more professional in conveying their message to the media, especially the Czech and the Baltic ones. Countries which do better on freedom of the press seem also to be more careful in dealing with the media, while a great difference between the time allocated to discussing media (73, 64, respectively) as in Romania and Slovakia and the relative carelessness towards communicating to media (24, 14, respectively) might be because other informal means of handling the media are preferred. The survey of East European ministers seems to confirm what Robert Dahl wrote in his classic, *Who governs?*: 'The more uncertain a politician is about the state of public opinion or the more firmly believes in the "power of the press" the more reluctant he would be to throw down the gage to a newspaper publisher'.[18] *In other words, power of the media in normal times depends on the extent that decision-makers believe in it*, and this might explain the wide variation of media effects studies, as this belief varies greatly across national media environments, and from one moment in time to another.

Conclusion

Research often ends up in more questions. Rather than asking ourselves if the media is influential,[19] and if investment in freedom of the media by the international community can bear fruit — it clearly is, and it clearly does — I suggest we focus on the circumstances that empower the media. This means that a comparative politics research design across a broad interval of time, rather than generalizations from the cross-sectional study of one country might provide better answers as to what specific set of circumstances makes a politically influential media. I also suggest that informal aspects of media control and media behaviour should not be neglected in favor of classic ones, and that corruption of the media is an underrated and under-studied phenomenon.

Does the history end if a country reaches the relatively happy phase of accommodation, and we witness far less interaction between media and politics, as in liberal democracies? By and large, judging by the EE experience, I would say it does, but actors in the field might not agree. The media in most of the countries discussed here differ sharply in style from the rest of continental Europe. The violent critical tone and the poignancy of the investigative journalists in Eastern Europe (as well as their inaccuracy) are hard to accept in some Western European countries, such as France or Switzerland, with their mild media, and are closer to the British press only from 'old Europe'. One would be tempted to say that such governments deserve the media that they get, and the other way around. It would be an easy way out, though. East European governments rule through exceptional times, when the constitutional and economic order is daily overhauled to push transition further towards what their citizens black-humouredly call 'the light at the end of the tunnel'. Politicians are often amateur policy-makers trying to acquire some skill during office. Publishers and journalists often picture themselves as better at the job of government and give strong indications what policy decisions should be taken. Some may even get a position in the next government. Until the process of consolidation of new professional elites make such shifts between professions the exception rather than the norm, governing in Eastern Europe would remain a sort of athletic game in which spectators are allowed to throw in various objects and even descend from the amphitheatre into the playing field, while the results of the game are established by their open vote. It would sound anarchic and unprofessional, indeed, if the mere word 'democracy' was not actually born precisely in such amphitheatres.

Notes

1. Siebert, and Peterson and Wilbur, *Four Theories of the Press*. 1–2.
2. Hallin and Mancini, *Comparing Media Systems. Three Models of Media and Politics*.
3. Robinson, *Theorizing the Influence of Media on World Politics. Models on Media Influence on World Policy. European Journal of Communication*, vol 16 (4) 523–544.
4. Lucan A. Way, 'Authoritarian State Building and Transitions in Western Eurasia'. A paper prepared for the workshop on "Transitions from Communist Rule in Comparative Perspective", Encina Hall, Institute for International Studies, Stanford University, CA. USA, 15–16 November.
5. Correlation between Nations in Transit Corruption Score for 26 post-communist states (scores range from one to seven, with seven the most corruption) and the FH Freedom of the Press scores (scores ranged from 17 for Estonia and Latvia, as the most free, to 96 for Turkmenistan and 86 for Belarus), where the greatest infringements of media freedom were found. The correlation was highly significant with a Pearson index of 0.81. The two scores are both 'subjective', but as they are computed through two different methodologies they can be correlated.
6. Belin, L. (2001). "Verdict against TV-6 is Latest Warning to Opposition Media", in Radio Free Europe/Radio Liberty: *Russian Political Weekly*. 1: 25.
7. *The Standing Committee of PSD*, Oct 20th 2003. *Stenogramele PSD*. Editura Ziua, 3 volumes, Bucureflti: 2004. The leaked transcripts of the Romanian Social Democrat (post-communist) Party, in power at the time, were under investigation by the national anticorruption prosecutor beginning 2005. Former Affairs Minister Mircea Geoana was quoted by BBC World Service acknowleging the transcripts are genuine. Several others PSD members made similar statements to the Romanian press. The Prime Minister Adrian Nastase (after January 2005 chair of the Chamber of Deputies) denied their authenticity. See the review of transcripts in *Romanian Journal of Political Science*, Fall 2004, pp. 54–56, www.sar.org.ro/polsci/.

8. Sükösd and Bajomi-Lázár, *Reinventing Media. Media Policy Reform in East Central Europe*: 11 and Hall, Richard A. and O'Neil, Patrick "Institutions, Transitions, and the Media: A Comparison of Hungary and Romania", in *Communicating Democracy: The Media and Political Transitions*: 143.

9. Mungiu-Pippidi, '*State into Public: the Failed Reform of State TV in East Central Europe*', http://www.ksg.harvard.edu/presspol/publications/pdfs/alina.PDF.

10. Based on Olena Prytula, *Journalism at the Heart of the Orange Revolution*, an address to Knight Fellowships Reunion and Conference.

11. Anable, '*The Role of Georgia's Media – and Western Aid – in the Rose Revolution*'.

12. Idem note 11.

13. Office of the Coordinator of U.S. Assistance to Europe and Eurasia, U.S. Dept. of State.

14. O'Connor and Hoffman, *International Herald Tribune*, "Media in Iraq: The Fallacy of psy-ops".

15. Cobb and Elder, "*The politics of agenda-building: an alternative perspective for modern democratic theory*". *Journal of Politics* 33: 892–915. Also, Kingdon, J. W. *Agendas, alternatives and public policies*.

16. Dearing and Rogers, Communication Concepts 6: Agenda-setting. Thousand Oaks, CA, Sage: 74.

17. Walgrave and Nuytemns, "*Specifying the media's political agenda-setting power. Media, civil society, parliament and government in a small consociational democracy*".

18. Robert Dahl, *Who Governs?*: 259.

19. Novak, 'Effects no more?' in U. Carlsson (ed.) Beyond Media Uses and Effects, 31–40.

References

Belin, L. (2001). "Verdict against TV-6 is Latest Warning to Opposition Media", in Radio Free Europe/Radio Liberty: Russian Political Weekly.

Cobb, R. and T. Elder (1971). "The politics of agenda-building: an alternative perspective for modern democratic theory". *Journal of Politics* 33.

Dahl, R. (1974). Who Governs? New Haven: Yale University Press.

David A. (n.d.) 'The Role of Georgia's Media – and Western Aid – in the Rose Revolution'.

Joan Shorenstein Center on the Press, Politics and Public Policy Working Paper Series 3:2006 Cambridge, MA: Harvard University.

Dearing, J. W. and E. M. (1996). Rogers Communication Concepts 6: Agenda-setting. Thousand Oaks, CA, Sage.

Hall, R. A. and O'Neil, P. (1998). "Institutions, Transitions, and the Media: A Comparison of Hungary and Romania", in O'Neil, P. ed. Communicating Democracy: The Media and Political Transitions. Boulder and London: Lynne Rienner Publishers.

Hallin, D. and C. Mancini. (2004). Comparing Media Systems. Three Models of Media and Politics. Cambridge: Cambridge University Press.

Kingdon, J. W. (1995). Agendas, alternatives and public policies. Boston: Little Brown.

Lucan A. W. (2002). 'Authoritarian State Building and Transitions in Western Eurasia'. A paper prepared for the workshop on "Transitions from Communist Rule in Comparative Perspective", Encina Hall, Institute for International Studies, Stanford University, CA. USA, 15–16 November.

Mungiu-Pippidi, A. (2004). 'State into Public: the Failed Reform of State TV in East Central Europe', Shorenstein Center on Press and Politics, Harvard University, Working paper 2000#6. http://www.ksg.harvard.edu/presspol/publications/pdfs/alina.PDF.

Novak, K. (n.d). 'Effects no more?' in U. Carlsson (ed.) Beyond Media Uses and Effects, Gothenburg University: Nordicom.

O'Connor, E. and Hoffman D. (2005). *International Herald Tribune*, "Media in Iraq: The Fallacy of psy-ops" 16 December.

Olena Prytula (2005). Journalism at the Heart of the Orange Revolution, an address to Knight Fellowships Reunion and Conference, Stanford, California, 9 July.

Robinson, P. (2001). Theorizing the Influence of Media on World Politics. Models on Media Influence on World Policy. *European Journal of Communication*, vol 16.

Romanian Journal of Political Science, Fall (2004), pp. 54–56, www.sar.org.ro/polsci/.

Siebert, F. S and T. Peterson and S. Wilbur (1956). Four Theories of the Press. Urbana: University of Illinois Press.

Sükösd, M. and P. Bajomi-Lázár (2003). Reinventing Media. Media Policy Reform in East Central Europe. CPS Books. Budapest: Central European University Press.

The Standing Committee of PSD, 20th Oct 2003. (2004). Stenogramele PSD. Editura Ziua, 3 volumes, Bucureflti.

Walgrave, S. and M. Nuytemns (2004). "Specifying the media's political agenda-setting power. Media, civil society, parliament and government in a small consociational democracy" (Belgium, 1991–2000). Paper presented at ECPR's Uppsala Workshop Session.

Finding the Right Place on the Map: Prospects for Public Service Broadcasting in Post-Communist Countries

Karol Jakubowicz

Central and Eastern European students of post-Communist media change universally express disappointment – as we seek to show below – when it comes to assessing progress in the introduction of public service broadcasting in their countries. There is no question that the process has been part of what may be called "mimetic" or "imitative" transformation (see Jakubowicz 2007; Splichal 2000, 2001). It was clear from the start that transplantation of the legal and institutional frameworks of PSB would have to be followed by a long period of development of the kind of political and journalistic culture required for PSB to be able to flourish. The initial assumption was that as democratization proceeded, and as the new democratic political system matured, the required conditions for PSB to operate successfully would gradually be created. Accordingly, there was recognition of the fact that in this field, at least, new broadcasting laws proclaiming the need for PSB to be independent, and seeking to create a legal and institutional framework for this independence, were defining a long-term goal to be achieved gradually, over time, rather than immediately.

How long is "long", however? And are we seeing "an enabling environment" for PSB emerging, as we thought we would? And, if not, perhaps we are being too impatient and should be prepared to wait some more?

It is, thus, time we asked ourselves: could more have been achieved since 1989? In other words, is disappointment with progress achieved in developing PSB in the context of post-communist transformation fully justified?

Since the most disappointing feature of PSB performance in post-communist countries is the perceived lack of independence of these broadcasting organizations, especially from political forces and the power establishment, we will – in seeking answers to these questions –

concentrate primarily on that aspect. Our purpose here is to see whether some answers can be found by conducting a comparative analysis of political and media systems in different countries and regions. If a degree of similarity with conditions prevailing in other countries and regions can be established, perhaps an understanding of the process unfolding there can inform our examination of developments in Central and Eastern European countries.

One possible framework for such a comparative analysis is provided by Hallin and Mancini's (2004) analysis of media systems. It shows that media systems display a high degree of what we may broadly call "systemic parallelism", i.e., reflect the systemic features of the society within which they operate. We will seek to apply it here in order to see whether it can indeed offer an insight into the process of media system evolution. We will do so on the assumption that if the systemic features of the socio-political situation in post-communist countries are found to correspond, at least to some extent, to those defining one of Hallin and Mancini's systems, then there should be a degree of correspondence between their PSB systems as well. This would then provide a framework of assessment of progress achieved in the process of developing public service broadcasting after the collapse of communism.

However, how should we reconcile this approach with the warning sounded by Sükösd and Bajomi-Lázár (2003: 15) that "it would be a mistake to suggest that East Central European media systems are 'half way' to some final media state of reform, an end point of the Western institutional pattern. In our view, such a final destination does not exist and democratization of the media remains an open-ended, normatively oriented project". Also Mungiu-Pippidi (2003: 33) argues, along with many other scholars, that a clear model for the transformation of public service broadcasting is missing in Europe and that the "idealized Western European model" has either vanished or become inaccessible.

The answer to this quandary is that while it is true that post-communist transformation and democratization of the media are open-ended processes, Hallin and Mancini's analysis suggests that the range of options is not limitless. Historical experience shows that specific clusters of macro-structural circumstances tend to result in the emergence of specific media systems. The purpose here, therefore, is not to measure the situation in post-communist countries against some supposed western ideal. Rather, we agree with Sükösd and Bajomi-Lázár (2003) that some of the problems presently found in post-communist countries are shared by many democratic media systems, including those in countries with sustained, or at least significantly longer, democratic institutions and traditions. Accordingly, the goal here is to understand those similarities and the reasons for them, using Hallin and Mancini's typology as a framework of comparative analysis.

In doing so, we will also seek to view the Hallin-Mancini framework against a broader historical context. We will therefore begin with an attempt to correlate what we believe were the three main models of PSB introduction in various countries and historical contexts with Huntington's three waves of democratization, as well as with three models of "media and political system" identified by Hallin and Mancini (2004).

Introduction of PSB in Different Social and Historical Contexts

We may identify three main models of the creation of public service broadcasting, or of the transformation of state broadcasting into public service broadcasting:

■ Paternalistic – as in the UK, where PSB was originally born in 1926 in the form of the BBC, an independent public corporation with a public-service remit, understood in part as promoting public enlightenment, playing a clearly normative role in the country's cultural, moral and political life, and as promoting "the development of the majority in ways thought desirable by the minority" (Williams 1968: 117);

■ Democratic and emancipatory – as in some other Western European countries, where erstwhile state broadcasting organisations began to be transformed into public service broadcasters in the 1960s and 1970s, a time when state (government) control of the then monopoly broadcasters could no longer be justified or claim legitimacy, and a way was sought to associate them more closely with the civil society and turn them into autonomous PSB organizations.

■ Systemic – as in West Germany after World War II; Spain, Portugal and Greece in the 1970s; and in Central and Eastern Europe after 1989, when change of the broadcasting system was part and parcel of broader political change, typically transition to democracy after an authoritarian or totalitarian system.

As we will seek to show, more than one model may, over time, operate in one country. One example of that is the evolution of PSB systems in response to broader change in society, leading, e.g., to democratic and emancipatory change in an existing paternalistic (or state-dominated and politicized) PSB system.

In the group of countries representing the systemic model of PSB introduction, we may additionally distinguish cases where the system of public service broadcasting has been imposed by outside forces. This includes Germany as well as, to some extent, Japan (Kato 1999; por. Shimizu b.d.w.).

The United States and New Zealand offer another special case of PSB being created (or, as in the latter case, recreated; see e.g., Comrie, Fountaine 2006) for reasons other than the progress of democratization (as in the democratic and emancipatory model) or loss of legitimacy of state media (as in the democratic and emancipatory or systemic models). Here, we have to do with a clinical case of the market failure rationale for PSB: a conviction that commercial broadcasting alone is not enough, as it fails to meet all the needs of society.

The three main models of PSB introduction obviously emerged in different socio-political circumstances, arising out of the history of political development of particular countries. There is clear interdependence between this process and the level of democratic consolidation in a particular society. Accordingly, this might perhaps suggest a strong correlation between particular models and the three "waves of democratization" identified by Huntington (1995; see also Balcerowicz 1995; Eckstein 2001):

■ The years 1828–1926 which saw the democratization of Australia, Canada, Finland, Iceland, Ireland, New Zealand, Sweden, the United States, Switzerland, Great Britain, Austria, Belgium, Denmark, France, the Netherlands, Norway (as well as others, which, however, reverted to non-democratic rule);

■ The years 1943–1964, when Allied occupation helped impose democracy on some countries (Germany, Japan, Italy, Austria, South Korea); when other countries (Greece, Turkey, Brazil, Argentina, Peru, Ecuador, Venezuela and Columbia) advanced to democracy; and when the beginnings of decolonization also promoted the process;

■ The years after 1974, when the fall of the Soviet Union and the final phase of decolonization were the prime movers of the process.

And yet, despite some chronological parallels, Huntington's three "waves of democratization" are not a sufficient guide to prospects for PSB emergence and development. This is because Huntington accepts the Schumpeterian formal and procedural definition of democracy and that, as we will try to show below, is not in itself enough to create propitious conditions for PSB independence. Moreover, not even consolidation of democracy is enough for PSB properly so called flourish. After all, Linz and Stepan (1996) regard Southern European democracies as consolidated, and yet – as we will see – PSB has had immense difficulties in those countries. What is needed is a stable, mature liberal democracy. However, given that the United States is such a democracy and yet has a very weak system of PSB, even that in itself is not enough. What is also required is a tradition of concern for the public interest and of a strong State role in meeting the society's needs. McQuail (2005: 239–241) has identified three phases of media policy development in Europe, including a public service phase, lasting from the 1920s to the 1970s and – not coincidentally – largely overlapping with a long period of social democratic rule in many of those countries. That was the period when PSB emerged and developed. The triumph of neoliberalism in the 1980s, again not coincidentally overlapping with a new phase of the evolution of media policy, has shaken PSB and raised doubts as to its future.

In Huntington's first-wave countries, PSB was introduced in line with the paternalistic model. Later, however, there were no clear-cut chronological or societal parallels. The democratic and emancipatory model emerged primarily in first-wave countries, but before and during of the third wave of democratization. Those countries were already displaying all the characteristics of procedural democracy, but without the requisite socio-political conditions allowing PSB either to have already been introduced at all, or to be really independent and engage in impartial journalism. In some countries, the democratic and emancipatory phase followed the much earlier introduction of PSB in line with the paternalistic model, due to progress of democratic consolidation.

The systemic model has been most conspicuous in third-wave countries (which is not to say that PSB is now present in all those countries), but was equally evident in other countries, where – as in Germany, for example – democratization was followed by reversion to totalitarian/ authoritarian rule and only its subsequent collapse paved the way to transforming State into public service media. Depending on the strength of democratic tradition in a particular country, or on the pace of democratic consolidation, while it typically produced a polarized pluralist model, it did also, in some cases (e.g., Germany), lead to the democratic-corporatist model

Simple correlations are equally elusive in the case of waves of democratization and media systems as classified by Hallin and Mancini (2004). True, the liberal system is to be found exclusively in the first-wave countries (the United States, the UK, Canada and Ireland). However, other first-wave countries (Austria, Belgium, Denmark, France, the Netherlands, Norway, Switzerland etc.) developed the democratic-corporatist system. The obvious reason for this is that their socio-political systems, traditions, cultural and religious divisions required the accommodation of various group interests.

In turn, third-wave countries have so far, as a rule, developed "Mediterranean systems" (polarized pluralism). In Hallin and Mancini's analysis they are Greece, Spain and Portugal, but in addition, also, France and Italy.

All this confirms the assumption that the media display "systemic parallelism" in the sense that they are shaped by the socio-political and cultural features of the countries in which they operate, including notably the level of actual or potential societal conflict and the degree of democratic consolidation.

Table 1 provides a schematic and simplified depiction of the interrelationships we discussed above.

Table 1: "Systemic parallelism" and public service media

Waves of democratization	Models of PSB introduction	Media systems
First	Paternalistic or Democratic-emancipatory	Liberal; democratic-corporatist
Second	Systemic (possibly followed by democratic-emancipatory)	
Third		Polarized pluralist

Incidentally, the concept of "systemic parallelism" would suggest that a future wave of democratization should bring about the emergence of PSB organizations in new countries. This could perhaps be the logical conclusion, especially as concerns countries and regions oriented to imitating European models, though we need to note that while some authors do look forward to a "fourth wave" (Diamond 1997), others expect only a "fourth trickle" (Bunce 2002), and still others are saying that the next wave is already happening and is producing "illiberal democracies" (Zakaria 1997). Illiberal democracies are certainly not a natural habitat for PSB.

Liberal, democratic-corporatist, "polarized pluralist" systems: Vive les (petites) différences

To gain a better understanding of the interrelationships discussed above, but primarily to establish whether Hallin and Mancini's typology can serve as a framework of comparative analysis of post-communist media change, let us recall the main features of the three systems they analyse (see table 2).

The fact that polarized-pluralist and democratic corporatist media systems often operate in the context of consensual (consociational) systems of government is a manifestation of the "systemic parallelism" we mentioned above. Consociationalism is essentially a strategy for conflict management and the choice of a majoritarian or consociational form of government is predicated primarily on the level of actual or potential conflict within society (due, e.g., to divisions of various nature within society) or on political tradition (e.g., most former British dependencies have adopted the Westminster, or "Westminster adapted" models; Lijphart n.d.). Where there is a high level of actual or potential conflict, PSB organizations will be affected by the political and institutional solutions designed to cope with it, inter alia, involving politicized and pluralistic governing bodies of PSB ("politics-in-broadcasting"), serving as a an arena for the negotiation and resolution of such conflicts.

Incidentally, as Marletti and Roncaloro (2000) point out, Italy has evolved from a consensual, quasi-consociational system of government to a majoritarian one under Berlusconi, so change from one system to another in the same country is, of course, not impossible.

Marletti and Roncaloro (2000) note that consociational and majoritarian politics differ significantly with regard to the relationship between politics and the media. Under multiparty systems and especially consociationalism, direct appeals to public opinion occur relatively infrequently, and their political impact is seldom decisive. Multiparty systems develop their own

Table 2: The Three Models: Main Political and Media System Characteristics

	Polarized pluralist model	Democratic- Corporatist model	Liberal model
Political system			
Political history: conflict vs consensus	Late democratization, polarized pluralism	Early democratization, moderate pluralism,	Early democratiza-tion, moderate pluralism
Consensus or majoritarian govt.	Both	Predominantly consensus	Predominantly majoritarian
Individual vs. organized pluralism	Organized pluralism	Organized, democratic corporatism	Individual representation
Role of State	Dirigisme	Strong welfare state	Liberalism
Rational Legal Authority	Weak, clientelism	Strong	Strong
Media system			
Political parallelism	High Politics-over-broadcasting	External pluralism, politics-in-broadcasting with substantial autonomy	Internal pluralism (external in the UK), professional broadcast governance, formally autonomous system
Professionalization	Weak	Strong	Strong
Role of State in Media	Strong	Strong, but freedom of media protected	Market-dominated (but strong PSB in UK and Ireland)

Adapted from Hallin and Mancini, 2004: 67–68

internal mechanisms, some formal and some informal, for accommodating economic and social interests and resolving controversial issues. Moreover, the parties commonly prefer these conflict management mechanisms to those offered by the media because they do not entail the same risk of loss of control that is associated with going public.

In "Mediterranean" majoritarian systems, by contrast, direct appeals to public opinion as a means of resolving controversial partisan issues are common and accepted as normal arenas for the articulation of conflict. Broadcast media are one instrument of pursuing this practice, resulting in elite control of them.

In liberal systems, on the other hand, majoritarian systems of government operate without direct, hands-on control of the media exercised by politicians.

Linz and Stepan's (1996) concept of consolidated democracy helps portray the systemic interdependencies between the five arenas of democracy (political, civil and economic societies, state administration and the rule of law) needed for (representative) democracy both to operate properly, and to create propitious conditions for media freedom and autonomy.

As a minimum, these conditions must include:

- Sufficient separation of all these arenas (which is not to deny their interdependence) so that proper separation of powers is achieved, all the countervailing forces operate properly, and the economy (and PSB) is outside direct political control;
- The existence of a strong civil society which, as Linz and Stepan put it, "helps monitor the state apparatus and economic society", resisting the expansionist tendencies of political society and state apparatus which always, when given a chance, seek to control more and more of social and public life. If this condition is met, an independent public sphere outside the control of politicians and/or state apparatus may emerge as the social space where independent media, operating as emanations of civil society, rather than political society, may develop;
- The effective operation of the economy and economic society and markets, so that the media can be sustained by the market and financially successful, as a prerequisite of their independence and development;
- Effective rule of law, so that the legal framework designed to protect media autonomy and proper performance is respected, both by the media as well as political society and state apparatus.

While this is all true, we must be conscious of the fact that these conditions can never be met fully. The experience of Western European countries and of the United States suggests that "clinical" separation of political and civil society, or political and economic society, can hardly be expected. It would be no exaggeration to say that precisely because these conditions can never be met fully, the importance of a strong, aware and engaged civil society is all the greater, as the only countervailing force capable of bringing influence to bear on the other arenas of democracy so as to prevent takeover of the democratic process.

As far as the prerequisites for PSB independence are concerned, let us note that in 1979 the following conclusion emerged out of an analysis of the relationship of politics and television in six Western European countries: "What happens in practice is often very different from constitutional theory and political intention. The way in which television presents politics and the ways in which politicians influence television have to be explained in terms of the political and journalistic culture of the societies concerned" (Smith 1979: ix).

More than a quarter of a century later, a Danish report on PSB governance in the UK, Norway, Sweden and Finland (liberal system) and the Netherlands, Austria and Germany (democratic-corporatist system) produced similar conclusions regarding the relationship between PSB and the political class:

- "Political influence and control of public service broadcasting is in reality taken for granted in all the countries studied;

- The responsibility of the politicians in this respect is to ensure that the political influence in/on public service broadcasting does not take on the character of any political party;
- Assuming that it is unbiased, political influence on public service broadcasting is harmless, and can be an advantage because public service broadcasters operate in a political environment" (Mediesekretariatet 2005: 2).

If the concept of "unbiased political influence" strikes one as odd, an explanation is offered by Hallin and Mancini (2004: 52) who point out that often the same institutional arrangements for broadcast governance produce different political results in consensus and majoritarian systems. Thus, they say, a governing board appointed by parliament according to proportional representation will result in power sharing in a consensus system, such as Italy, or government control in majoritarian system, such as Spain. More to the point, we could add, is that while the appointment of the director general of RTVE by the Spanish government (the system has now changed, as we will see below) served precisely the goal of direct government control, that of the director general of RUV by the minister of culture in Iceland most likely does not.

It is equally obvious that, depending on other circumstances, institutional arrangements may produce different political results, regardless of the intended purpose for which they were created. In Poland, in order to prevent capture of PSB by the government of the day, the supervisory board (which then appoints the board of management) of a public service broadcaster is appointed by the broadcasting regulatory authority (itself appointed by the two houses of parliament and the president). Yet, because of informal mechanisms and political clientelism (as well as executive dominance over the legislature – a feature not only of majoritarian, but also of unconsolidated democracies), the Polish government finds it easier to control PSB than the UK government which, to all intents and purposes, appoints the BBC Trust (which appoints the director-general).

As a general principle, "systemic parallelism" means that a country's system of government is translated into a corresponding system of PSB governance ("politics-over-broadcasting", "politics-in-broadcasting" etc.). Whether or not the particular set of institutional arrangements for PSB governance will lead to the organization's subordination to, or independence from, politicians, depends on the degree of consolidation of democracy and even more so on the concomitant political culture.

So, the decisive element is not the fact of involvement by politicians, e.g., in the appointment of the governing bodies of PSB organizations, or in other relations with them (as this is very common in all systems), but the quality of that involvement or relations. This is where political culture comes in.

According to Paletz and Lipinski (1994), political culture consists of widely shared, fundamental beliefs that have political consequences. Political culture shapes how individuals and the society act and react politically. It is political culture, to a great extent, that determines whether the society is able to maintain and operate a viable and enduring constitutional democratic system of government, or whether the society must choose between authoritarianism and domestic disorder.

Political culture sets the framework, the intellectual environment, within which government and politics take place. Among other things, it should constrain the actions of politicians and public officials: even if inclined otherwise, they usually refrain from taking positions or from implementing policies that blatantly violate the elements of the political culture. This underscores the need for a strong civil society, capable of contributing to the development of a political culture and of imposing limits on political behaviour. Without such a countervailing force, political society will be less constrained in its actions and policies.

However, acceptance by politicians and office-holders of restrains on their power is also very clearly a function of advanced consolidation of democracy, as explained by Diamond (1997: 4):

> Consolidation [of democracy – K.J.] involves not just agreement on the rules for competing for power but <u>fundamental and self-enforcing restraints on the exercise of power</u>. This, in turn, requires a mutual commitment among elites, through the "coordinating" mechanism of a constitution, related political institutions, and often an elite pact or settlement as well, to enforce limits on state authority, no matter which party or faction may control the state at any given time. Only when this commitment to "policing" state behavior is powerfully credible, because it is broadly shared among key alternative power groups, does a ruling party, president, or 'sovereign' develop a clear *self-interest* in adhering to the rules of the game, which then makes those constitutional rules "self-enforcing" …This in turn involves not just tactical calculations of long-term benefit in a repeated game but, again, a <u>normative shift</u> as well (emphases added – K.J.)

Restraints on the exercise of power are hardly likely to be accepted, unless there is long-term stability of a polity and the satisfactory resolution of fundamental societal issues. A recurrence of conflicts or the reappearance of profound divisions within society may potentially lead to rejection of these restraints. Nevertheless, there is little doubt that elite acceptance of restraints on the exercise of power and of limits on state and political authority is indispensable for the successful introduction and operation of PSB as an independent broadcaster. Otherwise, as shown by countless examples, a nominal PSB organization will become, in one way or another, an extension of the state or of the power establishment.

From our point of view, acceptance of restraints on the exercise of power over or on attempts to influence the media, in general, and PSB, in particular, are a necessary part of political culture as a prerequisite of media independence.

To conclude this line of thought, then, differences between political and media systems analysed by Hallin and Mancini range between macro-structural features on the one hand, and, on the other, nuances of political culture which may give an entirely different meaning and practical effect to identical institutional solutions applied in the organization of PSB. It is especially this second aspect which requires a long period of gestation. Politicians, civil society and media practitioners need time – measured in decades – to institutionalize the values and standards of consolidated democracy and to use transplanted patterns of public service broadcasting in the proper way.

Comparing Southern European and Post-Communist Political Development

The foregoing general analysis of some salient elements of Hallin and Mancini's media systems in the context of political systems is our point of departure for a comparative analysis of the situation in Central and Eastern Europe and southern Europe. In line with the "systemic parallelism" concept, this needs to begin with a brief look at political development in the two regions.

Sitter (2005) discusses two approaches to comparative analysis of political systems in Western and Eastern Europe. One consists in looking at "similarities with earlier developments in Western Europe. Perhaps the most obvious comparison was to the Mediterranean transitions to democracy in the 1970s, or even post-war democratisation in Germany and Italy, but others look to Lipset & Rokkan's classic analysis of the development of party systems in Western Europe". The other concentrates on "East European exceptionalism", a view based on the conviction that post-communist developments are so different from previous episodes of democratization, let alone the dynamics of party political competition in Western Europe, that comparative analysis may well be misleading.

Sitter's own view, based on the study of competitive politics in post-communist Central and Eastern Europe, is that developments over the last decade and a half have been less "exceptional" than is sometimes argued. Also Dryzek and Holmes (2002: 256) argue – rightly, we believe – that "differences between at least the more democratized CEE states and the West look to be of degree rather than kind".

In short, then, valid comparisons should be possible, even given all the differences between the two regions. Let us, therefore, proceed from the suggestion that what is happening in Central and Eastern Europe can most obviously be compared to Mediterranean transitions to democracy and their results. If we can establish some parallels between the Mediterranean variety of democracy and the resultant media system of polarized pluralism and those of post-communist countries, we will have a framework of assessment of PSB development in the latter. Of course, we cannot go here beyond unavoidably cursory and general remarks on this subject.

To begin with southern Europe (for an extensive analysis of the process of democratic consolidation in the region, see Linz and Stepan 1996: 87–150), Statham (1996) says that Italy is a case of an unfinished process of modernization. Marletti and Roncaloro (2000) add that in Italy the elite-led nation- and state-building process has not succeeded in bringing about a unitary civic culture, but rather has created a gap between the political cultures of the masses and the elites, accentuated by the centralism of the state. Italy remains a fragmented and pluralistic country, with various territorial identities and political subcultures, in which state centralism is only a heavy superstructure. The First Republic (the period which goes up to the *Tangentopoli* scandals and the disappearance of the traditional party structures at the beginning of the 1990s) was characterized by a sort of *panpoliticismo*, i.e., a situation when politics pervades and influences many social systems, the economy, the judicial system and so on (see also Mancini 2000).

Papatheodorou and Machin (2003) point to similarities in historical experience, level of economic development and political culture between Spain, Greece, Portugal and, occasionally, Italy. Greece and Spain, they say, were – due to delayed and uneven economic development – sites of intense social conflict and upheaval during a large part of the twentieth century. Social and ideological divisions culminated in civil strife. After several decades of authoritarian rule, stable democratic institutions were only established in the last quarter of the twentieth century.

In these circumstances, it is no surprise that, as – Papatheodorou and Machin (2003) put it – the political elite and the media are joined by a "umbilical cord" that remained in place (as in Portugal, Spain and Greece) even after the overthrow of dictatorship and subsequent political change. Despite efforts towards political and economic modernization, patronage channels have remained. Even after the downfall of dictatorial governments, and despite the extensive renovation of political personnel, the persistence of social incoherence and of traditional political practices imposed limitations on the establishment of mass political parties in the West European fashion. As a result political parties in government have always relied heavily on the resources of the state in order to consolidate their power. Patronage has thus remained a crucial means for mobilizing and maintaining political support.

Papatheodorou and Machin conclude that the central role of the state in south European societies, the organizational weakness of political parties and the insecurity caused by the fluidity of their electoral base are a key to understanding both the pattern of development of media institutions and their place within the overall configuration of power.

Southern European countries display features of "state paternalism" (Papatheodorou, Machin 2003) or, indeed, "political clientelism" (as in Latin America), defined as "a pattern of social organization in which access to resources is controlled by patrons and delivered to clients in Exchange for deference and various kinds of support. It is a particularistic and asymmetric form of social organization, and is typically contrasted with forms of citizenship in which access to resources is based on universalistic criteria and formal equality before the law" (Hallin, Papathanassopoulos 2002: 184–185). Cases of clientelism can be found anywhere, but in some countries – and this applies to southern Europe – it is described as the dominant feature of the social order.

Hallin and Papathanassopoulos (2002) associate certain features of the media system with political clientelism:

- A tradition of advocacy reporting (see also Mancini 2000);
- Instrumentalization of privately owned media;
- Politicization of public broadcasting and broadcast regulation;
- And limited development of journalism as an autonomous profession.

As for post-communist countries, they share some of the features of southern European countries: late democratization, insufficient economic development, weak rational-legal authority combined with a <u>dirigiste</u> state. Their modernization is also incomplete or (in some cases) little advanced.

The pace of democratization in Central and Eastern Europe has been very uneven. In fact, according to Carothers (2002: 6) "Many countries that policy makers and aid practitioners persist in calling 'transitional' are not in transition to democracy". Instead of "transitioning" to democracy, many countries so described, says Carothers, have entered "a political gray zone", encompassing two main broad syndromes:

- "feckless pluralism", where democracy remains shallow and troubled (Carothers lists Moldova, Bosnia, Albania and Ukraine as belonging to this category, with Romania and Bulgaria teetering on its edge).
- and "dominant-power politics", where one political grouping dominates the system in such a way that there is little prospect of alternation of power in the foreseeable future, and the line between the state and the ruling political forces is blurred, with the state's main assets in the direct service of the ruling party (Armenia, Azerbaijan, Georgia, Kyrgyzstan and Kazakhstan).

And then, there are the out-and-out authoritarian systems, including the other Central Asian republics and Belarus.

The "colour revolutions" have changed the picture as far as some of these countries are concerned (see McFaul 2005), as has the EU accession process for some of these countries, but there is no doubt that democratization is stalled in many post-communist countries. According to Krastev (2006), countries like Russia are not democracies, but "democracy's doubles" – regimes that claim to be democratic and may look like democracies, but which rule like autocracies.

Still, there are also examples of relatively successful post-communist democratization. Indeed, Sükösd (2000) argues that Hungary's democracy can be regarded as consolidated in each of the dimensions listed by Linz and Stepan (1996). Other assessments are less optimistic. One argues that "no doubt, prospects for successful consolidation can be found in the countries which were admitted to the EU in 2004, and those that are to join in 2007, i.e. Romania and Bulgaria. As for the others, we can rather speak of the beginnings of democratic transformation (Ukraine, Croatia, Serbia and Montenegro), or of attempts to consolidate some hybrid forms (Russia, Albania), or of an authoritarian system (Belarus)" (Cichosz 2006: 66; see also Antoszewski, Herbut 2004).

Cichosz goes on to say that most post-communist countries have developed hybrid forms of democracy:

■ Formal democracy – no counter-elites to oppose those in power, low level of political competition (Russia, Ukraine before 2004; Serbia before 2000);
■ Elite democracy – competing oligarchies with low political participation of the citizens (Romania before 1996; Albania, Bulgaria);
■ Partitocrazia – monopolization of public life by political parties which exclude other social actors from decision-making processes; rule by political oligarchs often connected to economic pressure groups. This amounts to political party capture of the state, corruption and low legitimacy of the system (just about everywhere in post-communist countries);
■ Tyrannical majority – forces returned to power disregard the political views and interests of other political or social forces; display no willingness to compromise and accept no restraints on their power. This type of hybrid democracy is promoted by "leaders convinced of their 'historic and moral mission', consisting in imposing a direction of the country's development on the rest of society" (Cichosz 2006: 64). Examples include Hungary in 1990 to 1994; Slovakia under Meciar; Croatia under Tudjman; Slovenia after 2004; Poland after 2005).

This last tendency and its very recent upsurge in some of the "leader" or "trailblazer" countries, such as Poland, may indicate regression, rather than progress. In 2005–2007, Poland was certainly been the scene of the "etatization of democracy", delegitimization of civil society and all opposing political and intellectual elites as democratic actors and far-reaching concentration of power, including that over the public media. This amounts to de-consolidation of democracy, rather than anything else. According to some commentators, Poland may have been turning then from a prospective liberal democracy into an illiberal one.

It is in this context that media policy has been formulated and implemented in post-communist countries. First, they had to settle on a model of the media system, with underlying normative media theory(ies) and concepts of the role of the media and journalism in society (see Jakubowicz 2007). They had a choice mainly of three media policy orientations:

■ Idealistic (a radical vision of direct, participatory communicative democracy);
■ Mimetic (straight transplantation of the generalized western media system with a free press and a dual broadcasting system), and
■ Atavistic (the unwillingness of new power elites to give up all control of, or ability to influence, the media).

In the circumstances described above, it is not surprising that the atavistic orientation proved very popular. As already noted, post-communist countries break down into several groups in terms of their democratic development. Vachudova (2005) simplifies this by distinguishing liberal and illiberal democracies.

In the liberal ones, partitocratic systems, together with the politicization of all spheres of public life (the post-communist version of *panpoliticismo*) and the political culture of post-communism favoured control of the media by political elites. In the illiberal democracies, autocratic systems of government, involving the power of state administration or the oligarchs over the media and an underdeveloped civil society, largely undermined prospects for media freedom, turning them into the voice either of the state or of political or other vested interests.

As a result, the media model characteristic of the present stage of transformation is a combination of the mimetic and "atavistic" media policy orientations. It is hard to describe precisely which elements of which model shape the media most in particular countries, but as a general rule liberal democracies countries have acquired more features of the mimetic model, while the illiberal democracies retain more of the atavistic model. Meanwhile, the authoritarian states represent a straight and unadulterated atavistic orientation, allowing the media little, or no, freedom and independence at all.

PSB in Southern Europe

We may now take a look at the development of public service broadcasting in southern Europe, bearing in mind the political context briefly described above.

With regard to Spain, Gunther, Montero and Wert (2000: 47) make the point that media liberalization after the end of the franquist period "did not include a reform of the structural relationship between the government and TVE". Also Bustamante (1989) has pointed out that the formal democratization of state television showed a curious delay in relation to other institutions in the country, with TVE remaining the centre and basic arena of political struggle. The "heavy legacy of Franco's television model" continued to exert its influence long after the demise of Franco's system of government, despite repeated (but perhaps only half-hearted) attempts to introduce institutional arrangements guaranteeing greater independence for TVE (all the while, however, the director general of RTVE was still appointed directly by government).

Thus, Bustamante (1989) concluded, the transition to democracy partially, and belatedly, reformed that model without breaking from the traditional concepts of broadcasting, generically identified with authoritarianism. But, above all, he said, Spanish television joined the wave of commercialization, but without having previously consolidated a public service stage.

Students of public service broadcasting in post-communist countries may find it instructive that it was only in 2004, nearly 30 years after the collapse of the authoritarian regime and the "systemic" model of PSB introduction, that "democratic and emancipatory" changes were launched in Spain by the new Zapatero government, designed to promote the "degovernmentalization of RTVE" (Caffarel, de Castro 2006).

This may confirm Eckstein's (2001) view that "a plan to democratize fully should probably cover some twenty-five years - more or less, depending on local conditions". After a period of about fifteen years of democratization, Eckstein continues, just about anything is still about equally likely to occur, from quick demise of democracy to something approaching permanence. After that, however, persistence becomes more likely as time from the start increases. This seems to have been the case in Spain.

A "Report on the reform of the publicly owned media", commissioned by the Zapatero government, confirmed that the appointment of the upper management by the government not only implied distortions in the programming or suspicions concerning the independence of the news, but also resulted in an inefficient power structure. Its chronic instability (twelve directors in little more than twenty years, a new one every two years) has been, moreover, incompatible with a rational management of a public company permanently destined to increase its level of debt. And in the same way, the composition and functions of an Administrative Council made up of political supporters with no more competence than the ability to permanently reiterate their political views, has substantially aggravated the situation.

As Caffarel and de Castro put it, the main purpose of the reform is to put an end to the political control within the public broadcaster, respond to the public demands for truthfulness, plurality and transparency, and endow it with internal practices that will bring back the confidence of its professions, guaranteeing them respect for their rights and duties. To this end, a new RTVE corporation has been formed, autonomous with regard to its management, acting independently of the government and under the control of Parliament and the new State Council for Audiovisual Media, with a new Administrative Council formed by highly qualified professionals, appointed by Parliament for six years (longer, therefore, than the life of a legislature). A key aspect is participation of the citizens, with the new law calling for the creation of an Advisory Council made up of thirteen members appointed by social organizations, the Social Economic Council, consumer and user organizations and associations of various types, professional and civic. Finally, with regard to control over the management of public resources by the state, a framework mandate for a duration of nine years is proposed, operated under a programme agreement with the state in which the objectives, the management and administration of the public service and the relevant economic arrangements would be specified.

A strikingly similar situation can be found in Portugal. Writing in 1996, Sousa had this to say about Portugal's public service broadcasters:

> RTP has never had a balanced and impartial political output, it has been financed mainly (and now almost totally) by advertising revenue; thus, it has never had a high degree of financial and political independence. Finally, its statutory requirement to educate, inform and entertain has not been taken seriously. In general terms, the Portuguese PSB has been controlled by the government and operates like the other commercial channel.

She went on to say that both RDP and RTP had been under the control of successive governments, with the result that between 1974 and 1986 the eleven seats on the board of governors and the twenty directors posts at RTP and RDP has been held by 80 and 130 different people respectively, whose qualifications for the job were considered less important than their party membership cards.

As in Spain, it took nearly 30 years for serious attempts to reform the situation to be launched. In 2002, the Portuguese government accepted a report drawn up by a panel of independent experts on the restructuring of public service broadcasting and redefinition of its remit. A sign of the new approach is that one of the two national public service television channels will from now on include partnerships with civil institutions such as universities, foundations, museums and associations, for the cession of their archives or copyrights, sponsoring and other forms of contributing for the production of programmes.

The 2003 Television Broadcasting Act has a special section on access to airtime on public television, guaranteeing political parties, the government, trade unions, professional organizations and those representing economic activities and environmental and consumer protection associations the right to broadcast time on the public television service, in accordance with strictly calculated quotas. Moreover, a variety of the now-defunct American Fairness Doctrine was introduced, with opposition parliamentary parties enjoying the right to refute, in the same programme service, to the political declarations made by the government on the public television service which affected them directly. Another new departure is the fact that the law calls for the appointment of "the Listener Ombudsman" and "the Viewer Ombudsman" who are to represent the public, its complaints and grievances vis-à-vis the management of public radio and public television. Their annual reports are to be considered by the regulatory authority.

By contrast, Italy is still waiting for its "democratic and emancipatory" process of change in RAI, the public service broadcaster. The story so far is well known. After decades of Christian Democratic Party hold on society and RAI, an attempt to democratize public service broadcasting and free it from government control led in the 1970s to the introduction of the *lottizzazione*, turning a system of "party domination" into one of "party partition" (Cavazza 1979), a paragon of "political parallelism". After the collapse of the Christian Democrats and the Socialists (two of the three parties which had held RAI in its grip) in the *Tangentopoli* scandal in 1992, the old *lottizzazione* system was replaced by "individual *lottizzazione*" (Hibberd 2001), with political appointees placed in the management of RAI to promote party interests. The many years of Berlusconi rule in reality meant the return of "party domination" over RAI: "Berlusconi and his coalition allies...adopted majoritarian, winner-take-all policies in appointing directors and overseers of the RAI broadcasting empire" (Marletti, Roncarolo 2000:197).

Under the pressure of the Italian president, the European Parliament and the Parliamentary Assembly of the Council of Europe, all concerned with insufficient pluralism in the Italian broadcast media, the Italian Parliament adopted the Gasparri Law, ostensibly designed to improve the situation. However, the European Commission for Democracy through Law of the Council of Europe had this comment to make:

In conclusion, the Commission notes that change at RAI will allow for government control over the Public Broadcaster for an unforeseeable period of time. For as long as the present government stays in office, this will mean that, in addition to being in control of its own three national television channels, the Prime Minister will have some control on the three public national television channels. The Commission expresses concern over the risk that this atypical situation may even strengthen the threat of monopolisation, which might constitute, in terms of the case-law of the European Court of Human Rights, an unjustified interference with freedom of expression (Venice Commission 2005)

In June 2006, the Prodi government announced it would undo Berlusconi's media reforms, but it was not clear whether that would lead to enhancing PSB independence. In January 2007 it was reported that according to government plans, RAI would be controlled by a Foundation "in order to avoid direct control by the Italian government" (Pekic 2007). The Foundation is to guarantee autonomy of government, represent the citizens-viewers, defend the company's independence, define the statutes of RAI and nominate the top management. It is proposed that the Foundation's Board of Directors be composed of seven members, with candidates screened by Parliament. The Board will have a six-year mandate, a third being renewed every two years. Another idea is that the Board will be appointed by other institutions as well, such as regions, universities and trade unions: in that case the number of members would be bigger. Following a public consultation, a government bill providing for these changes was to be submitted to Parliament.

It remains to be seen whether this will mean a democratic-emancipatory turn in Italy's policies vis-à-vis PSB, reducing what is now full political control of the broadcasting organization.

PSB in Post-Communist Countries

Despite the strong impact of the "atavistic" orientation, the mimetic orientation, combined with considerable pressure (or "leverage", as Vachudova 2005, prefers to call it) exerted on particular governments by the European Union, the Council of Europe and other international organizations, has – as shown in table 3 – produced a significant result in terms of the legal and institutional introduction of what is described as PSB in the region.

The World Bank (2002) assigned particular countries to one of the categories on the basis of the situation in 1999. Some countries have evolved since then and have moved or are moving towards other categories. Introduction of PSB could be an indicator of this change of status. The table does not include Mongolia, where PSB has also been introduced.

The precarious situation of PSB in post-communist countries is illustrated by the situation in Armenia, where "although in 2001 the state TV was transformed into *Channel H1*, the first public-service broadcaster in the CIS region, the channel still has yet to play its role as a public-service broadcaster...It is problematic that all five members of its board are appointed by President Kocharyan. The lack of political independence of the Board is seen as one of the main causes for the lack of objectivity and diversity in the news coverage of the public-service broadcaster, as confirmed by recent civil-society monitoring endeavours" (Haraszti 2006). In Azerbaijan, the Parliament first adopted a law on PSB which did not indicate that PSB would in reality be established. Then, in 2004, a presidential decree provided for transformation of one channel of

Table 3: Presence of PSB (*) in Post-Communist Countries

Competitive democracies	Concentrated political regimes	War-torn regimes	Noncompetitive political regimes
Czech Republic*	Slovak Republic*	Armenia*	Kazakhstan
Slovenia*	Bulgaria*	Albania*	Uzbekistan
Hungary*	Romania*	Georgia	Belarus
Poland*	Ukraine	Macedonia, FYR*	Turkmenistan
Lithuania*	Russia	Azerbaijan*	
Estonia*	Croatia*	Tajikistan	
Latvia*	Moldova*	Bosnia-Herzegovina*	
	Kyrgyz Republic		

The World Bank (2002) assigned particular countries to one of the categories on the basis of the situation in 1999. Some countries have evolved since then and have moved or are moving towards other categories. Introduction of PSB could be an indicator of this change of status. The table does not include Mongolia, where PSB has also been introduced.

state television into a PSB organization, alongside state television. Its independence is seriously in question. In Kyrgyzstan, Parliament adopted a law on public service broadcasting on 8 June 2006, but it was not sure the president would sign it (see also Richter, Golovanov 2006).

It is clear that where modernization and consolidation of democracy are incomplete, only a hybrid political system can emerge. As a consequence, also PSB stations in the more advanced post-communist democracies are in reality hybrid constructs, combining disparate (public service; political elite mouthpiece; political battlefield; commercial) elements within one organization. That is not a feature of post-communist countries alone: many PSB organizations in older democracies are also hybrid constructs, combining these and other elements in various degrees.

In general, public service broadcasting – where it exists – is, so far, generally seen as failing to deliver on its promise of independence and political impartiality, as well as of serving as a mainstay of the public sphere, and of delivering diverse and pluralistic content of high quality. Many of the stations are heavily in debt and their audience share is falling, especially in countries where national commercial radio and television stations have been licensed. Many are facing enormous challenges caused by, among other things:

- Traditional and badly designed organizational and management structures, involving many collective bodies divided along party lines, incapable of fast decision-making and mainly concentrating on blocking each other's actions;
- Heavy political control, resulting both from the politicization of the process of appointing top governing authorities, turning former state radio and television into "parliamentary" rather than public broadcasters, or indeed amounting to its "re-nationalization";
- Frequent management and leadership crises and changes of top management, resulting from political interference;
- Lack of funds and programming know-how required to compete with commercial broadcasters, sometimes coupled with exaggerated insistence on non-commercialism which additionally weakens those stations' ability to hold their own in the face of aggressive competition by commercial broadcasters;
- Self-censorship of journalists and programme-makers who can expect little protection from their superiors when they run afoul of politicians or some influential organization.

These outward manifestations of crisis are accompanied by problems of a far more fundamental nature: lack of social embeddedness of the idea of public service broadcasting and lack of a social constituency willing and able to support public service broadcasters and buttress its autonomy and independence. Transplanted into post-communist countries in the process of "transformation by imitation", they have not, generally speaking, been able to win support and a constituency in civil society. All this is well documented (see, e.g., Galik 2003; Hrvatin 2002; Jakubowicz 1995, 2003, 2007; Mungiu-Pippidi 2003; Ociepka 2003).

Hallin and Mancini (2004: 73) identify the following features of the "Mediterranean" media system:

- An elite-oriented press with relatively small circulation and a corresponding centrality of electronic media;
- High political parallelism, with the press marked by a strong focus on political life and a tradition of advocacy journalism, and with public service broadcasting tending to follow government or parliamentary models;

- Low development of the professionalization of journalists, with journalism not very distinct from political activism;
- Strong role of the state in the media as an owner, regulator and funder of the media.

Of these four features, items 2 through 4 can be said to relate directly to the situation in PSB. And indeed, PSB systems in post-communist countries display very much the same features as those in Southern European countries.

Thus, we may have found a place on the map for post-communist media systems. Contrary to what an encyclopaedia may tell you, post-communist countries appear to be located – figuratively at least – around the Mediterranean, and on both its sides, too, as some of them are politically closer to North African regimes than to any southern European country. After all, it is not by accident that Splichal (1994) has coined "Italianization of the media" as a phrase to describe the process of media change in those countries (even if he later decided that the comparison was too facile; see Splichal 2004).

Prospects for PSB in Post-Communist Countries

We noted above that according to Eckstein democratization should, in favourable conditions, be more or less complete after a quarter of a century. Given that hypothetical "benchmark" what, one may ask, are the prospects that around 2015–2020 (i.e., around 25–30 years after 1989), we may see a wave of democratic-emancipatory changes in the PSB systems of post-communist countries, replicating those in some southern European countries? This would reduce political pressure on, and interference in PSB. If it were to be accompanied by evolution of polarized into moderate political pluralism, it could, metaphorically speaking, send post-communist media systems, including public service broadcasting, "northwards", towards the democratic-corporatist system of moderate pluralism. If so, how far could they go, and how long would it take them to get there?

Of course, this is not to posit a unilinear view of media system evolution. Still, given the framework we have adopted, this is one possible option.

In any case, one should also remember that according to Dahrendorf (1991, p. 86), transformation in post-communist Europe towards the goal of creating a liberal democracy and market economy would be complete when "social foundations" have been laid "which transform the constitution and the economy from fair-weather into all-weather institutions which can withstand the storms generated within and without" – and that can take the better part of 60 years.

One of the theories of democratization is known as the discontinuity-hypothesis (Eckstein 2001). This says that highly discontinuous social change (rapid change, broad in scale) generally has pathological consequences. Also, that certain crucial political issues lead to especially intense conflicts. They include issues of national identity, the relations of church and state, regime-structure and popular participation, and redistributive social policies. These involve deep and broad questions of the boundaries, nature, and purpose of the polity, and of legitimacy.

It is difficult to imagine a more discontinuous and conflict-generating process of social change than the triple transition of post-communist countries – encompassing, according to Offe (1999) issues of nationality and territoriality; constitutional issues; and of economic order, or, as Ekiert (1999) puts it, simultaneous transformation of political, economic and social structures. Kuzio (2002a) says that there are two kinds of transition in post-communist countries: post-authoritarian and post-colonial, in the latter case involving quadruple transformation: democratization, marketization, state institution-building and civic nation-building. This has produced even more tension and conflicts (for an overview, see Hann 2002). According to Eckstein, no one should be surprised if anomic pathologies in behaviour follow such discontinuous change — as, indeed, they have in the region under discussion. It is clear that the media, and PSB in particular, have no hope of independence and impartiality at such a time.

In Eckstein's view, democratization should proceed gradually, incrementally, and by the use of syncretic devices, i.e., adapting the old to the new and vice versa.

Earlier waves of democratization have shown that viable democracy requires an appropriate political and general culture, and this, in turn, a social structure appropriate for such a culture, and that, therefore, the speed with which democratization can be carried out successfully varies directly with the extent to which pre-existing culture and social structure are conducive to it.

It is a well-established tenet of transition studies that the lack of a pre-communist corporate or national identity is a major barrier to successful change, as Kuzio (2002b) shows clearly by comparing Ukraine with Belarus, where "an ethno-cultural identity never developed prior to its incorporation into the USSR".

However, Eckstein's (2001) understanding of the cultural and structural prerequisites of successful democratization is broader. These include:

■ The democratic culture is a <u>mixed culture</u>, in which disparate, perhaps even contrary, elements are balanced. Liberal and participant elements always play a vital role in it, but they require balancing by other norms and practices;
■ Democratic political culture coexists, and probably is based on, a more general culture, in which major themes are (a) high social trust and (b) what might be called "civicness": the tendency to act "horizontally", viz., cooperatively, with others rather than "vertically" through hierarchical relations, such as patron-client relationships;
■ Democratic culture and structure are constituted by substantially congruent segments, in which the norms and practices of smaller entities substantially resemble those of national governance, especially those smaller entities that play important roles in political socialization and the recruitment of politicians and leaders. Society in this way can be a school for learning democratic citizenship and governance. From this it follows that political democratization should be accompanied by a good deal of social democratization - the democratization of social life in a more general sense.
■ Democratic political culture is based on a highly developed associational life in society, the hallmark of what is now generally called "civil society".

It would be foolish to try to predict timelines for the full emergence of these cultural and structural prerequisites of democratization, but it is clear that the process will not be fast. In Poland, for example, transformation has turned the country into a "loving mother" for some and into a "wicked stepmother" for many others:

Some Poles have found their feet in the post-communist Polish realities and others have got bogged down. Some have found their feet quickly and easily, others slowly and with great difficulty.... Today we are in the best condition we have ever been in, since the very beginning of transformation. The pitiful condition of the state itself is another matter. However, in theory at least, the state is easier to fundamentally reform than society as a whole. But only in theory, because instead of a public-oriented society, we have seen the rise of what we might call a self-oriented society. This self-orientation, or resourcefulness, of Poles too often allows them to improve their own situation at the expense of the state...If the divorce of citizens from their state is just passively observed, this could lead to an even more dangerous consequence, namely that the chance of a sustainable development is missed (Czapiński 2004: 288).

It will thus be considerable time before the cultural and structural prerequisites listed by Eckstein fully develop in many post-communist countries.

One of the versions of "Eastern European exceptionalism" focuses on the destruction of civil society under communism, and the effect of weak or absent civil society. Leaving the question of "exceptionalism" aside, it is true that civil society cannot provide a counterweight to the dominant role of the State and "political society". As noted by Pleines (2005), the number of civil society groups relevant to policy-making is comparatively small in post-communist countries. Their possibilities of exerting influence are, with a few exceptions, limited to a consultative role, i.e., a cooperation strategy. Exceptions are above all those cases where lobbying structures existed already in the socialist system, in concrete terms the agriculture lobby, coal mining and the Polish trade unions. Due to their weak state of development, Pleines concludes, non-state actors can pit little against unified state actors. Moreover, as shown by an overview of civil society development in Central and Eastern Europe (Solarz 2006), the state and civil society organizations, where they exist, often operate alongside each other, with the state unwilling to recognize them as partners and with citizens displaying little interest in civic engagement. Civic activities focus primarily on areas of importance to the financial well-being of individuals. Moreover, the low credibility of elected authorities combined with a high level of corruption lead to low societal identification with democratic processes and procedures.

If so, then acceptance of restraints on the exercise of power – and, thus, the emergence of cultural prerequisites of full PSB development – will be long in coming.

Conclusion

On the strength of this comparative analysis we could say that disappointment with PSB performance in post-communist countries is one more reflection of the great, but also to some extent unrealistic expectations created by the process of post-communist transformation, especially as concerns the pace of change and the success of transformation.

Given that the creation of PSB is one of the hardest tests of the success of the general process of political and media change, it is doubtful whether, realistically, more could have been achieved since 1989.

There is a price to be paid for disappointed expectations, however. Much of the mimetic strategy of transformation was based on a hope that, with time, the cultural and axiological underpinnings of transplanted institutions could be added to enable those institutions to operate as intended. As we saw on the example of Spain or Portugal, change in media, especially public service media, may lag behind a more general process of democratization. So, this soon becomes a race against quickly growing disillusionment with the way the institution operates. Such disillusionment may prove dangerous, as public opinion may not be prepared to accept the existence of a flawed institution, failing to bring the expected benefits.

Frustration with the unending controversies surrounding PSB, combined with the lack of a clear answer as to what can be done to remedy the situation, may prove destructive. Assuming the original legal and institutional framework created by legislation is appropriate, the question then becomes whether it is possible to maintain this framework for long enough (i.e., several decades) for it to bear fruit. More likely, however, that framework will be changed because of the atavistic tendencies on the part of successive governments wishing to gain greater control of PSB, usually with little resistance from civil society (though one has to mention the 2005 battle in Slovenia against changes in the broadcasting law, leading to greater parliamentary control of PSB, ending with a nationwide referendum that was narrowly won by the government). That may deepen the frustration on the part of civil society and cynicism about the concept of public service broadcasting.

Spain, Portugal, Italy and France have been the scene of this vicious circle for many years. It can be broken through. It can also persevere. Eventually, we will know whether PSB has taken root in post-communist countries.

References

Antoszewski, Andrzej, Ryszard Herbut (2004). *Systemy polityczne współczesnego świata*. Gdańsk: Arche.

Arato, Andrew (1996). "The Hungarian Constitutional Court in the Media War: Interpretations of Separation of Powers and Models of Democracy (in:) A. Sajó, M. Price (eds.) *Rights of Access to the Media* (pp. 225–242). The Hague: Kluwer Law International.

Brečka, S. (1993). *Transformation of the Slovak Television*. Paper presented to a conference on "Restructuring TV in Central and Eastern Europe, University of Westminster, London, October 20–23.

Bunce, Valerie (2002). *Democratization after the Third Wave*. The Kim Okil Memorial Lecture at Ewha Women's College, Seoul, South Korea, May 16, 2002. http://kcri.ewha.ac.kr/webapps/culture/scholar/valH.doc.

Bustamante, Enrique (1989). TV and public service in Spain: a difficult encounter. *Media, Culture and Society*, 11(1): 67–88.

Caffarel, Carmen, Mario Garcia de Castro (in print). "Editorial autonomy and public control – the debate over reform" (in:) Christian Nissen (ed.) *Making a Difference. Public Service Broadcasting and the media landscape in Europe*. Geneva: EBU.

Carothers, Thomas (2002). The End of the Transition Paradigm. *Journal of Democracy*, 13(1): 5–21.

Cichosz, Marzena (2006). "Transformacja demokratyczna – przyczyny, przebieg i efekty procesu" (in:) Andrzej Antoszewski (ed.) *Systemy polityczne Europy Środkowej i Wschodniej. Perspektywa porównawcza*. Wrocław: Wydawnictwo Uniwersytetu Wrocławskiego, pp. 35–66.

Comrie, Margie, Susan Fountaine (2006). "Back to the Future in New Zealand: Can a "third way" compromise reinvigorate public service broadcasting?" (In:) Christian Nissen (ed.) *Making a Difference. Public Service Broadcasting and the media landscape in Europe*. Eastleigh: John Libbey Publishing, pp. 147–162.

Czapiński, Janusz (2004). Conclusion: New Poland – Loving Mother Or Wicked Stepmother? (In:) Janusz Czapiński, Tomasz Panek (eds.) *Social Diagnosis 2003. Objective and Subjective Quality of Life in Poland*. Warsaw: University of Finance and Management. http://www.diagnoza.com./files/report/report.html.

DCMS (2006). *A public service for all: the BBC in the digital age*. White Paper. London, Department of Culture, Media and Sport.

Diamond, Larry (1997). Is the Third Wave of Democratization Over? The Imperative of Consolidation. Working Paper No. 237, http://www.nd.edu/~kellogg/WPS/237.pdf.

Dryzek, John, Z., Leslie Holmes (2002). *Post-Communist Democratization. Political Discourses across Thirteen Countries*. Cambridge: Cambridge University Press.

Eckstein, Harry (2001). Lessons for the "Third Wave" from the First: An Essay on Democratization. http://www.democ.uci.edu/publications/papersseriespre2001/lessons.htm.

Ekiert, Grzegorz (1999). *Do Legacies Matter? Patterns of Postcommunist Transitions in Eastern Europe.* East European Studies Program, Woodrow Wilson International Center for Scholars, Occasional Paper No. 54 (http://wwics.si.edu/ees/papers/1999/54osb_p.pdf).

Galik, Mihaly (2003). "Evolving the Media Market: The Case of Hungary" (in:) David L. Paletz, Karol Jakubowicz (eds.) *Business as Usual: Continuity and Change in Central and Eastern European Media.* Cresskill, N.J.: Hampton Press. pp. 177–204.

Gunther, Richard, Jose Ramon Montero, Jose Ognacio Wert (2000). The Media and Politics in Spain: From Dictatorship to Democracy (in:) Richard Gunther, Anthony Mugham, (eds.) *Democracy and the Media. A Comparative Perspective.* Cambridge: Cambridge University Press.

Hallin Daniel C., Paolo Mancini (2004). *Comparing Media Systems: Three Models of Media and Politics.* Cambridge: Cambridge University Press.

Hallin, Daniel C., Stylianos Papathanassopoulos (2002). "Political clientelism and the media: southern Europe and Latin America in comparative perspective". *Media, Culture and Society*, 24(2): 175–196.

Hann, C. M. (2002) (ed.) *Postsocialism. Ideals, Ideologies and Practices in Eurasia.* London: Routledge.

Haraszti, Miklos (2006). *The State of Media Freedom in Armenia. Observations and Recommendations.* Vienna: The Representative on Freedom of the Media, OSCE. http://www.osce.org/documents/rfm/2006/07/20007_en.pdf.

Hibberd, Matthew (2001). The reform of public service broadcasting in Italy. *Media, Culture and Society*, 23(2): 233–252.

Hrvatin, Sandra B. (2002). *Serving the State or the Public. The Outlook for Public Service Broadcasting in Slovenia.* Ljubljana: Peace Institute.

Huntington, Samuel P. (1995). *Trzecia fala demokratyzacji.* Warszawa: Wydawnictwo Naukowe PWN.

Jakubowicz, Karol (1995). Lovebirds? The Media, the State and Politics in Central and Eastern Europe. *Javnost/The Public*, 2(1), 75–91.

Jakubowicz, Karol (2003). "Ideas In Our Heads: Introduction of PSB as Part of Media System Change in Central and Eastern Europe", *European Journal of Communication*, 19 (1): 53–75.

Jakubowicz, Karol (2007). *Rude Awakening: Social and Media Change in Central and Eastern Europe.* Cresskill, N.J.: Hampton Press, Inc.

Kato, Hidetoshi (1999). "The Birth of A 'Free Radio'—Broadcasting Under Military Occupation" (in:) *Media, Culture, And Education In Japan [A Collection Of Papers].* Tokyo: National Institute of Multimedia Education. http://homepage3.nifty.com/katodb/doc/text/2598.html.

Kivikuru, Ullamaija (2006). "Top-Down or Bottom-up. Radio in the Service of Democracy: Experiences from South Africa and Namibia". *The International Communication Gazette*, 68(1): 5–31.

Krastev, Ivan (2006). Democracy's "Doubles". *Journal of Democracy*, 17(2): 52–62.

Kuzio, Taras (2002a). *National Identity And Democratic Transition In Post-Soviet Ukraine And Belarus: A Theoretical And Comparative Perspective* (Part 1). RFE/RL East European Perspectives, 4(15), 24 July (www.rferl.org/eepreport).

Kuzio Taras (2002b). *Is Nationalism Always a Bad Thing? National Identity and Democratic Transition in Post-Soviet Ukraine and Belarus.* http://www.taraskuzio.net/lectures/columbia_nationalism.pdf.

Lijphart, Arend (n.d.) *The Westminster model and Westminster adapted*, http://www.aph.gov.au/senate/pubs/pops/pop34/c04.htm.

Linz, Juan J., Alfred Stepan (1996). *Problems of Democratic Transition and Consolidation. Southern Europe, South America, and Post-Communist Europe.* Baltimore and London: The Johns Hopkins University Press.

McFaul, Michael (2005). Transitions From Postcommunism. *Journal of Democracy*, 16 (3): 5–19.

McQuail, Denis (2005). *McQuail's Mass Communication Theory*. London: Sage Publications.

Mancini, Paolo (2000). Political complexity and alternative models of journalism: The Italian case (in:) James Curran, and Myung-Jin Park (eds.), *De-Westernizing Media Studies*. London and New York: Routledge, pp. 265–279.

Marletti, Carlo, Franca Roncarolo (2000). Media Influence in the Italian Transition from a Consensual to a Majoritarian Democracy (in:) Richard Gunther, Anthony Mugham, (eds.). *Democracy and the Media. A Comparative Perspective*. Cambridge: Cambridge University Press, pp. 195–240.

Mediesekretariatet (2005). Executive Summary. Public Service-Ledelse i Andre Lande. Copenhagen. http://www.mediesekretariatet.dk/bilag/oevrproj/psrapport.pdf.

Mungiu-Pippidi, Alina (2003). From State to Public Service: The Failed Reform of State TV in Central Eastern Europe (in:) Miklós Sükösd, Péter Bajomi-Lázár (eds.) *Reinventing Media. Media Policy Reform in East-Central Europe*. Budapest: CEU Press, pp. 31–84.

Nikoltchev, Ivan (1998/99). Journalists as Lawmakers: Grassroots Initiative for Media Regulation in Bulgaria, 1996–1998. *International Journal of Communications Law and Policy*, issue 2, Winter (www.digital-law.net/ijclp).

Ociepka, Beata (2003). *Dla kogo telewizja? Model publiczny w postkomunistycznej Europie Środkowej*. Wrocław: Wydawnictwo Uniwersytetu Wrocławskiego.

Offe, Claus (1999). *Drogi transformacji. Doświadczenia wschodnioeuropejskie i wschodnioniemieckie*. Warsaw-Kraków: Wydawnictwo Naukowe PWN.

Paletz, D. L., and Lipinski J. (1994). *Political Culture and Political Communication* (http://www.diba.es/icps/working_papers/docs/WP_I_92.html).

Papatheodorou, Fotini, David Machin (2003). "The Umbilical Cord That Was Never Cut: The Post-Dictatorial Intimacy between the Political Elite and the Mass Media in Greece and Spain". *European Journal of Communication*. 18(1): 31–54.

Pekic, Branislav (2007). RAI to be controlled by a Foundation. http://www.advanced-television.com/2006/news_archive_2006/Jan08_Jan12.htm.

Pleines, Heiko (2005). "The Political Role of Civil Society Organisations in Central and Eastern Europe" (in:) Heiko Pleines (ed.) *Participation of Civil Society in New Modes of Governance. The Case of the New EU Member States*. Part 1: The State of Civil Society. Arbeitspapiere und Materialien, no.67. Bremen: Forschungsstelle Osteuropa Bremen.

Richter, Andrei, Dmitry Golovanov (2006). Public Service Broadcasting Regulation in the Commonwealth of Independent States. Special Report on the Legal Framework for Public Service Broadcasting in Azerbaijan, Georgia, Moldova, Russia and Ukraine Strasbourg: European Audiovisual Observatory.

Sitter, Nick (2005). *Finlandisation Or The Danish Model? Party Competition And Euroscepticism In East Central Europe*. Paper presented at a One-Day Workshop *Enlargement and Civil Society* University of Nottingham. http://www.bi.no/FellesFiles/Nottingham-paper.pdf.

Smith, Anthony (1979). "Introduction" (in:) Anthony Smith (ed.) *Television and Political Life. Studies in Six European Countries*. London: Macmillan.

Solarz, Radosław (2006). Kształtowanie się społeczeństwa obywatelskiego w krajach Europy Środkowej i Wschodniej" (in:) Andrzej Antoszewski (ed.) *Systemy polityczne Europy Środkowej i Wschodniej. Perspektywa porównawcza*. Wrocław: Wydawnictwo Uniwersytetu Wrocławskiego, pp. 243–278.

Sousa, Helena (1996). *Communications Policy in Portugal and Its Links with the European Union. An Analysis of the Telecommunications and Television Broadcasting Sectors from the Mid-1980's until the Mid-1990's*. London. http://bocc.ubi.pt/pag/sousa-helena-chap-7-broadcasting.html.

Sparks, Colin (2000). Media theory after the fall of European communism. Why the old models from East and West won't do any more. In James Curran, Myung-Jin Part (eds.). *De-Westernizing Media Studies*. London: Routledge, pp. 35–49.

Splichal, Slavko (1994). *Media Beyond Socialism: Theory and Practice in East-Central Europe*. Boulder: Westview Press.

Splichal, S. (2000). Reproducing Political Capitalism in the Media in East Central Europe. *Media Research*, 6(1), 5–18.

Splichal, S. (2001). Imitative Revolutions: Changes in the Media and Journalism in East-Central Europe. *Javnost/The Public*, VIII(4), 31–58.

Splichal, Slavko (2004). Privatization: The Cost of Media Democratization in East and Central Europe? (In:) Pradip N. Thoas, Zaharom Nain (eds.) *Who Owns the Media. Global Trends and Local Resistances*. Penang: Southbound.

Statham, Paul (1996). "Television News and the Public Sphere in Italy. Conflicts at the Media/Politics Interface". *European Journal of Communication*, 11(4): 511–556.

Sükösd, Miklós (2000). Democratic Transition and the Mass Media: From Stalinism to Democratic Consolidation (in:) Richard Gunther, Anthony Mugham, (eds.) *Democracy and the Media. A Comparative Perspective*. Cambridge, England: Cambridge University Press, pp. 122–164.

Sükösd, Miklós, Péter Bajomi-Lázár (2003). The Second Wave of Media Reform in East-Central Europe. In: Miklós Sükösd, Péter Bajomi-Lázár (eds.) *Reinventing Media. Media Policy Reform in East-Central Europe*. Budapest: CEU Press, pp. 13–30.

Vachudova, Milada Anna (2005). *Europe Undivided. Democracy, Leverage, and Integration after Communism*. Oxford: Oxford University Press.

Venice Commission (2005). *Opinion on the compatibility of the laws "Gasparri" and "Frattini" of Italy with the Council of Europe standards in the field of freedom of expression and pluralism of the media*. Opinion no. 309/2004, CDL-AD(2005)017. Venice: European Commission For Democracy Through Law. http://www.venice.coe.int/docs/2005/CDL-AD(2005)017-e.asp.

Williams, Raymond (1968). *Communications*. London: Penguin Books.

World Bank (2002). *Transition. The First Ten Years. Analysis and Lessons for Eastern Europe and the Former Soviet Union*. Washington, D.C.

Zakaria, Fareed (1997). The Rise of Illiberal Democracy, *Foreign Affairs*, November/December, http://www.foreignaffairs.org/19971101faessay3809/fareed-zakaria/the-rise-of-illiberal-democracy.html.

Dances with Wolves: A Meditation on the Media and Political System in the European Union's Romania[1]

Peter Gross

Romania's media — their independence, nature, role(s), professionalism and the laws that pertained to them — have had a rollercoaster ride since December 1989, when they and the society they are supposed to serve were freed from communism. They showed promise one day, only to regress the next day and then raise hopes again before once more disappointing expectations. Their short history in a period of tentative, timid democratization defies easy conclusions or facile classifications and typecasting.

This paper briefly focuses on the problems related to the general status of the media, their nature, independence, professionalism and role in society in 2005 and 2006 and just as briefly on developments in the media sphere since January 2007; it then turns its attention to how Hallin and Mancini's (2004) three models of media and politics may relate to the Romanian media. In that context, it endeavours to provide the most succinct, preliminary answers to the question, why is the Romanian media system the way it is, operates in the fashion and plays the role(s) it does and is burdened by laws, regulations and handling by its owners that are inimical to independence, a democratic role and professionalism.

Romania is one of two countries to join the EU in January 2007 and has had a difficult candidacy. It continues to have a media whose nature, system and legal supports put into question the nature of the country's democracy and of the political class' understanding of and commitment to it.[2] Romania had a protracted courtship and a relatively short engagement with the EU; during both periods the country was pushed and cajoled to meet certain standards in the economic, legal, political, social and other realms. Freedom of the press, in question for a number of years, was one of the core issues in the negotiations for Romania's membership in the EU.[3]

After first attempting to Potemkinize the realization of these standards, Romania embarked on small, tentative changes in 2004 after Traian Basescu's election as the nation's third post-communist president.[4] No degree of perfection in any of these standards was achieved but the real efforts that were made, together with political considerations specific to the EU, led to the consummation of the arranged marriage between the EU and Romania. For Romania it was a triumph; for the EU the new member may prove to be a continuing problem. It took only weeks after Romania's official entry into the EU for Romania's political elite to signal that the *status quo ante* that dominated the pre-engagement period was to be restored, including how issues of freedom of the press and other media-related matters are being handled.

1. Media, politics, freedom of the press and the (instant) end of the EU-Romania honeymoon

As Romania prepared in 2005 and 2006 to join the EU, a laundry list of issues continued to plague Romania's journalists, journalism and media outlets, and the laws that apply to journalists and, by extension, society. According to studies of Romanian media (Coman 2004, 2003, 1998; Gross 1996, 1999a, 1999b; Marinescu 2002; Stanomir 2003; Zarojanu 2001) and a report released by the Agentia de Monitorizare a Presei (May 2007), in 2006 the important developments and continuations of sixteen-year-long trends included,

- The overt increase in attacks against press freedom by some state institutions
- A relatively high number of attacks and threats against journalists
- Changes in the media marketplace; the appearance of new media/media owners and the consolidation of the media concentration phenomenon[5]
- Attempts at political control over the National Audiovisual Council
- The lack of political will to modify the law addressing the functioning of public radio and television in ways that would assure their true independence
- The initiation of a legislative project by the Ministry of Justice that would legalize the access of public prosecutors to data in computers systems without a court ruling (OUG nr. 131/2006)
- The press being increasingly perceived as an instrument for obtaining certain political and economic advantages;
- The persistent continuation of politicization of news coverage and the dominance of opinion rather than fact-based journalism, practiced in the name of partisan interests, continued as did the tabloidization trend begun in the 1990s;
- The manipulation of media; sometime censorship by owners and editors/director of and self-censorship in the media;
- The lack of protection for and anonymity of news sources;
- Either bad relationships between politicians and the media or relationships in which media are subordinate to politicians;
- The absence of bona fide ethical codes, the means and willingness to enforce them;
- The lack of real solidarity and organization among journalists;
- Poor pay for journalists, particularly when compared to the exorbitantly high pay for editors, directors and other media elites.

These and other problems have made the overall professionalism of Romanian journalism and the independence of media and their journalists doubtful; concrete examples of professionalism and independence are indeed few and far between.

A study of television news from the perspective of the public interest and journalistic practices, for example, conducted from November 2006 to January 2007 (Codreanu and Dobre 2007), presents a mixed picture of broadcast journalism, if we are to believe the data. Analyzing the evening news coverage of the most significant television outlets, Antena 1, Antena 3, Prima TV, Pro TV, Realitatea TV and TVR 1, the study concludes that

- sensationalizing stories is highest at Antena 1(21% of stories and lowest at Antena 3 (1% of stories);
- respect for the value of presumption of innocence in crime stories is highest at Antena 3 (100% of stories) and lowest at Antena 1 (54% of stories);
- respect for privacy is highest at Realitatea TV and TVR 1 (100% of stories) and lowest at Pro TV (50% of stories);
- respect for the principles of non-discrimination/the out-of-context mentioning of ethnicity or disabilities of a story's protagonists is highest at Pro TV (50% of stories) and lowest at Antena 1, Prima TV, Realitatea TV and TVR 1 (100 % of stories); and
- presenting opposing points of views is highest at TVR 1 (75% of stories) and lowest at Antena 3 (48% of stories).

Some progress was also discernible in 2005 and 2006, however, in regard to overall media issues:

- Improvement in the access to information law and the relatively better access to information, particularly government information; the transparency in domestic affairs, judiciary and the prime minister's office;
- The government resolved the issue of government loans and subsidies to media enterprises by working out a new set of regulations "with representative of media institutions and media NGOS", and made distribution of public advertising "more transparent", and set "criteria for its distribution" (Media Monitoring Agency 2006);[6]
- The Romanian Parliament, after considerable efforts by the reform-minded Romanian Justice Minister Monica Macovei, decriminalized defamation and insults;[7]
- Romanian Public Television was to some degree set free from the clutches of the governing party/parties for the first time since its brief, two to three weeks of certifiable independence in December 1989–January 1990;
- Increased debates about internal media problems, spurred on by blogs that analyze media (Codreanu and Dobre May 2007);
- The continuation of the now decade-old debates within professional organizations regarding the definition of instruments for self-regulation and the mechanism of applying them (Codreanu and Dobre May 2007).

Unfortunately, as Romanian's post-communist history has repeatedly shown, whenever progress is registered, so is some regression or a relapse to old ways. Thus, in January 2005, it was discovered that Romania's intelligence service tapped the phones of two Romanian journalists working for foreign media outlets, in "violation of the right not to reveal journalistic sources", as noted by Reporters Without Borders (28 January 2005), which called on the government to comply with European standards in the matter. And during summer 2006, a website created by two foreign desk reporters of the daily *Ziua*, parodying the website of the Ministry of Foreign

Affairs, was shut down by the privately owned Internet service provider CHL at the request of the Ministry. To make matters worse, CHL violated the law protecting personal data by handing over information about the journalists; no action was taken against CHL. In response to these developments, Reporters Without Borders (21 July 2006) said: "It is astonishing that Romania, a future European Union member, has not respected free expression and the confidentiality of personal information in this case, although these rights are guaranteed by the European Convention on Human Rights and Romania's own Law 677–2001."

Thus, the fundamental issues related to a meaningful, positive transformation in the media field remained unresolved: the values, attitudes, mentalities and behaviour of media owners, editors and directors, politicians and political parties, parliamentarians and others who have an influence in defining the media system, its nature, role(s) and operations, the integrity of the judicial system and that of the private business sector. Media owners, for instance, by and large agree that the "theory of independent media is a chimera", as the president of the Conservative Party and one of a handful of media moguls, Dan Voiculescu, said. Voiculescu, who serves in the Romanian Parliament, says, that in Romania "there are many newspapers that are politically partisan [belonging] to certain groups" and that there is no press outlet that is independent (Agentia de Monitorizare a Presei Oct./Dec. 2007, p. 14).

Stating the obvious, Voiculescu fails to recognize his own role in creating the reality that he so accurately describes. As the head of a parliamentary group that sought to impeach President Basescu in spring 2007, Voiculescu uses his media empire with alacrity and vigor in pursuing his and his political party's political goals.[8] A former agent of the notorious Securitate, Romania's version of the KGB, he is not alone to use his media outlets for political purposes, while claiming to be the victim of a system he is innocent of creating; Sorin Ovidiu Vantu, Dinu Patriciu, Valentin Paunescu, Viorel and Ioan Micula, Liviu Luca, Verestoy Attila, Sorin Marin and Adrian Sarbu own major media enterprises and are also leaders of political parties, parliamentarians or businessmen with strong political interests, ties or ambitions.[9] Without any understanding of, or care for, social responsibility, they wield their media outlets like broadswords in the interest of politics and profit.

The excessive mediatization of politics in spring 2007 has decreased television audiences and Ioana Avadani, head of the Independent Journalism Center in Bucharest, points out that the public is supersaturated with political messages by an "editorial machinery" that is a veritable "noise machine" whose product is "crude, superficial and more aggressive than explanatory" (Iancu 14 May 2007).

Together with a small group of politicians and businessmen, President Basescu is somewhat of an anomaly among the country's political elite for his pursuit of real, meaningful democratization and his battles against the corrosive corruption that is at the core of the nation's many ills. In a speech to the Romanian Parliament (14 February 2007), he told parliamentarians and the country,

> I should also mention the close ties between some businessmen and some politicians, …through which the transfer of political power from politicians to these businessmen was accomplished. These are the same businessmen that we find in continuous power through the influence they have obtained on top politicians. In addition, these businessmen are the same ones that can start or stop press campaigns. From this point of view, it is essential that politicians de-couple themselves from this tag team and work for the general interest and not for the interests of these clients.

President Basescu's understanding of the relationship between businessmen and politicians is an accurate one; this relationship, however, goes well beyond a symbiotic one. Individuals who wear two hats, those of media owner and politician, now control major news media outlets.[10]

The growth and accentuation of political control over media enterprises increased after 2000 and so did the pursuit of economic windfalls. Consequently, it is not only the political power of news media outlets that is being protected and perpetuated by the overwhelming control exercised by media owners but also "The mafia-like structures within the advertising industry and influential media outlets are operational and effective" (International Research and Exchanges Board 2006).

There is also general agreement among politicians, media moguls and the leadership of their media enterprises – editors, directors and managers – that the Romanian media are the country's "public opinion". The public is clearly not part of public opinion or its formation. This is a perpetuation of the pre-communist and communist mentalities that disregarded the will and opinions of the people and considered the elites as the makers and embodiment of public opinion.

The foreign media enterprises that own outlets in Romania or have major media investments have brought little change to how the role(s) and nature of media are defined, how the media system functions, and how journalism is practiced. They have, in fact, conducted themselves in a very Romanian fashion since their injection into the Romanian media market in the very late 1990s, much later than in most other post-communist countries in the region. They are now a significant presence at the local and national level; most own specialized magazines and weeklies play little or no role in the political arena.[11]

The Romanian media have not established themselves as an institution in its own right, a necessity in any democracy. The assessment of the state of the media in Romanian by the head of the Romanian Cultural Institute and a respected public intellectual, Horia-Roman Patapievici (15 Feb. 2007), is on target: "the source of legitimacy for politics has come to be only the press, and the press' [legitimacy] only politics, society having stopped being the objective of the press and the subject for politics." It is hardly a surprise that – despite showing promise more than once since 1989 that they might evolve as bona fide platforms for news, information and varied opinions – most news media outlets persist being organs of dis-information, misinformation, intimidation, trivialization, rumours, advocacy and propaganda on all so-called controversial issues, i.e., the political and economic interests of the elites.

Consequently, we cannot talk about the media having influence on the political class, whose direct and indirect influence over the media has grown since 2003 and 2004, a short period during which it appeared to be waning. Writes Tapalaga (10 November 2006):

> [Media] owners, managers, involve themselves in an impermissible way in editorial matters, deciding what appears and does not appear in a newspaper. They order positive or negative article about the potentates of the day, as a function of their own interests. Most of them write copy for the newspaper with one hand and sign advertising contracts with the other hand. For years [politicians and their minions] in the press did not do more than obey on command, unleashing press campaigns according to their own political or economic interests.

The news media are a "sophisticated propaganda machine", according to Alexandru Lazescu (5 March 2007). There is less parallelism between media and political parties and politicians than there was in the 1990s and more a form of political press that belongs to politician-businessmen who use it for their own purposes; a situation in which in the culture of the media owners, the political and media functions overlap rather than proceed in parallel to one another. In April 2007, in the wake of Parliament's month-long suspension of President Basescu,[12] the head of the foreign department of the daily *Evenimentul Zilei*, Victor Roncea, claimed that the director of the newspaper told him of a secret understanding among the media oligarchs to eliminate all supporters of the president from their media enterprises (Scanteie 24 April 2007). Roncea was not the only journalists to make that claim.

And the television stations owned by politician-businessmen are fully engaged in the battle between the major political parties, the Social Democratic Party (PSD) and the National Liberal Party (PNL) and President Basescu.[13] Rodica Culcer (11–17 May 2007), the former head of TVR 1 news programmes, writes in the weekly 22 that the political battles are being carried out in the media, particularly on television stations such as Realitatea TV and Antena 3 but also

> On the Internet and wherever [they can] find a microphone, PSD and PNL politicians carry out a ferociously negative campaign, attempting to create Traian Basescu's image as sick with power, with an errant mind, possessed of a desire to rule a slave people...They are counting on an electorate that is less informed, less active and uninvolved.

Journalists see the involvement of politics and economic issues as the biggest problem that the Romanian media face; two-thirds view journalism as a dangerous profession, one that does not pay well, but one that is relatively objective, an ironic claim given their complaint of political manipulation and influence. The same journalists say, if we take them at their word, that they feel an affinity with liberalism (21 per cent), social democracy (8 per cent), the ecological movement (4 per cent), Christian-democracy (4 per cent), nationalism (2 per cent), communism (1 per cent), populism (1 per cent), conservatives (1 per cent), and almost half say they have no political preferences (49 per cent) (Lazaroiu 16 Oct. 2006).

By joining the EU, an expectation of progress in all aspects of the media was present both inside and outside the country and proved to be misplaced. By 18 January 2007, only days after Romania became an official EU member, the country's Constitutional Court re-criminalized defamation and insults, overturning the hard-won progress made on this issue in June 2006. "This ruling is a significant step backwards, coming just a few weeks after Romania joined the European Union and after big improvements last year...Reinstating press offences in the criminal code will bring serious threats to bear on the work of journalists", rightly opined Reporters Without Borders (2 February 2007). Romania's supreme court cited rulings made by the European Court of Human Rights in support of its decision and also similar laws in France, Germany and Italy to justify its position, highlighting the need for the "decriminalization of press offences throughout Europe", which are "more necessary than ever" (Reporters Without Borders 2 February 2007).

In March 2007, the Romanian Parliament lifted the accreditation of the intellectual weekly 22, which has been a consistent critic of Romania's new political elites and the system that has evolved since December 1989. It was yet another sign that Romanian parliamentarians have little understanding of the nature of a free press or sympathy for it, its duty to cover the workings of state and government institutions and, even more overwhelmingly, of the need for these institutions to establish transparency.

Also in March 2007, Rodica Culcer, since August 2005 the head of the news department of the Romanian Television (RTV), formally speaking, a public service broadcaster, was fired.

RTV, which was for almost its entire post-communist life controlled by the government of the day, lags in ratings behind most of the major private television stations and thus has eroded its political relevance and value to the ruling parties in the last two to three years.[14] RTV resurfaced as a political football in spring 2007, precisely because it is one of the few national media outlets that are no longer entirely controlled by politicians and it was an easy political target for the opponents of President Basescu. Spearheading the attack on RTV were Voiculescu's newspaper, *Jurnalul National*; the parliamentarian/media mogul is siding with Prime Minister Tariceanu against President Basescu in an escalating political battle that caught RTV firmly in its jaws and made Rodica Culcer its first victim (and, even more dishearteningly, reformist Minister of Justice Monica Macovei its second and most important victim in April 2007).

Romanian audiences profess confidence in the media, ranking it just below the Church and the Army as trustworthy institutions. Yet, the media are in a veritable identity crisis, as are their journalists, a reality that can only be explained by the intersection of several developments, including the re-politicization of journalism in the last sixteen years (Coman and Gross 2006, pp. 110–120 and p. 54):

(a) The journalists' inability to offer a convincing concept of their mission or their achievements in defending the public interest,
(b) The tabloidization of the media and of journalistic styles, leading to the admixture of journalism and entertainment, and
(c) Widespread corruption.

Romanian audiences, therefore, have few credible means of informing themselves, reliable platforms to express their views and champions for their concerns and welfare, not to mention the welfare of the democratization process. Journalism in Romania may not be too free — the Freedom House report (2006) places Romania's media in the "Partly Free" rubric — but neither does it exercise much social responsibility.

2. Hallin and Mancini in Romania

Why are Romania's media system, the nature, role of media in society and journalism as they are today? Is biased, politicized, advocacy journalism an outgrowth of the political system and politics or a historical-cultural artefact adjusted to the needs of a new Romanian reality? Explanations invariably are offered by pointing to politics and the political system and/or by focusing on the ownership of media outlets and their dependence on the market.

The latest such approach is Hallin and Mancini's (2007) major scholarly contribution, a brilliant, nuanced work. However, it has two shortcomings from my perspective: (1) it excludes the Eastern European nations from its considerations, and (2) it fails to consider culture as a key element of the political systems and politics, of institutions such as the media, and of other aspects of society. For Eastern Europe, post-communist culture with its still undigested experiences, the battle to purge itself of non-democratic and illiberal mentalities, attitudes, habits, values and behaviour has only begun emerging, and the *new* political systems, politics and institutions are in large measure still driven by *unchanged* institutional, professional, political and general societal cultures.[15] The notion that the fall of communism left a *tabula rasa* upon which one can build "democracy from scratch" (Fish 1995) all of its institutions and more importantly the way they function, interpret and apply the new rules and exigencies, and react and act in the new, non-communist reality, is unfounded.

I argue, therefore, that Hallin and Mancini's models are incomplete and insufficiently universalizable to allow them to describe and explain Eastern European media systems and their journalism. What I offer here is but the *beginning of a process* of assessing the applicability (or otherwise) of Hallin and Mancini's work in Eastern Europe and in Romania, specifically. I leave to another time the more in-depth analysis of their models vis-à-vis the Eastern European media and, equally as important, their testing on the nature and practices of journalism in the region that is also addressed in their work.

At first glance, Romania's media appear to fit Hallin and Mancini's (2007, pp. 73–75, pp. 89–250) Mediterranean or Polarized Pluralist Model (MPPM) but almost instantly anomalies appear, as the two authors indeed recognize is possible in systems that are not stagnant.[16] More importantly, however, what quickly surfaces is a disconnect between the Romanian reality and the MPPM model. In Romania, the media system has changed over time – from the appearance of the first newspapers and the formal end of feudalism in the nineteenth century to the introduction of radio in the early twentieth century and the timid flirtation with democracy that ultimately led to fascism, then royal dictatorship and ultimately communism. But the quasi-feudal, undemocratic mentalities, values, attitudes and behaviours have simply been adapted to the changes in political systems and politics and, thus, to all societal institutions.[17]

Hallin and Mancini's main points that describe the Mediterranean or Polarized Pluralist media model find little congruence with the Romanian realty and this is instructive both for signaling the differences between the Romanian media and the Hallin/Mancini model and the reasons or explanations that may buttress those differences (see table I):

1. As in the MPPM, Romania's press was elite-oriented before World War II but not so during the communist era and even less so in the post-communist one. Having said that, I hasten to add that the institutional, professional and general cultures that drive the news as opposed to the entertainment media have not entirely shaken their feudal, kleptocratic and undemocratic parentage (Gross 1996; Coman and Gross 2006). And journalism has not distanced itself too much from that practiced in the nineteenth century when it was, according one of Romania's literary and journalistic giants, Mihai Eminescu, "too vehement in tone, disproportionate personal attacks, excessive forms of political versions...hyperbolism which resembles at once that of the great prophets of the Old Testament and that of the un-matched Dante" (as quoted in Cretia 1990, p. 4).

The electronic media have unquestionably become central in Romania's media world, and now the Internet is slowly but surely making inroads with effects that are yet unclear for the varied endeavours in public life.

2. Freedom of the press did indeed come late in Romania's history with the 1923 Constitutions guaranteeing the widest latitude to press freedom and forbidding censorship; the press laws were altered in 1922, 1923 and 1925 to the benefit of press freedom "but the promise these changes held never fully materialized and were not institutionalized" (Coman and Gross 2007, p. 15).

One can argue that in 2007 freedom of the press is to some extent still stuck at the (shaky) level of the 1920s and has yet to be institutionalized in juridical, institutional and cultural terms. Freedom of the press in Romania has always been defined in a culture in which the notion of social responsibility was lacking; the interests of the few were paramount and largely accepted by a fatalistic populace.[18]

3. Commercial media was introduced at the beginning of the twentieth century but this commercialization was not allowed to fully develop anymore than the process of democratization and attendant cultural changes that might have been possible after World War II, had the communists not taken over the country (Gross 1996); Romania's commercial media constitutes a bifurcated system: the entertainment and general consumption media are strictly commercial, and the news media are predominantly political in nature and often keep functioning even if they are not economically viable on their own;

4. Unlike in the MPPM, the state does not really have a strong role. The state provides some subsidies, mostly to ethnic media, and has an economic presence in the broadcast field thanks to state advertising and even more significantly in subsidizing public radio and television; its strongest role is in the application of law. The extant culture does not permit the real separation between the legislative, executive and judiciary, despite its codification in the constitution, and this is why the state could still play a potentially negative role;

5. The notion that newspapers in the MPPM have often been economically marginal and in need of subsidies was/is a generalization with many exceptions in pre and post-communist Romania. In the 1990s, many newspapers were quite profitable, while others required financial assistance, which they received mostly from political parties; the print media's market share declined by the turn of century (Coman and Gross 2007, pp. 63–69). The important point, however, is that the economic viability of many newspapers may be a function of too many newspapers per number of available readers, rather than any other reason.

6. Political parallelism was, indeed, high in the pre-communist period, as well as in the post-communist 1990s. The period of parallelism that dominated the 1990s, however, has mutated in the twenty-first century to a form of party press or party-media overlap, in this case a media that are controlled by businessmen/politicians for their own political and economic ambitions. This, too, may be an expression of that marriage of political, general, institutional and professional cultures that have not had an opportunity to change sufficiently to have an influence on how the media system is constituted, what its nature, role(s) and workings are.

7. Not all of the Romanian press is marked by a strong focus on political life, external pluralism and a tradition of commentary-oriented or advocacy journalism, as in Hallin and Mancini's MPPM. There is a great deal of focus on political life and external pluralism, but an approximately equal amount of tabloidization and, yes, a very strong commentary-oriented or advocacy journalism legacy that remains at the core of Romanian journalism. It has always been that way even during the communist era (with the exception of external pluralism, of course) and is culturally ingrained and, therefore, perpetuated.

8. The government has had limited and uneven success in its attempt to instrumentalize the media, and the political parties lost the party press in the mid-1990s. Other institutions such as non-governmental and civic groups have also instrumentalized the media, but have been far less successful. Here, again, one can argue that the kleptocracy has always been a part of the fabric of society and, therefore, one of many cultural artefacts that remain unchanged regardless of systemic and institutional changes and with deleterious affects on the media.

It looks like the instrumentalization of the media by government, by political parties and by industrialists with political ties in common, as found in the MPPM, is only partially true in Romania.

9. Romania's public broadcasting does indeed fit into the MPPM by following the government or parliamentary models and there is little change in sight because, one can clearly argue, the culture of the political elites cannot and does not allow a change.[19]

10. Professionalization in journalism is not as strongly developed in the MPPM, as in other models, journalism is not as strongly differentiated from political activism and the autonomy of journalists is often limited (in this model there are explicit conflicts over the autonomy of journalists – power and authority within news organizations has been more openly contested in the Polarized Pluralist systems). Indeed, this is true in Romania, but attempts at professionalization are ongoing and we have also seen the contestation of power and authority within news organizations in the last few years, when we consider the overall turmoil in the profession, the resignations from a number of media outlet, the turmoil at RTV and, to a lesser extent, the three major press scandals involving *Romania Libera*, *Evenimentul Zilei* and *Adevarul* (Gross 1996, pp. 73–80).

11. The state *does not* play a large role as an owner and founder of media, and its capacity to regulate effectively is often limited in Romania, a radical departure from the MPPM.

12. The MPPM model suggests a rapid and uncontrolled transition from state controlled to commercial broadcasting. This is most certainly a unique feature of a transition from no mere authoritarianism but from a Romanianized Stalinism, i.e., a very specific socio-political and economic culture.

13. In the MPPMs there is a high degree of ideological diversity and conflict and this is both true and false in Romania, because on the one hand ideological diversity is only superficial and a clear understanding and articulation of ideological differences is yet to be achieved, although there is a clear distinction between the proto-communist inclinations of some and the democratic inclinations of others. Conflicts are due more to personal and party ambitions and interests than to pure ideological differences.[20]

14. There is delayed development of liberal institutions related to the strong role of the state in society (often in an authoritarian form), a strong role of political parties, a continuing importance of clientelism and a weaker development of rational-legal authority in the MPPM. In Romania, there is ample evidence that the lack of success in developing liberal institutions, including the media institution, has little to do with a strong role of the state, whereas the negative role in this respect on the part of political parties and the economic and political elites is certainly true. I should also mention the less than helpful role of a civil society that has not yet garnered enough power to be effective. Does this not contribute to proof that institutional changes can occur without the kind of liberalization that would make democracy truly workable? Does this not point to the illiberal culture stifling the evolution of "democratic" institutions?

On the other hand, while there are elements of the MPPM that may be discernible in Romania, there is nothing in that country's media system or journalism that might fit the North Atlantic or Liberal Model either. There are some elements that are similar to what Hallin and Mancini see as exemplifications of the Northern European or Democratic Corporatist Model, albeit in a wholly different historical and cultural milieu:

Table 1: Presence of PSB (*) in Post-Communist Countries

In Mediterranean/Political Pluralist Model	In the Romanian Media World
Media are elite-oriented & the electronic media have become central	News media are elite-oriented; the entertainment media are not; electronic media are central to the non-elites
Freedom of the press came late in the country's history	Press freedom remains at pre-communist/dictatorship/ fascist levels & is not institutionalized in juridical, institutional & cultural terms
Commercial media industries also came late	Commercial media was introduced in the early 1900s, eliminated by communism in 1947 & resurrected in 1989
The role of the state is strong	Not really
Newspapers have often been economically marginal & in need of subsidies	That is a generalization with many exceptions
Political parallelism tends to be high	The period of parallelism dominated the 1990s & has mutated in the twenty-first century
The press is marked by a strong focus on political life, external pluralism & a tradition of commentary-oriented or advocacy journalism	There is much focus on political life & external pluralism, an equal amount of tabloidization & a very strong commentary-oriented & advocacy journalism
Instrumentalization of the media by government, by political parties & by industrialists with political ties in common	Government attempts to instrumentalize the media had little success; political parties lost the party press in mid-1990. Non-governmental, civic groups et al. have also instrumentalized the media
Public broadcasting tends to follow the government or parliamentary models	True & there is little change in sight because the culture of the political elites cannot allow a change
Professionalization is not well developed; little separates journalism from political activism; journalists' autonomy is often limited but there are explicit conflicts over it; power & authority in news media are openly contested	True
The state plays a large role as an owner, regulator & founder of media, though its capacity to regulate effectively is often limited	Not at all true, with the exception that the state has & does regulate the public broadcast media
Rapid and uncontrolled transition from state-controlled to commercial broadcasting	A particularly unique feature of a transition from a Romanianized Stalinism
High degree of ideological diversity and conflict	Yes and no
Delayed development of liberal institutions related to strong role of state in society (often in authoritarian form), strong role of political parties, continuing importance of clientelism, weak development of rational-legal authority	The lack of success in developing liberal institutions, including the media institution, has little to do with a strong role of the state; the strong role of political parties etc. has delayed the development of liberal institutions

1. A history of strong party newspapers (before and during communism) and other media connected to organized social groups,
2. A political press that coexisted with the commercial press, that is, until the communist era; today the political and commercial press are one and the same,
3. Political parallelism is historically high but, as pointed out above, it has muted to overlapping; there is a moderate degree of external pluralism, and commentary-oriented journalism persists but in Romania it is not "mixed with a growing emphasis on neutral professionalism and information-oriented journalism", except, perhaps, on issues that do not in one way or another touch on politics and the corruption in the political, economic, governmental, state and judicial systems,
4. Journalism is not subject to either institutionalized or non-institutionalized self-regulation.

None of these seeming similarities, however, make the Hallin/Mancini models relevant to the Romanian media. In short, the model that must be constructed to explain and exemplify the Romanian media, and I would argue the media in the post-communist world of Eastern Europe, should be specific to the historical and cultural patrimony upon which the media system, its values, nature and workings are based. These are the elements that explain how the media institution in this post-communist era, now constructed similarly to those in western democracies, relate to the state, government, political parties, politicians, media owners, journalists and their sources and audiences.[21] In turn, these relationships explain the nature of journalism.

Hallin and Mancini's work, as worthwhile as it is, continues the long-standing trend of ignoring the cultural element in constructing a model of media systems and explaining why they may be as they are and journalism is being practiced as it is. Vladimir Tismaneanu (1998, p. 5), one of the world's most astute students of Eastern Europe and, specifically, of Romania, points out that "The avalanche of studies and reports about the emergence of markets and Western-style institutions have tended to dismiss the role of political traditions, memories, and deeply entrenched attitudes – in one word, the role of political culture."

Hallin and Mancini construct their three models of media on the basis of differing types of democracy, specifically Lijphart's (1968, 1971, 1977, 1999) distinction between consensus and majoritarian democracy, which they say is "probably of considerable use in understanding relations between the political and media system." True, but only if we first understand the relations between history and culture and the political system and politics. First and foremost, the classic definitions of majoritarian and consensus politics are not easily discernible in Romania, where elements of both may hold sway.[22] For instance, majoritarian politics appears to dominate, yet it is not a purely two-party system and elements of consensus politics – such as power-sharing, in the context of coalition politics, and a multiparty system – are present. Romania is a semi-presidential republic.[23] It also has a relatively weak welfare state, another legacy of communism and, perhaps, the result of the "wild capitalism" (might this also be explained in cultural and historical terms?) installed after 1989, and more akin to what is found in the North Atlantic or Liberal Model than in the other two posited by Hallin and Mancini.

In other words, Romanian politics is a hybrid or, more accurately, a system still in the making and suffering from its communist past, one that is a social organism in gestation and not just a legacy (Wyrda 2007). Wyrda points to the fact that democratization is not solely a matter of institutional re-design; it is more importantly a matter of consciousness and leadership, which means that we need to focus on culture to understand how the new non-communist society is working and how its institutions function. And echoing Tismaneanu (see above), Wyrda (2007,

p. 279) writes, "any substantial analysis of the chances for democracy and market capitalism in Eastern Europe" must grasp "the cultural, political, and economic 'inheritance' of forty years of Leninist rule." Culture, of course, is not an inheritance apart from the political and economic ones, it is part and parcel of these and of other societal endeavours.

The mere study of politics and the political systems of nations, therefore, does not well serve as an explanation for the nature of the media system or of the journalism that it is practiced. Politics and political systems – and, more importantly, how they are carried out and function, respectively – are an expression of attitudes, beliefs, habits, behaviours and values. The great Italian intellectual Umberto Eco (22 June 1995, p. 12) made that point all too well when he wrote: "even though political regimes can be overthrown, and ideologies can be criticized and disowned, behind a regime and its ideology there is always a way of thinking and feeling, a group of cultural habits, of obscure instincts and unfathomable drives." Perhaps this explains the crisis in values that has dominated Romania's post-communist years and the resulting simulated democratization that some like Tismaneanu, among many others, judge to be the post-communist reality. Furthermore, it explains, in my view, the crisis of values and identity in the Romanian media and journalism, elements that are insufficiently reflected in the media models in general and in Hallin and Mancini's models in particular.

Thus, the cultural inheritance of both the pre-communist era and even more certainly the communist or Leninist one, as Ken Jowett (1992) points out, must be taken into consideration when judging the nature of Romania's new political system and politics. Only then can one better understand the nature and ways of the new non-communist media, their system, nature, role(s), functioning, influencers and influence. In short, institutional cultures combine with professional cultures, political culture and the general societal culture to establish how systems are organized, how they function, who and what affects them, and the effects they may have on their constituencies. A country's political system and its politics are directly shaped by this admixture of cultures and, in turn, the media as an institution and platforms for mass communication are the children of these cultures almost no matter how the system is organized and how many institutional changes are made. Daniel Etounga-Manguelle (2000, p. 75) states emphatically that "culture is the mother; institutions are the children."

Yet, the centrality of institutions to the transition and transformation from communism is touted by a number of institutional determinists – and Hallin & Mancini approach to the media institution suggest a similar outlook – who argue that the state and the new post-communist institutions can create new habits, customs, values and behaviours, i.e., new cultures (Fukuyama 1992; Balcerowicz 1995; Fish 1996; Agh 1998; Elster, Offe and Preuss 1999). I have now long argued that despite the reconfigured make-up of the post-communist Eastern European media and the new rules under which they function, they have not shaped a new media and journalistic cultures by creating a new reality and new incentives, nor have they changed the way the new rules are applied. For the institutional deterministic position to prove itself, one must presuppose "that institutional change also renews the opportunities political actors have, in turn changing their behavior. Of course, this presupposition in turn assumes a positive, democratic-oriented change in behavior, something that could happen only if the institutions are liberal" (Gross 2002, pp. 6–7).

But how are liberal democratic institutions to be created when their systemic make-up is dependent on the cultures that do not allow them to function in a democratic, liberal way? Crawford and Lijphart (July 1995) stress that "liberal institutions can structure preferences and constrain choices in ways that create new political and economic cultures." Perhaps, yet what else needs to occur and over how much time is required to make the institutions "liberal" before they have the Crawford/Lijphart imprimatur? It is clear that in Romania these institutions are not liberal, because the absence of cultural changes impede them from being so and, therefore, they are actually preventing or at least slowing down the cultural changes required for democratization and claimed to "structure preferences and constrain choices". At the very least, there must be a reciprocally promoting relationship between democratic institutions and democratic or democracy-fostering culture.

If we are to understand Romania's media as a system, its nature, role(s), how and why it works the way it does, with what affects it and what the effect of all that is, the starting point cannot be the study of politics and the political system or the media as an institution. Rather, the starting point has to be history and the extant cultures that underline the nature, role and workings of institutions, i.e., values, attitudes, behaviours, modes of thinking and so forth. In this regard, Huntington's (1997, p.158) notion that "Europe ends where Western Christianity ends and Islam and Orthodoxy begins" may be a good (if, perhaps, exaggerated) starting point.

A peoples' or nation's fundamental culture is established over a long period of time in the crucible of historical experiences and circumstances, geography, religion and so on. Thus, the "history recorded is the history of peoples and nations, but the patterns that emerge are patterns of cultures" that, in turn, enable us to understand how these patterns "in general affect the economic and social advancement of the human race" (Sowell 1994, p. 7 and p. 1). History shapes culture (values, attitudes, behaviour etc.), which configures not only the nature of politics and political and economic systems but the way elites and non-elites behave; in turn, both the nature of these systems and the behaviour of elites contribute to the establishment of the institutional cultures that ultimately define the professional cultures functional in a society. There are outside influences that affect fundamental cultures to be sure, but the latter have a way of adapting these more than adopting them.

In short, the study of a media system such as Romania's must begin with the study of Romanian history and the cultural patterns that were established and which affect the political and economic systems and the political and economic cultures. Only then can we begin to understand the overall institutional culture that exists, how it shapes the media and other institutions and the media culture, both contributing mightily to defining the professional culture (see table II).

Table 2

Political culture ⇒ politics & political system ⇓	
	⇑ Institutional cultures ⇒ institutions ⇒ ⇓
History/culture ⇒ ⇒ ⇒ ⇒ ⇒ ⇒ ⇒ ⇒ ⇒ } ⇒ { Media culture ⇒ media ⇒ ⇓	
	⇓ Professional culture ⇒ journalism
Economic culture ⇒ economic system ⇑	

Cultures (institutional, political, professional etc.) are difficult to measure; this is partly why most scholars shy away from using them as indices for measuring changes and evolutions. The study of cultures often succumbs to the "cultures are relative" and "cultures are equal" schools of thought, partly because it is politically incorrect to suggest that one culture may be superior or inferior to another. Yet without identifying and understanding the dominant values, attitudes, behaviours and mentalities that fuel the functioning of politics, political, economic and social systems and institutions, we cannot possibly construct a credible model of post-communist media.

Conclusion

That Romania and its media have still a long way to go before they can claim to have completed a transformation to a true democracy, and to a media and journalism capable of exemplifying and supporting it, is true and an often repeated sentiment. We will not be able to understand why and how that transformation may proceed unless we inject the study of culture in the examination of the Romanian media and their journalism. Nor for that matter will we be able to construct a theoretical model that allows for a more in-depth, nuanced, sophisticated and accurate description and explanation of media systems and journalism unless we begin their study with an examination of the history and culture that gave them birth, and now nurtures and defines them.

Notes

1. This paper is based on a presentation made at the "Hour of Romania" conference organized by the Russian and East European Institute at Indiana University, Bloomington, 22–24 March 2007.
2. Bulgaria is the other. Romania applied for EU membership in 1995 and at the end of 2004 completed the negotiations started in 2000. Many in the EU expressed misgivings about Romania's preparedness for membership and a cabinet reshuffle by the Romanian government in August 2005 was meant to speed up EU reforms.
3. A Reporters Without Borders report authored by Blatmann and Julliard (April 2004) proclaimed: "Press freedom does not yet occupy the position it deserves between the old habits inherited from the dictatorial period and the strides actually made toward implementing European standards."
4. Ion Iliescu served two and a half terms; Emil Constantinescu served one term.
5. It should be noted that the media market is still fragmented and, despite the trend of media concentration, one cannot speak of a media oligopoly. The relatively few individuals who owned most major and minor media outlets are politicians or businessmen, who have direct ties to politicians and political parties.
6. The Public Procurement Law was modified in May 2005 and there is a new website dedicated to public advertising, and a Guide to Good Practices, which addresses public institutions or companies that expend public funds on advertising.
7. See Law 278/2006.
8. A referendum on the impeachment was scheduled to be held on 20 May 2007.
9. Politicians at the local level are also in the media business; see Coman and Gross, p. 66.
10. For a recent description of the media system, its economic and other aspects, see Coman and Gross (2006).
11. The foreign media owners include the Dogan Group (Turkey), Ringier (Switzerland), Burda (Germany), Hachette (France), Springer (Germany), Sonoma-Hearst (US), Gruner & Jahr (Austria), Playboy (US), Hustler (US), Westdeutsche Allgemeine Zeitung (Germany), and News Corporation Europe (US).

12. Romania's supreme court made it clear there are no constitutional reasons for President Basescu's suspension, yet the parliament proceeded to suspend him.

13. The main objections to President Basescu is that he (1) continued to fight against corruption, which will implicate many members of Parliament, (2) requested that the files of the Securitate be made public and (3) made a declaration condemning the former communist regime and acknowledged its faults.

14. See Badicioiu and Lazar (17 April 2007) for an analysis of TVR's report of its activities in 2006 to the Romanian Parliament.

15. When it comes to the media and their journalism, these may include the inclination to control, manipulate, politicize, be intolerant, proselytize and editorialize (instead of inform), dis-inform, mis-inform, propagandize and so on.

16. The obvious should be noted: the trajectory of media and journalism evolutions after World War II in countries that were not under the communist yoke is quite different from those only recently having the opportunity to construct societies and institutions that also require a change in cultures in order to make them viable, as in and for a working democracy.

17. For the most update and complete report on Romanian media developments, see Coman and Gross 2006.

18. For an interesting and informative explication of press freedom in Romania, see Petcu, ed. (2005). "A free people will be showing that they are so, by their freedom of speech", remarked Trenchard and Gordon (1995, vol. 1, p. 74) speaking as Cato. And when people demand a voice in their own governance, it means there is a need for a free press. Romanians are not quite as demanding of a voice in their own government as they should be, but they do enjoy freedom of speech, while lacking the independent media that can serve as (a) platforms for such a freedom and (b) as suppliers of information to fuel public opinion formation and the ability for self-governance.

19. Culture is not an independent variable and there are development-resistant cultures that, among other things, shape the behaviour of elites, who in turn have a profound effect on how societies evolve. See Grondona (2000).

20. Besides, it is not the degree of ideological diversity that counts, at least not if we define ideologies as Tismaneanu (1998, p. 28) does; a description with which I wholeheartedly agree: "Ideologies are all-embracing and all-explanatory: they refuse dialogue, questioning, doubt. In this respect liberalism is an ideology only in name: with its incrementalism and skepticism regarding any ultimate solutions to human problems, it lacks the soteriological, apocalyptic power of radical visions of change."

21. Ronald Inglehart (1997) has long argued, for example, that there is strong connection between cultural values and performance in a nation's political and economic realms. See also Inglehart (2000) and Landes (1999).

22. In their analysis, Hallin and Mancini acknowledge the existence of hybrid systems.

23. Vladimir Tismaneanu, Professor in the Department of Politics and Government at the University of Maryland and the most astute observer of the Romanian scene, told me that "[President] Basescu has tried to move it toward a two-party system, which would stabilize the political situation and make it more predictable and transparent, but he has encountered the opposition of all the networks of interest. Therefore his solitude these days. He has become the president of civil society (which is great), but he [deals with] the challenges of a corrupt and cynical political society. Articulating the two, without giving up principles, is difficult. Compromise between government and opposition is not very clearly delineated. There is no wining party: the Alliance 'D.A.

References

Agentia de Monitorizare a Presei (2007). *Press Freedom in Romania 2005.* Academia Catavencu: Bucharest, Romania.

Agentia de Monitorizare a Presei (2006). *Press Freedom in Romania 2005.* Academia Catavencu: Bucharest, Romania.

Agentia de Monitorizare a Presei (2004). *Cartea Alba a Presei II.* Academia Catavencu: Bucharest, Romania.

Agh, Attila (1998). *Politics of Central Europe.* London: Sage.

Badicioiu, Alexandru and Diana Lazar (17 April 2007). "Cit a primit TVR pe Ceausescu", in Cotidianul. www.hotnews.ro/articol-69974. Accessed 19 April 2007.

Balcerowicz, Leszek (1995). *Socialism, Capitalism, Transformation.* Budapest, Hungary: Central European University.

Basescu, Traian (14 February 2007). "Mesajul Presedintelui Romaniei, Traian Basescu, adresat Parlamentului Romaniei", 14 Februarie 2007. Departamentul de Comunicare Publica, Administratia Prezidentiala, Bucharest, Romania.

Blatmann, Soria and Jean-Francois Julliard (April 2004). "Caught between Old Habits and Democratic Strides: Romanian Press at a Crossroads". Reporters Without Borders. Mimeo.

Codreanu, Ionut and Gabriel Dobre (2007). "Un om a muscat of stire. Raport de analiza a stirilor TV din perspectiva interesului public si a practicilor jurnalistice". Bucharest, Romania: Agential de Monitorizare a Presei.

Coman, Mihai (2004). "Media Bourgeoisie and the Media Proletariat in Post-Communist Romania", in *Journalism Studies,* 5 (1), pp. 45–58.

Coman, Mihai (2003). *Mass media in Romania post-comunista.* Iasi, Romania: Polirom.

Coman, Mihai (1998). "Les Journalistes roumains et leur ideologie professionelle". In K. Feigelson and N. Pelissier eds., *Tele-revolutions culturelles: Chine, Europe Centrale, Russie.* Paris, France: L'Harmattan, pp. 183–200.

Coman, Mihai and Peter Gross (2006). *Media and Journalism in Romania.* European Journalism Review Series. Berlin, Germany: Vistas Verlag.

Crawford, Beverly and Arend Lijphart (July 1995). "Explaining Political and Economic Change in Post-Communist Eastern Europe: Old Legacies, New Institutions, Hegemonic Norms, and International Pressures", in *Comparative Political Studies* 28, pp. 177–99.

Cretia, Petru (3 August 1990). "Ce nu este vremelnic in ziaristica lui Eminescu", in 22, p. 4.

Culcer, Rodica (11–17 May 2007). "Superoferta electorala", in 22. www.revista22.ro. Accessed 15 May 2007.

Eco, Umberto (22 June 1995). "Ur-Fascism", *The New York Review of Books,* p. 12.

Elster, Joh, Claus Offe and Ulrich K. Preuss (1999). *Institutional Design in Post-Communist Societies: Rebuilding the Ship at Sea.* NY: Cambridge University Press.

Fish, M. Steven (1995). *Democracy from Scratch.* Princeton, NJ: Princeton University Press.

Fukuyama, Francis (1992). *The End of History and the Last Man.* NY: Free Press.

Grondona, Mariano (2000). "A Cultural Typology of Economic Development". In Lawrence E. Harrison and Samuel P. Huntington eds., *Culture Matters. How Values Shape Human Progress,* pp. 44–55.

Gross, Peter (2002). *Entangled Evolutions. Media and Democratization in Eastern Europe.* Washington, D.C. and Baltimore, MD: The Woodrow Wilson Center Press and the Johns Hopkins University Press.

Gross, Peter (1999a). "Limping to Nowhere: Romania's Media Under Constantinescu". Washington, D.C., USA: The Woodrow Wilson Center for International Scholars, East European Studies, Occasional Paper 51.

Gross, Peter (1999b). *Colosul cu picioare de lut*. Iasi, Romania: Polirom.

Gross, Peter (1996). *Mass Media in Revolution and National Development: The Romanian Laboratory*, Ames, IA: Iowa State University Press.

Huntington, Samuel P. (1997). *The Clash of Civilizations and the Remaking of World Order*. N.Y.: Touchstone (Simon & Schuster).

Iancu, Bogdan (14 May 2007). "Agandonul TV", in *Romania Libera*. www.romanialibera.ro/index.php?page=13&aid=95023. Accessed 14 May 2007.

Inglehart, Ronald (2000). "Culture and Democracy". In In Lawrence E. Harrison and Samuel P. Huntington eds., *Culture Matters. How Values Shape Human Progress*, pp. 80–97.

Inglehart, Ronald (1997). *Modernization and Postmodernization*. Princeton: Princeton University Press.

International Research and Exchanges Board (2006). Media Sustainability Index. www.irex.org.msi. Accessed 14 February 2006.

Jowett, Ken (1992). *New World Disorder: The Leninist Extinction*. Berkeley: University of California.

Landes, David (1999). *The Wealth and Poverty of Nations: Why Some Are So Rich and Some So Poor*. N.Y.: W.W. Norton & Company.

Lazaroiu, Sebastian (16 October 2006). "Cu cine voteaza ziaristii", in *Jurnalul National*. www.jurnalul.ro/articol.php?id=64081 Accessed 29 March 2007.

Lazescu, Alexandru (5 March 2007). "Lectia de propaganda", in 22. Hotnews.ro/articol_print_10_-1-Lectia-de-propaganda-de-Alexandru-Lazescu.htm. Accessed 5 March 2007.

Lijphart, Arend (1999). *Patterns of Democracy: Government Forms and Performance in Thirty-Six Countries*. New Haven: Yale University Press.

Lijphart, Arend (1977). *Democracy in Plural Societies*. New Haven: Yale University Press.

Lijphart, Arend (1971). "Comparative Politcs and the Comparative Method", in *American Political Science Review* 65(3), pp. 682–93.

Lijphart, Arend (1968). *The Politics of Accommodation*. Berkeley: University of California Press.

Mancini, Paulo (1991). "The Public Sphere and the use of news in a 'coalition' system", in Peter Dahlgren and Colin Sparks (eds.), *Communication and Citizenship*. London: Routledge, pp. 133–54.

Marinescu, Valentian (2002). *Mass media in Romania: O lectura sociologica*. Bucharest, Romania: Tritonic.

MediaSind Trade Union Organization (2006). The Freedom and Independence of [the] Romanian Press. Report for 2005–2006. Bucharest, Romania.

Patapievici, Horia-Roman (15 February 2007). "Senatul EVZ: Presa si politica", in Evenimentul Zilei Online. www.evz.ro/article?arti/=292316. Accessed 2 March 2007.

Petcu, Marian, ed. (2005). *Cenzura in spatial cultural romanesc*. Bucharest, Romania: Editura Comunicare.

Reporters Without Borders (2007). *Romania - Annual report 2007*. www.rsf.org/article.php3?id_article=20821&Valider=OK. Accessed 12 March 2007.

Reporters Without Borders (21 July 2006). "Government closes down foreign ministry spoof website". www.rsf.org/article.php3?id_article=18337. Accessed 12 March 2007.

Reporters Without Borders (8 January 2005). "Secret police tap phones of two journalists". www.rsf.org/article.php3?id_article=12402. Accessed 12 March 2007.

Scanteie, Floriana (24 April 2007). "Roncea spune ca Rosca Stanescu l-a povestit cum au pus la clae 'oligarhii de presa' 'eliminarea' lui Basescu" in *Evenimentul Zilei*. www.hotnews.ro/articlo-70641. Accessed 28 April 2007.

Splichal, Slavko (1994). *Media Beyond Socialism. Theory and Practice in East-Central Europe*. Boulder: Westview Press.

Stanomir, Ioan (2003). "Libertatea de exprimare si dreptul la informatier". In M. Coman ed., *Manualul de jurnalism*, 2nd edition. Iasi, Romania: Polirom.

Tapalaga, Dan (10 November 2006). "Santajisti, santajati si santajabili d presa", in 22.

Tismaneanu, Vladimir (1998). *Fantasies of Salvation. Democracy, Nationalism, and Myth in Post-Communist Europe*. Princeton, NJ: Princeton University Press.

Trenchard, John and Thomas Gordon (1995). *Cato's Letters, or Essays on Liberty, Civil and Religious, and Other Important Subjects*, vol. 1 (Paperback edition edited by Ronald Hamowy). Indianapolis, Indiana: Liberty Fund.

Wydra, Harald (2007). *Communism and the Emergence of Democracy*. Cambridge University Press.

Zarojanu, Tudor Catalin (2001). "A fi ziarist and Romania", in *Romania Literara*, nr. 48, p. 2.

Democratizing Media, Welcoming Big Brother: Media in Bosnia and Herzegovina[1]

Aida A. Hozic

Ever since the end of the Cold War, the United States of America and the European Union have been actively (some would say aggressively) engaged in democracy promotion and assistance around the world. Often diverging in their means, and just as often in their interpretations of democracy, Europe and the United States have poured billions of dollars and euros into political and economic reforms all over the globe; dispatched thousands of experts and consultants on matters from law to healthcare to environment into Eastern Europe, Africa, Asia and the Americas; deployed military forces, waged wars, and hired the best public relations firms to sell those wars at home and abroad – all, ostensibly, in order to ensure that the third wave of democratization continues unabated.

In such a world, framed by violence, on the one hand, and benevolence, on the other, Bosnia and Herzegovina occupies a special place. The most touted case of peacemaking and democracy promotion during the Clinton administration (Talbott 1996), Bosnia is, in the words of Ambassador Douglas Davidson, appointed in 2004 as head of OSCE Mission in Bosnia and Herzegovina, "a kind of a laboratory for how to rehabilitate and even reconstruct a state after a conflict." (Davidson 2006) Governed by the UN and EU-appointed Office of High Representative, ethnically and institutionally divided, economically and politically paralyzed, Bosnia has nonetheless held a series of democratic elections since 1995, which have passed without any major incidents. Thus, although "the experiment underway in the laboratory that is Bosnia and Herzegovina is not quite complete", (Davidson 2006) the lack of violence and the attainment of minimum democratic standards seem sufficiently well grafted to ponder a graceful exit of the international community from Bosnia and, thus, end its quasi-protectorate status, by June of 2008.

One of the most contradictory aspects of democratization efforts in Bosnia and Herzegovina, at least since 1997, has been media reform. On the one hand, Bosnia is consistently moving up on the scale of the Worldwide Press Freedom Index, annually updated by Reporters Without Borders. In 2006 Bosnia and Herzegovina shared the 19th spot with Denmark, New Zealand, Trinidad and Tobago and was well ahead of France, Italy, UK, USA or its neighbours Croatia and Serbia. Bosnia's regulatory framework is now considered exemplary in the region, and its well-respected Communications Regulatory Agency is one of the few institutions that have successfully transitioned from international to local governance. Bosnia boasts one of the most diverse and plural media environments in Europe (Basic Hrvatin et al. 2004) – 43 public and private television stations, 142 radio stations, 7 daily newspapers, a plethora of political and entertainment magazines.

On the other hand, both Bosnian and international media experts question the economic sustainability of such a colourful and plural media landscape (Brunner 2003; Udovicic R. 2005; Henderson et al. 2003). Reform of the public broadcasting system is still one of the three outstanding issues (the other two being police reform and cooperation with the Hague Tribunal), blocking Bosnia's Stabilization and Association Agreement with the European Union. Representatives of the international community in Sarajevo and many local journalists privately assess the state of Bosnian media as abysmal. Lack of professionalism, poor quality of investigative reporting, even outright media illiteracy, low salaries and lack of social protection for most journalists are all often cited as signs that Bosnian media have simply turned from bad to worse since the outbreak of the war. Asked to discuss the current state of media in Bosnia and Herzegovina, one of the former directors of Bosnian television shrugged his shoulders and said, "What is there to discuss?" Said off the record, a high-ranking American representative, "We have poured a billion dollars into this place, and look at what we've got". "We are exactly where we were when the war started fifteen years ago", complained one of the editors of BHRT, Bosnian public service broadcaster. As if to confirm such perceptions, in January of 2007, Milorad Dodik, Prime Minister of Republika Srpska (one of the ethnically defined entities in the country), instructed the members of his government to boycott BHRT because of its alleged discriminatory treatment of RS on joint public airwaves, and forced the resignation of BHRT's general manager, Mr Drago Maric.

Has media reform in Bosnia and Herzegovina really been such a failure? Or is it, perhaps, that the difficulties in assessing the state of Bosnian media stem from inherent difficulties of establishing standards of media performance (Sükösd and Bajomi-Lázár 2003), constantly shifting global media terrain and technology, and essentially contested nature of media representation? In this paper, I would like to urge for a different perspective on Bosnian media by moving the lens through which it is observed from what editors of this volume call "political demand" to "market demand" as the main force shaping the media. This is not to say that overt political pressures on media no longer matter in Bosnia and Herzegovina (as Karol Jakubowicz states in his chapter on public service reform, where don't they?); rather, it is to suggest that commercial concerns and "soft news" have become just as important in Bosnia and Herzegovina as they have elsewhere in the world. In other words, Bosnia's media landscape may have become much more similar to the commercialized American and European media sphere than to the idealized Western European models of public service upon which its assessments are usually based. Democratization of the media has yet to produce a satisfactory public service system in Bosnia and Herzegovina – but it has definitely helped usher Latin American soap operas, Serbian turbo-folk, *Desperate Housewives*, Bingo, karaoke and reality TV shows, such as *Big Brother*, onto its TV screens.

The chapter provides an overview of the current media landscape in Bosnia with particular focus on the unintended consequences of international media assistance – complicity of international community in the slide towards commercialization of Bosnian, and regional, media; increased technological gap between Bosnia and Herzegovina and Europe (not to mention the US); and, finally, broader impact of de-politicization of media sphere in countries in transition. Taking a cue from Karol Jakubowicz's chapter on public service reform in Central and Eastern Europe, I will argue that Bosnia and Herzegovina represent yet another case of media's "systemic parallelism" with the country's political and social institutions, and yet another case where disillusionment, frustration and cynicism about the functioning of public service broadcasting, and media in general, may have severe consequences for political developments in the region – all the more so as the international community constitutes an inextricable factor in that disappointment.

Post-Dayton Bosnia

The Bosnian war ended with a peace accord reached at Wright-Patterson Air Base in Dayton, Ohio, on 21 November 1995, and signed into an agreement on 14 December 1995 in Paris. Construed, primarily, as a document whose purpose was to end violence, the Dayton Peace Agreement appeased territorial ambitions of nationalist leaders in the former Yugoslavia and "devolved rapidly from an interim solution to a virtually fossilized governing instrument." (Hitchner 2005, p. 2.) The Agreement created a state comprising two ethnically defined entities – Republika Srpska, where the majority of the population is Serbian, and Bosniak-Croat Federation, where ten administrative units – called cantons – have either Bosnian Muslim (Bosniak) or Croat majority population. Both the state and the two entities have been endowed with multiple layers of government and multiple venues for ethnically based political representation. The most important bodies on the state level are presidency of Bosnia and Herzegovina, which is comprised of three representatives of the three 'constitutive peoples" – a Croat, a Serb and a Bosniak; and the Council of Ministers, elected by the bicameral Parliament, whose upper House also upholds the principle of ethnic parity with five members each from the three "constitutive peoples". The Bosniak-Croat Federation, due to its checkered ethnic character, also has a bicameral Parliament while ethnically far more homogeneous Republika Srpska has a unicameral Assembly.

Cantonal and local governments often replicate the complex structure of state and entity parliaments and governments, while a combination of the first-past-the post and proportional electoral systems encourages parties to compete for a large number of positions in various government offices. Thus, although ethnically based parties continue to dominate political life in an institutional structure which stimulates ethnicity as the dominant political feature, in the last October 2006 elections, electorate could choose among 9,000 candidates in 47 different political parties and eleven coalitions as their representatives in fifteen institutions on three levels of government. (Dnevni Avaz, cited in Jusic 2006) A recent study of electoral process in Bosnia and Herzegovina from 1996 till 2005 provocatively – but correctly – characterized it as "ten years of democratic chaos" (Arnautovic 2007)

To make things even more complicated, Bosnia is still de facto run by the Office of the High Representative, an ad hoc international institution created by the Dayton Peace Agreement and responsible for the implementation as well as interpretation of the Agreement. Initially a joint appointee of the United Nations and European Union, the High Representative is now simultaneously the European Union's Special Representative, "working with the people and institutions of Bosnia and Herzegovina and the international community to ensure that Bosnia and Herzegovina evolves into a peaceful and viable democracy on course for integration into Euro-Atlantic institutions." (OHR website). Over the years, duties and responsibilities of OHR have varied – depending as much on the political and economic circumstances in Bosnia as on the personality of the High Representative himself. Paddy Ashdown, former leader of the British Liberal Democrats, who reigned over Bosnia between 2002 and 2006, was frequently accused of attempting to run a British Raj in the Balkans (Knaus 2003). His successor as High Representative, Christian Schwarz Schilling, German parliamentarian with decades of experience in humanitarian work in the region, is deemed much too passive. But regardless of the character of individuals who occupy the position, the institution of the High Representative is still endowed with enormous powers – from vetting and, if necessary, removing candidates for all key political offices to imposing laws as s/he sees fit.

Given the persistent and institutionally perpetuated ethnic gridlock, the Office of the High Representative (OHR) was forced frequently to intervene in domestic politics. The OHR was, thus, responsible for the creation of nearly all attributes of statehood that Bosnia has attained thus far – from the national anthem and the flag to common currency, car licence plates, tax system, border control, military reform and even the final design of the Bosnian passport. The OHR and other representatives of the international community have been criticized, both within Bosnia and outside of its borders, for being too heavy-handed, hypocritical and outright colonial in their dealings in Bosnia. Several years ago, Canadian political scientist David Chandler (2000) persuasively argued that the presence of the non-accountable law-making international community in Bosnia and Herzegovina also takes accountability away from Bosnian politicians, thus stimulating all political actors to simply engage in the game of "faking democracy" instead of genuine democratization. More recently, Bosnian political scientist Nermina Sacic (2007), at a conference devoted to the role of international community in Bosnia and Herzegovina, simply concluded that "the politics of the international community has been reductionist and non-democratic, i.e. in defiance of the democratic spirit which governs its mission, since most of the laws and regulations have been created without consulting the public. Therefore, it may be important to see that similar mistakes are not repeated in other countries of Southeastern Europe."

Faced with the existence of two powerful internal entities on the one hand, and just as powerful representatives of the international community as inventors of statehood on the other, Bosnian public intellectuals often bemoan the weakness of the state in Bosnia and Herzegovina. In words of Asim Mujkic (2007a, 2007b), professor of political science at the University of Sarajevo, Bosnia has become an "ethnopolis" with no hope for the construction of a civic state any time soon. His colleague, and former editor of the independent weekly *Dani*, Nerzuk Curak (2006), argues that Bosnians have to forget about the contested ideas of state and sovereignty in order to learn to live together. At the same time, international financial institutions criticize the multilayered government institutions for being much too expensive, taking 50 per cent of the GDP and draining the limited budget of the Bosnian state of its revenue. Privatization, cuts in social welfare, reduction in payments for veterans and pensioners, are all recommended as parts of standard neo-liberal package to improve the state of the Bosnian economy. Bosnian citizens, meanwhile, are struggling for survival: 20 per cent of national income comes from remittances of family members and workers abroad – by far the highest percentage in the region; trade deficit is 3.6 times higher than in the rest of the region; the official unemployment rate is 44 per cent in the Bosniak-Croat Federation and 37 per cent in Republika Srpska; and it is estimated that more than 50 per cent of Bosnian population lives below the poverty line (World Bank and UNDP data). This, therefore, is the complex, difficult and often depressing political, social and economic context in which media reform in Bosnia and Herzegovina has to be examined.

Reforming Bosnian Media

Transformation of media in Bosnia and Herzegovina under the tutelage of the international community – the OHR , OSCE and European Commission – has already been described and assessed in detail in several academic studies (Kumar 2006; Kurspahic 2003; Thompson and De Luce 2002; Jusic 2005) and numerous reports commissioned by international agencies (USAID, OSCE, IREX, Stability Pact). It is continuously scrutinized in local magazine and newspaper articles. Based on these accounts, the key features of the intervention of the international community into the media sphere in Bosnia and Herzegovina can be summarized as follows. Intervention into the Bosnian media – both financially and in terms of personnel – has been the most ambitious incursion into journalistic practices and institutions by the international community in any post-conflict society thus far. However, the attempt to transform media in Bosnia started only in 1997, two years after the Dayton Peace Accord, which, in view of some analysts, may have been much too late (Thompson and De Luce 2005). The intervention has been focused on the creation of alternative media outlets to the prevailing nationalist press and TV stations – initially, by fostering independent media and then, later on, by creating regulatory bodies and transforming the existing state-TV stations into a single public broadcasting service for entire Bosnia and Herzegovina. The greatest failure – and the most expensive experiment – of the international effort was the creation of the independent TV channel OBN, envisioned in 1996 as the network of independent stations from all over Bosnia and as the replacement for state-wide TV. Twenty million US dollars of international aid later, and with almost 70 per cent of coverage of the territory of Bosnia and Herzegovina, OBN was forced to shut down as it never found its audience (Kumar 2006; Ranson n.d.). As we shall see below, OBN was later sold in London under some very strange circumstances and now, as a private TV station, it has many more viewers than it ever did while lavishly sponsored by the international community.

Three aspects of the international community's intervention seem worth emphasizing in this chapter. First, international efforts have been seriously thwarted from the outset by deep divisions between the US and EU officials over the course of desired media transformation (Brunner 2003; Jusic 2005; Thompson and De Luce 2002). While the United States representatives insisted on commercial viability and economic independence of media from the state, EU officials were primarily interested in the establishment of public service broadcasting. The failure of OBN may, at least in part, be ascribed to this discord between the US and EU over the future character of the media system, particularly public television, in Bosnia and Herzegovina. Even today, the clash between the "European model" (viable public service sector which exists alongside with commercial TV), which has become a sine-qua-non of accession into EU, and American insistence on media sustainability, which governs US decisions on further donations, permeates the international community and colours their reports on and assessments of Bosnian media.

Second, many international advisors often assumed that media outlets and journalists they were working with in Bosnia and Herzegovina had no worthwhile and relevant pre-war professional experience. Political subservience of some journalists and media outlets during the war were interpreted as symptoms of the communist legacy, and of the underlying lack of professionalism, political opportunism, and overall lack of standards in media circles of the former Yugoslavia, and Bosnia and Herzegovina in particular (Taylor and Kent 2000; 2003). As Kemal Kurspahic (2003), renowned journalist and former editor of Sarajevo daily *Oslobodjenje*, puts it:

> foreign 'media interventionists' have fully ignored the fact that Bosnia and Herzegovina had a respectable radio-television before the war, as well as journalists who had fought for and succeeded in gaining an enviable level of independence in the twilight of the single-party state. This is why Bosnian journalists themselves have never been brought to the position of equal and decision-making partners in that project.

Jenny Ranson, CEO of OBN (1998–2000), conceded that most "internationals involved were inexperienced" and "had no knowledge of local history or sensitivities." Yet, she also thought that

> finding qualified (local) staff, especially managers, was a constant problem. Older people had been trained under communist centralized system and so found it hard to adjust to a Western management regime including delegation and responsibility. (Ranson n.d.)

Needless to say, for journalists who struggled throughout the war to do their job with integrity, and for all those who were recipients of major international awards before the war, or who superbly organized the coverage of the XIV Winter Olympic Games, or who had worked for years as equal partners with their European counterparts on various Eurovision projects – such assumptions by their international colleagues seemed offensive and caused unnecessary frictions and tensions in their joint endeavors. "Repeatedly", cites Ranson Alyson Scott's interview, "I heard from my Bosnian colleagues, 'They think we're animals', and 'They think we're idiots', and sadly, there were elements of truth to this." (Ranson n.d.)

The tendency of international advisors and reformers to underestimate local journalists and staff also determined the character of aid. According to the Media Task Force of the Stability Pact for south-eastern Europe, 40 per cent of financial support in the region was spent on training, an additional 26 per cent on association building, media centers and law reform. Only 34 per cent was direct aid to media. Roughly a third of all funds listed by Stability Pact went on training programmes or direct support of media for stories on corruption and criminality in the region. Training programmes, however, often proved problematic. Jenny Ranson expressed the frustration of international advisors with local attitudes towards training, when she wrote that "many staff, including journalists, editors and managers, did not believe they needed training, and used it to enjoy study visits abroad or time off with no discernible changes in practice." Yet last year, local magazine *Dani* exposed a USAID and New York University joint programme in investigative journalism as a hoax. The Center for Investigative Journalism or CIN, as it was called, had a budget of 1.8 million US dollars, was run by barely qualified individuals from the United States, and in two years of its existence produced 62 stories of which only twelve were published. After a brave and critical internal USAID assessment in August of 2006 (Cornell and Thielen 2006), management of the Center was kindly asked to leave Bosnia, and leadership positions transferred to several local staffers. Hopefully, the Center itself will soon be folded under the successful and reputable umbrella of Sarajevo Media Center. Interestingly enough, with all the money spent on training programmes, international donors never thought that more money should be invested in local education, especially journalism schools at Bosnian universities, which remain understaffed and with very limited resources for technical or practical training of their students.

Finally, and for the purposes of this paper, most importantly, the entire project of media transformation of Bosnia and Herzegovina has been based upon the same political premises as the Dayton Peace Agreement. The UN, EU, US and other powers and organizations generally viewed the wars in the former Yugoslavia and Bosnia as ethnic wars and as the product of "ancient hatreds". Therefore, the solution sought at Dayton was to de-ethnify Bosnian politics by creating institutionally enshrined ethnic parity in two territorial entities, parliaments and the presidency. Likewise, media reform was also essentially perceived as the process of ethnic neutralization and de-politicization. Hence, aside from the fact that "ethnic hatred" and "ethnic warfare" were never the only possible explanations for the wars in the former Yugoslavia (Gagnon 2004; Bowen 1996) – and that, consequently, solution offered at Dayton simply institutionalized ethnicity as the basis of all politics rather than neutralizing it (Curak 2004; Mujkic 2007a and 2007b) – such interpretations also relied on a very narrow understanding of politics and of the media. By limiting their conceptualization of politics to ethnicity and institutions, media reformers created strict rules of language use and election coverage, banished some compromised journalists from public life, established principles of ethnic representation in public media outfits, funded numerous training programmes for local journalists and fostered development of associations and regulative agencies. They have failed, however, to recognize the persistently important link between entertainment and politics in former Yugoslavia, and infused a fear of politics to such a degree that news and even election coverage have become "politically neutered".

Thus, Tarik Jusic, programme director of Sarajevo Media Center, warned before elections of 2006 that media should do their civic duty and move beyond passive reporting of political events and statements of political candidates as has been the case in previous elections (Jusic 2006). Radenko Udovicic, programme director of Journalism School MediaPlan, correctly noted that no matter how painful it might be, media should finally address and confront extremist political views, which are still obviously present in Bosnia but rarely analyzed in media. According to Media Plan research, TV news on all three public television stations simply avoid themes around which there is no consensus of all three constitutive peoples (Bosnian Muslims, Serbs and Croats) (Udovicic R. 2006).

These three factors – conflict between European and American models of media system; tensions and mutually dismissive attitude between local journalists and international advisors; and political neutralization of media (particularly broadcast, which is strictly regulated by Communication Regulation Agency) – have all contributed to an environment in which superficial entertainment and tabloid journalism appear far more appealing to journalists than in-depth analysis of events. As a consequence, they have helped create an incredibly complex, fragmented and diverse media system, which is a far cry from ideals of public service and unsustainable by market forces alone – a system, which, in words of a senior American official, "is not bad, but also not good – just OK", and as such no longer considered worthy of substantial international investments. USAID expects that donor assistance will be dramatically reduced in the future, with funding going only to tried-and-proved institutions such as Media Plan Institute, Media Center and the key regulatory body – Communications Regulatory Agency (Cornell and Thielen 2006). Thus, in Bosnia and Herzegovina, as in many other cases examined in the present book, the liberal, market-driven model of the media will, most likely, by default – if not by design – eventually become the dominant one.

Public Service Broadcasting Reform in Bosnia and Herzegovina

If intervention into the media in Bosnia and Herzegovina came much too late, the process of transforming Bosnia's state television and radio into public service broadcasters has been even further delayed. The delay was initially caused, in part, by the near-exclusive focus of the international community and the Office of High Representative on the creation and maintenance of alternative broadcasting venues – OBN and Radio Fern. In 1996 when OBN was created, the hope of the OHR was that OBN would become the state-wide commercial television broadcaster, linking a number of independent private TV stations throughout Bosnia. Radio Fern, on the other hand, was created as the information service for the first elections in 1996. It became a talk radio in 1997. When it folded in 2001, its personnel moved to BH Radio 1. Thus, it was not until 2000 and 2001, when it became obvious that OBN could not compete with entity broadcasters RTV BiH and RTRS, and when Radio Fern shut down, that the international community put real emphasis on the creation of the public service broadcasting system in Bosnia and Herzegovina.

Yet the crux of the problem in the creation of PSB actually rested in the Dayton Peace Agreement itself. The Dayton Peace Agreement barely mentioned media, and its subsequent interpretations, particularly the so-called Madrid declaration of the Peace Implementation Council (the body that oversees activities of the OHR), allowed for the placement of state media under the entity and municipal control. Not surprisingly, any attempt to create a new legal framework and a state-wide public broadcasting service, met with resistance from these vested interests, interlocked with pressures from Bosnia's powerful nationalist parties which treated entity media as their own parlors.

Thus, more than a decade after the war, a series of decisions towards the creation of PSB taken by the OHR, numerous highly paid foreign media experts who acted as the HR's special appointees in charge of PSB reform, an expensive BBC consultancy project, and tremendous EU pressure – Bosnia and Herzegovina still does not have a fully functional public service broadcasting system. The plan created in 2000, under the guidance of John Shearer (a much disliked BBC expert who was the HR's Broadcasting Agent between 2000 and 2003), envisioned the creation of four distinct units. This plan included two entity television and radio broadcasters, one each in Republika Srpska and in the Federation, a state-level public broadcaster, and a state-level corporation for public broadcasting which would act as a technical coordinator and distributor or programming, advertising, and funding among the three emitters. The two entity broadcasters were created in 2001. Radio-television in Republika Srpska simply continued its existence as an entity broadcaster. Federal TV was created on the ashes of BHTV – once upon a time, Television of Bosnia and Herzegovina, successor of pre-war RTV Sarajevo, which many Bosnians, especially in Sarajevo, continued to view as the symbol of unity and resistance to Serbian aggression during the war. Newly created BHRT, a state-wide public service broadcaster, which has strict rules of ethnic parity in terms of language (Bosnian, Croat, Serbian) and script (Cyrillic and Latin) use, as well as the ethnic background of its journalists, transmitted the first newscasts on 7 May 2001. It did not start full-time programming on a countrywide frequency until August 2004. The fourth, joint, corporation for public broadcasting has not yet been created.

The process is now stalled mostly because of the demands of the main Croat nationalist parties that Croats, too, deserve their own public service channel. In 2005, Bosnian Parliament and the National Assembly of Republika Srpska adopted three laws, which govern the creation of a single state-wide public broadcasting system – the law on Public Broadcasting System, law on state-wide Public Service Broadcaster of BiH and entity Public Service Broadcaster of the Republika Srpska. The fourth law, on the entity Public Service Broadcaster of the Federation, was adopted in the Federation Parliament in June of 2006, but Croat representatives voted against it on the grounds that the vote "violated the Vital National Interest of the Croat constituent people" (Haraszti 2007). The disputes over the law, and its interpretation continue, blocking in the meantime the creation of the public service system and, particularly, the joint corporation – or the "fourth channel" as it is sometime referred to (Kulenovic 2006).

But public broadcasters are facing even more difficult issues. Many analysts contend that the system, as envisioned, and even without an additional channel for Croats, is not sustainable – either financially or in terms of programming (Henderson et al. 2003). BHRT is in dire financial situation since collection of subscription fees never reaches beyond 65 per cent (Haraszti 2007). Croats in western Herzegovina, where they are majority population, are instructed by their political parties not to pay for the public service system, which, in their view, does not represent their interests. The rate of collection in the rest of Federation and in Republika Srpska is also very low. The fee, which is about a half of the fee assessed before the war when the collection rate was between 85 and 90 per cent, and Bosnia had only one state-level broadcaster, is paid with utility bills (electric or telephone), but consumers have the right to refuse to pay that part of the bill. Already heavily indebted and overstaffed, public service system is, therefore, just as dependent on advertising revenue as its commercial competitors.

Dependence on advertising revenue and its distribution are also a source of contention. By far, the highest share of advertising revenue is collected by Federal TV, followed – though remotely – by RTRS. BHRT receives only 4 per cent of total advertising expenditures on television stations (see table 1).

Revenue distribution agreement, on the other hand, states that BHRT should receive 50 per cent of overall (fees and advertising revenue), while FTV and RTRS should receive 25 per cent. FTV, which has already written off all of its equipment and the building to BHRT in the process of liquidation of BHTV, is now in the position of subsidizing the state-wide broadcaster.

Table 1: Television advertising revenue Bosnia and Herzegovina – January 2007

	Total	Share %
OBN	4 757 920.00	30.41
PINK BH	2 972 003.50	19.00
FTV	2 962 540.00	18.94
NTV HAYAT	1 453 573.50	9.29
ATV	1 323 364.00	8.46
RTRS	786 607.00	5.03
MREZA PLUS	772 633.00	4.94
BHT	616 446.00	3.94
Total	15 645 087.00 KM	100.00

Source: Mareco Index Bosnia, 2006

Needless to say, such institutional structure and sharing agreements put the two television stations, housed in the same building, and sharing the same equipment, in competition with each other and create resentment among their employees. Just as importantly, the pressure to attract advertising impacts programming decisions of all three public broadcasters. All three struggle to reach the quota of 40 per cent of public service programming, all three have difficulty acquiring 10 per cent of programmes from local independent producers, and all three prefer cheap, in-studio shows, reality and game shows, sports and popular foreign TV series to documentary or education programmes. Local critics are particularly keen to stress that BHRT, the flagship state-wide public broadcaster, does not even have a desk for children and education programming, as was the case before the war.

Sliding into Commercial Reality: Financial Interests over Ethnic Loyalties

Although the tendency towards media commercialism permeates public service broadcasting in Bosnia and Herzegovina, PSB is still unable to compete with private television stations. Between 2002 and 2006, audience share of public broadcasters has slid down from 37.9 per cent to 23.7 (see table 2).

As table 2 shows, foreign TV stations from Croatia and Serbia – to the degree to which they can be considered foreign given linguistic similarity – have made major inroads into BH audiences, mostly legally but sometime illegally. In some cases, it seems that Croat TV stations, HRT 2 and Nova TV in particular, have made tacit agreements with local cable providers in Bosnia that they can carry their signal for free. In exchange, by promising to deliver larger audiences, they are increasing their advertising revenue in Croatia. Questions of exclusive broadcasting rights and their re-transmission on cable are also often at stake – from sports events to popular TV series – and Bosnian private TV stations, fearful of the loss of audience and advertising revenue, are now demanding from the Communications Regulatory Agency to block local cable providers from carrying HRT2 and Nova TV signals. The question has become politicized, as Bosnian Croats feel that, having been deprived of a public TV channel, they are now being deprived of the most popular Croat TV programmes as well.

Permeability of Bosnian media borders has been an issue of concern for years. It was heightened in 2003, when Ivan Caleta, at the time owner of TV Nova in Croatia and TV3 in Slovenia, purchased OBN. That same year, Zeljko Mitrovic, owner of the highly popular TV Pink from Belgrade, purchased four smaller TV stations in Bosnia and Herzegovina. OBN and Pink brought reality TV shows into Bosnian households – both have claimed their own versions

Table 2: Television stations in Bosnia – Market share of audiences, 2002–2006

TELEVISION STATIONS	2002	2003	2004	2005	2006
PUBLIC – BHT, FTV, RTS	37.9	33.5	31.8	24.8	23.7
LOCAL/REGIONAL	42.6	45.0	48.9	40.6	40.3
FOREIGN (Serbian and Croat) TV	14.3	16.3	14.6	30.8	33.3
OTHER SATELLITE TV	5.2	5.2	4.7	3.8	2.7

Source: Mareco Index Bosnia, 2006

of Big Brother thus far – and successfully attracted audiences. TV Pink has in just four years become the most popular TV station in entire Bosnia and Herzegovina (see table 3).

Both also reveal, along with a few Bosnian counterparts, the degree to which commercial interests can eventually trump ethnic loyalties, and the strange ways in which the slide into entertainment has been, perhaps unintentionally, entwined and helped by the presence of the international community in Bosnia and Herzegovina and the region.

OBN, for instance, that stillborn child of the international community, was, as mentioned, sold under very murky circumstances in London, in 2003, where the company had been registered as a trust. OBN went into liquidation in January of 2001, but the first hurried attempts to sell it proved to be disastrous. One of the potential buyers was a businessman from Republika Srpska, Gavrilo Bobar, known for his ties with war criminals Ratko Mladic and Radovan Karadzic. When the scandal broke out, OBN trustees went in search of another buyer. In 2003, the company was sold to Mr Ivan Caleta, but the details of the deal were kept away from the public, and his identity was not immediately revealed. Indeed, OBN is still registered in Sarajevo, under the name of Gabrijel Vukadin, general manager of OBN. Mr Vukadin is, however, just the fictitious owner, whose name is there to satisfy the 51 per cent rule of domestic ownership over media companies in Bosnia. Mr Caleta, who also owns Slovenian TV3 and several marketing agencies in Croatia and Bosnia (he lost control over Nova in 2004 after being knee-capped in front of his house in Zagreb), cleared OBN's debt and equipped the company with transmitters to ensure coverage over the entire territory of BH. In 2004, Mr Caleta linked Nova, TV3 and OBN in the first and mega-successful reality show – *Story Super Nova Talents* – and the show created a marketing windfall for OBN's owner. Other media companies in Bosnia now argue that Mr Caleta uses his advertising agency in Zagreb to link advertising sales in Croatia and Bosnia, and that way offers advertising minutes on OBN at significantly lower prices than his media competitors in Bosnia can. Dumping, thus, may be one of the reasons why OBN still attracts over thirty per cent of all TV advertising sales in Bosnia (see table 1). According to a USAID assessment team, OBN "unabashedly claims to target its programming towards women aged 17–48, particularly those employed and living in urban areas – as those women make household choices regarding consumer goods, and are therefore sought after by firms that OBN covets as advertisers." Consequently, the programming consists of films, serials and telenovelas, while "the network provides the minimum amount of news and information content prescribed by CRA regulations in order to concentrate on entertainment programming." (Cornell and Thielen 2006)

Table 3: Top TV Stations in Bosnia and Herzegovina – Audience shares, 2002–2006

	2002		**2003**		**2004**		**2005**		**2006**	
1	FTV	30.1	FTV	26.9	FTV	23.8	FTV	13.7	PINK BH	12.5
2	RTRS	7.3	OBN	6.9	PINK BH	10.4	PINK BH	11.6	FTV	11.8
3	OBN	5.8	RTRS	6.5	OBN	7.7	TV BN	6.1	BHT	7
4	NTV HAYAT	5.5	NTV HAYAT	6.2	NTV HAYAT	6.6	BHT	6	OBN	6.4
5	TV TK	3.9	TV BN	4.2	RTRS	5.2	OBN	5.3	TV BN	5.6

Source: Mareco Index Bosnia, 2006

The other successor to OBN is USAID/IREX-sponsored Mreza Plus, a network which links five BH TV stations (Alternative TV from Banja Luka, TV Hayat from Sarajevo, RTV Mostar, HTV Mostar Oscar C and TV Tuzla), originally linked through OBN. Mreza Plus also thrives on commercial programming – from *Desperate Housewives* to Formula 1 races – which, frequently, puts it at odds with above-mentioned Croat stations and Mr Caleta's OBN. Mreza Plus, also, did not start producing a 30-minute daily news programme until 2006. Mr Darko Aleksic, network manager, attended USAID management training programmes and is proud of the fact that the network – with its commercial, mostly American, programming – overcomes all ethnic barriers in Bosnia and Herzegovina.

Mr Zeljko Mitrovic and his TV Pink are another example of ambivalent relations between commerce, ethnicity and international community. Mr Mitrovic was once a member of JUL, a political party in Serbia founded by Slobodan Milosevic's wife, and his television station the favourite of Mr Milosevic's family. The building, which housed TV Pink, was strategically bombed during the 1999 NATO raids on Belgrade as it also housed TV Kosava, owned by Mr Milosevic's daughter. During the Milosevic years, TV Pink was broadcasting an entertaining mix of talk shows, pirated movies and soap operas, with the message "enjoy life, forget politics". The key element of Milosevic's media strategy was to destroy alternatives to his own political vision (Gordy 1999). Pink also promoted and celebrated the turbo-folk genre in popular music, infamous for its underlying nationalism and numerous links of its stars with key figures of Milosevic's regime, including immensely popular Svetlana-Ceca Raznatovic. After the so-called October revolution in Serbia, in 2000, Mr Mitrovic switched political sides and joined Milosevic's opponents. No longer on the US Treasury list of individuals with whom US companies cannot trade, Mr Mitrovic befriended a number of western diplomats and hired a lobbyist in Washington to take care of his business interests on the other side of the Atlantic (Manasek 2005). Pink continues to feed films, reality TV shows and turbo-folk music to its audiences – just as in Milosevic's years – but this time around in support of Serbia's budding democracy.

As mentioned, in 2003, Mr Mitrovic purchased four smaller stations in Bosnia and Herzegovina. He subsequently opened a TV studio in Bijeljina, Republika Srpska, and then later in Banja Luka and Sarajevo. Within just four years, and with 12 per cent audience share, TV Pink has become the most popular TV station in Bosnia and Herzegovina (see table 3). Media analysts now claim that "although there was a lot of repulsion for this TV station in Sarajevo before it started broadcasting because of its owner's ties with Slobodan Milosevic, the station's programming has proven to be diverse, entertaining, good quality and all-Bosnian with particular emphasis on events in Banja Luka and Sarajevo." (Udovicic R. 2006) In the fall of 2006, TV Pink brought the Serbian version of *Big Brother* show to Bosnian audiences with a multi-ethnic cast of characters, including a young man from Sarajevo, in fierce competition for a 100,000 euros prize. The show's ratings exceeded all expectations. Ironically, the original Serbian *Big Brother* was produced by B92, staunch opponent of Milosevic's regime, the bastion of independent journalism with public service orientation in Serbia. The director of B92, Veran Matic, justified the decision to produce *Big Brother* by saying that if reality TV is our reality – that is, if all TV stations in the world broadcast reality shows, and if *Big Brother* remains absolute champion in programming formats and the global phenomenon of reality TV – then B92 wants to produce the best of the best of reality TV shows.

But, perhaps, the best example of the ways in which financial interests eventually overcome ethnic loyalties – and the most paradigmatic figure of Bosnia's media landscape – is Mr

Fahrudin Radoncic, owner of the daily newspaper *Dnevni Avaz* in Sarajevo. Started as an occasional publication of the leading Muslim party in Bosnia — SDA — during the war, *Dnevni Avaz* has since grown into the newspaper with the highest circulation in Bosnia and Herzegovina, with an estimated daily average of 40,000 and weekend circulation of 80,000 copies. Mr Radoncic, a former journalist and a war-time assistant to Mr Sefer Halilovic, commander of the Bosnian army, is frequently attacked by the Bosnian political elite and other media outlets because of his aggressive business strategies and transparent desire to influence public opinion and politics in Bosnia and Herzegovina.

The origins of Mr Radoncic's capital, with which he started the paper, are still unknown, and his financial dealings have been subject of several (in Mr Radoncic's view, politically motivated) investigations. Frequently accused of shady business practices, and equally shady alliances with shady Balkan characters, Mr Radoncic's greatest sin, however, seems to have been his fascinating business acumen. He has built his press and media empire by undercutting opposition (e.g., by purchasing the largest printing press in Sarajevo in 2001, thus making all other magazines and newspapers published in Sarajevo dependent on Avaz press), fierce pursuit of advertising share, excellent distribution network of his papers in Bosnia and abroad, paternalistic care for his deeply loyal employees, and lowest-common-denominator journalism. (See table 4 for advertising share among daily newspapers.)

Aside from Avaz, Mr Radoncic's company A-Roto Press also publishes a weekly magazine for women, *Azra*, a weekly tabloid, *Express*, a daily tabloid, *AS*, and a weekly sports newspaper, *Sport*. In 2007, after some years of promise and delay, Mr Radoncic also re-launched his TV station, TV Alfa, which boasts objectivity as its greatest asset. Interestingly, TV Alfa was penalized in 2004 by CRA for anti-Semitic content of some of its programmes.

Mr Radoncic has been known for his shifting political preferences, as he has backed different candidates over the past ten years. His opponents are convinced that his political moods, which powerfully colour the news in his publications, correlate with prospects for the expansion of his business empire. In the last election, held in October 2006, he was accused of influencing and even outright determining the election outcome, especially the victory of presidential candidate Haris Silajdzic. Representatives of the international community are also concerned about Mr Radoncic's political influence and, in private conversations, reject any comparisons between

Table 4: Major daily newspapers in Bosnia and Herzegovina and their advertising revenue — January 2007

Daily	TOTAL	SHARE %
Dnevni Avaz	418 318.38	34.00
Dnevni List	296 914.00	24.13
Oslobodjenje	206 090.00	16.75
Nezavisne Novine	156 583.00	12.72
Glas Srpske	109 780.00	8.92
Vecernji List	42 832.00	3.48
TOTAL	1 230 517.30	100.00

Source: Mareco Index Bosnia, 2006

Mr Radoncic and Ruppert Murdoch as an insult to Mr Murdoch. At the same time, however, they too believe that they depend on Mr Radoncic's paper as the link to the hearts and minds of ordinary Bosnians. Avaz has been the favourite outlet of all High Representatives thus far, especially Paddy Ashdown. In the contest of mutual adoration, Avaz named Ashdown 'Personality of the Year' in January 2003, while in his acceptance message Ashdown crowned Avaz 'newspaper of the year' and 'the clearest example of professional and business success.'

Although OHR representatives claim that the paper is no longer privileged as much as it was during Ashdown's reign, Christian Schwarz-Schilling also has a weekly column in Mr Radoncic's paper. For years, Mr Radoncic rented one of his villas as a residence to American ambassadors and some suspect that Avaz's increasingly critical stance towards the US is a result of the broken lease agreement. Nonetheless, Fahrudin Radoncic was invited as a Bosnian representative to President Bush's Prayer Breakfast in Washington D.C. in 2007 and was the first Bosnian to attend.

All media outlets linked to Mr Radoncic display a mix of gossip, entertainment, brief news, brisk comments, blunt views and little analysis – a Daily Mirror recipe for broadening of media appeal and attracting readers. And yet, despite his success, Mr Radoncic's ambitions at the moment seem to go beyond the media. He has transformed a half of his newly built Avaz building (which envelops the ruins of Sarajevo's oldest, and now barely surviving, daily newspaper, Oslobodjenje) into a hotel. He also plans to build the tallest office towers on the Balkans in Sarajevo and has signed an agreement with the richest man in Serbia, Miroslav Miskovic, to build twenty shopping centres around Bosnia within the next four years. Public outcry over Mr Radoncic's decision to join forces with a man who made a fortune under the reign of Slobodan Milosevic – and, thus, place his financial interests above ethnic solidarity – has not yet ceased.

And, finally, to conclude this survey of Bosnia's slide into commercial reality, let me just mention that most Bosnian newspapers and political magazines – including those that were once heavily subsidized by the international community – now have sister gossip, sports or specialized magazines, perfectly suited for waiting rooms in beauty salons or increasingly privatized medical service offices. While exact circulation data in Bosnia and Herzegovina do not exist (publishers are resisting any attempt to create market research instruments for the press), a recent IREX study of media sustainability shows that women's magazines from Bosnia and Croatia have taken a lead in terms of circulation (see table 5).

Political magazines, on the other hand, which used to live off foreign donations, are now increasingly engaged in media wars. This is not surprising. In the highly saturated media market,

Table 5: Reading rates of magazines

Magazine	Reading rate
Azra (women's magazine, affiliate of Avaz)	14.7%
Gloria (Croatian women's magazine)	12.5%
Dani (independent political magazine)	9.4%
Slobodna Bosna (independent political magazine)	7.2%
Express (weekly tabloid, affiliate of Avaz)	5.3%

Source: IREX, Media Sustainability Index 2005; Mareco Index Bosnia

with advertising revenue valued at approximately 80 million euros (or one-fifth of the Croatian market which has only four TV channels with national coverage), battle for readership and eyeballs is becoming fierce. Thus, if international subsidies were a major factor in proliferation of media outlets in Bosnia, and international community already a midwife of media commercialization, it is hard to see how anything but a race to the bottom will become Bosnia's media future once the subsidies completely disappear.

Digital Laggards
And while the choice between public service broadcasting and mindless entertainment, ethnic interests and money-making continues to preoccupy both media observers and practitioners in the region, a few Bosnian media analysts have noticed that such preoccupation only deflects attention from a far more serious problem – Bosnia's technological lag behind an increasingly digitized media world. As Boro Kontic, director of Sarajevo's Media Center noted, "EU plans to move from analog to completely digital TV broadcast by 2012, while Bosnia and Herzegovina remains the only country in Europe, including our neighbors, which has not even raised an issue of a pilot digital TV signal." According to Mr Kontic (2007), the Bosnian public service broadcaster is already an anachronistic institution, with too many channels that cannot be sustained by the Bosnian advertising market, too many employees, an enormous BHT building in Sarajevo, which is not used to its capacity, and rapidly declining audiences. "Debate about two or three or four channels with national markings (...) will be pointless in a digital environment with hundreds of thematic channels. In fact, paradox of current public service broadcasting debate in Bosnia, is that it is already outdated in Europe – it's just that nobody has told us this secret."

Mr Kontic's article prompted a response from Ms Dunja Mijatovic (2007), Director of Broadcasting at the Bosnian Communications Regulatory Agency. She also suggested an opening of discussion about new information technologies and their use in communications and politics, the digital divide, and ways in which Bosnia, and its citizens, may benefit from new technologies. But a serious initiation of such debate may have to wait for years. After the national elections of 2006, Bosnian citizens had to wait more than six months to have a government, since the complicated coalition of their elected representatives could not decide on distribution of all available ministerial portfolios. If the newly formed government continues with that pace, it is difficult to expect that any major decisions regarding any of the pressing social and economic issues will be made under their mandate. And the low level of Internet penetration in Bosnia – according to ITU data it stands at only 17 per cent of population – makes it unlikely that pressures for comprehensive digital strategy would come from citizens themselves. Thus, the key concern of Rupert Murdoch and his look-alikes in contemporary global media environment – how to keep audiences in face of Internet competition – has no serious bearing on Bosnia's media executives as yet.

Bosnia's dismal Internet situation reveals deeper political, social and economic problems of its post-Dayton existence. Twelve years after the war, more than half of Bosnian population is still excluded from the social mainstream. A daily purchase of one newspaper would cost a pensioner one-tenth of monthly pension, while a monthly Internet connection would take up one-fifth. Poverty, poor transportation links and the strict visa regime imposed on Bosnian citizens keep the country and its peoples disconnected from developments in Europe and the rest of the world. One cannot, therefore, but wonder – and media reform and democratization may be a great example – if millions of dollars spent on Bosnia's re-integration into the world did not have the opposite effect – turning the country inwards, to its own reality shows, with entertainment, on the one hand, and nationalism, on the other, as ways of bridging otherwise extreme economic divisions and structural inequalities.

Conclusion

In his chapter on public service broadcasting reforms in Central and Eastern Europe, Karol Jakubowicz relies on Hallin's and Mancini's notion of "political parallelism" between media and political systems. Jakubowicz's analysis is further enriched with the introduction of political culture as a variable as well as with his reliance on dynamic, rather than static, accounts of political institutions in countries of transition. He is skeptical about the future of public broadcasting in post-communist countries.

Although Bosnia's situation, at the first glance, may seem different because of its post-conflict situation, deep involvement of international community, and politically – not just economically – porous borders to neighbouring Serbia and Croatia, its complex political system, fragmented political culture and weak political society seem perfectly reflected in the cacophonic media environment. Twelve years of international guidance have helped fracture the Bosnian media landscape, politically neutralize its messages, and introduce market-driven wars over advertising and audience shares into its saturated media space. In a peculiar symbiosis with Bosnia's nationalist leaders, just as in politics, they were not able to bring Bosnia into global economic and infrastructural trends, which are now deemed necessary for Bosnia's integration into the European Union. De-politicization of commercial media in Bosnia may have succeeded, and may constitute a progress in comparison with inflammatory wartime propaganda. However, just as elsewhere in the world, and the United States in particular, de-politicization of media and the shift towards entertainment have also helped maintain a political status quo, nationalist and globalist at once, feeding off each other in perpetual complicity.

And to the degree to which space, architecture and landscapes speak about power, particularly in the inherently fluid media worlds, it may be appropriate to end this chapter with the images of two buildings, perhaps the best representation of Bosnia's shifting media environment. One building is Mr Radnocic's shiny blue *Avaz* high-rise, half-hotel, half-media headquarters, with a rotating panoramic restaurant, saunas, gyms and a printing press, swirled around the devastated building of Sarajevo's other daily newspaper, *Oslobodjenje*. And just a kilometer down the street, the other building, that of Bosnia's public broadcasters, BHRT and FTV, which was in the early 1980s one of the most technologically advanced radio and television centres in Europe, is now half abandoned, full of outdated and poorly maintained equipment. The building no longer displays a sign, "NOT FOR SALE", placed by its employees at the time when the international community demanded the sale of the premises in order to fund the PSB. But the question is how long will it take before the building and the institutions it houses are not – both literally and metaphorically – put up for grabs, sold perhaps to Mr Radoncic or one of his business associates from Serbia or Croatia.

Note

1. I would like to thank Miklós Sükösd and Karol Jakubowicz for their guidance and patience in the course of my writing of this chapter. I would also like to thank Tarik Jusic and the staff of Sarajevo Media Center, colleagues at the Faculty of Political Science in Sarajevo, where I was a Fulbright scholar in 2006 and 2007, numerous Bosnian journalists and representatives of OHR, USAID, OSCE and the US Embassy in Sarajevo who agreed to share their view on media reform and the political situation in Bosnia and Herzegovina. All mistakes and errors of judgement in this chapter are mine.

References

Arnautovic, S. (2007). *Ten Years of Democratic Chaos: Electoral Processes in Bosnia and Herzegovina from 1991 to 2006* (Sarajevo: Promocult).

Babic, D. (2005) 'Economic Pressure – A Tool for Achieving Political Aims', mediaonline.ba, 20 April 2005 available at http://archiv2.medienhilfe.ch/News/2005/BiH/MOL_ECONOMIC.pdf.

Bamburac, N. M., Jusic, T. and Isanovic, A. (eds.) (2006). *Stereotyping: Representation of Women in Print Media in South East Europe*, Sarajevo, Mediacentar.

Basic Hrvatin, S., Petkovic, B. and Jusic, T. (2004). *Vlasnistvo nad medijima i njegov utjecaj na nezavisnost i pluralizam medija*, Sarajevo, Mediacentar.

Bose, S. (2002). *Bosnia After Dayton* (New York: Oxford University Press).

Bowen, J. R. (1996). 'The Myth of Global Ethnic Conflict,' *Journal of Democracy* 7:4, pp. 3–14.

Brunner, R. (2002). *How to Build Public Broadcast in Post-Socialist Countries*, Medienhilfe, June 2002, available at http://archiv2.medienhilfe.ch/topics/PBS/pbs-1st.pdf.

Chandler, D. (2000). *Faking Democracy After Dayton*, 2nd edition (London: Pluto Press).

Cornell, S. and Thielen, T. (2006). Assessment of USAID Bosnia and Herzegovina Media Interventions, Final Report, prepared by ARD, Inc., USAID, 14 August.

Curak, N. (2004). *Dejtonski nacionalizam* (Sarajevo: Buybook).

Curak, N. (2006). *Obnova Bosanskih Utopija* (Sarajevo-Zagreb, Synopsis).

Davidson, D. (2006). OSCE BiH Head of Mission, Monitoring of Media Reporting in the Countries of the "Dayton Triangle:" Remarks to the Thirteenth Igman Initiative Regional Conference, 19 June available at http://www.oscebih.org/public/default.asp?d=6&article=show&id=1814.

De Luce, D. (2003). Assessment of USAID Media Assistance in Bosnia and Herzegovina, 1996–2002, Bureau for Policy and Program Coordination, USAID.

Dzihana, A. (2006). 'Digitalni jaz i reforma javne TV,' *Puls Demokratije*, 1 November available at http://www.pulsdemokratije.net/clanak.php?sifra=061101007&lang=bh.

Gagnon, V. P. (2004). *The Myth of Ethnic War: Serbia and Croatia in the 1990s* (Ithaca: Cornell University Press).

Gordy, E. D. (1999). *The Culture of Power in Serbia: Nationalism and the Destruction of Alternatives*, University Park, PA, The Pennsylvania State University Press.

Hadzifejzovic, S. (2002). *Rat Uzivo* (Sarajevo).

Hitchner, B. R. (2005). The Process and Prospects of Constitutional Reform in Bosnia and Herzegovina, Report to the Peace Implementation Council, Paris, France, 14 December.

Haraszti, M. (2007). OSCE Representative on Freedom of the Media, 'The State of Media Freedom in Bosnia and Herzegovina: the Public Service Broadcasting,' 29 March available at http://www.osce.org/documents/rfm/2007/03/23751_en.pdf.

Hallin, D. and Mancini, P. (2004). *Comparing Media Systems: Three Models of Media and Politics* (Cambridge, UK, New York: Cambridge University Press).

Henderson, G., Kilalic, J. and Kontic B. (2003). The Media Environment in Bosnia and Herzegovina: An Assessment for USAID/Bosnia, January, available at http://usaid.ba/DemoAnnex%20IV%20media%20assess.%20report.doc.

IREX (2005), Media Sustainability Index: Europe and Eurasia 2005, available at http://www.irex.org/programs/MSI_EUR/index.asp.

Jusic, T. (2005), 'Televizija u Evropi: regulative, politika i nezavisnost - Bosna i Hercegovina' in OSI/EU Monitoring and Advocacy Program/Network Media Program, Televizija u Evropi: regulativa, politika i nezavisnost, Monitoring izvjestaj (translated from English by Kanita Halilovic), Budapest, Open Society Institute.

Jusic, T. (2006). 'Izbori i javna sfera: mediji kao akteri,' *Puls Demokratije*, 1 September available at http://www.pulsdemokratije.net/clanak.php?sifra=060901007&lang=bh.

Kontic, B. (2006). 'Šarafcigerom na sistem, ili zašto u BiH nikada neće funkcionisati javna RTV,' *Puls Demokratije*, 1 November, available at http://www.pulsdemokratije.net/clanak.php?sifra= 061101010&lang=bh.

Knaus, G. (2003). 'Travails of the European Raj?, *Journal of Democracy*, 14:3, pp. 60–74.

Kumar, K. (2006). *Promoting Independent Media: Strategies for Democracy Assistance* (Boulder, CO: Lynne Rienner Publishers).

Kurspahic, K. (n.d.) 'Building Public Television in BiH', Medienhilfe, available at http://archiv.medienhilfe.ch/ Projekte/BiH/Monitoring/BiH-PBS.htm.

Kurspahic, K. (2003). *Prime Time Crime: Balkan Media in War and Peace* (Washington D.C.: USIP Press).

Lindvall, D. (2006). 'Imposed Reform Facing its Ultimate Test', *SEE Online*, 8 February, available at http://www.southeasteurope.org/subpage.php?sub_site=2&id=16326&head=if&site=2.

Manasek, J. (2005). 'The Paradox of Pink', *Columbia Journalism Review*, January/February, available at http://www.cjr.org/issues/2005/1/manasek-paradox.asp.

Mijatovic, D. (2007). 'Digitalna televizija (II): Tehnologija u funkciji razvoja', *Puls Demokratije*, 14 February, available at http://www.pulsdemokratije.net/clanak.php?sifra=070214001&lang=bh.

Mujkic, A. (2007). *Mi, gradjani etnopolisa* (Sarajevo: Sahinpasic).

Mujkic, A. (2007). 'We, the Citizens of Ethnopolis', *Constellations* 14 (1), pp. 112–128.

Omerovic, S. (2003). 'Bolna rekonstrukcija javnog RTV servisa: analiza razvoja javnog TV servisa u BiH,' Mediacentar, Sarajevo, September, available at http://195.222.62.54/mediacentar/documents/ Rekonstrukcija%20Javnog%20servisa.pdf.

Paletz, D. and Jakubowicz, K. (2003). *Business as Usual: Continuity and Change in Central and Eastern European Media*, Cresskill, NJ, Hampton Press, Inc.

Pejanovic, M. (2005). *Politicki razvitak Bosne i Hercegovine u postdejtonskom periodu* (Sarajevo: Sahinpasic).

Price, M. E. and Thompson, M. (2002). *Forging Peace: Intervention, Human Rights, and the Management of Media Space*, Edinburgh, Edinburgh University Press.

Ranson, J. (n.d.) 'International Intervention in Media: The Open Broadcast network. A Case Study of Bosnia and Herzegovina', available at http://www.mediapeace.org/archive/RANSON%20MA% 20THESIS%20_4_.pdf.

Sacic, N. (2007). 'Medjunarodna zajednica u Bosni i Hercegovini (decembar 1995-maj 2007) – politoloski uvidi', paper presented for a conference on the role of the international community in Bosnia and Herzegovina, organized by Heinrich Boll Foundation, Sarajevo, 17 April.

Sacic, N. (2004). *Politicka de(re)socijalizacija i mediji*, Sarajevo, Internews BIH.

Sparks, C. with Reading, A. (1998). *Communism, Capitalism, and the Mass Media*, London, Sage.

Splichal, S. (1994). *Media Beyond Socialism: Theory and Practice in East-Central Europe*, Boulder, Westview Press.

Stability Pact for South Eastern Europe, Media Task Force, 'Overview of Media Support to South Eastern Europe 2003', available at http://www.stabilitypact.org/media/default.asp.

Sükösd, M. and Bajomi-Lázár, P. (eds.) (2003). *Reinventing Media: Media Policy Reform in East-Central Europe*, Budapest, CEU Press.

Talbott, S. (1996). 'Democracy and the National Interest', *Foreign Affairs*, November/December, pp. 47–63.

Taylor, M. and Kent, M. L. (2000). 'Media Transition in Bosnia: From Propagandistic Past to Uncertain Future', *International Communication Gazette*, 62:5, pp. 355–378.

Taylor, M. and Napoli, P. M. (2003). 'Media Development in Bosnia: A Longitudinal Analysis of Citizen Perceptions of News media Realism, Importance and Credibility,' *International Communications Gazette*, 65:6, pp. 473–492.

Thompson, M. (1999). *Forging War: The Media in Serbia, Croatia, and Bosnia and Herzegovina* (Luton: University of Luton Press).

Thompson, M. and De Luce, D. (2002). Escalating to Success: Media Intervention in Bosnia and Herzegovina in Price, M. E. and Thompson, M. *Forging Peace: Intervention, Human Rights, and the Management of Media Space*, Edinburgh, Edinburgh University Press, pp. 201–235.

Turcilo, L. (2006). *ON-line komunikacija i off-line politika u Bosni i Hercegovini*, Sarajevo, Internews BIH.

Udovicic, R. (2006). 'Izmedju novca i politike: medijska slika BiH u 2005 godini', mediaonline.ba, 27 January, available at http://www.mediaonline.ba/ba/?ID=418.

Udovicic, R. (2004). 'Public Service Under International Protectorate, Press Beyond Any Control, Statistically Speaking Pressure on Journalists Declining', *Media Online*, available at http://archiv2.medienhilfe.ch/News/2004/BiH/MOL9475.pdf.

Udovicic, Z. (2001). Comment: Wasted Millions, IWPR's Balkan Crisis Report, NO. 275, Part II, 29 August, available at http://archiv.medienhilfe.ch/News/2001/BiH.IWPR275M1.htm.

Udovicic, Z. (1996). 'Radio i TV difuzija u BiH', Media Plan Institut, mediaonline.ba, available at http://www.mediaonline.ba/ba/arhiva/arhiva_izvjestaja/izvjestaji/difuzijaubh96.pdf.

UNDP (2004). Democratic Governance Group, Supporting Public Service Broadcasting: Learning from Bosnia and Herzegovina's Experience, United Nations Development Programme, Bureau for Development Policy, available at http://www.undp.org/governance/docs/A2I_Pub_PublicService Broadcasting.pdf.

Media Concentration Trends in Central and Eastern Europe

Zrinjka Peruško and Helena Popoviç

Acknowledgements

Research for this chapter was conducted as part of the project "Media, Cultural and Communication Aspects of Civil Society" at the Department for Culture and Communication, Institute for International Relations, Zagreb, financed by the Croatian Ministry of Education, Science and Sport in the 2002–2006 period, and of the project "Media culture in contemporary Croatia: pluralism in media and media policy", financed by the Ministry of Education, Science and Sport (2007–2009) at the Faculty of Political Science, University of Zagreb. Both projects were led by Zrinjka Peruško.

The study on Croatian Media Markets was supported by a grant from the Media Division of the Council of Europe, thanks to the voluntary contribution of the government of Norway within the Media Component of the Stability Pact for South-Eastern Europe.

1. The Media, Markets and Democracy

Global media development in recent decades highlights several trends with potential impact on the role of the media in democratic societies. Globalization, in the sense of the integration of world markets, is playing out in the media field as well. The global expansion of media industries leads the increased concentration of media owners as well as the ever bigger media companies. The concentration of media industries is the main contemporary trend at the global level, with the consequence that a smaller number of media companies are controlling an ever larger number of media products and world markets.

The premise prevailing in contemporary media policy theory is that ownership concentration leads to diminished diversity of media content, leading in turn to diminished plurality of programmes in cultural as well as social and political terms.[1] In democratic political systems the media should enable citizens to learn and become involved in political processes, as well as to enable communication of diverse ideas, communicated by diverse actors. This is why pluralism and diversity in the media are one of the fundamental topics of media policy in European democracies.

Early modern theorists viewed the market as that balancing factor which would hold in check the despotic governments and provide a free press.[2] As in the beginning, so in the transitions of the 1990s, the market was perceived in the new post-communist democracies of Central and Eastern Europe as that balancing factor that could prevent the recurrence of the erstwhile overarching rule of the political realm. In the early modern times, the belief in "decentralized market competition as a vital antidote to political despotism" (Keane 1991, pp. 45) was extrapolated on to the media enterprise and freedom of expression. And without a doubt, this early hope was initially fulfilled. The power began to slowly shift from the realm of politics to that of the market – "…the market being an alternative to politics (up to a point) for making decisions, or an alternative for reaching outcomes as by-products or 'as though by a hidden hand' instead of as decisions" (Lindblom 1998, pp. 20). Democracy and market economy should not be conflated, but also cannot be dissociated (Le Goff 2002) in the empirical experience of modern societies. The pluralism of contemporary democracies is necessarily based on the cooperating/competing roles of different social institutions and not on the all-encompassing role of only one (i.e., the state). Thus, the market as a social institution figures importantly in the practice of democracy as a social and political system. This role of the market and free enterprise is perhaps even better appreciated in Central and Eastern Europe which has experienced the failure of the "planned economy" of the socialist system.[3]

Although a comprehensive analysis of the region's media market development in the 1990s is yet to be written, the growth in the number of media outlets, types of media content and products as well as the diversity of owners is a direct consequence of the introduction of the market system of free enterprise. Where there were once party/state-controlled broadcast monopolies new media companies entered. The political realm is no longer restricting the free flow of information in Central and Eastern Europe. However, the opening of the media markets of the countries of the region (many of whom are now also members of the European Union) brought them into the global media environment. There, competition is not perfect and the large players and technological and policy liberalization trends leading to market concentration are creating conditions where the market is increasingly seen as producing negative effects for the freedom and diversity of information in the public sphere.

The essential aspect of democracy is in the pluralism of social institutions and in the sharing of their power. Accordingly, full control of the media by a market-based institution is as undesirable as full total control by the state. At the European level, the quest for media pluralism and diversity is built into the European Convention on Human Rights (Article 10), in which the freedom of expression and media are guaranteed. The application of this article through the judgements of the European Court for Human Rights obliges all the member states to protect pluralism of the media in order for them to carry out their democratic function. All the ensuing political texts and recommendations of the Council of Europe are developed from this basic understanding. Based on this premise many European media policies control concentration of ownership in the media (and not only in terms of ensuring market competition), as well as support diversity by other measures (including support for public service broadcasting).

Concentration is in economic terms a characteristic of a market in which the competition of companies is constrained, to different degrees, with monopoly position being the drastic example in which the access to a given market is totally barred for other players. In this text, we are interested not in the economic aspects and ramifications of concentration in the media sector, but in the social and political consequences that these developments possibly have on the fulfilment of the media's social role.

In addition to structural diversity (of owners, companies, types of media, different territorial coverage – from local to national), diversity and pluralism needs to be in the final analysis reflected in media content, in order to enable the development of a democratic society. In the realm of media content, diversity implies types of programme genres (different news genres, documentaries, movies, new genres), topics that are covered (politics, economy, culture, science, education, religion), audiences they address (majority and minority, children, groups with special needs), actors with access to the media and the political orientations and world-views they present. The last element of diversity begins to describe media pluralism as that quality of the media necessary for public debate, for a culture of democracy that enables democratic governance and the development of democratic societies.

The effects of concentration on pluralism of content relate to the diminishing of choice and diversity in the number of titles (in the press) and in the mainstreaming of the remaining titles in order to maximize audiences. Another aspect is editorial concentration, a practice of "diversified" media conglomerates: media content is produced in one central place and distributed to local audiences. The diversity and pluralism is at risk again, as only one viewpoint is presented in different kinds of media (press, TV, radio, Internet). Concentration also has negative effects on programming quality, as was shown in an analysis of the US entertainment programme diversity and quality after recent mergers (Einstein 2002). Standardization of the cultural content in the media is also a result of concentration: all media companies use the same audience-attracting strategies (Humphreys 1996). If we take a more radical view, the very essence of the corporate media ownership is a threat to the development of civil society (Roth 2004). The media follow editorial policies that are commensurate with the aims and social values of their corporate owners (Bagdikian 2000). Views that are contrary to these interests have less of a chance of entering the public sphere, or may be blocked altogether, even if they represent the majority of civil society (McChesney 2000).

Other studies have analyzed the relationship between type of the market and the content of the media. Roth (2004) shows the correlation of the structure of the media market and the diversity of the media system in the Netherlands. Comparative research on the quality of programming (Ishikawa 1996) showed (as was to be expected) a higher level of diversity for public television channels, while the lowest results were scored by American commercial television networks. The relationship is, however, not uncontroversial: repeated analysis in Sweden in 1996 showed that "in the presence of increasing competition from commercial channels, Sweden's public service television system increased its diversity, while her public service radio system decreased in diversity" (Hillve et al. 1997).

The process of media concentration can be observed at three different levels: *horizontal merger* – whereby two firms combine forces which are at the same position in the supply chain and are engaged in the same activity; *vertical* growth – which involves "expanding either 'forward' into succeeding stages or 'backward' into preceding stages in the supply chain (creation of media output and distribution or retail of that output in various guises)" (Doyle 2002, pp. 4); *diagonal* expansion which occurs when "firms diversify into new business areas" (like merging of a telecommunications operator and a television company) (Doyle 2002, pp. 4). In media policy terms, diagonal expansion translates into rules on cross-media ownership.

Arguments in favor of media concentration are that concentration (which means fewer competing suppliers) implies a more cost-effective use of resources. That, in turn, means that the availability for innovation enables an increased range of output (Doyle 2002, pp. 13). The OFCOM review of media ownership rules lists the following potential benefits of media consolidation:

- economies of scale and scope in news gathering and dissemination, which can reduce news costs and improve access to international news;
- access to better news management and superior talent;
- improved access to overseas capital for investing in the news function;
- improved access to news gathering, editing and dissemination technology. (OFCOM 2006, sec. 2.20, pp. 7)

However, as Dowd (2004) emphasizes, tendencies in media concentration to constrain diversity are connected to the fact that media production only presents a small segment of a conglomerate's potential product. Another constraint on diversity is the fact that media firms "face inertial pressures in the production process", which results in the repeating of previously successful content (Dowd 2004, pp. 1412).

Doyle (2002) points out several determinants of media pluralism:

- Size and wealth of market (research shows that larger and wealthier markets can afford greater diversity, for example there is a positive correlation between size of population in EU countries and the number of daily newspaper titles available). These variables are taken into consideration in media ownership regulation on national, regional and local level, however, no solution has yet been found on a supra-national European level;
- Diversity of suppliers – important because the reduction of the number of media suppliers can "translate into media power." (Meier and Trappel 1998, pp. 39; in Doyle 2002, pp. 19). The influence of the owner is visible in the selection of editors as well as the decision about investments and "arrangements for sourcing or distributing content". (Meier and Trappel 1998, pp. 39; in Doyle 2002, pp. 19) – decisions which results in the over-representation of the owner's values and interests;
- Consolidation of resources – the question about how media resources will be managed, especially consolidation of editorial functions: in order to gain diversity of input for a media product has to be gained from different sources;
- Diversity of output – the main aspect of political and cultural pluralism. Since diversity of ownership does not necessarily results in output diversity (for the reasons stated earlier), the latter is additionally regulated through other policy instruments (obligations to source a percentage of output from independent producers).

2. From Politics to Markets in Central and Eastern Europe

Media pluralism and diversity was a fundamental aim of European media policies (Ward 2002) even before it became the central value of the (European and global) countertrend to media globalization and the increasing commercialization and unification of the world media market. In a post-socialist context, attempts to ensure and protect media diversity and pluralism are burdened by the difficulties that occur regarding the democratization of the media in general, connected both to economic and political changes.

Media policy developed during the transitions of the 1990s in the European post-socialist countries in three, sometimes overlapping, phases. The first was focused on de-linking the media from the state, and included the achievement of freedom and independence from the political realm. This phase in most of the countries included the creation and restructuring of public service broadcasting systems and introducing structures that guarantee its independence from the political and economic forces (the success has been varied). In the initial phase of post-socialism, the battle was fought "in the political and administrative domain, and the 'enemy' was the state." (Jakubowicz, in Paletz et al. 1995, pp. 137).[4] The second phase was marked by attention to market developments and includes liberalization of telecommunications and broadcasting markets and the increased entry of the foreign capital in the media markets. This was also the time when attention starts to shift to threats from market developments, and the realization that pluralism is (surprisingly) at lesser risk from political than market pressures. The third phase is marked by European integration, and the main activity is harmonization of media legislature with the EU *acquis* in the audio-visual field. This phase includes more attention to the implementation of media legislation (a sore point for many countries of the region). The direction of post-communist transitions as well as the media development in CEE was without a doubt streamlined, organized and defined by the "magnetic pull of the EU".[5]

Regime change in Eastern and South-Eastern Europe has had a huge impact on media systems. The transformation from state-controlled, highly centralized media system, to the opening of the market formally started in the beginning of the 1990s, with the abolition of censorship and the implementation of new media regulation. However, elements of market privatization in CEE are recognizable already in the eighties, when new commercial enterprises started to appear.[6] In this period, Western European media firms started to show interest in Eastern European media markets, but, as Hans Heinz Fabris (Fabris in Paletz et al. 1995) pointed out, they were faced with problems in connection with "currency convertibility, poor economies, limits on western participation in joint ventures, poor working conditions, and the lack of new media legislation" (pp. 223). Nevertheless, at the end of the 1980s, after the overthrow of the regimes in 1989, foreign investors were attracted to enter these markets, populated by publics interested in their novel media content, by workers willing to work for lower salaries, as well as by the advantages offered by well-developed audio-visual production facilities in several of the CEE countries.

The domestic players involved in the changes of the CEE media systems, embraced the opening of the markets in an optimistic, even idealistic manner, firstly – because it meant autonomy from the state; secondly – because it was believed that the "demands of the market would prevent political partisanship" (Sparks 1998, pp. 172); thirdly – because it ensured employment security, and lastly – because it was believed that competition would raise the quality of programme output. Overall, the opening of the market was, in a general sense, positively accepted. In the media landscape, these changes resulted in the mushrooming of new titles in the newspaper market, the urge for new policy regulations of the area and the appearance of foreign investments in the media markets. The produced resentment as foreign investors gained control over media enterprises at low cost and were seen as social actors that could jeopardize the newly gained national sovereignty of the states.

If we look specifically at the common denominators of the media markets in the post-socialist states, they could be described as fragmented and small, with a large number of media. In addition, parallel media markets exists, divided according to linguistic/ethnic lines. The region is also burdened with the expansion of tabloid media, local and regional market concentration, and "close links between the largest and the most influential media on the one hand, and local owners of capital and political parties on the other" (Hrvatin & Petkovic, in Petkovic 2004, pp. 20).

Even though the old media system was in most countries instantly replaced by a market-oriented system, this applies more to the press than the broadcasting media. In regards to the press, as Jakubowicz points out, there were no "provisions governing foreign involvement in the press or against concentration of capital" (in Paletz et al. 1995, pp. 40), nor were there any policies that would promote the rights of minorities or other interest groups, which all resulted in a "wild" privatization of the press enterprises. However, the press boom that occurred in the initial phase of the post-socialist period was soon dampened by the introduction of tax systems, the increase of the production, print and distribution costs and other factors resulting in a decline of readership (Prevratil, in Paletz et al. 1995, pp. 162).

Broadcasting was not so easily released from political control. The newly elected political parties continued to control the broadcasting systems, due to the fact that "they believed that, as the new democratically elected governments, they deserve the support and have the right to use, radio and television to promote the process of reform." (Jakubowicz, in Paletz et al. 1995, pp. 40), In Croatia the early debates around the liberalization of the television sector centered additionally on the issue of sovereignty, as well as on the envisaged role of television in national cohesion building (Peruško Culek 1999a).

As Sparks has emphasized, the differences between the development of the press media markets and the broadcasting markets can, partially, be explained by the size of the media institutions: particular newspapers were smaller and, therefore, subjugated to particular division among private investors, while "the broadcasting institutions were so large, and so politically sensitive, that they could not simply be seized by one group or another" (Sparks 1998, pp. 104) – thus, all the political actors had to reach a consensus on how to set the rules for broadcasting operations, since they all claimed right to gain and sustain political power. The

Table 1: First launch of main western investors in television in Central and Eastern Europe

Country	Group	Channel	Launch
Bulgaria	News Corporation	bTV	2000
Croatia	Central European Media Enterprises (CME)	Nova TV	2000
Czech Republic	Central European Media Enterprises (CME)	TV Nova	1994
Estonia	Modern Times Group (MTG)	TV3	1993
Hungary	RTL Group	RTL Klub	1997
	SBS Broadcasting	TV2	
Latvia	Modern Times Group (MTG)	TV3	1998
Lithuania	Modern Times Group (MTG)	TV3	1992
Poland	–	–	–
Romania	Central European Media Enterprises (CME)	PRO TV	1995
Slovakia	Central European Media Enterprises (CME)	Markiza TV	1996
Slovenia	Central European Media Enterprises (CME)	Kanal A	1991

Source: EUMAP: Television across Europe: regulation, policy and independence (2005, pp. 173)

countries of the region introduced new broadcasting acts that enabled commercial television from the early 1990s — Czechoslovakia in 1991, Poland in 1992 and Hungary in 1995.[7] In some countries (Croatia is a good example), the early legislative framework was not sufficiently liberal for foreign investments: even though the legal framework for commercial television was in place in 1994, and the first licences (at the local and regional level) were already awarded in the next year, the limit of 25 per cent share in ownership of a television licence of any company (domestic or foreign) precluded serious interest of foreign investors until the change in the law after 2000.[8]

The prevalence of this "nation-building approach" in which media was seen as a tool of the state, playing an integrative role in the society, and establishing stability, control and homogeneity, by focusing on state interests (Peruško-Čulek 1999a, pp. 246–247) presented a mixture of new and old values and beliefs — one that embraces a new multi-party political system, and another that still claims the right to control communication channels. No wonder, then, that scholarly interests in the first decade of post-socialism were more oriented towards the question of media independence, freedom of speech, and — more generally — towards the establishment of a new media including the implementation of new media regulations modeled on "old" democracies. In addition, one practical research problem appeared as a result of the institutional changes: the lack of new, systematically classified and collected data. At the same time, as a reminiscence of the past, scarce existing data were not transparent to the public.

As market development in the media field was seriously tackled only after the political framework for media freedoms was more or less firmly established, studies dealing with media markets in CEE countries started to appear only at the end of the 1990s.[9] At the turn of the century, scarce data was available on media markets in the post-socialist region, regardless of the fact that CEE and the Baltic States were deeply penetrated by foreign investments. On a regional level, the existing data on European media markets referred to the "old" democracies, while CEE countries were briefly touched upon, as a matter of comparison and prediction of market trends.[10]

After 2000, with EU accession nearing, and with the issue of ownership concentration increasingly viewed in terms of media diversity and pluralism (mainly thanks to the sustained effort and activity of the Council of Europe, as well as repeated pressure from European Parliament), studies increasingly began to focus on the Central and Eastern European region.[11] After the EU enlargement to the East in 2004, more detailed analysis of media ownership regulations and the media market players in the Member States started to appear.[12]

At the same time, research and studies that focused on South-Eastern European countries were still more oriented towards the media landscape and its legislation, professionalism in the media associations that operates in the area, as well as towards the donor activities — still

Table 2: Number of households and different type of television channels

	TV households	Basic Cable	DTH Satellite	Terrestrial
Western Europe	142.7m	29% (40.6m)	6% (8,6m)	65% (93.5m)
Eastern Europe	92.1m	15% (14.0m)	6% (5.8m)	79% (72.3m)

Source: Pluralism in the Multi-Channel Market: Suggestions for Regulatory Scrutiny 1999/2000, p. 10

present in some of the analyzed states, due to slow changes in the processes of institutional change.[13] After 2000 studies with comparative data started to uncover the profile of the developing media markets of post-socialist Europe.[14]

The shape of media markets is related to general market strength and size of the economy. In the new Member States of the EU, market strength (in terms of per capita revenues) is between 25 and 75 per cent of the older Member States. The markets are smaller in terms of audiences as well as the populations in individual countries are generally smaller. That being said, the main characteristics of the present media markets are defined by the role in its development of advertising investments and by the predominant role of television (IMCA 2004).

Advertising revenues are the primary source of revenues in the audio-visual industry across the board, with a few exceptions where the public funds make up for significant percentages (i.e., in Slovenia with 44 per cent and Slovakia with 34) (IMCA 2004).

The strength of the audio-visual market (including public sources, television subscription fees, advertising and other revenues in radio, television, cinema and Internet) is still below the EU

Table 3: Share of advertising revenue within the media sector

Country	Television/market share in%	Press/market share in%	Radio/market share in%	Outdoor and other/ market share in%
Croatia***	49,7%	34,4%	7,0%	8,8%
Czech Republic*	43,8%	25,1	5,42	3,0%
Estonia**	26,0%	56,0%	9,0%	9,0%
Hungary*	62,0%	26,6%	4,2%	13,1%
Latvia **	33,0%	46,0%	12,0%	9,0%
Lithuania**	41,63%	43,17%	7,26%	7,9%
Poland*	50,0%	37,0%	8,0%	5,0%
Slovakia**	70,8% – gross	18,4%	6,8%	4,0%
	47,2% – net	33,1%	9,9%	9,7%
Slovenia*	43,3%	41,8%	7,0%	7,2%

*data from 2002

**data from 2003

***data from 2004

+ The data in the tables compiled from different country reports and the sums are sometimes not a 100 per cent; also, it is not clear if the data are for gross or net revenues.

Source: Final report of the study on "the citizen in the EU: obligations for the media and the Institutions concerning the citizen's right to be fully and objectively informed" European Parliament, prepared by the European Institute for the Media in 2004 (Kevin, D., Ader, T., Carsten Fueg, O., Pertzinidou, E., Schoenthal, M.).

Source for Croatia: Hrvatsko medijsko tržište: Regulacija i trendovi koncentracije, eds. Peruško, Z., Jurlin, K. [2006].

Source for Lithuania: The Baltic Media World, eds. Richard Baerug, author: Halliki Harro-Loit: The Baltic and Norwegian Journalism Market, pp. 90–121.

15 average of 182 euro per capita. The CEE audio-visual revenues are highest in Hungary (137), followed by the Czech Republic (99), Slovenia (88) and Poland (70), while the smallest are in Romania and Lithuania (15) (IMCA 2004). Television revenues account from 60 per cent in the Baltic countries, to more than 75 per cent in the largest market countries, and even more in others – up to 92 per cent (in Romania). The main composition of the television market in CEE includes one public service broadcaster with two channels and two commercial broadcasters at the national level. Public service channels show market strength in smaller and less developed markets (Bulgaria, Romania, Slovenia, and we could include Croatia as well), and the predominance of private commercial channels in larger audio-visual markets (with the exception of Poland, where public television is a major force on the market). These data point to the still-developing media markets in the CEE, as the characteristic of a developed market is a lower rate of television participation in advertising revenues, with a stronger influence of the print and other media. The IMCA study points to longer viewing times in many CEE countries in comparison to the EU 15 (average of 186 min. a day). The distribution of viewing times in CEE follows roughly the North-South divide in media consumption also seen in Western Europe – the northern countries' audiences read more, and the southern audiences spend more time with TV.

The EFJ report showed that the main investors in the CEE radio, television and press markets are German, Scandinavian and Swiss but also US-based and US-owned media groups. While US-based media groups conquered the audio-visual sector (Viacom, the Walt Disney Company, AOL Time Warner, Liberty Media, Central European Media Enterprises Ltd – CME, Scandinavian Broadcasting System SA SBS), European based media groups took control of the press market in CEE countries, especially the regional press (Passauer Neue Presse-PNP, Westdeutsche Allgemeine Zeitung-WAZ, Axel Springer Verlag, Ringier, Orkla) (EFJ 2003, pp. 7).

The main investors in television are foreign media groups: SBS (Viacom), CME (Estée Lauder), MTG (Kinnevik), RTL (Bertelsmann), LARI (Lagardère, HBO (Time Warner), UPC (Liberty Media), as well as the Canal+ group, Murdoch's News Corp, Endemol and AGB Italia (IMCA 2004, pp. 35). In many countries the global companies are in partnership with local players in the ownership/control of licences and broadcasting rights, but the know-how, technological and programme modernization as well as the imports of programme bouquets are determined by the foreign partners who provide the financial input.

Commercial operators have the highest audience share in Bulgaria (bTV, 31,8%, News Corporation), Czech Republic (Nova TV, 42,2%, CEM), Estonia (TV3 – 23,6% Modern Times Group), Hungary (RTL Klub, 29,4%, RTL Group), Latvia (LNT, 22,1%, Polsat, Janis Azis, Baltic Media Holdings), Lithuania (Tele 3 – 27,5%, MTG), Slovak Republic (TV Markiza – 33,7%, CME) and Slovenia (Pop TV – 27,0%, CEM) (however, the sum of audience share of the PSB (all channels) is higher than the commercial (PSB – 37,8%) in Slovenia).

PSB television (TVP) is more popular in Poland (TVP 1 has the highest audience share of 24,9%, and the total audience share of all four PSB television channels being 51,9%), Romania (TVR1, 22,1 %) and Croatia (HRT 1, 38,6%) with both PSB channels sharing 54,2% of the audience.

The level of concentration is high in most of the states, except for Latvia and Romania. However, one has to take into consideration that it is difficult for more than a few broadcasters to survive in smaller markets, due to financial reasons (low advertising spending). Hence, in smaller countries, external media pluralism, involving a large number of competing channels

Table 4: Foreign media companies operating in CEE markets (2003/2004)

Country	Press	Television	Radio
Bulgaria	WAZ (Germany) Springer (Germany)	Antenna TV SA (Greece) News Corporation (US) Eurocom (cable)	
Croatia	WAZ (Germany) Burda (Germany) Sanoma Magazines International (Finland) Styria Media Group (Austria)	Central European Media Enterprises Ltd (CME) RTL Television*	
Czech Republic	Vltava-Labe-Press (VLP) Ringier (Switzerland) Rhenische Post Group Sanoma Magazines (Finland) Passauer Neue Presse (PNP) (Germany) Burda (Germany) Springer (Germany) Bauer (Germany) Bertelsmann (Germany)	Central European Media Enterprises Ltd (CME) (without concession)	Lagardere (France)
Estonia	Schibsted (Norway) Marieberg (Sweden) Bonnier (Sweden)	Schibsted (Norway) Modern Times Group (MTG) (Sweden)	
Hungary	Bertelsmann (Germany) Axel Springer Verlag (Germany) WAZ (Germany) Heinrich Bauer Verlag (Germany) Sanoma Magazines (Finland) Ringier (Switzerland)	Scandinavian Broadcasting System (US) Bertelsmann (RTL) (Germany) Tele-Munchen Gruppe (Germany) Scandinavian Broadcasting System (US) Modern Times Group (MTG) (Sweden)	Marquard Media AG (Switzerland) Lagardere Group (France)
Latvia	Bonnier (Sweden) Orkla (Norway)	Modern Times Group (MTG) (Sweden)	Modern Times Group (MTG) (Sweden)
Lithuania	Bonnier (Sweden)	Bonnier/Marieberg (Sweden)	Modern Times Group (MTG) (Sweden)

Country			
Poland	Orkla (Norway) Passaueer Neue Press (PNP) (Germany) Bauer (Germany) Springer (Germany) Bertelsmann (Gruner+Jahr) (Germany) West Allgemeine Deutsche Zeitung Group (Germany) Edipresse (Switzerland) Marquard (Switzerland) Bonnier (Sweden)	Bertelmann (RTL) (Germany) Vivendi Universal (France) Scandinavian Broadcasting Systems (SBS) (US)	Lagardere Group (France)
Romania	WAZ (Germany) Burda (Germany) Ringier (Switzerland) Edipresse (Switzerland) Sanoma (Finland)	News Corporation (US) Central European Media Enterprises (CME) (US) Scandinavian Broadcasting System – SBS (US and Luxemburg)	Lagardere Group (France)
Slovakia	Passauer Neue Presse (PNP) (Germany) Bertelsmann (Gruner+Jahr) (Germany) Bauer (Germany) Holtzbrinck (Germany) Ringier (Switzerland) Sanoma (Finland)	Millennium Electronics Ltd. (UK) Central European Media Enterprises (CME) (US)	
Slovenia	Motopresse (Germany) Burda (Germany) Bonnier (Sweden) Leykam (Austria)	Central European Media Enterprises (CME) (US)	

* In 2003, RTL Group applied for the second national commercial channel in Croatia. The RTL Television was launched in 2004.
Adapted from: Medijska koncentracija: izazov pluralizmu medija u Srednjoj i Istočnoj Europi (Peruško 2003a, pp. 48–50; and the *Final report of the study on "the citizen in the EU: obligations for the media and the Institutions concerning the citizen's right to be fully and objectively informed"* European Parliament, prepared by the European Institute for the Media in 2004 (Kevin, D., Ader, T., Carsten Fueg, O., Pertzinidou, E., Schoenthal, M.).

Table 5: Television markets in Central and Eastern Europe: players and concentration levels

COUNTRY	Ownership of operators	Audience share – main channels	C3[15] – level of concentration
Bulgaria*	PSB: BNT (channel – Kanal 1) Main commercial operators: News Corporation: Bolkan Nyuz Korporeushan EAD (channel – bTV); CME (channel Nova TV)	bTV –31,8 Kanal 1 – 24 Nova TV – 17,9 Planeta – 2,3 Diema+ – 2 Evrokom – 1,3	C3=73,7 High concentration 32,6% – PSB 67,4% – foreign commercial operators
Czech Republic*	PSB: Ceska Televizie (CT), (channels CT 1 and CT 2) Main commercial operators: CET 21 (channel Nova TV) (PPF); FTV Primiera S.r.o., channel: Prima TV	Nova TV – 42,2 CT 1 – 21,5 CT 2 – 9,0 Prima TV – 21,1 Others – 6,1	C3= 84,8 High concentration 25,4% PSB 74,6% – domestic commercial operators
Estonia*	PSB – Eesti Televisioon (ETV) (channel – ETV) Main commercial operators: TV3 AS, (channel TV3) (Modern Times Group); Kanal 2 AS (channel – Kanal 2) (Schibsted Group) Perviy kanal Estonia – channel in Russian YLE – Finnish PSB	Eesti Television –18,0 TV3 – 23,6 Kanal 2 – 19,6 Pervyi Baltiiski Kanal – 9,6 RTR/Rossiya/RTR Planeta – 4,6 YLE – 1,4	C3= 61,2 High concentration 29,4% – PSB 70,6% – foreign commercial operators
Hungary*	PSB – Magyar Televizio (MTV) (channels – MTV 1 (free-to-air), MTV 2 (available on cable and satellite) and Duna TV). Main commercial companies: Magyar RTL Television, (channel – RTL KLUB); MTL SBS Televizio, (channel – TV 2); Duna TV Rt. (channel Duna TV); Viasat Hungaria, (channel: Viasat 3)	M1 – 15,5 M2 – 1,9 Duna TV – 1,7 TV2 – 27,4 RTL Klub – 29,4 Viasat 3 – 3,1 Video – 3,5 Minimax – 1	C3= 72,3 High concentration 21,4% – PSB 78,6% – foreign commercial operators

Latvia **

PSB – Latvijas Television, (channels LTV 1 and LTV 7)
Main commercial operator:
Latvijas Neatkariga Televizija (channel – LNT)(Polsat, Polish company – 60% share)
MTG (channel – TV3)
Channel 3+Baltic, Prevy Baltiysky Kanal Latvia and Perviy Baltijskyi Muzykalnyi Kanal – channels in Russian language

LTV 1 – 13,8
LTV 7 – 4,9
LNT – 22,1
TV3 – 17,1
PBK – 9,6
TV 5 RIGA – 2,9
3+Baltic – 2,4
Video – 2,7

C3= 53
Moderate concentration
26,0% – PSB
74,0% – foreign commercial operators (LNT, 60% share of Polsat – Polish company)

Lithuania **

PSB – Lietuvos Nacionalnis RAdijas ir Televizija (LRTV), (channels – LTV and LTV 2)
Main commercial operators:
LUAB Laisvas ir nepriklausomas Kanalas, (channel – LNK)
Tele-3, (channel – Tele 3);
UAB TV 1, (channel – TV 1)
Pervy Baltiysky Kanal Lithuania – Russian-language channel

LTV – 12,5
LTV 2 – 0,6
Tele 3 – 27,5
LNK – 26,2
Baltijos TV – 8,8
PBK – 3,6
5Kanalas – 1,6
Tango TV – 1,4
TV 1 – 1,4
Video – 0,6

C3=66,2
High concentration
18,9% – PSB
39,6% – domestic commercial operator
41,5% – foreign commercial operator

Poland **

PSB – Telewizja Polska SA (TVP) (channels – TVP 1, TVP 2, TVP 3 and TVP Polonia)
Main commercial operators – Canal + Cyfrowy SP (channel – Canal +); TelewiPolsat, RTL polska, (channel – RTL 7)
Telewizja Wisia SP, (channel –TV Wisla)

TVP 1 – 24,9
TVP 2 – 20,5
TVP 3 – 5,1
TV Polonia – 1,4
PolSat – 16,2
TV Wisla – 14,0
TV4 – 2,8
RTL 7/ TVN7 – 2,0
Canal + – 0,2

C3=61,6
High concentration
73,7% – PSB
26,3 – domestic commercial company

Romania*	PSB – TVR (TVR1, TVR2, TVR Cultural, TVRi) Main commercial operators: Media Pro International SA (Pro TV, Acasa), (CME), TV Antena 1 S.A. (Antena 1) (CCAI)	TVR1/Romania 1 – 22,1 TVR2 – 4 PRO TV – 16,7 Antena 1 – 16,6 Acasa TV - 9,2 Prima TV – 5,1	C3=55,4 Moderate concentration 39,9% – PSB 30,1% – foreign commercial company 30,0% – domestic commercial company
Slovakia**	PSB – Slovenska televizia STV, (channels – STV1 and STV2) Main commercial operators: Markiza, MAC TV – (channel TV Joj) Czech and Hungarian channels have an important market share	Jednotka STV 1 – 19,9 Dvojka STV 2 – 4,7 TV Markiza – 33,7 TVF Joj – 13,6 TA 3 – 1,1 CZ Channels – 11,2 HU channels – 8,5	C3= 67,2 High concentration 29,6% – PSB 50,2% – foreign commercial company 20,2% – domestic commercial company
Slovenia**	PSB – RTVSLO, (channels – TVS1 and TVS2 and third regional channel TV Koper Capodistria) Main commercial operators: Central European Media Enterprises Ltd, (channels Pop TV and Kanal A); TV3 Televizijska Dejavnost, (channel – TV3) Croatian channels available	TVS1 – 26,0 TVS2 – 10,4 Pop TV – 27,0 Kanal A – 8,1 Koper – 0,4 TV3 – 1,9 Croatian channels – 6,4	C3= 63,4 High concentration 57,4% – PSB 42,6% – foreign commercial company
Croatia***	PSB – Hrvatska radiotelevizija (HRT), (channels: HRT 1, HRT 2) Main Commercial operators: Central European Media Enterprises Ltd, (channel – Nova TV); RTL Group, (channel – RTL Televizija)	HRT 1 – 38,6 HRT 2 – 15,6 RTL – 24,4 Nova TV – 13,6 Other – 7,8	C3 = 78,6 High concentration 69,0% – PSB 31,0% – foreign commercial company

* Audience share main channels 2005 (based on the data provided in the Commission Staff Working Document, Media pluralism in the Member States of the European Union, Brussels, 16 January 2007, SEC(2007) 32).
** Audience share main channels 2004 (based on the data provided in the Commission Staff Working Document, Media pluralism in the Member States of the European Union, Brussels, 16 January 2007, SEC(2007) 32).
*** Source: Hrvatsko medijsko tržište: regulacija i trendovi koncentracije, eds. Peruško, Z., Jurlin, K. (2006) (*The Croatian Media Market: Regulation and Concentration Trends*, unpublished study for the Media Division of the Council of Europe).

controlled by different players is harder to sustain. Thus, one should focus more on internal pluralism (SEC(2007) 32).

The introduction of markets and democratic political systems in CEE countries has led to the creation of commercial privately owned media, which have vastly increased the media system diversity in comparison to socialist times. Media concentration trends, however, also appear in Central and Eastern Europe. Media markets in most countries of the CEE region are highly concentrated and with a very significant foreign ownership. In addition to concentration, in this region the transnational media concentration is particularly apparent, the extent of which as well as the consequences are not yet clear (AP-MD 2004).

The data presented above mainly speak to structural diversity of media systems in CEE and do not say much about the issue of internal pluralism and diversity of media content. It is in this area where, in the final analysis, we truly find the conditions for pluralism in the political and social sphere. So far, little evidence about diversity and pluralism of media content is available from the Central and Eastern European region, apart from statistics on broadcast programme genres (for instance, in the Yearbook of the European Audiovisual Observatory). The Croatian case will serve as an example of a more in-depth look at pluralism in a new media market. The data we base the analysis on come from two recent studies: Media markets in Croatia (Peruško, Jurlin 2006) and "Study on the assessment of content diversity in newspapers and television in the context of increasing trends towards concentration of media markets".[16]

3. From structural to content diversity in a new media market: the Croatian case

The adjustment of Croatian media to a democratic political system started with the transitional changes in the 1990s, but the consensus to embrace the pluralistic paradigm (as opposed to previously dominant state-building paradigm) was reached only after 2000.[17] With the acceptance of Croatia's application for membership in the EU and the commencement of the candidacy procedure, Croatian media policy entered its third phase, increasingly aware of the globalization and integration context.

The interest for analysis of media markets in Croatia appeared in the research community at the end of the 1990s, at the time of the first significant foreign investments in the media. The first study including market data – shares of the audience (viewers, listeners, circulations in the press), and shares in advertising – was published in 1999.[18] Thereafter, several research projects and published texts focused on the issues of concentration of ownership, pluralism and diversity.[19] All were based on scarce publicly available data, and none performed a systematic economic market analysis.

The television market in Croatia is clearly national, as fourteen regional and local television stations have an audience of less then 9 per cent. In radio broadcasting, however, the market is regionally structured (the study on media markets in Croatia identified 21 regional markets). Based on the Croatian average, 47 per cent of radio audiences are held by the local station, 18 per cent by the regional station, and 24 per cent by national commercial stations. Three national public channels have a joint share of 10 per cent of the radio audience. On average, in each county there are two or more strong radio competitors (Peruško, Jurlin 2006).[20]

Two commercial televisions at the national level are majority-owned by foreign companies (RTL Group in RTL Television, and CME in Nova TV). Public service television HTV operates two national terrestrial channels. The television market in Croatia is highly concentrated: the C3 for audience shares of the first three television channels in Croatia in 2004 was 78 per cent (Ward

2006), while the H index in 2005 was 0,54 (Peruško, Jurlin 2006). Croatian public television still has the leading market share of television audiences in Croatia, and, in spite of a decline, has retained the highest audience ratings among countries of comparable size. Adult audiences (over 34) predominantly watch two public television channels (HTV 1 and HTV 2) (59%). Young adults prefer RTL Televizija, followed by HTV 1, HTV 2 and Nova TV. Children are true fans of RTL (34.7%), followed by HTV 1, Nova TV and HTV 2.

The Croatian case differs (at the level of the media system) somewhat from the rest of the Central European countries in several pre-transition respects.[21] Television Zagreb (to become Croatian television HTV after 1990 and part of the public service broadcaster Croatian Radio Television HRT) was (unlike the television stations of the Soviet bloc countries which formed the Intervision exchange) part of the Western European EBU-based Eurovision programme exchange, along with all of the television centres of the former Yugoslavia. This afforded not only a glimpse into the news and documentary productions of Western European countries, but also into their fiction and entertainment productions (BBC productions especially). Programme scheduling also included American television programmes and films. *Peyton Place, Bonanza, Dallas* and some other well-known examples in the new television genres were familiar to Croatian audiences in the decades preceding the transition. Technological development of the Television Zagreb was before the 1990s on a par with that in smaller Western European countries (i.e., Austria). Both of these factors influenced the future development of the television market in Croatia,[22] making it a much harder prospect for commercial stations to obtain quick profits from old western soaps and quiz shows.

In terms of programme genres, the television market is very highly concentrated in the genre of cultural programmes, art and religion (where the HTV has almost 100% market share); and sports, music, information and political programmes, documentaries, science and education programmes (80% contributed by HTV). With those programmes, HTV contributes significantly to the diversity of the television programmes in Croatia.

In the information genre (news and political magazines), HTV 1 and HTV 2 combined have 80 per cent of the television audiences; followed by Nova TV (14%). The share of RTL in this genre is less than 7 per cent. In the entertainment genre, the leader is RTL (almost 50% of the audiences), followed by HTV (25%), and Nova TV with 20 per cent. There is strong competition in the markets of films, series and, to a lesser degree, in the entertainment and children's programming.

A further view into pluralism of content was afforded with the analysis of the genre output and news programme content.[23] Diversity and pluralism of media output can be said to exist if there is balance between the representation of actors carrying characteristics of race, ethnicity, gender, sexual orientation, educational background, ideas, beliefs etc. Diversity inspiring tolerance and respect among citizens can only be accomplished if these groups and categories are presented in an unbiased way.

At the level of content diversity, we present here only the distribution of programme genres and the diversity of topics and actors (i.e. direct speech) in television news programmes as they play out in the programmes of two privately owned broadcasters operating at the national level (NOVA TV, RTL TV) and the Croatian public service television (HTV).

Even though all three broadcasters give most space in direct speech to the anonymous general public (i.e., *vox populi*) in their news, the percentage is lower in the news of PSB (22%) compared to the privately owned broadcasters (Nova TV, 27% and RTL TV, 26%). Differences are visible in that the PSB gives more space to actors representing state institutions and public employees, government and ministers, national defense and security forces and civil servants, while privately owned broadcasters gives considerably more space to the general public, as well as to celebrities. They also give more space to company representatives and independent experts, but the differences are small. The division between commercial broadcasters' tendency towards infotainment (Delli Carpini, Williams 2001) and HTV's policy of giving more space to actors and institutions representing the state is clearly visible.

The most frequent topic covered in the news bulletins is that of home security and crime. This topic, a mainstay of tabloid media, is most present in RTL TV news (36,8% of all news topics) followed by HTV (33,3) with the lowest percentage in Nova TV (26,9). According to our sample, Nova TV seems to give importance to social issues (15,7% as opposed to 9,4 on RTL and 12,9 on PSB) while RTL TV gives a considerable amount of space to sport – 16,6 per cent (HTV has a special sport news programme broadcast after the evening news which was not part of this sample). Politics accounts for 12,9 per cent of the public service news, 11,5 on Nova TV and 8,1 on RT TV, while international affairs and politics gets around 4 per cent on all programmes. PSB gives more importance to business and economy compared to the commercial broadcasters (PSB 14,1 Nova TV 9,1 and RTL TV 7,6). Arts and culture are equally covered in the news of Nova TV and HTV, but neglected in RTL TV news (only 1,4%). The latter gives more space to human interests topics.

In the analysis of genre, the differences in the programme output of commercial and PSB television is most visible. While commercial broadcasters show 17,9 per cent (RTL TV) and 13,6 per cent (Nova TV) of light entertainment, HTV only has a percentage of 2,4 per cent of this genre. The differences are also visible in the time provided for soap operas: Nova TV – 25, 9 per cent, RTL TV – 19 per cent and the PSB – 8,2 per cent. RTL TV gives more space to comedy (15,1%), drama (9,4%) and chat and talk shows (6,6,%) compared to Nova TV and HTV, while Nova TV gives considerably more space to movies, 27,2 per cent, than RTL TV (18,8%) and HTV (16,9%). However, movies are the most frequent genre in Croatian national broadcasters programme viewed in total. HTV differs from the commercial broadcasters in that it has the highest percentage of news (5,5,%), children's television (9,7%), quiz and panel games (3,6%), political interview and discussion (3,4%) and documentary (3,3%). It also contributes to the diversity of content, and thus fulfils its role as to serve the public, since it is the only broadcaster that broadcasts school and educational programmes, breakfast television, magazine, arts and culture, current affairs, nature and wildlife, religion, cinema, history and hobbies and leisure.

4. What future for media pluralism and diversity?

The Croatian data clearly show that the majority of genres with socially important content (news and information, culture, political discussion and other topics not in the category of light entertainment – mainly devoted to reality television) are broadcast on the public service broadcasting channels HTV 1 and HTV 2. Not surprisingly, audiences at the national level are highly concentrated in these segments on the public service broadcaster. This highlights the important role of public service broadcasting in providing diversity of non-entertainment content, and the unwillingness of commercial broadcasters to invest in this type of programming. In this respect, the implementation of media policy needs to be questioned, as all broadcasters are obliged to contribute to cultural identity, the promotion of cultural creativity, and development of education, science and the arts.

Within the Croatian television market, the public service broadcaster is clearly more diverse in its programming that its commercial competitors. When we compare the findings, however, with the programmes of public service broadcasters in Norway, UK and Italy, HTV shows the smallest percentage of news and current affairs programmes (Ward 2006). HTV's largest programme segment is movies, as opposed to news programmes which are the largest segment in the other PSBs studied. The study of the Croatian media markets showed that in the segment of movies and series, the Croatian market is very well segmented and similar shares are held by all three companies broadcasting at the national level. This would tend to show that the public service broadcaster is giving in to commercial pressure. Whether the reason is the size of the market or the level of concentration, or both, Croatian PSB (still one with the highest audience ratings among CEE PSBs) is finding it difficult to cope with commercial pressure.

Regarding the diversity of topics and actors presented in the news, the differences between the public service broadcaster and the commercial stations are only slight, with some more emphasis in HTV on the economic and business news, political affairs and public service topics. HTV also gives a little more voice to "official sources" and none to celebrities. This could be assessed in two ways: the need of the public service broadcaster to compete for news audiences brings about the mainstreaming of its news output (although they have 80% of the national audience in news and current affairs programmes) or as improvement in regard to political independence shown in a greater similarity of news selection choices of the PSB to commercial broadcasters. The second evaluation is rather stretched, though, and even if partially correct – i.e., the news selection values have indeed changed in Croatia in the past decade (Stantić 2003) – the trend should not lead to the exclusion of hard news from the television news programme.

The Croatian data further tend to show a high degree of similarity of the largest programming segments of public service television and the commercial broadcasters, which could support the first thesis that commercial competition in a highly concentrated market brings about the convergence of programme output. The public service broadcaster is still producing the majority of socially important content. Media policy in Croatia should take further steps to ensure that the programming obligations in this respect are met also by the commercial broadcasters.

The Ward (2006) study of four European countries showed that a linear relationship could not be claimed between the content diversity in television news coverage and newspapers and the level of market concentration; and that resources, size of market and the regulatory framework are important elements in determining the diversity of the programming. One of the reasons for this honest conclusion is, of course, in the nature of the study: a snapshot of one moment in time. Media concentration is a process and not an event, and longitudinal data are necessary to analyse it. The Ward study for the Council of Europe is one of the rare attempts to directly link concentration and diversity and pluralism of content and is in that respect not only interesting for its results but also as a methodological basis for further work. Further study and attention to this issue are necessary, not only for a policy perspective, but from the research one as well.

Diversity and pluralism of the media in terms of their social and political role is increasingly linked to the growing consolidation of media industries at the international level. Some evidence of the negative relationship has been already accumulated. Recent European reports on media concentration and/or pluralism[24] point to several transversal conclusions:

■ The trend of global media consolidation shows up in national markets as growing concentration of media ownership/control by a relatively small number of media companies;

■ The trend is evident in the press markets, as well as in television broadcasting, cable and satellite transmission;

■ European countries are attempting to control the concentration by limiting market shares in regard to mergers and (sometimes) cross media ownership; this is showing not to be effective in terms of limiting the market presence brought about by performance (i.e. growth of companies);

■ Different models of regulatory measures are employed in different countries; there is no European model of ensuring diversity and pluralism;

■ There is as yet no discernible pattern of media concentration types in different models of media markets;

■ Though no causal relationship (in terms of empirical methodology) has yet been shown to exist, as regards the impact of concentration on diversity and pluralism of media content, the relationship is implicitly (and sometimes explicitly) assumed to be negative;

■ The role of public service broadcasting is highlighted in terms of securing diversity and pluralism at the level of media systems;

■ Regular monitoring is necessary at the European level of concentration, pluralism, and transnational aspects of media consolidation.

Regarding Central and Eastern European countries, we could add several more conclusions/concerns which emerge from studies and texts on the topic and apply specifically to post-socialist Europe:

■ The media markets are still developing and have not reached the levels of the EU 15;

■ Most of the media companies participating in the consolidation/concentration of media markets are of foreign origin;

■ This transnational aspect of media concentration is more pronounced in the East than in the West, where the media industry developed indigenously over decades. There is no clear conclusion if this is a negative development;

■ The issue of pluralism and diversity – in terms of the political and social role of the media in democracy – is compounded by the political history of state intervention and oppression of freedom of expression. Pluralism and diversity was after 1990s first provided by market-based media rather than the former state media and broadcasters, now transforming into public service broadcasters;

■ The transformation of state broadcasters into PSB is difficult – for political and financial reasons;

■ Across all the media in CEE, the professionalization of journalists has not yet been attained, making them more vulnerable to influences from both the owners and the political pressures;

■ Market data are still not thorough or transparent enough, and the analysis of concentration trends is only in an initial stage;

■ Studies on diversity and pluralism of content are almost non-existent (or not published in international journals or English-language publications).

In his discussion on market concentration and its effects, Timothy J. Dowd points out two different standpoints which could be applied to the analysis of CEE media markets as well:

a) the "cyclical account" (Peterson and Berger 1972, 1975; in Dowd 2004) emphasizes the negative effect, in which there is a negative relationship between concentration and diversity. As Peterson and Berger point out, long periods of high concentration are followed by short periods of de-concentration which occur when "unique historical factors produce a gap in the "majors' control" (Dowd 2004, pp. 1416) and the audiences demands different products that are not to be found in the supplies of the majors. This short period of competitiveness is then replaced by high concentration again, that occurs when the majors "absorb the new challenge." (Dowd 2004, pp. 1416)

The cyclical account might be used to explain the boom in the media sources and companies in the early transition years, when the market was open but not yet regulated. State media (old "majors") were deprived of their market dominance by the collapse of the communist system and market competition began. Commercial media (new "majors") then entered by a different door (the market) and the process of concentration began anew.

b) the "open system account" emphasizes the importance of the interaction between concentration and decentralized production: centralized production and high concentration dampen diversity, while the "expansion of decentralized production reduces the negative effect of concentration on diversity" (Dowd 2004, pp. 1444). According to this standpoint, the effects of concentration are softened by the logic of production: the ability of small independent firms to respond to new demands resulted in decentralized production of big firms (establishment of semi-autonomous divisions, or signing contracts with independents, project-based approaches, inter-firm alliances); in this way, the majors are able to keep track of new trends and demands of the market.[25]

We still lack sufficient data to test the second thesis. Even though we are seeing a growing number of studies focusing on CEE media markets, the data available are still not as detailed, comprehensive and, of course, cover a short time span (so it is difficult to show trends). Data on media markets and ownership structure need constant updating, due to constant changes of the dynamic environment in which they exist. There is no doubt about the importance of the media in contemporary societies; in a general sense, it reflects a society as a whole, since it provides "cues about the nature of social reality, for the agendas of our concerns, and for the climate of public opinion" (McLeod, Kosicki, Pan 1996, pp. 246). The latest European Commission (2007) document on media pluralism in Member States highlights the need to focus more on the study of internal pluralism, which means that new indicators for assessing pluralism should be developed.

In order to show the influence of ownership concentration on content, it is necessary to study both. While there is ample evidence of the concentration trend worldwide as well as in the region of Central and Eastern Europe, the relationship to content has not often been studied, especially in new European democracies. While this paper, based on data concerning Croatia market structures and content diversity, cannot be said to prove that the concentration of the television market reduces the diversity of programme content, some conclusions on the influence of competition and the structure of the media policy in respect to diversity of content have been drawn.

If we agree with Le Goff's thought — "L'illusion selon laquelle nous en aurions fini avec l'histoire et la barbarie, que nous pourrions désormais vivre dans un *monde pacifié et unifié par les lois du marché*, a fait long feu" (Le Goff 2002, pp. 188),[26] there is work to be done. The "invisible hand of the market" let loose in the field of media and communication cannot, on its own, produce the necessary conditions for pluralist democracy to flourish. Conscious reflection and democratic decision-making is necessary. Thus, the future level of diversity and pluralism in the media will reflect the (political and policy) decisions that we make today. This responsibility cannot be avoided.

Notes

1. See AP-MD reports *Media Diversity in Europe* and *Transnational Media Concentration in Europe*.
2. See the account of the early modern ideas in chapter 1, "Liberty of the press", and the relationship of the market to the liberty of the press especially pp. 44–50. J. Keane "The Media and Democracy". Polity Press. 1991.
3. The (few) positive impacts of communism/socialism on modernization (especially in Russia), or the negative impacts on freedom of expression or individual action cannot be elaborated here.
4. For comprehensive analyses of these changes, see Paletz & Jakubowicz (eds.) *Business as Usual*, and L. D. Paletz, K. Jakubowicz, P. Novosel eds. *Glasnost and After*.
5. Jurgen Kocka's phrase in the lecture on the "European project" at the Goethe Institute Zagreb, 1 February 2007.
6. For example, in Hungary, 1986, Radio Danubia.
7. See the introductory chapter by Sükösd and Bajomi-Lázár, "The second Wave of Media Reform in East Central Europe", in *Reinventing Media* for an account of the newer media policy developments in East Central Europe.
8. In the Croatian case the political framework before 2000 was probably an even more serious barrier to investment in the media.
9. For example, the publication *The Economics of the Media: The Convergence of the Transition Countries with EU Member States*, Hruby et al., deals with the ownership in new democracies of CEE, with a special emphasis on broadcasting markets in the 90s. A short general overview of television markets in Bulgaria, Czech Republic, Hungary, Poland, Romania, Russia and Slovakia is given, with a more detailed focus on Slovakia and, to a lesser extent, Czech Republic.
10. An example of this is the report *Pluralism in the Multi-Channel Market: Suggestions for Regulatory Scrutiny*, by C. Marsden, in which the author deals with media pluralism and convergence in Europe, with a main focus on western and northern European countries.
11. The European Federation of Journalists published a report in 2002, on media groups in "old" democracies, with data on the media landscape in regards to the broadcasting platform, cable, satellite and multimedia platform and the press platform, in order to identify the main players in the media markets. This was followed by a complementary report in 2003, named *Eastern Empires*, which concentrated on foreign media ownership in the press and broadcasting media markets in post-socialist countries.
12. The Final report of the study on "The Citizen in the EU: Obligations for the Media and the Institutions Concerning the Citizen's Right to Be Fully and Objectively Informed", prepared by the European Institute for the Media in 2005, includes data on broadcasting (radio and television) operators, press and publishing companies, cable and satellite companies and the share of advertising revenues. Probably the most comprehensive study on the structure of audio-visual media markets in the CEE was published in April 2004, commissioned in 2002 by the DG Culture of the European Commission prior to the last wave of accession and conducted by IMCA international media consultants & associates (*Etude du paysage audiovisuel det des politiques publiques des pays candidats dans le*

secteru audiovisuel. Rapport transversal, version definitive. IMPCA pour la commission européenne – DG EAC Etude DG EAC/59/020). Individual country reports are available for Cyprus, Estonia, Hungary, Latvia, Lithuania, Malta, Poland, Czech Republic, Slovakia, Slovenia, Romania, Bulgaria and Turkey. Among the first transversal publications on the regional developments in the audio-visual sector was published in 1992 by Eurocreation & IDATE, offering a view into the territory of the former Central and Eastern European film and audio-visual industries, new policies and international cooperation. The 1996 book *The Development of the Audiovisual Landscape in Central Europe since 1989* (John Libbey Media University of Luton Press), presented by the EU Commission in cooperation with Eureka Audiovisual, includes authored chapters on different countries with some data, but not in a comprehensive comparative mode. The 2005 EUMAP study (OSI/EU Monitoring and Advocacy Program) "Television across Europe: regulation, policy and independence" provides in-depth accounts of the country-by-country television systems with the greatest emphasis on the regulatory aspects and independence. The texts include market data as well, but the sources and methodologies are not always comparable. The latest study with market data is the Commission staff working-document *Media Pluralism in the Member States of the European Union* from 2007 which gives an analysis of EU Member States, including the two new ones: Bulgaria and Romania.

13. An example is the report *Media in South Eastern Europe: Legislation, Professionalism and Associations* of the Stability Pact for South Eastern Europe, conducted by the Media Task Force (2003). The report covers the media landscape in Albania, Bosnia and Herzegovina, Bulagarai, Croatia, Macedonia, Moldova, Montenegro, Romania, Serbia.

14. The first thorough attempt to assess media ownership in connection to pluralism in former socialist states, which includes South-Eastern Europe, is the *Media Ownership and its Impact on Media Independence and Pluralism* (ed. B. Petkovic). The report mapped eighteen European countries covering the legislative framework, the privatization processes and the media markets (press, television and radio), giving an important view on the situation in the whole region. A year later, in 2005, the monitoring report *Television across Europe: regulation, policy and independence* was released, focusing on the policy, regulatory, market and institutional aspects of commercial and public service television. It covers eight CEE countries that acceded to the EU in May 2004 (Czech Republic, Estonia, Hungary, Latvia, Lithuania, Poland, Slovakia and Slovenia), Bulgaria and Romania (which joined the EU in 2007), Turkey and Croatia (two candidate countries), four "old" EU Member States (France, Germany, Italy and the UK) and the potential EU-candidate countries in South-Eastern Europe (Albania, Bosnia and Herzegovina, Republic of Macedonia and Serbia).

15. Indicator of concentration of the three strongest players on the market, by which 0–35 represents low level of concentration, 36–55 moderate level of concentration and above 56 high level of concentration.

16. "Study on the assessment of content diversity in newspapers and television in the context of increasing trends towards concentration of media markets", by David Ward, Centre for Media Policy and Development (London), for the Media Division of the Council of Europe. The Croatian research was performed at the Department for Culture and Communication, IMO, Zagreb. The content analysis was performed simultaneously in Croatia, Italy, Norway and the UK. A quantitative content analysis was conducted in the period of two weeks (24.10.2005 – 06.11.2005), through the monitoring of daily newspapers and television news coverage, as well as genres appearing in the programmes of the broadcasters. For the purpose of this paper, the data set on television news coverage and genres was used.

17. For more information on the development of the Croatian media system and policy in the 1990s, see Z. Peruško Čulek (1999) *Demokracija i mediji*, Barbat: Zagreb and Z. Peruško 2003. "Croatia: The

first ten years. In Paletz & Jakubowicz eds., *Business as Usual*, Hampton Press, p. 111–145. For a detailed account of the television policy and sector in contemporary Croatia, see Z. Peruško 2005. "Croatia". In *Television Across Europe: Regulation, policy and independence*. EUMAP & NMP: Budapest.

18. Peruško Čulek, Z. ed. Nova medijska agenda: za europsku medijsku politiku u Hrvatskoj. *Medijska istraživanja*, vol. 5, no. 2: 1999.
19. Peruško, Z. «Medijska koncentracija: izazov pluralizmu medija u Srednjoj i Istočnoj Europ», Medijska istraživanja (god. 9. br.1) 2003 (39–58). Round Table on Media Pluralism IMO & Council of Europe http://www.imo.hr/culture/conf/medconf02/Media_Diversity_and_Pluralism.pdf; Malović, Stjepan, Report on Croatia, u Brankica Petkovic ur., *Media Ownership and its Impact on Media Independence and Pluralism*, Ljubljana, Peace Institute and SEENpM, June 2004. Peruško, Zrinjka. Mediji. Otvorenost društva Hrvatska 2005. ur. Simona Goldstein. Institut otvoreno društvo Hrvatska, 2005. Peruško, Jurlin, *Hrvatsko medijsko tržište*, (unpublished study).
20. Peruško, Jurlin, *Hrvatsko medijsko tržište*, (unpublished study).
21. Vesna Pusic on defining the transition in relation to the pre-transition character and history as well as to the post-transition dominant aim in the 1990s., also see Jakubowicz's interpretation and Peruško Čulek for a more detailed analysis of the 90s decade of transition in media and media policy in Croatia, in Paletz, Jakubowicz eds., *Business as Usual* (2003).
22. For a recent account of the Croatian television market, see Z. Peruško, "Croatia" in *Television across Europe: Independence*, 2005.
23. The data base set for the analysis of content diversity was created in the comparative "Study on the assessment of content diversity in newspapers and television in the context of increasing trends towards concentration of media markets", by David Ward.
24. Ward 2006, Ward 2004, EIM 2004, OSCE 2003, AP-MD 2003, AP-MD 2004, EFJ 2002, EFJ 2003, Commission Staff Working Document (SEC(2007) 32).
25. Dowd's research on one specific media market – that is, on the US recording industry – with a focus on new performing acts and new recording firms in the mainstream market, confirms the open-system account. This approach can be applied to other media markets as well, even though the network television companies (ABC, CBS) "increasingly rely on in-house production in the wake of deregulation and high costs" (p. 1445), thus, centralized production combined with increasing concentration results in the diminishing of program diversity
26. Le Goff, *La démocratie post totalitare*, 188.

References

Bagdikian, B. H. 2000. *The Media Monopoly*. Sixth Edition. Boston: Beacon Press.

Bennet, W. L. 2000. "Introduction: Communication and Civic Engagement in Comparative Perspective". *Political Communication*, vol. 17, no.4 (2000): 307–312.

Corcoran, F. and Preston, P., eds. 1995. *Democracy and Communication in the New Europe. Change and Continuity in East and West*. Cresskill: Hampton. Press, Inc, 1995.

Delli, C. M. X. and Williams, B. A. 2001. "Let us Infotain You: Politics in the New Media Environment" in *Mediated Politics: Communication in the Future of Democracy*, eds. Bennett, W. L. and Entman, R. M. (Cambridge, UK: Cambridge University Press, 2001), pp. 160–181.

Dowd, J. Timothy. 2004. "Concentration and Diversity Revisited: Production Logics and the U.S. Mainstream Recording Market, 1940–1990". *Social forces*, 82(4):1411–1455.

Doyle, G. *Media Ownership: The economics and politics of convergence and concentration in the UK and European media*. London: SAGE Publications, 2002.

EFJ, *European Media Ownership: threats on the Landscape. A survey of who owns what in Europe*, Brussels, European Federation of Journalists, 2002.

EFJ, *Eastern Empires: Foreign Ownership in Central and Eastern European Media: Ownership, Policy Issues and Strategies*. Brussels, European Federation of Journalists, 2003.

Einstein, M. *Program Diversity and Program Selection Process on Broadcast Network Television*. FCC, Media Ownership Working Group, 2002.

Etude du paysage audiovisuel des politiques publiques des pays candidats dans le secteur audiovisuel. Rapport transversal, version definitive. IMCA pour la commission européenne. DG EAC Etude DG EAC/59/020. 2004.

Guide du cinéma et de l'audiovisuel en Europe Centrale et Orientale. Eurocreation Production & IDATE, Institut d'Études Slaves, Paris. 1992.

Harcourt, A. "The Regulation of Media Markets in selected EU Accession States in Central and Eastern Europe". *European Law Journal*, vol. 9, no. 3. July 2003, pp. 316–340.

Harro-Loit, H. "The Baltic and Norwegian Journalism Market." ed. Baerug, R. *The Baltic Media World*. 2006. pp. 90–121.

Hillve, P. Majanen, P. and Rosengren, K. E. "Aspects of Quality in TV Programming: Structural Diversity Compared over Time and Space." *European Journal of Communication*, vol. 12, no. 3 (1997): 291–318.

Hruby et al. *The Economics of the Media: the Convergence of the Transition Countries with EU Member States*. Research Centre of the Slovak Foreign Policy Association Prešov, 1999.

Humphreys, P. J. *Mass Media Policy in Western Europe*. Manchester and New York: Manchester University Press, 1996.

Ishikawa, S. ed. *Quality Assessment of Television*. London: John Libby Media, University of Luton Press, 1996.

Keane, J. *The Media and Democracy*. Polity Press. 1991.

Kevin, D., Ader, T., Carsten Fueg, O., Pertzinidou, E., Schoenthal, M. *Final report of the study on "the citizen in the EU: obligations for the media and the Institutions concerning the citizen's right to be fully and objectively informed"* European Parliament, prepared by the European Institute for the Media (2004).

Le Goff, J.-P. *La démocratie post totalitare*. Paris: La Découverte, 2002.

Libbey, J. *The Development of the Audiovisual Landscape in Central Europe since 1989*. Media, University of Luton Press, 1996.

Lindblom, Ch. E. *Democracy and Market System*. Norwegian University Press, 1998.

Marsden, T. C. "Pluralism in the Multi-channel Market: Suggestions for Regulatory Scrutiny". *International Journal of Communications Law and Policy*, Issue 4, Winter 1999/2000.

McChesney, R. W. *Rich Media, Poor Democracy: Communication Politics in Dubious Times*. New York: New Press, 2000.

McLeod, M. J., Kosicki, M. G. and Pan, Z. "On understanding and Misunderstanding Media Effects", in *Mass Media and Society*, eds. Curran and Gurevitch. London and New York: Arnold, 1996.

Media pluralism in the Member States of the European Union. Commission Staff Working Document Commission of the European Communities Brussels, 16 January 2007 (SEC(2007) 32).

Media Diversity in Europe. Report Prepared by the AP-MD. Strasbourg; Council of Europe: Media Division; Directorate General of Human Rights, 2002.

Media diversity in Europe. Council of Europe: AP-MD Report prepared by the. Media Division, Directorate General of Human Rights, Strasbourg, December 2002 (H/AP-MD (2003) 1).

Media in South Eastern Europe: Legislation, Professionalism and Associations. The Stability Pact for South Eastern Europe, Media Task Force, 2003.

Review of Media Ownership Rules, Ofcom: Office of Communication, 2006.

OSI, EUMAP: Television across Europe: regulation, policy and independence. EU Monitoring and Advocacy Program, Network Media Program, vol. 1–3. 2005.

Paletz, L. D., Jakubowicz, K., Novosel, P. eds. 1995. Glasnost and After: Media and Change in Central and Eastern Europe. Cresskill, New Jersey: Hampton Press, Inc.

Petković, Brankica (ed.) 2004. Media Ownership and its Impact on Media Independency and Pluralism. Peace Institute, Ljubljana.

Peruško Čulek, Z. Demokracija i mediji. Zagreb: Barbat, 1999a.

Peruško Čulek, Z. ed., et al. 1999b "Nova medijska agenda: za europsku medijsku politiku u Hrvatskoj", Medijska istraživanja, vol. 5, no. 2. (1999).

Peruško, Z. 2003a. "Medijska koncentracija: izazov pluralizmu medija u Srednjoj i Istočnoj Europi". Medijska istraživanja, vol 9, no 1 (2003): p. 59–75.

Peruško, Z. 2003b. "Croatia: The first ten years". In Business as Usua, eds. Paletz, D. and Jakubowicz, K., Hampton Press.

Peruško, Z. 2005a. "Mediji" Otvorenost društva Hrvatska. Ed. Simona Goldstein. Institut otvoreno društvo Hrvatska.

Peruško, Z. 2005b. "Television across Europe: Regulation, Policy and Independence: Croatia" in Television across Europe: Regulation, Policy and Independence, ed. OSI, EU Monitoring and Advocacy Program (Budapest: Open Society Institute, 2005), pp. 427–481.

Peruško, Z., Jurlin, K. et al. eds. 2006. Croatian Media Markets: Regulation and Concentration Trends. IMO:Zagreb (unpublished study).

Roth, A. 2004. "The Ecology of a Dual Television Market: Competition and Diversity in the Netherlands." 6th World Media Economics Conference, 12–15 May 2004, HEC Montreal, Canada, 2004.

Sparks, C., Reading, A. Communism, Capitalism and the Mass Media. London: Sage, 1998.

Stantić et al. Politika u programu HTV-a. Zagreb: Hrvatski Helsinški odbor za ljudska prava, 2003.

Sükösd, M., Bajomi-Lázár, P. "The Second Wave of Media Reform in East Central Europe" in Reinventing Media: Media Policy Reform in East Central Europe, eds. Sükösd, M. and Bajomi-Lázár, P. (Budapest: CEU Press, 2003), pp. 13–27.

Transnational media concentrations in Europe, report prepared by the AP-MD, Media Division, Directorate General of Human Rights, Council of Europe, Strasbourg, February 2004, AP-MD (2004).

Ward, D. 2002. The European Union Democratic Deficit and the Public Sphere. An Evaluation of EU Media Policy. Amsterdam, Berlin, Oxford, Tokyo, and Washington D.C.: IOS Press, 2002.

Ward, D. Final Report: Study on the assessment of Content Diversity in Newspapers and Television in the context of increasing trends towards concentration of media markets. Media Division. Council of Europe. MC-S-MD (2006)001, 2006.

Whipple, M. "The Dewey-Lippmann Debate Today: Communication Distortions, Reflective Agency, and Participatory Democracy". Sociological Theory 23:2 June 2005: American Sociological Association, Washington.

Williams, G. European Media Ownership: Threats on the Landscape. A Survey of who owns what in Europe. European Federation of Journalists, Brussels, Belgium, 2002.

Zakon o medijima, Narodne novine br.: 59, 10.5.2004.

Zakon o elektroničkim medijima, Narodne novine br.: 122, 30.7.2003.

Zakon o telekomunikacijama, Narodne novine br.: 122, 17.07.2003.

Zakon o Hrvatskoj radioteleviziji, Narodne novine br.: 25, 07.02.2003.

Zakon o zaštiti tržišnog natjecanja, Narodne novine br.: 122, 30.07.2003.

PART THREE: OBJECTIVITY VS PARTISANSHIP AND FANDOM

HOW WILL IT ALL UNFOLD? MEDIA SYSTEMS AND JOURNALISM CULTURES IN POST-COMMUNIST COUNTRIES

Epp Lauk

The fall of the communist regimes in the Central and Eastern European (CEE) countries nearly two decades ago opened completely new avenues for the development of their media systems and journalistic professionalism. The processes that ensued – adaptation to free market conditions, opening up of a variety of information sources that had been inaccessible before, seemingly unlimited freedom of expression, an accelerating new technological revolution (the Internet and digitalization) – were rapid and simultaneous. The media and journalists found themselves in a certain normative vacuum, and there was confusion as to how to behave in the changing public sphere where the old patterns did not work and new ones were yet to be introduced or adapted. Furthermore, journalists and other media professionals also faced emerging generation tensions, pressures from the new political elites, media owners and investors, and the uncertainty of employment conditions. At the same time, post-communist media systems have been affected by global trends: market concentration, (hyper)commercialization, fragmentation of channels and audiences and drastic newsroom cutbacks. These general factors have influenced the development of journalism cultures in all post-communist countries, albeit in different ways

The core of *journalism culture* comprises journalistic discourse in its various formats and practices (such as textual norms, genres, writing styles etc.), written and unwritten ethical norms and values, and perceptions of the roles and functions of journalists and journalism in society (Hallin & Mancini 2004; Mancini 2000). Broadly speaking, journalism culture has been defined as the character and performance of journalism as an institution, profession and discourse in a concrete economic, political and cultural context (Carey 1969; Croteau & Hoynes 1997; Weaver 1998).

Hallin and Mancini (2004) compare professionalism in different media systems, clearly demonstrating the connections between the characteristic features of journalism cultures and the contexts of the media systems. A number of universal aspects exist against which journalism cultures can be compared at the macro level: conditions of the freedom of expression and the extent of state intervention (media policy and appropriate legislation), market development, the nature of links between the media and political parties ('political parallelism'), and aspects of professionalization (codes of conduct, self-regulation etc). In addition, technological and organizational factors play an increasing role. Local political, economic and cultural peculiarities, however, create specific journalism cultures in particular countries.

Arguably, one can find a broader variety of journalism cultures in Central and Eastern European countries than in established Western European democracies, which derive their professional philosophy of journalism predominantly from the Anglo-American or 'liberal' model. In the early years of rapid transition to the free market and open society in at least some post-communist countries, there was no consensus among journalists as to how the newly achieved press freedom was to be used or what guidelines to follow. Although journalists were generally aware of the principles of 'good journalistic practice' and ethically responsible reporting, the legal and/or conventional framework that would have motivated them to follow these principles was still missing. Both the functions and roles of journalists as professionals and the media system as such in the changing society needed to be redefined and reshaped. Therefore, it was quite natural to look for the models to emulate in the more developed western democracies.

Attempts to export western models

The Anglo-American or 'liberal' model of journalism has been generally accepted by media practitioners and theorists as an ideal of responsible and professional journalism. Being widely discussed and theorized in scholarly books and textbooks, this model has also become, as pointed out by Paolo Mancini (2000: 267), an 'ideology' for professionalization and for interpretation of the mass media system. This model views the media as a communication channel between government and citizens. They are to provide citizens with objective, balanced information, necessary for individual decision-making. They are also to form and mediate public opinion and scrutinize and criticize the activities and performance of politicians and the power elite generally. In order to fulfil these functions, the media must have legal and institutional support from the state, such as protections of freedom of expression, access to information and an independent judiciary. In turn, the media are expected to use their power responsibly and to establish self-regulatory institutions in order to safeguard this responsibility. The international principles of journalists' organizations define professional journalism as 'supported by the idea of a free and responsible press' and call 'for professional autonomy of journalists as well as a measure of public accountability' (Nordenstreng 1998: 132).

It became a common assumption both in the East and West that journalism in post-Communist countries would naturally develop towards this model and would adopt professional values and standards recognized by the media in developed western democracies. Western experts and journalists took it for granted that the 'liberal' journalism model would be the best goal to achieve. Efforts were made to export it to East-Central European new democracies. A veritable army of professionals from the West and the US travelled to the newly liberated countries in the early 1990s to offer their knowledge and experience in 'profession-building'.

These efforts at exporting the philosophy and elements of the 'liberal' model became, however, for various reasons much less successful than anticipated. In many instances and unexpectedly for all parties, a good deal of misunderstanding and irritation emerged. This happened largely because the western experts did not have an adequate picture of the traditions and history of local journalisms and of the level and content of journalists' education. They also tended to underestimate the professional experience of their local colleagues. They seemed to believe that nothing but propaganda journalism had existed in these countries until the collapse of communism swept it away, leaving an empty space to be filled up with a new professional culture. A Polish journalist, Wojciech Maziarski, reflected the feelings of many Eastern European journalists in the following words: "Western journalists decided to be good to us, assuming that we are people coming from the bush and it is necessary to enlighten us" (Kwiatkowski 1995, quoted by Hadamik, 2005: 212). Journalism culture in Poland, as demonstrated by several authors (Curry 1990; Oledzki 1998; Johnson 1999; Klossowicz 1999; Jakubowicz, 2003; Hadamik, 2005), had long and rich traditions that had helped to maintain the opposition spirit and professional values during the years of the communist regime. 'Fact-centred' journalism, which is the core of the 'liberal' model, has by no means superseded advocacy journalism and political engagement that are deeply rooted in Polish journalism (Hadamik 2005). According to Jakubowicz (2003: 238–239), many journalists "still think that it is their duty to take sides in the many divisions within Polish society and promote the cause they support". Convinced they are better informed, due to their access to various exclusive sources, journalists feel responsible for fostering what they think is politically 'right' and good for the development of democracy in their country. Such a perception, however, is not conducive to neutral and objective analysis or 'fact-based' reporting. Furthermore, mere reporting has not really been regarded as true professional work; lots of emphasis is put on commentary (Hallin & Mancini 2004). Gross (2003: 267–268) describes something similar in post-communist Romania, where journalists perceive themselves as an elite and are convinced that they are not only transmitters of accurate and balanced information, but discoverers of the truth and providers of opinion. The result may be highly politicized journalism of views and of partisanship.

It is only to be expected that in countries that had experienced long periods of restricted freedom of expression and censorship, where journalists simultaneously fulfilled an ambiguous role of propagandists of the official ideology on the one hand and the public's advocates on the other, opinionated journalism is very much viable. According to a survey, conducted in Latvia in 1998 (Shulmane 2000), journalists still largely saw themselves as providers of opinion and interpretation (53 per cent of Russian-speaking journalists and 32 per cent of Latvian-speaking journalists) and guardians of the public's interests (53 per cent of Russian-speaking journalists and 36 per cent of Latvian-speaking journalists). In Estonia, a quarter of journalists in 1995 believed that helping people to form opinion, to influence their value assessments and attitudes is a very important task of journalists, while 58 per cent considered it important. There is clear parallel to the pre-independence decades when in 1988, 45 per cent of Estonian journalists regarded opinion-formation as a very important function (data from the surveys carried out by the Department of Journalism and Communication of the University of Tartu in 1988 and 1995).

In the case of Russia (but also in Ukraine and Belarus), unfavourable conditions for the freedom of expression and the disastrous financial situation of news organizations in the early 1990s prevented the emergence of the free media on a large scale (except for a few independent newspapers and television stations). By the middle of 1995, more than 85 per cent of Russian newspapers had failed to achieve financial independence and most of the 10,500 newspapers in the country had a print run of fewer than 10,000 (Mills 1999: 125).

The press and broadcasting still remain largely controlled by the economic and political forces and serve their interests. Russian journalists, according to a study in 2005, largely believe that it is their natural role to serve as collaborators of those in power. The idea that journalism should function as an extension of the government is still alive and well (Pasti 2005: 93, 101).

Another reason why the 'liberal' model could not take root in Russia is close to that of the Polish case – western values were neither applicable nor adaptable to the existing cultural context. According to Mickiewicz (1998: 52–53), some Russian journalists at Russia's largest private television network, NTN, "engaged in a deliberate effort to impose Western journalistic values and styles", but it appeared to be something from outer space. Mickiewicz quotes a Moscow television critic: "They think we – this provincial lot, undisciplined, unnecessarily emotional, unable to organize – need to adapt Western intellect and only then will Russians finally learn how to live, work, think and feel, as in America". Culturally, journalism in Russia seems to develop within the influence of two opposing forces: deeply rooted 'Eastern' values such as collectivism, respect for central authority, social harmony and unity etc., and 'Western' values such as individualism, creativity, market economy and the rule of law. These 'Eastern' values and patterns of behaviour go far back in the history of Russia and have become a part of its people's identity (cf. de Smaele, 1999). Russian journalism will gradually adopt many features of democratic journalism, but may never be entirely replaced by the 'Western' model.

Also of importance in this context is a significant feature of journalism in the CEE nations, going back to the nineteenth century – its engagement in nation-building processes and its enlightening and instructive character, which is not typical of Anglo-American journalism. From the mid-nineteenth to the early twentieth century, the Czech, Slovak, Hungarian, Romanian, Estonian, Latvian and Lithuanian press strongly contributed to the development of national identities and culture in national languages. For the Baltic nations, the press also served as a safeguard of national languages during the periods of Russification in the late nineteenth century as well as at the end of the 1970s and beginning of the 1980s. The nineteenth-century Polish press became an important national institution and political forum during the partition periods. The Polish press also served as a safe haven for the Polish language at a time when the Polish state was non-existent (having been partitioned by the three neighbouring powers: Russia, Prussia and Austria) and a source of employment for the members of the elite (more in: Johnson 1999). It was a mission of the press in these (oppressed) nations to educate their readers, to teach them about their own history, literature, language and to keep national values alive. Lots of original *belles lettres* and translations from other languages were published in the newspapers and magazines. Literary traditions had their impact on newspaper discourse with valuing characteristically individual style and expression, polished language and use of various linguistic methods. In many ways, these features are still alive in journalism cultures where there has been certain continuity of traditions throughout history.

Development of journalism culture in the Baltic countries has differed to an extent from the rest of the post-communist countries and has probably come closest to the concept of the 'liberal' model. Traditions of the nineteenth-century enlightening and instructive journalism, as well as the short and rapid period of modernization of journalism between the two world wars, became almost entirely forgotten during the 50 years of the Soviet occupation. There was no one to ensure the continuity of old traditions, since during the first year of the Soviet rule (1940/1941) and during World War II, as all the journalists perished and the profession of journalism ceased to exist. In the course of the Sovietization of the press, all journalists who had worked in the 'bourgeois' press were fired. New people were employed (even if they had no journalistic experience) from amongst those who demonstrated loyalty to the new regime. Journalists who did not want to co-operate or had been involved in political life during Independence, were arrested and deported in 1941 or shot. In Estonia, for example, nearly 700 journalists worked for 281 newspapers and magazines at the beginning of the Soviet occupation in 1940. After World War II, only a score or so of the pre-war journalists who deserved the trust of the new authorities continued to work in the re-established Soviet press. Several escaped to the West at the end of the war. There is still no information about the destiny of 211 Estonian journalists who disappeared during 1940 through 1946.

For ten years after World War II, journalists for the Estonian communist press were trained in the journalism schools and faculties of the Communist Party colleges and journalism faculties in Moscow and Leningrad. However, most of the journalists were inexperienced, with insufficient education and with limited knowledge of languages (there were even "journalists" without sufficient command of the Estonian language). Loyalty to the communist authorities was more important than professional skills and knowledge. The situation changed when journalism education was established at Tartu University. The birth of journalism education in Estonia in 1954 can be seen as resulting from a mistake of the ideological supervisors of the time. They underestimated the importance of the mother tongue as a means of national survival and maintenance of a spirit of opposition to the ruling regime. The Ministry of Education permitted journalism to be included in the curriculum of Estonian language and literature. Consequently, journalism education was based on subjects that could not be faulted on ideological lines — linguistics, the history of Estonian culture and the traditions of national press. At the same time, research into Estonian journalism history was launched. During the ensuing decades, several generations of critically minded journalists started their careers, many of them in key positions in the Soviet Estonian media system. A significant group of these journalists were committed to 'telling the truth' to the people; they challenged the constraints of the official ideology, using metaphorical language, allegories and allusions. This generation left the scene during the first five years of the new Independence because of age and retirement. Interestingly, the generation replacement in Estonian journalism coincided with the beginning of the political and societal transition (see more in: Lauk 1996).

Concurrent with the generation shift of journalists in the early 1990s and an influx of untrained young newcomers into the field (51 per cent of journalists entered the field between 1990 and 1995), the fact-centred news concept was gradually adopted. Journalists learned to use the American invention of the inverted pyramid. In Estonian journalism, this structure of news became especially popular after a university teacher had spent half a year in the editorial office of *Newsweek* and started to teach it at the University of Tartu and on mid-career training courses. The journalists, however, fail to fully apply this concept in practice. As text analyses confirm, too often, the news contains value-loaded expressions and judgements that replace facts, and the use of unidentified sources is beyond control.

Estonian journalists also readily identify themselves with the roles of being a 'neutral transmitter of information' and a 'watchdog'. According to a 1995 survey, the vast majority of Estonian journalists (99 per cent) considered getting information to the public quickly and investigating the wrongdoing of the powerful (87 per cent) as their most important tasks (Lauk 1996). However, journalists seem to lack a clear understanding of their watchdog role. In many cases, coverage of political scandals, presented by the newspapers as investigative journalism appears to be simply leak-driven reporting. Similar phenomena are depicted also in the other Baltic countries (Balčytiene 2005) as well as in Slovakian and Czech journalism (Školkay 2001:114).

Extremely liberal media policies and unrestricted freedom of expression in the Baltic countries have created relatively favourable preconditions for the adaptation of the principles and features of the 'liberal' model. New generations of journalists have no experience of Soviet journalism; their education follows the same principles of democratic journalism as elsewhere in Europe and many have also completed a part of their studies abroad. Thus, they are no strangers to the ideas of objective journalism, public service and impartial reporting. However, there are also forces, especially market pressures and growing commercialization, that work against the realization of these professional values in practice. Professionalization is a long process with its ebbs and flows, and less than two decades of the free press is only the beginning of this process in Estonia as well as in the other post-communist countries.

As discussed above, the Eastern and Central European experience clearly demonstrates that a universal model that can equally be applied to all media systems does not really exist. There are, indeed, similar characteristics and similar values that journalists in elective democracies share and that form a basis of common understanding of journalism, but they apply these characteristics and values in a variety of ways (cf. Deuze 2005). The special features and ways of development of journalism cultures in each country are determined by historical traditions, as well as specific local cultural, social and political conditions.

In the 1990s, under the pressures of the free market forces, where news organizations had enormous economic difficulties and were fighting for survival, they first adopted those practices and formats of 'western' journalism that helped them to survive in the market. This has involved, for example, changes of the layout of newspapers and magazines that received eye-catching front pages and covers in colour and with many pictures; headlines and subtitles became prominent and the news stories shorter. Many newspapers were changed from broadsheet to tabloid format that was regarded as being economically more expedient as well as more reader-friendly and attractive. This has also meant a change towards a more aggressive style of reporting that focuses on the details of the private lives of public figures, and even tends to use slang and vulgarisms. News in an entertaining format, mixing editorial content with advertising, sensational reporting and scandal-mongering, found its way into everyday journalistic practices. This was accompanied by disregard of the criteria and principles of 'good journalism practice' or ethical reporting, and of the borderline between justified public interest and privacy of individuals.

Values and norms cannot really be imported wholesale: they can only gradually become the guidelines of professional conduct in a long process of the development of journalism culture. Old traditions, where they exist, may support and foster this development. However, a rapidly changing environment, political and economic pressures on the media organizations and journalists have a contrary impact. Altogether, the nationally specific political and cultural circumstances will bring about diversity of possible directions of the development. It seems likely that a variety of models will take shape in post-communist countries, rather than simply the replacement of the communist model by the 'ideal' Anglo-American model, as predominant throughout this part of Europe.

Shift of the news paradigm

Together with the shift from total information control to an independent and free environment, journalists faced the need to re-define their professional values and standards, including a basic one – news presentation. It was not so easy for journalists to give up their old practices and norms or to adapt them to the new communication environment. Journalists in all post-communist countries had been subjected to the same set of rules, they had to follow the general "party line" if they were not part of the illegal *samizdat* sector; they were educated and socialized according to the principles of communist journalism, originating in the time of Lenin. It is not true, however, that the conditions were precisely the same everywhere; even censorship operated differently in different periods and regions. Therefore, the legacy of the communist era was not the same in all these countries.

The primary task of news presentation in former communist bloc journalism was not to chronicle daily events, but to glorify the Communist Party and its leaders. Thus, propaganda replaced information and public opinion – since it was the only opinion published (Lendvai 1981: 67). Propaganda is most effective when it is presented in journalistic formats, including news. As the main function of the news was to support the Communist Party's enterprise of building communism, this was also the leading criterion of newsworthiness. The consequence of the Party supervision and all-encompassing censorship was that bad news was not news, and the media reported primarily the achievements of "socialist construction" in industry, agriculture, culture, science and education. As news value was missing, most news items were not focused on topical details but presented as a homogeneous list of actions (Harro 2001: 109).

Manuals for censors with lists of forbidden subjects included accidents with human losses, public unrest, epidemics, crimes, jails, etc. There also existed a range of unwritten bans – facts, names, words and expressions that were not explicitly forbidden, but journalists were strictly advised not to use them. An old Estonian journalist recalled in his column in 1989: "For 30 years I was advised not to use the word 'Estonia' in my journalistic work. It was also wise to avoid using the words 'Estonian' and 'Russian'" (Lauk 2005: 315). According to a Romanian editor, "words such as *banana, orange, cheese, meat* and other food denominations were blacklisted because the censorship committees thought such words would inflame the hungry Romanian population at that time" (Dragomir 2003).

Information as an important component of power was the privilege of the Party elite in the former communist regimes. The elite decided what and when people were allowed to get to know. Political news reporting was especially centralized and controlled in all communist bloc countries. The media were obliged to use the news coverage provided by the central wire services (Sükösd 2000: 132) – MTI in Hungary, PAP in Poland, TASS in the Soviet Union etc. Using political news from the same sources, leading newspapers in all these countries conveyed basically the same world-view and the same stereotypes about a happy population, prospering citizens and a powerful economy (Lendvai 1981: 84). Filtering, rationing and delaying information was common practice. Independent, domestic or foreign political reporting was completely impossible, as was endorsement of any socio-political alternative to the existing socialist system (Sükösd op.cit.). The facts were interpreted in accordance with Party directives and very often, interpretations were offered as information. The Soviet *Pravda* was the model for all the main communist newspapers in the satellite countries and, indeed, in the former Soviet Republics; *Pravda*'s values and political priorities were reflected in Hungarian *Népszabadság*, Eastern German *Neues Deutchland*, Czechoslovakian *Rude Pravo*, Polish *Trybuna Ludu*, just to name a few.

According to Lendvai (1981: 90–91), there were also certain differences in what and how the communist press in these countries reported. The Hungarian *Népszabadság* was often "more outspoken about the many contradictions in a supposedly socialist society than any other Soviet bloc party organ"; the Romanian press demonstrated certain independence in some major foreign news reporting; Hungarian and Yugoslavian media could report about crimes, accidents and epidemics, while this was absolutely forbidden for the press within the borders of the Soviet Union.

In Hungary, Poland and Czechoslovakia, the party-state information monopoly was broken during the late 1970s and 1980s, when a growing number of independent sources and channels emerged. Most of these networks functioned illegally, creating a "second public sphere" of independent and foreign media (Sükösd 2000:135). In the Baltic countries, where large samizdat did not emerge, the opposition spirit was maintained in the cultural media that were less strictly censored and where rather strong social criticism was occasionally expressed. As Sükösd argues (2000:141), between 1988 and 1990 "the unrestricted political agenda of samizdat surfaced in the legal (official) public sphere and the two formerly separated public spheres merged into one". At about the same period of time, the hidden opposition discourse openly appeared in the weekly and regional press in the Baltic countries, and from 1989 onwards, the leading Estonian official daily, Rahva Hääl (The People's Voice), purposefully deviated from the communist party line (Høyer et al. 1993).

The change of the news paradigm was extremely rapid and dramatic. A new set of values suddenly governed the choice of news: the newsworthiness of events replaced ideology as the main criterion for publishing. Under the pressure of market competition, newspapers put a lot of stress on reporting and much less than before on commentary. Fact-based journalism, however, has not become the norm for several reasons: lack of reporting skills, various external pressures on journalists and editors, close connections with political or/and economic structures. Today, the main factor that influences the quality of news production seems to be economic dependence of the proprietors, both private and state. The need to make the newspaper into a profitable business is often the reason for deals with advertisers, enterprises or organizations, which seek positive coverage. A 1994 survey of 1,200 journalists in Russia's regional newspapers and television found that much news — positive stories and coverage — was covertly paid for by economic or political organizations. Nearly half of journalists in the survey (46 per cent) said that concealed commercial advertising in newspaper and television stories was "a standard practice". Another third admitted such practices took place (Mickiewicz 1998: 49). Koltsova (2001) describes how heavily news coverage in Russian television depends on journalists' and the owners' economic interests; and Pasti (2005) describes how often favourable coverage in the press has its origin in money changing hands. According to Koltsova (2001: 324, 330), Russian media organizations often have elaborate tariff systems for such services, with rates for hidden advertising ranging from 100 to 2,000 US dollars per story, depending on the size of audience. This is not only a Russian problem, but occurs also in other countries, even if less overtly. In 1996, the English-language weekly Budapest Business Journal reported that six out of seven leading daily newspapers in Hungary regularly accepted money for publishing promotional articles without identifying them as advertising or promotion (Hiebert 1999: 117).

In the Baltic States, where there is no direct political pressure on journalists, there is still very strong indirect economic pressure from the managers who want journalists to file stories that 'sell'. Publishers and editors commonly assess stories primarily in terms of their potential to attract as many readers as possible — and not of journalistic standards. The result is that journalists balance on the fine line between good and bad taste and very often sacrifice people's right for privacy in order to get a 'story'. For example, the Estonian leading daily, Postimees, reported in 2006 that doctors had diagnosed 'mad cow' disease in a woman in her sixties and that she had only a half a year to live. It was then added, however, that this was a different form of the Creutzfeldt-Jakob's disease from what is commonly known as the contagious 'mad cow' disease. There followed a statement by a doctor that an average person has only one-in-a-million prospect of catching this disease and that it would really take a post-mortem to confirm the diagnosis. The real point of the story – that Estonian doctors were able to diagnose a disease that occurs extremely rarely – was entirely missed.

Analysis of the news texts of Estonian newspapers also shows that journalists use anonymous sources more often for getting opinion than information, and that mixing facts and views is very frequent, especially in political reporting. There is also no need anymore for the use of carefully and subtly crafted language that was often the case under censorship for getting the message across between the lines. The news discourse has become more entertainment-oriented and sensationalistic and the style and language closer to colloquial – all features of tabloidization. This is, indeed, a global trend that does not leave journalism in post-communist countries untouched.

Impact of foreign investors on journalism cultures

The 'liberal' journalism model was, interestingly, not supported by the investors coming from western countries with developed journalism cultures. After the fall of communism, a new, untapped market opened up. The market's potential was estimated at 450 million consumers. As an American market analyst, William Dunkerley, put it: "The air is ripe for innovation and development. Investment capital is needed" (Dunkerley 1998). In 2007, Western European and Scandinavian media corporations controlled 85 per cent of the press markets in the CEE countries. As the advertising potential and revenues in Central Europe were much larger than in Eastern Europe (except Russia), the big western companies invaded these markets first and they dominate in all these countries (e.g., the print markets in the Czech Republic, Hungary and Poland are mostly controlled by German corporations), with the exception of Slovenia (see more: Hrvatin, Kučič & Petković 2004). It took some five to eight years for foreign investors to become interested in the smaller markets of Eastern Europe, like the Baltics. Norwegian Schibsted ASA and Swedish Bonnier Group in Estonia, for example, made their biggest investments as late as in 1998, by which time the market was shared among a handful of dominant national companies. Only then did they consider it safe to invest there. Today, Schibsted ASA owns 92.7 per cent of the largest national media company in Estonia. The Swedish Bonnier Group controls the largest Latvian national daily, Diena (readership of around 300,000), eleven regional newspapers and seven magazines, distribution and subscription services and printing facilities. Foreign investments in the CEE countries certainly bring benefits in terms of greater resources, product and management improvement and increased independence from national political elites.

There were also certain expectations that foreign owners' experience and know-how would be a good basis for the further development of journalistic professionalism and democratic media culture in the countries of their destination (Balčytiene & Lauk 2005:100). It was hoped that foreign investors would also invest in the improvement of journalism in their newly obtained outlets – in very many cases national opinion leaders. However, as Peter Gross claims, "there is no indication that the Eastern European media outlets that came under Western European ownership have in any way measurably improved their journalism" (Gross 2004:125). There are also strong indications that aggressive commercial policies are being pursued at the expense of journalistic standards. Dragomir (2003:36), in his report, refers to a Czech media manager claiming that his Swiss boss' motto was: "I do not care what you write, give them sex, gore, scandal, whatever, but bring me profit".

The main goal of foreign investors is, indeed, to make a profit, but should they ignore the questions: What kind of journalism develops as a result of their investment? How does their investment influence the local media culture and journalistic performance, the degree of editorial independence and journalists' professional autonomy? These questions become especially vital in small societies and less diverse media markets, where the largest national dailies are either wholly owned by foreign investors or, as in the Baltic countries, are co-owned with a national company. In such cases, the owners based in another country are likely to make strategic decisions about investment and staffing and, consequently, their commercial considerations dominate. Doug Underwood in his work "When the MBA's Rule the Newsroom" (1993) clearly demonstrates how owners can exert far-reaching influence on journalistic content through their economic strategies and newsroom organization. Their local managers and editors-in-chief are sitting simultaneously on two stools: they must guarantee profit to the foreign investors and they should be concerned about the quality of national journalism. Here, the conflict between the business orientation and social responsibility orientation becomes very obvious. Sometimes it even can become a political issue, as the Schibsted case in Estonia demonstrates.

Schibsted's Estonian flagship, the most influential opinion leader in the Estonian media — daily Postimees (The Postman) — claims to be a politically independent quality newspaper. In February 2005, the leaders of five mainstream political parties co-authored and sent an open letter to the management of the Schibsted Group claiming that Postimees had become a messenger of the political line of one particular party — the Reform Party. This letter was never published in Postimees. The competing daily Eesti Päevaleht (Estonian Daily) published it, and several hundreds of the readers' online comments reflected the politicians' concern. Postimees reacted with two articles — an emotional editorial diatribe against the co-authors and a commentary that criticized the competence of those who wrote the letter. All public comment to both the editorial and commentary on Postimees' online version was blocked. The response from Schibsted's headquarters was that they conduct business in Estonia and trust the local managers in their editorial independence without getting involved (Balčytiene & Lauk 2005: 101). Schibsted has not invested much effort to introduce the excellent journalistic standards that are so strictly followed in its home country, Norway, to its Estonian outlets.

This case is instructive in two ways. Within the conditions of a young democracy with underdeveloped political and media culture, the profit-making aims of foreign investors are inevitably accompanied by the growing power of their outlets in society and that certainly affects its politics and culture. It also demonstrates the importance of a carefully planned government media policy in the media systems where long traditions of public control over the media are absent. None of the Baltic States have imposed press ownership regulation or any other anti-monopoly provisions. The politicians in Estonia assumed that the owners would take responsibility, but were perhaps naively unaware that a liberal market policy and absence of an efficient accountability mechanism give the media, especially the press, nearly unlimited possibilities to set the agenda according to their business interests. Robert Picard (2004) has pointed out that managerial responses influence journalistic quality and produce practices that lower the social value of newspaper content. They also distract newspaper personnel from journalism to activities primarily related to the business interests of the press.

Self-regulation as a dimension of journalism culture

Legislation, public control and self-regulation are the three factors that together would be able to guarantee positive development towards a higher level of media's social responsibility – an important element of the 'liberal' concept of journalism – and support the development of journalism culture. However, governments and new political elites in the post-communist countries have been more concerned with gaining dominance over the media than to create conditions for their public service functions and respective accountability.

Media self-regulation emerged as a new development in some post-communist countries. The basic idea of self-regulation is that the media themselves are to ensure observance of rules of professional conduct and, in this way, increase their accountability and authority. Self-regulation is also aimed at preventing government interference. Voluntary adherence to the codes of ethics is motivated by the wish to gain and preserve the acceptance among the professional community and to demonstrate the awareness of journalists' responsibilities to society.

Developed democracies in Europe have introduced self-regulation institutions such as codes of professional conduct, press complaint commissions (or Press Councils) and the institution of the ombudsman. Codes of Journalistic Conduct are adopted today in seventeen post-communist countries, but the mechanisms or the bodies that would police their implementation are still missing in most of them. By itself, a code cannot influence the quality of reporting or prevent violations of ethical norms. It can simply be ignored or journalists may regard it as something irrelevant in their everyday work practice. A report on journalism in the south-eastern European countries says, "[...] people in the trade don't refer to the Code, they don't discuss or argue with it [...]; the Ethical Code seems not to have any practical meaning for Bulgarian journalists" (Širota 2005: 58). This seems to be typical of the vast majority of the post-communist countries (cf. Gross 2003).

The most developed self-regulation practices can be found in the Nordic countries, and they have also served as role models for establishing press councils in neighbouring countries. Thus, the Estonian Press Council and code of ethics largely follow the examples of Finland and Norway. The Swedish ombudsman institution has been an example for Lithuania, where, in addition, an Ethics Commission of Journalists and Publishers deals with the ethical issues of the media. Among former Soviet republics, self-regulation institutions have been established only in the Baltic countries and Russia, while Ukraine has a press ombudsman.

Bosnia-Herzegovina was the first country in south-east Europe to establish a Press Council in 2000, based on British experiences (and composed of representatives of journalistic organizations) and an enlarged Press Council with participation of publishers in 2006. Slovenia has an ethics commission of the journalists association. In Slovakia, a Press Council was established in 2002 by the Slovak Syndicate of Journalists and Association of Publishers of Periodical Press. In Slovakia, Association for Ethics in Journalism (also an NGO) was established shortly before the Press Council, but neither body has been able to make a strong impact on the ethical behaviour of Slovakian journalists. In the Czech Republic, the Union of Publishers took an initiative in 2000 to establish a Press Council, but it was never actually appointed because of disagreements among the members of the Union. In November 1998, the Union of Czech Journalists adopted a Code of Ethics and established an Ethical Commission (Kroupa & Smid 2004), but there is little evidence of its activities. Press Councils or respective bodies were also established in Hungary and Bulgaria as late as 2005. Also, in some countries, television or broadcasting councils deal with ethical issues in the electronic media (Slovakia, Lithuania and Poland).

Self-regulatory bodies in all these countries are relatively ineffective or have little real authority. Unstable, rapidly changing societies are not the proper environment for supporting the principles of self-regulation. The independence of news organizations and journalists is not efficiently protected by legislation, although the constitutions guarantee freedom of expression for all citizens and, more or less explicitly, also the freedom of the press. In some countries (e. g., Russia, Romania, Bulgaria) media laws are deliberately conceived to keep journalism under state control. In the early 1990s, the Press Law for Russia was so vaguely worded that many public figures took advantage by suing journalists for defamation. The Russian ultra-nationalist leader Vladimir Zhirinovsky alone filed over 100 defamation suits against journalists between the end of 1993 and the summer of 1994 (Mickiewicz 1997). Romania's Constitution of 1991 declares that the "freedom to express ideas, opinions, and beliefs" is "inviolable", but then adds that the law "prohibits defamation of the country and nation". In 2006, however, some steps were taken to decriminalize libel, but slander is still considered a criminal offence (Freedom House Report on Romania 2006).

Even where respective laws exist, their application is often inadequate. It takes time until the legislation becomes truly operative, and the same applies to the written and unwritten conventions, including journalistic professional standards. In the countries that are considered to have favourable conditions for press freedom (according to the Reporters Without Borders Press Freedom Index for 2006, the Czech Republic, Estonia, Slovakia, Latvia, Slovenia and Hungary rank among the top thirteen freest countries out of 168), corporate media seem to aspire to preserve the freedom of the press for their own ends. The crisis of the media self-regulation in Estonia today reflects these aspirations very clearly.

Within the context of unrestricted press freedom, the Estonian press enjoys the privilege to criticize everybody and everything, but is not tolerant of criticism of itself. The Rules of Procedure of the Estonian Press Council (established in 1991 and reorganised in 1997) oblige the news media to publish/air the full texts of its adjudications within seven days, in the case of a complaint. The publishers, however, in many instances, have ignored this commitment or when they did publish, they sometimes arbitrarily changed the wording. While the prestige of the press in general had been declining, editors-in-chief saw the rulings of the Press Council as a threat to the popularity of their own newspapers. Growing dissatisfaction of the publishers and editors-in-chief of six of the biggest Estonian newspapers with the adjudications of the Press Council resulted with a conceptual conflict between the Press Council and the Estonian Newspaper Association by late 2001. The Newspaper Association withdrew its membership and broadcasters (both private and public) followed suit. The Estonian Newspaper Association then established another press council – the Estonian Publishers' Press Council – for dealing exclusively with the complaints concerning its member publications. Public-service Radio and Television also joined this press council. Three of the nine members and the chairman of this PC are editors-in-chief and one member is a journalist of a Russian daily. The first chairman of it was the former managing director of the Estonian Newspaper Association.

The original Estonian Press Council, where seven members out of ten represent public NGOs and three are journalists, continues its existence and the adjudication of complaints. It provides expert opinion and evaluates the quality of the media content and performance. The adjudications of the complaints to the Estonian Press Council are published on its website (http://www.asn.org.ee).

According to the agreement within the Estonian Newspaper Association, newspapers refuse to publish the adjudications of the 'old' Press Council and do not respond to its requests for information. Furthermore, the editors-in-chief have told their journalists not to communicate with the Estonian Press Council, unless they want to lose their jobs. In this manner publishers and editors-in-chief gained full control over the adjudication and interpretation of the complaints. A broader discussion, critical of media, is effectively avoided as critical voices simply have no access to the newspapers. Cynical self-protection has thus replaced critical self-reflection. The latter, however, is an important means for improving quality of journalism and increasing the responsibility of journalists as professionals and the trustworthiness of their news organizations. The renewed Code of Ethics of the Norwegian Press states it very clearly (p. 1.4): "It is the right of the press to carry information on what goes on in society and to uncover and disclose matters, which ought to be subjected to criticism. It is a press obligation to shed critical light on how media themselves exercise their role" (Code of Ethics of the Norwegian Press 2005). The media themselves should initiate and carry on the public debate on the issues of the media quality and everyday performance. This is not, however, a popular practice in any of the post-communist countries.

The Internet and journalism culture

Societal transformation in the post-communist countries coincided with the global revolution in information and communication technology. Digitalization and the Internet have completely changed the information and entertainment production processes, the ways of consumption and the scope of potential audiences. The usage of the Internet in Europe in general, according to the Internet World Stats, has almost doubled (growth 199.5 per cent) during 2000–2007. Among the new democracies, the most advanced Internet countries are Slovenia and Estonia (positioned 29th and 30th in the world by Internet penetration, 55.5 and 51.8 per cent, respectively). They are followed by the Czech Republic and Latvia, with Internet penetration of 50 and 45.2 per cent (see table 1). Success in the spread of new technology and the Internet reflects the general economic advancement of the countries: in Albania, Serbia, Bosnia-Herzegovina, Macedonia, as well as Russia and Ukraine, the Internet is accessible to less than 20 per cent of the population. However, the Internet is spreading fast. Between the years 2000 and 2007, Internet penetration in Bulgaria, Lithuania and The Czech Republic quadrupled, while in Croatia, Latvia and Russia it grew about six-fold (Internet World Stats 2007). The growth of accessibility and usage of the Internet means a growing audience for the news media.

Technological innovations have always had an impact on journalism and journalistic work processes, enough to mention, for example, the introduction of the telegraph and the telephone. Today, the Web has become an integral part of newsrooms as an everyday information source and communication channel. The biggest impact of the Internet and World Wide Web on journalism is expressed by the emergence of online journalism. Does it bring new features into journalism cultures? Scholars, in general, agree that the main characteristics that functionally differentiate online journalism from other kinds of journalism are multimedia(lity), hypertext(uality) and interactivity (Dahlgren 1996; Paulussen 2004; Deuze 2001a, 2001b). The three differentiating dimensions of online journalism are strongly technology-bound and emphasize the role of modern communication technologies and their role in producing journalistic content. It can, therefore, be questioned whether this is a qualitatively new kind of journalism or just a new way of content presentation.

Most online journalism is not reporting, not generating story ideas and recording events, interviewing sources and gathering background information, but adapting stories for the Web and distributing them quickly (Singer 2003). This does not require traditional reporter's skills,

Table 1: Internet penetration by percentage of national population of CEE countries (March 2007)

Country	Internet Penetration
Slovenia	55.5
Estonia	51.8
The Czech Republic	50.0
Latvia	45.2
Slovakia	36.5
Lithuania	35.9
Belarus	35.1
Croatia	32.9
Hungary	30.4
Poland	29.9
Bulgaria	28.7
Romania	23.4
Macedonia	19.1
Bosnia-Herzegovina	17.3
Russia	16.5
Moldova	14.8
Serbia	13.9
Ukraine	11.5
Albania	6.1

Source: Internet World Stats http://www.internetworldstats.com/stats4.htm#europe

but much more technical knowledge. It has been argued that producing content online requires a different ability of writing – non-linear writing. This means that any story can simultaneously be spread out across a number of Web pages, having been 'cut' into smaller pieces. The users can access each of these pages separately, in any order they wish. A journalist must have the skill to make sure each content section offers the news as well as something else and is still part of the whole (Deuze 1999). The truth is that more specific technological skills and knowledge is required from journalists for producing content online than has ever been necessary in 'traditional' journalism.

How do journalists use the new technology and the possibilities of the Internet in the former communist countries? Estonia is one of the two most digitally advanced countries among them, so it is instructive to look at the surveys done among journalists in 2002 and 2005[1] (by the Department of Journalism and Communication of the University of Tartu).

In 2002, there were 64 per cent newspaper journalists among the respondents and a quarter of them said that they were, to various extents, involved in production of online content. In 2005, a similar amount of respondents (66 per cent) worked in newspapers and 98 per cent contributed to the online version.

The results of the two surveys demonstrate how fast the importance of the Internet as an information source for the journalists had been growing. In 2002, only one-third regarded the Internet an important information source in their everyday work. In 2005, all respondents reported the Internet being a very important or important source of information. It seems, however, that Estonian journalists still limit themselves to mostly national sources and do not make much use of international ones. Foreign media websites were not used at all by 32 per cent, news sites by 45 per cent and international databases by 85 per cent of respondents of the 2005 survey, and these numbers are only 2 to 4 per cent higher than they were in 2002. It is likely that a similar tendency can also be found in other countries, as the accessibility of the information on the Internet largely depends on the knowledge of foreign languages. In 2002, also the most popular search engine was Estonian (Neti.ee) and was used by 10 per cent more journalists than Google. In 2005, Google was the most popular search engine among all the respondents.

The three dimensions of online journalism (multimediality, hypertextuality and interactivity) presuppose specific technological skills of presentation (such as being able to write HTML, using picture processing and layout programs etc). It has also been argued that there is a direct correlation between possessing specific technological skills and job-finding success (Lowrey & Becker 2001; Harvey 2000). The results of the Estonian surveys, however, indicate that journalists are relatively slow in developing their IT skills: there is no significant progress in the skills of picture processing, using layout programs, writing HTML or updating data on the web-pages within the three years between the two surveys. All the journalists are the most confident in three basic IT skills – writing texts in Microsoft Word, using e-mail, and downloading data and files (99–100 per cent of respondents) that nowadays are regarded as a part of general education and are taught in high schools.

The editors and managers emphasize the importance of integration of traditional journalistic knowledge with technological and graphical knowledge. Multi-skilled journalists in 'converged newsrooms', however, are not yet common in either developing democracies or globally (Singer 2003). As Deuze (2005: 10) states, "The combination of mastering newsgathering and storytelling techniques in all media formats (so-called 'multi-skilling'), as well as the integration of digital network technologies coupled with a rethinking of the news producer-consumer relationship tends to be seen as one of the biggest challenges facing journalism studies and education in the 21st century."

It has also been assumed that the Internet could prompt a fundamental shift in journalists' role in the communication process (Singer 1998). The fact is that online journalists have wider possibilities to communicate with their readers and get immediate feedback. This is definitely a new dimension of the contemporary journalism culture and of people's participation in the public sphere.

The question whether online journalists have a different perception of their professional role is not yet exhaustively answered. American comparative surveys demonstrate that there can be found slight differences in role perceptions of online and print journalists. Two main conclusions emerge from these surveys. First, traditional 'public service' functions such as analyzing complex problems and investigating government claims are less important to online journalists than to their print colleagues (Brill 2001; Singer 2003; Cassidy 2005). Second, both the print and online journalists regard the information disseminator role the most highly, whereas the online journalists place a higher value on getting information to the public quickly than the print journalists (Cassidy 2005). Both tendencies may more reflect the different nature of the online work process than a real shift in role perceptions.

As to ethical standards, the studies seem to confirm that working under enormous time pressures online journalists put less effort into verifying facts and ensuring the reliability of the stories. Along with the enormous increase of the flow of information and speed of its transmission the intensity and speed of work of every individual journalist has been accordingly increased. In their survey on 203 American online journalists in daily newspapers, Arant and Anderson (2001) found that although nearly all respondents (97 per cent) agreed that journalism ethics and standards should be the same for both print and online publishing, almost half (47 per cent) claimed that they spend less time on checking the facts before publishing a story. Thirty per cent thought that the online sites of daily newspapers follow the general ethical standards less carefully than the print versions (see also: American survey 1999).

Journalists in the CEE countries do not yet have the same level of technologically advanced working conditions and training as their ICT-savvy colleagues in the Scandinavian countries, the Netherlands, the UK or Germany. New technology along with skills and knowledge of using it are, however, rapidly developing among the journalists in the CEE countries. It remains a question of future and further research, to what extent similar technological conditions in newsrooms and similar requirements for skills and knowledge would unify the working routines, understanding of news values and professional roles in various media systems, and to what extent journalism cultures develop along different paths due to local cultural, historical and socio-political circumstances.

Conclusions

After the fall of communism there were great expectations in both the post-communist countries and the established West that the model that would replace communist journalism would follow the Anglo-American paradigm. These expectations have not come true.

The export of the Anglo-American model failed for several reasons. This is the model for a stable society where the law of the freedom of the press is respected by the power elite and the public. The independence of the news organizations and journalists is not an exception, but protected by established legislation. It has taken the Anglo-American system almost 200 years to reach its current stage of development, based to a great extent on the progress and experience of several revolutionary developments such as the Age of Enlightenment, the Age of Reason, the social revolutions of the mid-nineteenth century, the hegemony of trade unions throughout the twentieth century, etc. Post-communist development has only lasted nearly two decades, the societies are in permanent flux, simultaneously fighting legacies of the past and searching for successful ways of building up the states based on the rule of law, as well as civil societies. Media systems and journalism cultures are an integral part of this development, and they reflect the character and level of political culture and economic progress that each of these societies has been able to achieve.

These societies have yet to achieve the stability and balance that have been preconditions for the development of the Anglo-American journalism model. In addition, this model has developed mainly for the press, but today the press is competing with other media for the public's attention.

In many cases (Russia, Ukraine, Romania, to a lesser extent Poland, Slovakia, Hungary, Lithuania, Bulgaria) there was almost unlimited freedom of expression in the first years after the fall of communism, but it was later reduced for legislative or economic reasons or both. Media self-regulation has not taken effect in any of the post-communist countries, although most of them have established codes of ethics and Press Councils or other self-regulatory bodies. Effective self-regulation needs an environment where the media organizations are ready to discuss media quality and ethical problems openly and publicly. Such conditions are still missing in these countries.

Foreign investments that the post-communist media systems so desperately needed and that have enormously contributed to their technological and economic progress, did not significantly support the development of journalistic professionalism. On the contrary, their pursuit of profit has fostered commercialization and homogenization of the contents and markets, in particular in the small media systems (e.g., the Baltics). The independence of journalists is hampered by the owners' interests in profit to the extent that they agree to contribute to the hidden advertising and give favourable coverage in exchange for money. This seems to be common practice in Russia, but there are similar cases also in other countries.

The failure in exporting the 'liberal' model of Anglo-American journalism also indicates that national, historical and cultural traditions, as well as the unique features of the progress of local journalism cultures, may have a stronger impact on the development of post-communist journalism than has ever been admitted. Such an admission would, however, lead to acceptance of the idea that the paths of future development can take very different directions in markedly disparate countries. We can, however, speculate that further digitalization and "Internetization" may ultimately have a unifying influence on journalistic work processes and consequently on how we view good journalism. This will not, however, occur because of the global standardization of technology and ideas, but as a result of the breathtaking decrease in the time delay from news occurrence through news production to audience reception and feedback.

Note

1. In 2002, the questionnaire was sent to all media organizations that had their e-mail addresses on the Web (71). In addition, 37 questionnaires were handed over personally and 269 requests were sent to the personal e-mail addresses of journalists. From a total of 377 requests, the feedback was 158 (42 per cent, which is approximately 13 per cent of the estimated number of journalists in Estonia). It was possible to choose between completing the questionnaire online, on the paper after printing it out from an attached Word file or to use body text of the e-mail. A total of 138 respondents gave permission to contact them later again. In 2005, 112 of them were accessible and they received a questionnaire that was slighty changed, but many questions were the same as in 2002. A total of 69 responded, which makes a 61 per cent response rate.

References

American survey (1999). Online news managers say small staff sizes and demand for speed and scoops erode standards', http://facstaff.elon.edu/andersj/summary.html (accessed 10.12. 2006).

Arant, D. & Anderson, J. Q. (2001). 'Newspaper Online Editors Support Traditional Ethics', Newspaper Research Journal 22, Fall, pp. 57–69.

Balčytiene, A. (2005). 'Media Modernization and Journalism Cultures in the Baltic States and Norway' in Bærug, R. (ed.) The Baltic Media World (Riga, Flera Printing House), pp. 169–184.

Balčytiene, A., & Lauk, E. (2005). 'Media Transformations: the Post-transition Lessons in Lithuania and Estonia', Informacijos Mokslai/Information Sciences 33, Vilnius University Publishing House, pp. 96–109.

Brill, A. M. (2001). 'Online Journalists Embrace New Marketing Function', Newspaper Research Journal 22:2, pp. 28–40.

Carey, J. W. (1969). 'The Communications Revolution and the Professional Communicator', The Sociological Review Monograph 13, pp. 23–38.

Cassidy, W. P. (2005). 'Variations on a Theme: The Professional Role Conceptions of Print and Online Newspaper Journalists', Journalism & Mass Communication Quarterly 82: 2, Summer, pp. 264–280.

Code of Ethics of the Norwegian Press (2005). http://www.presse.no/V%E6r%20Varsom% 20English.htm (accessed 31.03.2007).

Croteau, D. & Hoynes, W. (1997). 'Media/Society. Industries, Images, and Audiences', Thousand Oaks, London, New Dehli, Pine Forge Press.

Curry, J. L. (1990). 'Poland's Journalists: Professionalism and Politics', Cambridge, Cambridge University Press.

Dahlgren, P. (1996). 'Media logic in cyberspace: repositioning journalism and its publics', Javnost/The Public 3:3, pp. 59–72.

De Smaele, H. (1999). 'The Applicability of Western Media Models on the Russian Media System', European Journal of Communication 14: 2, pp. 173–189.

Deuze, M. (1999). 'Journalism and the Web. An Analysis of Skills and Standards in an Online Environment', Gazette 61:5, pp. 373–390.

Deuze, M. (2001). 'Understanding the Impact of the Internet: On New Media Professionalism, Mindsets and Buzzwords'. Ejournalist, 1:1, (a) http://www.ejournalism.au.com/ejournalist/deuze.pdf (accessed 05.07. 2006).

Deuze, M. (2001). 'Online Journalism: Modelling the First Generation of News Media on the World Wide Web'. First Monday, 6:10, October (b) http://firstmonday.org/issues/issue6_10/ deuze/index.html (accessed 05.07. 2006).

Deuze, M. (2005). 'What is journalism? Professional identity and ideology of journalists reconsidered', Journalism 6:4, pp. 442–464.

Dragomir, M. (2003). 'Fighting Legacy: Media Reform in Post-Communist Europe', Senior Fellows Publication, The Atlantic Council of the United States. http://www.acus.org/library-by_topic-eur.asp (accessed 03.03. 2007).

Dunkerley, W. (1998). 'East European Media: an Enigmatic Market', The Investor's Journal of Legislative Impact, 5, http://www.publishinghelp.com/rmedia/renigma.pdf (accessed 30.03. 2007).

Freedom House Report on Romania (2006). http://www.freedomhouse.org/template.cfm?page= 251&country=7043&year=2006, (accessed 31.03. 2007).

Gross, P. (2003). 'Romanian Mass Media and Journalism in the Midst of Transition' in Paletz, D. L. & Jakubowicz, K. (eds.) Business As Usual: Continuity and Change in Central and Eastern European Media (Cresskill, New Jersey, Hampton Press, Inc.), pp. 243–78.

Gross, P. (2004). 'Between Reality and Dream: Eastern European Media Transition, Transformation, Consolidation, and Intergration', East European Politics and Societies, 18:1, pp. 110–131.

Hadamik, K. (2005). 'Between East and West or Simply "Made in Poland"? The Many Different Styles of Today's Polish Journalism' in Høyer, S. and Pöttker, H. (eds.) Diffusion of the News Paradigm 1850–2000 (Göteborg, NORDICOM), pp. 211–226.

Hallin, D. C., & Mancini, P. (2004). 'Comparing Media Systems: Three Models of Media and Politics', Cambridge University Press.

Harro, H. (2001). 'Changing Journalistic Conventions in the Press. Empirical studies on daily newspapers under different political conditions in 20th century Estonia', Oslo, Faculty of Arts, University of Oslo.

Harvey, C. (2000). 'New Courses for New Media', American Journalism Review, December. http://www.ajr.org/Article.asp?id=252 (accesed12.12.2005).

Hiebert, R. (1999). 'Transition: From the End of the Old Regime to 1996, in Aumente J. et al., Eastern European Journalism: Before, During and After Communism (Cresskill, New Jersey, Hampton Press, Inc.), pp. 79–123.

Hrvatin, S. B., Kučič, L. J. & Petkovič, B. (2004). 'Media Ownership: impact on media independence and Pluralism in Slovenia and other post-socialist European countries' (Ljubljana, Mirovni Institut). http://www.mirovni-institut.si/media_ownership (accessed 12.12. 2006).

Høyer, S., Lauk, E., & Vihalemm, P. eds., (1993). 'Towards a Civic Society. The Baltic Media's Long Road to Freedom. Perspectives on History, Ethnicity and Journalism', Tartu: Baltic Association for Media Research/Nota Baltica Ltd.

'Internet World Stats' (2007). http://www.internetworldstats.com/stats4.htm (accessed 30.03. 2007).

Jakubowicz, K. (2003). 'Change in Polish Media: How Far to Go Yet?' in Paletz, D. L. & Jakubowicz, K. (eds.) Business As Usual: Continuity and Change in Central and Eastern European Media (Cresskill, New Jersey, Hampton Press, Inc.), pp. 205–242.

Johnson, O. V. (1999). 'The Roots of Journalism in Central and Eastern Europe' in Aumente, J. et al. Eastern European Journalism: Before, During and After Communism (Cresskill, New Jersey, Hampton Press, Inc.), pp. 5–40.

Klossowicz, J. (1999). 'Kulturelle Zeitschriften und die Kultur in den Medien' in Kopper, G., Rutkiewicz, I. & Schliep, K. (eds.) Medietransformation und Journalismus in Polen 1989–1996 (Berlin, Vistas), pp. 247–256.

Koltsova, O. (2001). 'News Production in Contemporary Russia. Practices of Power', European Journal of Communication, 16: 3, pp. 315–335.

Kroupa, V. & Smid, M. (2004). 'Co-operative regulatory systems in the media sector of the Czech Republic' (A report for the study on co-regulation measures in the media sector). http://www.hans-bredow-institut.de/forschung/recht/co-reg/reports/2/Czech_Republic2.pdf (accessed 31.03.2007).

Lauk, E. (1996). 'Estonian Journalists in Search of New Professional Identity', Javnost/The Public 3: 4, pp. 93–106.

Lauk, E. (2005). 'Restoring Democratic Discourse in the Estonian Press (1987–1990)' in Bolin, G., Hammer, M., Kirsch, F-M., Szrubka, W. (eds.) The Challenge of the Baltic Sea Region (Stockholm, Södertörn University College), pp. 307–322.

Lendvai, P. (1981). 'The Bureaucracy of Truth. How Communist Governments Manage News', London, Burnett Books.

Lowrey, W. & Becker, L. B. (2001). 'The Impact of Technological Skill on Job-Finding Success in the Mass Communication Labor Market', Journalism & Mass Communication Quarterly, 78: 4, Winter, pp. 754–770.

Mancini, P. (2000). 'Political complexity and alternative models of journalism: The Italian case' in De-westernizing Media Studies (London and New York, Routledge), pp. 265–278.

Mickiewicz, E. (1997). 'Changing Channels: Television and the Struggle for Power in Russia', New York, Oxford University Press.

Mickiewicz, E. (1998). 'Transition and Democratization: The Role of Journalists in Eastern Europe and the Former Soviet Union' in Graber, D., McQuail, D. and Norris, P. (eds.) The Politics of News: The News of Politics (Washington, D.C., CQ Press: A Division of Congressional Quarterly Inc.), pp. 33–56.

Mills, D. (1999). 'Post-1989 Journalism in the Absence of Democratic Traditions' in Aumente, J. et al. Eastern European Journalism: Before, During and After Communism (Cresskill, New Jersey, Hampton Press, Inc.), pp. 124–146.

Nordenstreng, K. (1998). 'Professional Ethics: Between Fortress Journalism and Cosmopolitan Democracy' in Brants, K., Hermes, J. and van Zoonen, L. (eds.), The Media in Question: Popular Cultures and Public Interests (London: Sage), pp. 124–134.

Oledzki, J. (1998). 'Polish Journalists: Professionals or Not?' in Weaver, D. H. (ed.) *The Global Journalist. News People Around the World* (Cresskill, New Jersey, Hampton Press), pp. 277–297.

Pasti, S. (2005). 'Two Generations of Contemporary Russian Journalists', *European Journal of Communication*, 20:1, pp. 89–115.

Paulussen, S. (2004). 'Online News Production in Flanders: How Flemish Online Journalists Perceive and Explore the Internet's Potential'. *Journal of Computer Mediated Communication*, 9: 4, July, http://jcmc.indiana.edu/vol9/issue4/paulussen.html (accessed 31.03.2007).

Picard, R. (2004). 'Commercialism and Newspaper Quality', *Newspaper Research Journal*, 25: 1, pp. 54–66.

Reporters Without Frontiers 2006 ranking. (2006). http://www.rsf.org/rubrique.php3?id_rubrique= 639 (accessed 20.03.2007).

Singer, J. B. (1998). 'Online Journalists: Foundations for Research into Their Changing Roles', *Journal of Computer Mediated Communication* 4: 1, 1, http://jcmc.indiana.edu/vol4/issue1/singer.html (accessed 31.03.2007).

Singer, J. B. (2003). 'Who are these guys? The online challenge to the notion of journalistic professionalism', *Journalism* 4: 2, pp. 139–163.

Shulmane, I. (2000). 'Professional Identities of Latvian and Russian Speaking Journalists in Latvia' (Riga); Manuscript.

Sükösd, M. (2000). 'Democratic Transformation and the Mass Media in Hungary: From Stalinism to Democratic Consolidation' in Gunther, R. & Mughan, A. (eds.) *Democracy and the Media: A Comparative Perspective* (Cambridge, Cambridge University Press), pp. 122–164.

Širota, J. (ed.), (2005). '*Ethics and Journalism in Southeastern Europe: a comparative analysis of the journalistic profession*', Belgrade, Media Center. http://www.seenpm.org/index.php?nav=ut.php&p=9 (accessed 24.01.2007).

Školkay, A. (2001). 'Journalism in the Czech Republic and Slovakia' in Bajomi-Lázár, P. & Hegedüs, I. (eds.) *Media and Politics. Conference Papers on the Interplay of Media and Politics* (Budapest, New Mandate Publishing House), pp. 111–134.

Underwood, D. (1993). '*When MBAs Rule the Newsroom. How the Marketers And Managers are Reshaping Today's Media*', New York, Columbia University Press.

Weaver, D. H. (ed.), (1998). '*The Global Journalist. News People Around the World*', Cresskill, New Jersey, Hampton Press Inc.

Changing Journalistic Discourses in the Baltic States – How to Deal with Cheap Journalism

Auksė Balčytienė

Foreword

This article addresses post-transitional development of the Baltic media. It shows that new structural changes unfolding in political, economic, social and technological realms directly affect the media and their practices, with an increasing emphasis on commercialized, elitist and entertainment-oriented content. A process of commercialization and commodification of news implies homogenization, monopoly, as well as increasing control, threatening democratic processes and development of civil society.

In this article, our analysis of Baltic media development proceeds in three stages.

First, general conditions for media systems convergence are assessed in order to shed some light on challenges that journalism is now facing. Second, three factors which have a decisive impact on journalistic discourse are discussed and examples of change across the small news markets of the three Baltic countries are given. The three factors are liberal media policy, changes in political communication and the impact of new technologies.

Finally, and most importantly, we argue that in this vulnerable and rapidly changing news environment it remains crucial to preserve professional journalistic discourse. Autonomous journalism should preserve the democratic functions of the media – citizens must recognize professional (independent, informed and critical) journalism which, indeed, should help them to make knowledgeable decisions and participate in the political public sphere.

The article proposes that, on the one hand, *open public debate and media criticism* is one logical path towards the development of accountable, autonomous and professional journalism in the Baltic States. On the other hand, in the modern and varied information space, various *ways and means* (such as public funding) should be applied to support new civic initiatives and thereby support media that serves the citizens' needs and is free from commercial interests.

This article is written from a Lithuanian perspective with comparative data from two other countries, namely Estonia and Latvia. The article aims at a systematic comparison between the three countries. It intends to identify and explain similarities between these countries' media with respect to the particular phenomena (e.g., media liberalism, changes in political communication culture and Internetization), being analysed. Hence, the emphasis here is on comparative theory building and testing, with the three countries themselves acting as cases.

1. General Introduction

A common understanding in contemporary media studies is that convergence of media systems and homogenization of journalism is becoming a worldwide trend. Authors advancing such views (Curran & Myung 2000; Hallin & Mancini 2004) have proposed that structural and organizational changes in the media systems (for example, ongoing media concentration, news commercialization, growth of infotainment and over-abundance of hybrid media) have taken place within the media of all countries, with more or less similar results.

The widely discussed commercialism of the media is, in fact, strongly related to social changes. One important argument for media commercialization is the idea that the centrality of organized social groups and importance of loyalty and solidarity to group interests is giving way to greater *individualism* (Hallin & Mancini 2003). As those scholars claim, the erstwhile mass audience is evolving into a new audience with personalized interests and the media are re-orienting towards producing news and information as a "saleable product".

Indeed, journalism is reported to be changing. Scholarly debates are now focusing on, and stressing, the process of homogenization of journalism, evident in practices of journalistic genre-mixing, shifting quality of news, more sensationalist and entertainment-oriented reporting, blurring boundaries between news, promotional writing and advertising (Erjavec 2005; Harro-Loit & Saks 2007). Mixed discourses (hybrid discourses of PR, advertising and journalistic texts) proliferate in magazines, broadcast media and online versions of newspapers. According to Scott (2006), new newsworthiness criteria seem to replace all others, meaning that journalism is no longer seen as just serving the public interest. Rather, the criterion guiding news selection is profitability.

The arrival of interactive technologies, too, contributes to the process of information "commodification": it provides means to personalized experience for information consumers.

At the same time, although the economic logic makes media similar to some extent, there still are certain differences due to history, traditions and culture of journalism which make media performance different in different national settings. In short, then, economics and technology are forces leading to the convergence of media systems, while specific political and cultural factors account for divergence. A historical perspective is very important, too: media institutions evolve over time; at each step of their evolution, past events and institutional patterns inherited from earlier periods influence the direction they take.

Thus, as we discuss post-transitional changes in the media of the Baltic countries, as well as professionalization of journalism, it becomes important to assess a number of issues. For instance, it becomes crucial to question whether economic liberalization, resulting from a laissez-faire media policy, has brought more pluralism and news diversity in the media of the Baltic States. Another concern is related to the changes in political communication cultures. While discussing the development of democratic media, it is important to ask whether professionalization of political communication amounts to a real shift in the communication of politics in both quantitative and qualitative terms, or is it simply related to the growth of specialized knowledge on political issue management? One more issue is related to the impact of the Internet on journalism. Wide application of Internet media and development of online journalism has a clear ability to transform journalistic discourse and journalistic culture. So, it becomes important to ask whether or not technological innovations and online journalism have changed and radically enhanced the Baltic public sphere, thus, leading to a more diverse picture of social reality by offering space for different opinions, topics, events and voices.

2. Studying Preconditions for Journalism Change: Observations on Economic, Political and Technological Realms

2.1 Laissez-Faire Policy as a Factor in Media Change, Development and Diversification

Since the re-establishment of independence in the Baltic countries in 1991, media systems in Lithuania, Latvia and Estonia have gone through a change of paradigm. The newly acquired political freedom brought along a libertarian media model, which promoted liberalism and very little regulation (see, e.g., Vihalemm 2002). A decade after the political breakthrough, a new wave of media re-structuring and orientation took taken place, with more diverse forms of ownership and cross-media concentration.[1]

In very general terms, news markets in all three Baltic countries are small, media regulation is very liberal and media accountability is weak (Harro-Loit 2005).

In all three Baltic countries, the desire to limit state intervention into the mass media can be traced back to, and explained by, the communist past, when everything was under strict government control. Compared to other parts of the world, mass media regulation in the Baltics is very liberal. In Lithuania, Latvia, and Estonia there is no law for the regulation of media concentration. There are also no restrictions for foreign capital investment into the media. So far, only concerns about restrictions on political advertising have appeared.[2]

In Lithuania as well as in other Baltic countries, state involvement in media matters is fairly limited (Balčytienė 2005). The level of state intervention is manifested in the public information policy in several ways, for instance, in the values which are promoted, in the types of subsidies (direct and indirect), in the regulation of media industry and power-sharing among various councils to regulate the broadcast sector. In Lithuania, the Law on Provision of Information to the Public (first accepted in 1996, new amendments as of July 2006) says that there is an institution authorized by the government to co-ordinate the implementation of national policy in the sphere of public information provision. Since 2001, this governmental institution has been the Ministry of Culture. The information policy seeks to increase openness and transparency of the media (as is indicated in Article 24 of the law), as well as to enable the widest range of views to be put forward in the media (diversity of the media), providing conditions under which they can have an equal chance of attracting public attention. Concerning transparency of the media, Article 24 of the law states that owners, producers and disseminators of public information are obliged to submit data to the ministry once a year, by 30 March, regarding the shareholders or co-owners of the enterprise.

In Latvia, by contrast, lack of transparency in the patterns of media ownership is a serious issue and the situation has not significantly improved since the period of the predominantly shadow economy of the early 1990s (see, for example, Nagla & Kehre 2004). Although partial information about owners can be obtained from the Company Register, lack of publicly available and updated information about real owners of different media companies is the main drawback on the Latvian media market.

In both Lithuania and Estonia the problematic issue concerns the lack of public discussion about the media, rather than lack of information on who actually owns what in the media.

The libertarian media model, with its principles of competition, pluralism and freedom of expression, confirms that all citizens have the right to express their opinions and receive information without any restrictions. While this may be true in theory, practice reveals something different.

On the one hand, the liberal news market opens new fields and forms for media development. On the other hand, liberal regulation and lack or state intervention into the media field create favourable conditions for the market-oriented logic to proliferate. The Lithuanian case shows that an information space governed by competition and market forces subordinates media operation to the profit motive. As media professionals themselves say,[3] the freedom of the press eventually becomes freedom of press owners instead of citizens' freedom.

The more the media organization is interested in profit, the more its journalism acquires the features of "market journalism". This is dangerous for democracy because, ultimately, the free press may degenerate, i.e., become dependent on advertisers, PR companies, orders from an imagined audience or simply be guided solely by the media owners' interests. Ultimately, this commercial virus may infect the whole information space, and information producers may rapidly notice that they need to present more of the same, i.e., celebrity news, lotteries, games, documentary programmes stimulating the emotions of ordinary people, chat and reality shows of various types. The fight for audience share is noticeable in the increase in the number of popular television talk shows and quiz shows, weekly lotteries and games. For example, statistics confirms that there was a steady increase from 1992 to 2001 in the number of television games produced originally by Lithuanian producers or adapted from foreign programmes. In 2003 alone, the increase in all kinds of television games and reality television shows was three times higher than during the previous years (Jasinevičiūtė 2004). Attempts are being made to introduce different television voting possibilities through mobile telephones, the viewers are encouraged to send SMS messages and vote during live television shows etc. Apart from direct economic revenue from SMS, the media also get an indirect profit: SMS helps to sell brands of television and radio programmes.

These examples testify to a process of *secularization* which is defined as the decline of a political order based on collective political actors and identities and their replacement by a more fragmented and individualized society (Hallin & Mancini 2004). With increasing secularization, news reporting is clearly seeking a more immediate connection to the everyday life of individuals – news reported by journalists must be relevant and have tangible consequences for ordinary citizens. Journalists also tend to think of people in terms of lifestyles and consumption habits. Indeed, for the Baltic countries, the newly discovered commercial logic is based on openly market-driven media, accommodating to pressures of audience demand.

In this context, small news environments are facing dramatic challenges. For some, media survival in such markets (especially in Lithuania and Latvia, where regional media concentration process is still going on) requires one of two things – they must get closely integrated either into political or business field or into a larger chain of newspapers. By seeking to remain on the market, many local media are overlooking the difference between paid and independently produced information. Indeed, local news is the most expensive to produce; therefore, having limited budgets journalists are "forced" to produce hybrid media by mixing journalism, promotional writing and advertising. The question of widespread proliferation of hybrid media (and also the indirect "legitimation" of such practice) is a sensitive matter, which has not been given sufficient attention by media scholars and policy-makers so far.

One particular dilemma that needs to be addressed here deals with the question whether media concentration – an issue widely debated and criticized by media scholars – is indeed a threat. One can claim that few but large and wealthy media firms could provide more and more innovative media products, with better editorial content and with more journalistic autonomy than many highly competitive small local media suppliers with only limited resources. At the same time, however, highly concentrated media ownership and business logics based on economic management of news production and distribution pose a threat to pluralism by concentrating more power into the hands of just a few suppliers (Doyle 2002).

As practice reveals, there is no one, or an easy, answer to this question.

With growing ownership and media concentration by foreign capital in the three Baltic countries, it was hoped that media owners from Nordic countries would transfer high journalistic standards also to small neighbouring markets (Balčytienė & Lauk 2005). Small societies with limited media markets, dramatically changing journalistic standards and weak professional ideologies, are especially vulnerable when foreign companies are concerned only about profits and distance themselves from issues of social responsibility. There exists a general understanding in media studies that foreign owners usually do not influence content – they, rather, control the finances. But through the control of editorial budget media content is affected indirectly.

In the long run, cultivation of consumerism, the market, class inequality and individualism tend to be taken as natural and often benevolent, whereas political activity, civic values and anti-market activities tend to be marginalized. Therefore, in any genuine democracy the question of who controls the media economy is an important issue of public debate. However, the public of Lithuania, Latvia or Estonia knows little about the mechanisms of financial and organizational performance of the media. There are only a few organizations monitoring and watching over the media's performance (in Lithuania, this is the role and function of the institution of the Inspector of Journalist Ethics, but his/her reports and decisions made, however, only seldom reach wider audience). In addition, changes in the media field such as mergers and acquisitions are mainly reported by the media themselves only as economic matters (with facts and data on the media company itself) and as a matter with no socio-political ramifications – thus, not interesting to the average citizen.

2.2 *The Pros and Cons of Political Communication Marketization*

We should also note that with professionalization of communication, values that are promoted in media – increase in political-marketing and image-oriented reporting – as well as the quality of interaction between journalists and their sources have changed substantially (Plasser 2005).

It is important to acknowledge that there are scholars who do not demonize the "softification" of political reporting, namely of bringing more emotional and personal aspects in political journalism. It is common to say that "permanent campaigns" nowadays are necessary in political issue communication, i.e., that politicians permanently have to seek voters' support. Thus, political campaigns have become much more expensive: political parties commission their own opinion polls and invest heavily in advertising, replacing the press medium more and more with television. Campaigns are "increasingly geared to media's needs", and political leaders are assessed in terms of their media appeal. In short, images dominate over ideas, and political coverage is increasingly personalized (Bielinis 2002; Donskis 2004).

Within an ongoing discussion of changes in political communication, the arguments of Murdock and Golding (1989) that identify three main kinds of relations between communications and citizenship seem to be important. According to those scholars, first, people must have access to information, advice and analysis that will enable them to know what their rights are and allow them to pursue these rights effectively. Second, they must have access to the broadest possible range of information, interpretation and debate on areas that involve political choices, and they must be able to use communications facilities in order to register criticism, mobilize opposition and propose alternative courses of action. Third, they must be able to recognize themselves and their aspirations in the range of representations offered within the central communications sectors and to be able to contribute to developing their representations in the media.

This may lead us to conclude that commercialized political journalism may become an alternative public sphere if it scrutinizes the power elite and helps formulate and consolidate grass-roots views and expectations. To put it more precisely – popular talk shows, political satire, infotainment and even the Internet blogs could work as instruments for otherwise marginalized groups to make their voices heard and help to extend the domain of public discourse. In other words, if popular journalism is a way to question the power elite and if it creates possibilities for different, perhaps marginalized, groups to come forward, then popular journalism's potential to become an alternative public sphere is legitimated.

Another aspect of changes in political communication as affecting journalistic discourse is related to shifts in professional standards of journalism, among which truth and transparency (or public accountability) are the fundamental ones. Now the biggest challenge for political journalists is to get behind the scenes and behind the "closed doors", to find adequate political sources who speak off the record and to use unofficial channels to get information etc. At the same time, this leaves journalists who are using scoops, leaks and other unofficial information which comes from confidential sources with the dilemma of how to verify such information and retain their credibility. In short, while there still may be differences in how journalists' and sources' relationships are managed on national (Lithuanian, Estonian or Latvian) levels and what happens on a transnational scale (Balčytienė & Vinciūnienė 2006; Tammpuu & Pullerits 2006), the tendency is clear – with professionalization of political sources (with increasing application of spin doctors and political issue management techniques) – journalists are increasingly denied direct access to important information; they are confronted with PR material instead of being allowed to discover conflicts within the actual decision-making process.

On the other hand, political institutions – also feeling they should constantly provide information and maintain proactive relations with the electorate – face difficulties in this regard. As research data from a transnational study on European news production "AIM – Adequate Information Management in Europe" indicates,[4] despite many direct and indirect efforts of political institutions (for example, the European Commission) to make more information available and apply sophisticated strategies of communication, the majority of people in Europe feel they are not sufficiently informed (AIM Research Consortium, 2007). Thus, in (European) political communication, one of the major problems faced by the media is certainly not one of availability of information but rather that of finding, selection and interpretation of relevant information. In other words, from the media's point of view, there is a lack of openness and transparency of the decision-making process at the political level (often resulting from the consensus-seeking approach and a "one-face" and "one-voice" policy of the European Commission). One of the policy proposals that the AIM project brings to political communication studies is that the contribution of journalism to enhancing transparency and openness of political reporting could receive a major boost if journalists would gain access to better insight into the very mechanisms and procedures of decision-making at the institutional level. As the research project found, correspondents working in Brussels need an alternative to the overload of so-called pre-cooked stories that are distributed via all kinds of well-developed and official channels (Web pages, e-mail, press releases, Midday Briefings at the European Commission etc.). If they were given access to the decision-making process, journalists could easily be motivated to invest more into investigative stories and approaches – something still an exception in the daily affairs of the reporting of European news. Whether political institutions are ready to accept this call appears to be an open question – so far, it looks like European institutions have instrumentalized the notion of a public sphere as only a PR concept and are not willing to disclose procedural aspects as well as get involved in national debates.

To conclude what has been said, the critical element within ongoing changes in political communication process is that, on the one hand, the market – with increasing commercialization – affects the media's performance. By translating social and political issues into personal experience and organizing them around the emotional state of the individuals concerned, by trivializing political matters etc., it stratifies information provision and fails to provide all citizens with the same quality of political information and opinion. In this respect, the media can be seen not only as a cornerstone, but also as a force inimical to democracy, as they can easily manipulate individual needs, desires and choices. On the other hand, the media themselves are forced to change and adapt to new working conditions, such as establishing new kinds of relationships with political news sources.

Thus, there are old (media as watchdog) and new (media as dealing with structural and organizational changes in the political communication process) issues that professional political journalism needs to address.

2.3 The Impact of the Internet: Conditions Inhibiting and Fostering Professionalization of Online Journalism

In all three Baltic countries news media products are between the top five visited websites. The Internet media are the fastest growing, with young audiences increasingly using online media as their first news source.

Though Internet audiences are growing fast and Internet advertising revenues are increasing, Internet media income from online advertising still remains very small. As comparative studies show, online journalists and editors are often using other kinds of publicly available information such as PR news, promotional writing, translations from other online information sources, rather than invest in development of original online journalism (Balčytienė & Harro-Loit 2006). Part of the reason is cost. Another is increased impact from new communication technologies on journalistic output. One of the biggest technological impacts on journalistic content production is the acceleration of dynamics in news cycle. The accelerated news cycle – the so-called 24/7 reporting model – and the pressure to fill the news hole online, allows less time for more serious reporting and fact-checking for journalists. Fast-changing news cycles cause more superficial use of sources and citations which highlights the "breaking news" character of news reporting. As a result, Internet media are considered one of the major news aggregators, with mixed discourses proliferating there.

Despite many drawbacks, a quality element in this complex situation with Internet media development is that conditions may be established for something entirely new to be born. On the Lithuanian Internet, for example, there are several online-only projects (Delfi.lt, Balsas.lt, Bernardinai.lt) where journalists and other public intellectuals enrich the information space by writing analytical articles or critical reviews. In this way, it is said, online-only media in Lithuania fulfil the role of many dailies which, in contrast to Internet media, are not open to external contributors (Balčytienė & Harro-Loit 2006). For example, content analysis of two national dailies, *Lietuvos rytas* and *Respublika*, conducted in the period of 1988 to 2000, shows that the number of outside actors in both newspapers has undoubtedly decreased (Nevinskaitė 2006). The analysis of actor's quotes in both dailies shows increasing domination of political figures, highly increased amount of commercial and industry organizations while, in the same period, opinions of individual and non-profit organizations occupy less space. On the Internet, on the other hand, public intellectuals are very often hired to write analytical online commentaries. Thus, online-only media become a serious alternative to newspapers where journalists seldom have time for long investigation and full-scale reporting. In addition, users of online news media (online versions of traditional newspapers and online-only media) often write online responses, actively participate in all kinds of public forums and communities. No doubt the Internet creates more opportunities for audiences in the Baltic countries to communicate and participate.[5]

Based on the foregoing, we can say that there exists a wide spectrum of Internet media, offering diversity of opinions (by journalists, public intellectuals, ordinary citizens) — in short, social connectedness, reader involvement, variety of opinions presented online etc. All this may have an important effect on the further professionalization of journalists in Lithuania (and also in other Baltic countries). As is often pointed out, while TV journalists have to be prepared to be recognized in public, online journalists must be ready to be criticized in public. Whether Internet media in general and original online journalism in particular do indeed create new conditions for the media to become more accountable remains to be assessed through practical studies.

3. Media Policy Proposals — How to Cultivate Good Journalism

In the context of changes unfolding in the Baltic media markets, our main concern, therefore, is this: Do economic restructuring, changing relationships with news sources, technological renovation as well as other factors, in fact, lead to democratization in the Baltic States?

As has been demonstrated, the fact that media organizations are driven primarily by market and financial considerations has a clear impact on the type of journalism that is produced in the Baltic countries. Market-oriented journalism has, indeed, found its way into public communication. With business interests dominating in the media organizations, the room for independent and free journalism is reduced.

Given that the cost of serious news-gathering and reporting is extremely high in small media markets, some media cannot and will not afford them. Journalists gradually learn a more market-oriented style of journalism, treated by the management as a commodity, and promoting the trend towards hybrid media production. Good journalism still exists, but against a growing background of a different style of journalism.

There are several mechanisms to keep the performance of media and journalism professionalization under scrutiny.

First, news organizations and journalists are subjected to the country's laws: if the media violate these laws, they are taken to court. Second, codes of professional conduct and self-regulation institutions for the media, e.g., commissions, councils and ombudsman institutions [6] have been introduced in many countries. The principal idea of self-regulation is that media themselves must preserve professional conduct and, in this way, boost their own accountability and authority.

In addition to legal acts and self-regulation, a very powerful instrument to check on the media is public control, i.e., its genuine and civic concern with the media, as well as public reflection and academic analysis of processes unfolding in the media. Thus, the third aspect of media's accountability is *media criticism*, which by producing quality and independent analysis can become a mechanism to watch effectively over the performance of the media (Harro-Loit & Balčytienė 2005). In some countries (for example, in Scandinavia) there is a long tradition of media watching over the media (especially the public service broadcaster): important media development issues are discussed among journalists and the public.[7] In addition, a special type of supervision takes place within the media through an in-house ombudsman. It is not customary for mass media companies in the Baltic States to have their own codes of ethics; however, some of them do have such codes (e.g., the daily *Diena* in Latvia).

In short, then, various means exist to encourage and support journalists' responsibility and reduce the pressure of market-driven journalism.

In the public sphere, the interests of at least three agents – state, media and public – intersect.

According to figure 1, the laws regulating the activities of the mass media reflect the interests of the state. For example, legislation regulates the amount of advertising on TV, media concentration, etc. The media, as market entities, have their own interests and seek more and more freedom to pursue their business interests. Self-regulation is directly attributed to the sector, and, as an external factor, public criticism on mass media influence the information quality. The different strata of society also have their own interests, e.g., to receive reliable information, which is the backbone of democracy.

If one of the three agents gains undue influence, it is impossible to find a consensus. It is tempting to indicate that lack of 'public control' (i.e. of informed public debate) is the weakest link in this system, but that would not be entirely true. The media themselves are also very vulnerable. Media accountability is very weak. Driven by commercial interests, unresponsive to the broader issues of public concern, overemphasizing sensational issues, the media set a public

The role of the *state* and its
policies on media performance
(e.g., requests on media
ownership transparency)

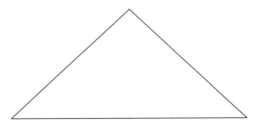

The *media* (the system of self-
regulation and media
accountability, norms and values)

The *public* and its control over
the media (public trust, public
criticism, etc.)

Figure 1: Main actors in the public sphere

agenda that is appropriate mainly for their own corporate interests. In addition, journalists themselves are reluctant to talk about the weaknesses of their profession. So it becomes obvious that the Nordic models of self-regulation[8] cannot work without strong traditions of democratic journalism and adequate professional culture in society. The audience is not very critical of the media, either. Why, then, should the media care, if consumers are happy?

In this situation a crucial question remains what can be done, by whom and, if possible, how to improve the current situation and to preserve good journalism.

The following issues appear to be of crucial importance in the debate of media policy development.

First, it appears crucial to find the means to foster journalistic accountability. In this respect, analysis of media performance and journalism quality to increase *informed* public and academic debates about media performance is of major significance. By extending public as well as academic discourse on media matters and media performance, it would be possible to open up new themes, issues and involve new actors in the debate. Thus, the role of media literacy becomes crucial in increasing public awareness of critical concepts of journalism; an informed public also plays a role in helping journalists find a balance between autonomy and freedom on the one hand and accountability on the other.

In addition, the role of training and education of journalists seems to be of particular significance in promoting practical training of student journalists, while at the same time promoting analysis and reflection that is necessary for journalism professionals fully to understand the social repercussions of the way they practice their profession.

One more way to promote debate on media matters is by popularizing academic research results. In this respect, the situation seems to be the most auspicious in Estonia, with the highest number of journalism and communication academics. Until now the higher education reform in the Baltic countries and the system of ranking of academic publications did not motivate scholars to write in their national languages and, thus, to increase popular public discussion on media matters and to widen knowledge and understanding of critical media concepts. The adopted system of assessment of academic results should be shifted into a more democratic one which also accepts participation of academics in the public life, for example, by writing popular articles or participating in TV programmes or round-table discussions on matters of the media.

Public service broadcasters should also play a much bigger role in diversifying the information space. In their organization and media logic (to serve the public interest), public service broadcasters (PSB) have the potential to resist market pressures. PSB should become a standard-setter for other traditional and Internet media. In addition, with further diversification of the media usage forms and channels there emerges a need to discuss and to promote other forms of *public service media*.

Another possibility to correct "market failure" — when media fail adequately to serve their audiences by seeking to maximize their profits — seems to be the *public funding*. Public finance (by funding non-commercial media projects) has a particular potential in fostering and enhancing pluralism, diversity and quality in content provision. Since 2005, for example, any natural person in Lithuania may, under the Law on Income Tax of Individuals, transfer up to 2 per cent of the amount of the income tax paid to the state to any public or business organization. This has allowed public financing of some traditional media projects (such as monthlies and weeklies) as well as specialized news media online (such as Bernardinai.lt, as well as other online-only media projects).

Conclusion and Outlook

A number of important observations about the Baltic media's post-transitional change emerge from the above discussion.

In the past few years, the Baltic media have rapidly diversified along different commercial lines and interests. At the same time, and in spite of rapid changes, there has been very little public and academic discussion about structural changes in the media and about the new responsibilities of both media professionals and media owners. A more systematic approach to the assessment of Baltic journalism has taken place only recently (for example, in Lithuania) when media and journalism studies were discovered by other disciplines (political sciences, sociology and psychology) and included in their discourses as objects of their scholarly concern. However, despite the change of focus in journalism research, new questions are mainly addressed in research articles, project reports and graduate theses, while a more thorough analysis of journalism is still missing. The conventional media, too, have gradually learned to "commercialize" media-related news by focusing on media business matters (mergers and acquisitions).

We have argued here that there is a tendency towards media convergence and homogenization of journalism and that the Lithuanian media (as well as the media in Latvia and Estonia) are not excluded from this general trend. The media in the Baltics are continuously affected by media concentration and news commercialization. The new technologies strongly influence the development of journalism as well. Professional media practice reveals that journalists spend more time and effort on the management of news (i.e., selection and presentation of information) than on preparing interviews or planning news reports.

To look for the reasons for the deterioration of contemporary journalism, we have looked into the liberal media policy as determining the hyper-commercialization of news, as well as the shifting values towards more hybrid and more entertaining reporting, the changing news cycles of reporting and the "breaking news" character of reporting which affects journalism, and the ongoing changes in political professionalization of sources which again has an impact on changes in reporting style and political news quality.

After examining the three factors and in particular their impact on journalism, we conclude that hybrid media and cheap journalism (cheap in many ways — in terms of the costs involved and as more entertainment-oriented) are on the rise in the Baltic States. Conventional genres belonging to journalism are being extensively used for other (promotional or political) purposes. Although this trend may look as universal it brings special challenges in a small news market. More issues need to be taken under critical assessment: for example, the growing power of news sources as determining the news agenda-setting function of the media needs to be clarified.

There is no need to stop media commercialization. Rather, it is important to find adequate means to open up the media field to other actors (media professionals, public intellectuals as well as the general public) to critically assess its structural changes, changing news values, general development and professionalization. Another avenue is to develop popularized professional discourse on media performance, thus enabling informed public usage of critical concepts such as news diversity, media concentration, commercialization, homogenization, marketization etc. In a secularized society, media discussion may attract wider public attention if it is presented in a way that is interesting to ordinary people. This skill should be acquired in journalism schools. Media scholarship should be discussed not in a banal, but interesting, way, which is one more challenge for comparative media studies to take into account.

Notes

1. If compared to the situation of few years ago, today media in Lithuania and Estonia is already more controlled by foreign multimedia groups (Schibsted from Norway with investments in newspaper, magazines and free dailies publishing) and local industrialists (very often having political alliances).

2. In Lithuania, requirements for political advertising and the procedure for announcing and designating it in the media is laid down by the Law on Funding of Political Parties and Political Campaigns and Control over the Funding (law enacted in 2004).

3. For comparison, see interview with Dainius Radzevičius, the Chairman of Lithuanian Journalists' Union, in the book *The Impact of Media Concentration on Professional Journalism*, published by OSCE 2003 (Dohnanyi & Moller 2003).

4. The European Commission's 6th Framework Programme project, "AIM – Adequate Information Management in Europe" (2004–2007), deals with mainstream journalism (in general) and specific news production processes (European information selection, analysis, editing, presentation) resulting in EU coverage in mass media (in particular) of eleven countries in Europe. Project website is http://www.aim-project.net.

5. Research study conducted in four geographically different countries in Europe (Italy, Bulgaria, Ireland and Estonia) confirms that online readers in Estonia (also in other Baltic countries) are very active online responses writers, while elsewhere such practice is rather marginal (Fortunati et al. 2005). A hypothesis whether Lithuanians and Estonians are active participants in online news commenting because traditional mass media (e.g., newspapers) in those countries restricts outside authors needs to be tested in other practical studies.

6. The number of councils and the functions that are delegated to them differ from country to country. In Lithuania, for example, there is an institution of ombudsman (Inspector of Journalist Ethics) as well as the Ethics Commission. In Estonia, two councils currently watch over the media. Different from Estonia and Lithuania, Latvia, so far, has no press council or other structure carrying out the according tasks. The idea has not come further than to discussions among Latvian journalists about the need of having a structure that among other things would have to evaluate ethical issues related to the media (cf. Dimants 2004).

7. For instance, in several Scandinavian countries there are programmes on both TV and radio where journalists discuss about the developments and changes in the media sector such as media concentration, crime journalism, sponsorship of TV programmes etc. Such "media watch" programmes create public forums, increase public knowledge and open journalistic profession to critical reviews from outside.

8. Lithuanian self-regulation system, "imported" from Sweden and Estonian, is a mixture of Finnish and Norwegian traditions (for more information, see Rossland 2005).

References

AIM Research Consortium (ed.) (2007). *AIM – Adequate Information Management in Europe Final Report*, AIM – Working Papers, Dortmund, Projekt Verlag.

Balčytienė, A., & Harro-Loit, H. (2006). 'New Media Environment and Journalism Cultures Online: Comparing Situations in Lithuania and Estonia' in *Proceedings of the Conference on the Impact of the Internet on Mass Media in Europe*, pp. 321–337, Abramis Publishing.

Balčytienė, A., & Lauk, E. (2005). 'Media Transformations: the Post-transition Lessons in Lithuania and Estonia', *Informacijos mokslai*, 33, pp. 96–110.

Balčytienė, A., & Vinciūnienė, A. (2006). 'The Case of Lithuania', in *Understanding the EU Reporting in Mass Media* (AIM Research Consortium, Projekt Verlag), pp. 107–123.

Balčytienė, Auksė (2005). 'Types of State Intervention in Media in the Baltic States and Norway' in Baerug, R. (ed.) *The Baltic Media World* (Riga, Flera), pp. 40–58.

Balčytienė, A. (2006). *Mass Media in Lithuania: Changes, Development, and Journalism Culture*, European Journalism Review Series 8, Berlin, Vistas.

Bielinis, L. (2002). 'Šou principų dėsningumai Lietuvos politiniame gyvenime' (Consistency of Show Elements in Political Life in Lithuania), *Politologija*, 1:25, pp. 22–40.

Curran, J., & Myung-Jin, P. (2000). *De-Westernizing Media Studies*, London, Routledge.

Dimants, A. (2004). 'The Future of Latvia's Mass Media in Enlarged Europe', in Jundzis, T. (ed.) *Latvia in Europe: Visions of the Future: Collection of Articles* (Riga: Baltic Centre for Strategic Studies, Latvian Academy of Sciences), pp. 334–352.

Dohnanyi, J., & Moller, C. (2003). *The Impact of Media Concentration on Professional Journalism*, Vienna, OSCE.

Donskis, L. (2004). 'Imagologija, manipuliacijos ir viešoji erdvė postmoderniojoje politikoje' (Imagology, Manipulation, and the Public Domain in Postmodern Politics), *Politologija*, 33 (the article is available electronically at http://www.leidykla.vu.lt/inetleid/politol/33/straipsniai/str1.pdf).

Doyle, G. (2002). *Media Ownership*, London, Sage Publications.

Erjavec, K. (2005). 'Hybrid Public Relations News Discourse', *European Journal of Communication*, 20:2, pp. 155–179.

Fortunati, L., Raycheva, L., Harro-Loit, H., O'Sullivan, J. (2005). 'Online News Interactivity in Four European Countries: A Pre-political Dimension (Comparing Practices in Bulgaria, Estonia, Ireland and Italy)', in Masip, P., & Rom, J. (eds.) *Digital Utopia in the Media: From Discourses to Facts* (Abalance, III International Conference Communication and Reality), pp. 417–430.

Hallin, D., & Mancini, P. (2003). 'Americanization, Globalization, and Secularization: Understanding the Convergence of Media Systems and Political Communication' in Esser, F. & Pfetsch, B. (eds.) *Comparing Political Communication*, Cambridge, Cambridge University Press, pp. 25–45.

Hallin, D., & Mancini, P. (2004). *Comparing Media Systems: Three Models of Media and Politics*, Cambridge University Press, Cambridge.

Harro-Loit, H., & Balčytienė, A. (2005). 'Media Accountability Systems: Ecological Viewpoint' in Baerug, R. (ed.) *The Baltic Media World* (Riga, Flera), pp. 25–40.

Harro-Loit, H., & Saks, K. (2007). 'The Diminishing Border between Advertising and Journalism in Estonia', *Journalism Studies*, 7:2, pp. 312–322.

Harro-Loit, H. (2005). 'The Baltic and Norwegian Journalism Market' in: Baerug, R. (ed.) *The Baltic Media World* (Riga, Flera), pp. 90–121.

Jasinevičiūtė, J. (2004). *Žaidimas kaip televizijos žanras Lietuvoje: aktyvios auditorijos kūrimo prielaidos* (Game as Television Genre: Assessing Active Audience Construction Prerequisites), Unpublished Master's Theses, Kaunas, Vytautas Magnus University.

Murdock, G., & Golding, P. (1989). 'Information Poverty and Political Inequality: Citizenship in the Age of Privatized Communications', *Journal of Communication*, 39:3, pp. 180–195.

Nagla, I., & Kehre, A., 'Latvia' in Petkovic, B. (ed.) (2004). *Media Ownership and Its Impact on Media Independence and Pluralism* (Ljubljana, Peace Institute, Institute for Contemporary Social and Political Studies).

Nevinskaitė, L. (2006). *Viešosios erdvės transformacija Lietuvoje 1988–2000 m.: laikraščių atvejis* (Transformation of the Public Sphere in Lithunia in 1988–2000: The Case of Newspapers), Unpublished Ph.D. Thesis, Vilnius, Faculty of Communication at Vilnius University.

Plasser, F. (2005). 'From Hard to Soft News Standards? How Political Journalists in Different Media Systems Evaluate the Shifting Quality of News', *Press/Politics*, 10:2, pp. 47–68.

Rossland, A. (2005). 'Accountability Systems and Media Ethics: Landscapes and Limits' in Baerug, R. (ed.) *The Baltic Media World* (Riga, Flera), pp. 14–25.

Scott, B. (2005). 'A Contemporary History of Digital Journalism', *Television & New Media*, 6:1, pp. 89–126.

Tammpuu, P., & Pullerits, E. (2006). 'The Case of Estonia, in *Understanding the EU Reporting in Mass Media* (AIM Research Consortium, Projekt Verlag), pp. 21–33.

Vihalemm, P. (2002). *Baltic Media in Transition*, Tartu, Tartu University Press.

Effect Seekers and Media Spectacle: Hungarian Audience Responses to Partisan Media

Péter Csigó

1. Introduction: audience attendance in the era of media "spectacle"

The apparently "spectacular" and "theatre-like" character of late modern media and politics received much academic interest in the last ten years. Scholars have pointed to the aesthetic and dramatic intensity of late modern media and political performances. Since these performances have absorbed the aesthetic qualities of popular film and theatre, the fields of popular fiction and popular politics have been compared as two arenas where truth, authenticity and loyalty are constructed in very similar ways (Street 1998; Corner-Pels 2003). However, the above conception of "aesthetic" politics in itself is easy to be re-appropriated by reductionist approaches, equating the theatrical element of late modern media with "spectacle" (Kellner 2001) or with "media logic" (which itself consists of "imperatives of speed and spectacle" [Moog, S.- J. Sluyter-Beltrao 2001; Altheide-Snow 1979]). In contrast to such reductionism, my aim in this chapter is to think further what is "theatrical" in late modern media and politics. My point is that in late modernity, media-audience encounters are becoming increasingly "theatre-like", and the aesthetic intensification of media discourse constitutes only one factor of this "theatricality".

The following chapter approaches the late modern transformation of politics "from below", and diagnoses the emergence of a new political audience, constantly exposed to intense, spectacular political appeals, and responding to them in a way similar to audiences of theatre or music performances. This new form of "audiencing" is defined by the practice of "attendance". The conception of "audience in attendance" draws back to Dayan and Katz's study (1992:114) on media events, the dominant form of "spectacular" media performance during the era of broadcasting. According to Dayan and Katz, media events call the audience to "attend", which means to actively transform the event offered by media actors into a collective, participatory "ceremony". Two fundamental aspects of "attendance" have to be highlighted here: first, that the attention and enthusiasm of the audience is a matter of deliberate choice; second, that once people engage themselves in great numbers, the resulting "epidemic" (1992:97) is intense enough to be discernable for media performers who adapt themselves to this feedback. Clear allusions can be drawn here with the "attending" activity of theatre audiences who, first, intentionally select a play by its presumable aesthetic qualities; second, expect an intense, "bigger-than-life", collective experience; third, give permanent feedback to the actors during the performance.

In the new media environment, spectacular media performances are the daily routine. Audiences, more than ever, have to actively select which appeal to listen to out of the loud "background noise" (Gitlin 2002) of competing performances. This competitive context is further strengthening the above "theatrical" practices: deliberate selection, a wish for enthusiastic engagement and the mutual adaptation of actor and audience. This mutuality is guaranteed by industrial mechanisms rating and monitoring the audience, which bring constant and quick feedback to media and political actors. The resulting, quasi real-time ability of performers to adapt themselves to audience reactions make room for an almost theatre-like interactivity. The above arguments suggest that late modern media foregrounds "attendance" as a typical form of audience behaviour. However, the "theatrical" mode of reception is incompatible with many of our conventional conceptions about the uses and effects of popular media. The following study explores, by the means of empirical analysis, how media power articulates itself when audiences are "attending" spectacular, intense media performances (about "attendance" and "reading" as two different metaphors of media use, see Csigó 2007).

In 2002, twelve years after democratic transition and five years after media deregulation, Hungarian citizens experienced the advent of a new era of mediatized politics. The 2002 election campaign – and, in fact, the right-wing government's "permanent campaign" during the year before – will be long remembered as an unprecedentedly dramatic period of Hungarian politics. The symbolic condensation of political discourse in the 2001 and 2002 period evokes the political "warfare" of the 2000 or 2004 presidential elections in the USA. In both countries, public opinion research evidence documents that most people felt the actual election uniquely important.[1] In 2002, in Hungary, public service television (m1) performed a heavily propagandistic mobilizing campaign in favour of the incumbent right-wing Government. The evening news of m1 echoed the themes and the language of the Government's "permanent campaign". As I will show, m1 news successfully mobilized its viewers – in spite of the fact that many of these viewers clearly recognized the programme's apparent political bias. This ambiguity signals that the political engagement triggered by late modern spectacular campaigns are not automatic, blind or merely imposed (Csigó 2006). The following chapter is aimed to interpret the double-faced performance of m1 (highly partisan and ambivalently received) from a "theatrical", "dramaturgical" framework.

The chapter continues by presenting what a "dramaturgical" approach may bring to empirical media analysis (section 2). A "theatrical" understanding of media reception is needed in the light of the fact that late modern political performance, highly dramatized and aesthetized, feeds "attendance" practices in the audience. My point is that "attending audiences", like spectators of theatre or musical performance, selectively plunge into an experiential space they do not have control over, willingly submit themselves to the aesthetic power of media performance, in the quest of a "bigger-than-life", cathartic experience. Audiences of spectacular media are "effect seekers". The conception of "effect seeking",[2] by simultaneously adhering to and transforming a classical idea of Uses and Gratifications (U&G)

research ("reality seeking"), expresses how the selective and active stance of media users may turn them into the object of media effects that surpass their intentional control. As made clear by dramaturgical theory, the power of all performance is conditioned by the willing collaboration of the audience. This allows for reconceptualizing the effects of "performance-like" media as contextual "alliances" between media actors and "effect-seeking" audiences.

"Effect seeking" is a hybrid concept, amalgamating what mainstream media research has presumed to be opposing: media effects and audience selectivity/activity. Most of mainstream empirical research has been lacking the above understanding of audience engagement as a choice-based, intentional activity making room for media influence exceeding the spectator's control. Still, several theoretical and empirical efforts have been done inside the mainstreams for transcending the inherited opposition of media effects and audience selectivity. Three "reconciliatory" attempts will be presented and welcomed in section 3. However, not all of these attempts have successfully transcended the mainstream opposition of media effects and audience activity. Out of the models presented, only John Zaller's has led beyond the mainstreams. Zaller's original, although rather dark, vision defines audience activity and competence as an almost tribal ability to "blindly" appropriate a performer's discourse.

The study will continue (sections 4–5) by exploring the effects of the greatly partisan performance of m1 news. I will argue that the symbolic power of m1 news diverges from what might be expected from a "mainstream" angle. One typical mainstream hypothesis would suggest that "passive" receivers are more exposed to propagandistic mobilization than competent, active viewers who recognize the bias of m1 news. Another mainstream assumption (inspired by U&G) would expect that the distorted, partisan discourse of m1 would attract those people only who have a right-wing identity "anyway". In contrast to both assumptions, the empirical evidence revealed underlies much of Zaller's model. However, it will also be argued that Zaller's too dark picture about the blindly tribal character of engagement needs reconsideration.

At this point of the analysis, the "theatrical", "dramaturgical" model will be re-introduced, as a model pointing to audiences' awareness and conditional engagements – in a word, "alliances" – with media actors. In the Conclusion (6), media effects will be theorized as emotionally heated "alliances" between media and audience, characterized by a deliberate permissiveness from the part of the audience willing to reach faith. This is the context in which the notion of "effect seeking" gains its meaning. The "effect-seeking" practices of audiences consuming factual media evoke the reception mechanism well known from studies of performing arts: the complicit establishment of an "alliance", the willing "suspension of disbelief" enacted by audiences thirsting for catharsis.

2. What a "dramaturgical" approach may bring to empirical media research

The following study connects two distinct traditions of media research by introducing some "culturalist" insights on drama, ritual and performance to the more positivist empirical research of the uses and effects of media. As suggested above, a "dramaturgical" approach may bring to empirical media research the idea, mostly lacking up to now, that media consumption evokes in many respects the experience typical to the "attendance" of live performances. What makes the "attendance" of live performances particular is its fundamental interactivity, the fact that spectators' active engagement and actors' mobilizing power stand in a cross-fertilizing relationship. Although actors follow highly calculated, almost manipulative, dramaturgical strategies, these latters' success does not imply at all that the emotional and mental response they trigger in the audience would be simply "imposed" by a top-down mechanism. This indicates a relation of complicity, rather than a pure opposition, between audience activity and dramaturgical "effects". On the whole, the practice of "attendance" may call forth engagements which are hard to explain with either of the two opposing "master narratives" of mainstream media research. What "attendance" activates is neither top-down, "message-driven media effects", nor audiences' autonomous, selective search for "value reinforcement" or "gratifications".[3]

The dramaturgical effects of theatre are much more complex than simply "imposed": they cannot work without the selective and willing engagement of the audience, without spectators' cooperation with actors, in the wish of cathartic experience. The very act of getting to the performance hall, in itself, implies a whole chain of selective acts (Schechner 2003): asking advice from fellow theatre-goers, choosing the play to be watched, following advertisements, going to the cash desk, inviting other people, attributing a certain sacrality, out-of-mundanity, to theatre. Moreover, audience activity is not confined to selecting the play, forming aesthetic expectations and going to the performance hall. The participatory, active stance of audiences does not vanish even during the performance, which guarantees spectators a co-performer status with the playing actors (for detailed argument about the complex status of the spectator,[4] see Schechner [2003]; see, also, Bennett 1997:106; Alexander 2006:73–6). In a word, audiences, with their motivation, attentiveness, expectations, competence, sensitivity and emotional mood take active part in the creation of a powerful, aesthetically condensed experience.

Meanwhile, it is not less obvious that the selective and active stance of viewers does not at all guarantee immunity from the dramaturgical power of the performance. Entering spaces of performance represents a deliberate step into an aesthetic power field which is beyond the audience member's intentional control. Audience "activity" in theatre cannot be simply reduced to selective "value reinforcement" or "gratification". In fact, these notions are almost irrelevant in the context of theatre: would it not be absurd to say "what I've got from today's Othello performance was a reinforcement of my faith in love"? Even if someone could account of nothing more than such a value reinforcement, it is obvious that this gratifying experience is, at least partly, an effect of how the play was actually performed. A different performance of Othello might have activated something other than the above gratification: either a disappointment that the play was boring, too modern, overplayed, mannered, routine, ridiculous or, on the contrary, a joy that it brought something unexpected and brilliant, something challenging the viewer's previous convictions. Thus, in theatre, no "gratifications" can be thought of as independent from the aesthetic power of the actual performance. Individual audience members' reactions to a play are highly exposed to the actual chemistry of the performance: the contingent interplay between actors, the script, the dramaturgy and the audience as a whole. Spectators are exposed to this contextual interplay, rather than merely following some a priori preferences or expectations which would be simply "gratified" by the performance.

Dramaturgical understandings of social action have always been interested in how people plunge, willingly and selectively, into the fictional world of play which, by its intensity and by its inner rules, excludes the ordinary world and offers a place where people may withdraw from the mundane and expose themselves to an intense experience (Goffman 1974; Burns 1992). Although the world of the play is fictional, an active involvement into it may result in very "real" emotional consequences, from joy to outrage, which are too unpredictable and too strong to be easily controlled by participants. Not only a play can trigger the above concurrent gain and loss of self-controlled agency. The same process may characterize all forms of involvement in communication, as it has been suggested by early social theories inspired by metaphors of theatre. Erving Goffman, theorizing the Self as a "dramatic effect" of interaction (Goffman 1990:253), recognized that the more actively people engage themselves in a conversation the more exposed they may become to its uncontrollable dynamics. Similarly, Kenneth Burke's (1969) understanding of dramatic identification presumes the coexistence of audiences' active engagement and their openness to persuasion.

This infiltration, or "fusion" (Alexander 2006), of agency and power characterizes not only theatre, play or symbolic interaction but also mediatized social dramas and those TV consumption practices which take the form of "attendance". Several important efforts have been done to explore those moments and sites where television programmes are not merely "watched" or "read" (like texts), but "attended" (like performances): standing out from the programme flow, being object of high attention and emotions of audiences, exposed to heated debates and enthusiastic commentaries. Extensive studies on media events and "audience in attendance" (Dayan-Katz 1992:114), media rituals (Cottle 2006), media performances (Alexander 2006), media pilgrimage (Couldry 2000) and fandom (Fiske 1992; Grossberg 1992b; Frith 1996) illustrate that engaged and "productive" consumer practices evade conventional oppositions like the one between user activity and media effects. Television audiences, in the above moments of "productive" engagement, are knowledgeable, motivated and competent media users who selectively get "taken over" by the force of appealing media contents. By "attending" television, they gain a new experience on life, without entirely controlling the production of its meanings and intensity. This ambivalent "productivity" characterizes all audience engagements with dramaturgically condensed media performances.

The arguments above are not easy to be translated to the empirical research of factual media. For social dramas, media events or fan practices all necessitate a dramaturgical momentum, a forceful heightening of emotions which are hardly predictable and, thus, researchable by the means of empirical analysis. However, as it will be argued in detail in the Conclusion, the above dramaturgical approach is getting inevitable in the light of recent media transformations. With the intensifying amalgamation of political/factual discourses and popular culture, highly expressive and partisan media performances proliferate, which trigger "attendance"-like audience practices.

3. Non-dramaturgical attempts to integrate 'effects' and 'uses' in mainstream media research

The theatre-like infiltration of effects and activity in emotionally heightened contexts is an experience hardly discernable by the mainstream approaches of empirical media studies. However, the idea itself that media effects and audience activity may mutually condition each other rather than being simply opposed did appear in mainstream media research (although with no reference to dramaturgical theories). In this section, three theoretical models will be presented, each aimed to transcend conventional polarities: the "systematic/heuristic processing" model, the "uses and effects" model and the "resonance" model.

The mainstreams of empirical media studies – although in a different form than 50 years ago – are still divided along the active-passive debate. Whether the media has power over the audience or whether audiences are "more influential than media" (Rubin 2002) has not ceased to be the number one dilemma for mainstream positivist media studies. Classical media theories have tended to overemphasize either media effects or audience selectivity at the expense of the other. This trade-off has been rightly criticized by Elihu Katz, disclaiming that "the power of the media tends to be considered limited whenever selectivity and interpersonal relations are thought to intervene" (Katz 1980:132). In spite of the development of research, the same author had to repeat the same critique sixteen years later (Katz 1996:19), together with another scholar noticing critically that "the ways in which viewers selectively interpret what they see, depending on their own experiences and cultural background [are taken to] undermine media effects" (Livingstone 1996:318).[5]

The above dilemma has been re- and re-tailored to newly emerging media formats. Accordingly, the difference of the "new" from the "old" has often been reduced to an active – passive dimension. (I am referring here to distinctions between public service and private media, print and television, broadcast TV and cable TV, TV and Internet, and so on). The above trade-off has led researchers to make highly diverging accounts about the media transformations of the last decades. The antagonism of "mediaoptimistic" and "mediapessimistic" narratives (Schulz et al. 2005) in connection to new media forms has resulted from the above basic trade-off. Accounts on active audiences, increasing viewer and user choice have hopelessly been diverging from reports on strong media power and increasing homogenization of media supply. However, the extensive hybridization of media undermines the above polarizing logic. The mainstream practice of polarizing reality along normatively loaded oppositions (Grossberg 1996) is becoming increasingly outdated in the light of intense cultural hybridization in late modernity.[6] In empirical media research, the once rigid opposition of 'media effects' and 'audience activities' has in the last decades unquestionably faded to some extent. Several important attempts have been done to understand media effects as a function of the motivations and intentions of audiences.

Scholars from the media effects research tradition have tried to integrate into their models the interest and knowledge of the audience as an important factor influencing the effects of media exposure and media content. According to the "systematic/heuristic processing" hypothesis, media is able to influence mostly those who are not sophisticated (i.e., interested and knowledgeable) enough to carefully consider the information received. Or, to put it the other way, "those who do view passively are more likely to show a cultivation effect as a result of heuristic processing" (Shrum 1995:421). Several experimental (Iyengar-Kinder 1987; Krosnick-Kinder 1990) and a few survey (de Vreese et al. 2006) researches have documented that news exposure produces more agenda-setting and priming effects among the passive and the less knowledgeable than among those processing information more systematically. Obviously, this approach owes much to the ELM model of persuasion (Petty-Cacciopo 1986).

The above presumption has been formulated in various combinations. The 'trap effect' hypothesis, for example, expects those with low expertise and high media exposure to be the most vulnerable to media effects. However, the trap effect model has received ambiguous empirical backing on survey data (Schoenbach-Lauf 2002; Lee-Cappella 2001).[7] On the whole, the most problematic aspect of the above approach lies in its adherence to classical definitions of media effects, a relation too strong to allow a real integration of audience activity and selectivity into the model. After all, cultivation effects have always been defined as acting upon those unselectively swallowing heavy doses of media (Gerbner-Gross 1976). Similarly, Jay Blumler, in his classical text on the political effects of television, has claimed that, in the main, the "uninvolved audience is a potentially persuasible audience" (Blumler 1970:86).

In sharp contrast to the model based on the media effects above, the U&G-based effort to link media effects to audience motivation presumed that audiences' active, selective and intentional media consumption amplifies rather than hampers media effects.[8] This idea was most fully developed in Alan Rubin's "uses and effects model" (Rubin-Perse 1987; Kim-Rubin 1997; Rubin 2002), presuming those to be more exposed to media effects who process information actively ("instrumental processing"). Accordingly, those not motivated enough to invest mental energies into appropriating the given media content will just pass away, uninterested, evading media effects ("routine processing"). The underlying idea, which can be found in various "culturalist" media theories (Silverstone 1994; Grossberg 1992a; Alexander 2006) is that accepting the world as presented by media results from the motivated and engaged mental work of audiences. Thus, Rubin has attempted to inject media effects into U&G research, and to create, so to speak, a motivational approach to media effects (surpassing Gantz's classic definition of U&G as a "motivational approach to learning" [Gantz 1978:665]; see, also, Chaffee-Schleuder 1986). Rubin's Uses and Effects model has had a considerable theoretical potential to integrate the opposing traditions of mainstream media research. Rubin, Perse and Taylor's suggestion that "activity is a catalyst rather than deterrent of media effects" and that, consequently, "cultivation evolves from active interpretation of messages" (1988:111) unquestionably opens a way beyond the polarizing logic of the mainstreams.

In spite of their innovative theoretical argument, Rubin's and his colleagues' empirical research has been too abstract precisely to grasp the place of media effects in audiences' engagements.[9] Rubin and Perse, themselves, have recognized this problem:[10] "the direction of associations was not established.... In our study...the politically disenfranchised may choose to watch more evening dramas because such programmes reinforce social alienation, instead of the argument that watching evening drama causes people to feel less efficacious politically" (Rubin-Perse 1987:128). Several empirical applications of the "Uses and Effects" model have left an opacity whether they surpass or merely recapitulate the classical "value reinforcement" thesis of selective perception and U&G theories.

Neither the systematic/heuristic processing model, nor the uses and effects model were able to transcend the mainstreams and step beyond the ideas of, respectively, message driven media effects and value reinforcement. Taking a route rather similar to that of "Uses and Effects", John Zaller has come the closest to an alternative conceptualization of media effects. Zaller's approach, named "resonance" model by Iyengar and Simon (2000), has focused on audiences' political engagement and expertise as two ultimate factors which mediate – amplify or vanish – media effects. Although Zaller himself has not referred to the above presented two models, his work might rightly be interpreted as an interesting combination of the two. As we have seen, the two above models have projected two antagonistic patterns by which audiences' competence and "activity" may relate to their exposure to media effects. The key moment in Zaller's work is the idea that engagement – people's political engagement – will define which pattern prevails. Accordingly, when active and motivated people ('experts') face ideologically consonant information, they will process it "instrumentally" (the more active they are, the more they will get involved in ideology). By contrast, the same people will relate critically and reflexively to ideologically dissonant contents (a kind of "systematic" processing). In short,[11] Zaller (1992, 1996, see also Lee-Cappella 2001: 372–3) has presumed that the politically aware 'experts' will recognize the bias of ideologically dissonant media, avoid viewing it and resist its message, while they will engage with consonant messages another way: treating it as 'real', watching it attentively and accepting its message.

Neither ME nor U&G's approaches fit Zaller's, who claims that active media users are able to intentionally avoid hostile media content, while the same activity makes them subject of effects pulling them into a closed ideological universe. Thus, what political awareness and expertise coincide with is a highly ideologized, predictable, ritualized and tribal disposition. Zaller draws a rather dark picture of the tribal, irrational character of political expertise when he notes that "any indication of independent thought among highly aware conservatives – or, for that matter, among highly aware liberals – is entirely absent" (Zaller 1996:57). Zaller's attempt to "fuse" ideological dependency and political expertise fulfils the somewhat unaccomplished promise of the Uses and Effects model to grasp audience activity as "catalyst" for media effects. This road leads toward a ritual understanding of media effects as triggering an active and engaged celebration of common and – temporarily – unquestionable values.

My analysis relies heavily on Zaller's arguments. Before turning to empirical data, it is worth to summarize the basic differences between the three preceding models.

In spite of all their seeming antagonism, the "systematic/heuristic" model and the "uses and effects" model are equally attached to the polarizing logic of the mainstreams. Their inner parenthood clearly manifests itself in their shared presumption that audiences' awareness of media bias hampers media actors to bring effects upon them. The two models, although diametrically opposing in many respects, share very similar presumptions about the perceived "realism" of media and the recognition of the distortion of reality by the media. The two models equally treat the former as amplifying, and the latter as hindering media effects.

The uses and effects model has grasped the "perceived realism" of television as an emotional catalyst of instrumental viewing, which mediates media effects (Rubin 1984; Rubin-Perse 1987;

Table 1: Three mainstream models amalgamating media effects and audience activities

	"systematic/heuristic processing" model	"uses and effects" model	"resonance" model
Audience activity and media effects	Activity hampers media effects	Activity catalyzes media effects	Activity hampers effects of dissonant media and catalyzes those of consonant media
What is activity?	*Systematic processing:* keeping critical distance, thorough evaluation of information	*Instrumental processing:* involvement, learning to apply a discourse	*Expert tribalism:* "systematic" avoidance of dissonant content, "instrumental" involvement in consonant content
What is passivity?	*Heuristic processing:* Passive media reception, open to effects	*Routine processing:* superficial media use, evading any media effects	*Lay bystanding:* passive and superficial media use
Bias awareness	Systematic: yes Heuristic: no	Instrumental: no Routine: yes (a sense of "unrealness", which hampers instrumental processing)	Experts: aware of the bias of dissonant media only, and this makes them object of consonant media effects

Kim-Rubin 1997). Given this interrelation, Rubin and Perse have hypothesized that "sensing television depictions to be unrealistic may contribute to discounting violent TV content" (1987:127) and evading its effects. Accordingly, awareness of distortion hampers the activation of "instrumental" processing and media effects. In general, bias and distortion, as negative attributes of media, have no place in the mainstreams of U&G research, presuming that people tend to reject unpleasant content (Zillmann-Bryant 1985) and look for gratifications in programmes they judge consonant, trusted and attractive.

The systematic/heuristic processing approach, although for diametrically opposed considerations, presumes a very similar relation between perceived realism and media effects. Accordingly, those processing actively and systematically would invest energies into considering the strength of arguments, the reliability of the medium, or the context of enunciation. Being too active naively to accept the verisimilitude of media, "highly politically sophisticated individuals are more likely to resist mass media messages" (de Vreese et al. 2006:22, cf. McLeod et al. 2002:239). This resistance consists in systematically considering "source-credibility cues" – like perceived self-interestedness – which may hamper media effects to rise (Groenendyk 2002:297–8). Reflexive resistance has been envisioned as arising from "awareness of the source of information (which) causes individuals to evaluate the verisimilitude of that information" (Busselle 2001:60, cf. Shrum et al. 1998). The presumption that bias recognition moderates media effects has been rather common in mainstream media research (in models of Agenda Setting and Framing). Learning-based models of persuasion (McGuire 1986), of priming and of "second-level agenda setting" (Kiousis-McCombs 2004:51) equally deduce the adoption of media-prescribed attitudes from the irreflexive acceptance of the media-presented world as undistortedly "real".

Semiotics-based media reception studies have equally attributed a prominent role to perceived realism in the efficiency of media. From the earliest classical texts onwards, researchers have defined submission to media as the naive acceptance of media contents as natural, in contrast to the reflexive recognition of their constructedness and bias (Hall 1997; Morley 1992; Allan 1999; for a creative rethinking, see Liebes 1995). This opposition echoes the classical distinction of modern literary theory between passive and deconstructive reading (Ryan 2001). On the whole, factual media effects have been supposed to be mediated by the illusion of their verisimilitude. As I have argued elsewhere (Csigó 2007), this "reality effect" hypothesis lies in the core of mainstream media studies. The mainstream paradigm of factual media research consists of various approaches verifying, refuting, contextualizing or modifying this model – but all accepting it as a starting point.

Even John Zaller's resonance model relates, partly, to the above mainstream presumption. Zaller's argument that political expertise implies a heavily tribal engagement excluding "independent thought" does not allow 'political experts' to keep distance from the discourses they engage with. They are affected by a media discourse, and they are not able to recognize its distorted nature. Not allowing any distance for the engaged, Zaller has made only a half-step from the idea of strong media effects which consist in the naturalization of "verisimilitude".

The empirical findings to be presented refute that the recognition of media bias would disactivate media effects. As it will be argued, the two can coexist and amalgamate. This ambiguity will be theorized by the dramaturgical model, to be re-introduced in the Conclusion. A dramaturgical approach may temper the sharpness of Zaller's model, by pointing to the reflexive, conditional, contingent nature of political engagements.

4. Bias awareness, media exposure and political expertise — an empirical analysis of partisan PSB-news effects in Hungary

The late modern "spectacularization" of popular media is present in Central and Eastern Europe just like elsewhere, however, it is certainly not the only factor accountable for expressive and harsh media performances. The other factor accounting for expressivity in factual television is media partisanship, due to the low autonomy of public service media from the state. While, of course, even the BBC, the prime model of public service broadcasting, has attracted criticism for its loyalty (see Curran 1996:15; McNair 2003:36–50; or the decades-long work of the Glasgow Media Group), it is no less certain that in Central and Eastern European democracies the state has been controlling public television by an immediacy never experienced in more established democratic systems (for extended information, see Sükösd – Bajomi-Lázár 2003; see, also, Jakubowicz 1995; Bajomi-Lázár 2002). Since the democratic transition in 1990, public service media in Hungary have been especially exposed to political influence and have fulfilled a mobilizing role in favour of the actual government. Since 1990, Hungary has had four governments, two left-wing and two right-wing, all with an equal hunger to control PSB media.

However, instead of exerting strong, message-driven 'media effects', PSB television brought contextually oscillating effects over its audience in the last seventeen years. In some moments, like in 2002, it successfully mobilized the audience, while in other moments it was object of audiences' self-conscious resistance, like in 1994 (Popescu-Tóka 2002). This contingency resulted, most importantly, from people's reflexive stance towards public media – which means a potential (although not a constant and explicit) awareness of its political bias. With their memories of socialism, Hungarian audiences are well aware of the "old" ideological function of state media. Moreover, since democratic transition in 1990, the governmental occupation of PSB television in Hungary has been aggressive and manifest enough to be obvious not only for common eyes in Europe (deliberately referring to m1 as "state" – and not "public" – television)[12] but also to Hungarian publics. People's awareness manifests itself in the widely used ironic term "royal television".[13] In the last seventeen years, people's awareness of PSB TV's bias, combined with their actual sympathy with the party currently controlling it, has resulted in various forms of audience engagement and disengagement with public media, and this oscillation has considerably affected its power potential. It is important to note that, although the strength of PSB-news bias was considerably fluctuating in the last sixteen years, this oscillation did not prove to correlate with the change of strength of propaganda in PSB TV. For example, in 1994 the extremely harsh pro-government propaganda on PSB TV decreased rather than increased audiences' loyalty to the government! (Popescu-Tóka 2002) After an only slight near-zero effect in 1998, public television news was rather successful in mobilizing political partisans in 2002.

The mobilizing power of m1 news in 2002 has proved quite different from mainstream expectations. Among the three national broadcast evening news available, only PSB television news affected the political attitudes of viewers. At the same time, only this news programme was recognized as politically biased by considerable audience segments! m1-news veracity was heavily contested: altogether, 41 per cent of the population named it as biased (to an open-ended question). As we shall see, those who recognized PBS news bias and those who were affected by this bias did not detach at all into two separate groups. In sharp opposition to mainstream expectations, widespread bias awareness did not hamper the power potential of m1 news. Meanwhile, private channel news programmes (RTL Klub news and TV2 news), although being much more trusted by the general audience than *m1*, did not bring significant effects on the voters.

Although in 2002, the audience ratings of PBS news was relatively low compared to its competitors on the two private channels, almost every second (47%) pro-government voters reported to watch it several times a week or every day. Meanwhile, only 29 per cent of pro-opposition voters and 34 per cent of the undecided and non-voters did so. *m1* news, reaching half of the right-wing electorate regularly, did play a considerable role in right-wing mobilization in 2002. This signals a considerable, although by far not overwhelming, mobilizing potential: *m1* news functioned as a successful mobilizing channel for pro-government voters. As it will be argued, however, the pro-government bias of public television (*m1*) in 2002 did not bring top-down, message-driven effects. At the same time, it can neither be argued that it merely "gratified" the needs of pro-government voters.

In the 2002 parliamentary election campaign, a right-wing government struggled with its left-wing opposition and heavily utilized *m1* news in this fight. Soon after the start of the campaign in the autumn of 2001, the programme became explicitly biased (for a detailed content analysis, see Csigó 2002). Unlike eight years previously, this strong bias efficiently mobilized the audience. Meanwhile, the same bias triggered large audience segments to reflect on the distortive effect of government control over *m1* news (41% of respondents named *m1* biased spontaneously, answering an open-ended question). Thus, the role of *m1* in the campaign equally consisted of mobilizing the right-wing electorate and triggering widespread bias awareness in the audience. Mainstream approaches might presume that bias awareness helped in evading the effects of *m1* news propaganda.

However, in contrast to mainstream expectations, the frequency of watching *m1* news and the chance of recognizing its bias have proved to be positively correlated in the overall sample (r=.11), as reported in table 2. Moreover, by decomposing the sample by political preference, the above association has disappeared among opposition voters and more than doubled among government voters (r=.24). The more government voters watched *m1* news, the more they recognized its bias. Meanwhile, left-wing opposition voters named *m1* news biased, independently of whether they watched it or not. (You may find detailed information on the construction of variables in the *Appendix*.)

The picture gets even more complicated if we consider the relation of political expertise to the above variables. Among government voters, *m1* exposure, bias recognition and political

Table 2: The interrelations of political expertise, *m1* news exposure and *m1* bias awareness.

		political expertise	m1news watching
Overall sample	m1 news watching	0.19	
	m1 bias recognition	0.29	0.11
Opposition Voters	m1 news watching	(0.06)	
	m1 bias recognition	0.36	(0.03)
Government Voters	m1 news watching	0.34	
	m1 bias recognition	0.22	0.24

Pearson correlation coefficients, values in parentheses are insignificant at <.05 level.

expertise were all positively correlated. The more politically aware people were, the more they were seeking the content of *m1* news and the more they recognized that it was biased. By contrast, among opposition voters, watching *m1* news was simply 'out of play': the politically aware did not evade it, and neither did those recognizing its bias. Meanwhile, awareness and bias recognition were very strongly correlated (r=.36): left-wing political experts were very highly aware of *m1*-news pro-government bias.

The above data suggest that political expertise and media use interrelate by very different patterns in the two electoral segments. Data on the absolute numbers of bias recognizers reinforce this suggestion. Figure 1 shows the association of *m1*-watching and bias recognition among right-wing voters, left-wing voters and the undecided.[14]

The bias perception of left-wing voters was consistently high regardless of whether they watched *m1* news or not (around 57–59%). The reason is clear: left-wing parties heavily criticized the government for occupying public service TV and made this critique part of their campaign. Meanwhile, among right-wing voters, only those found *m1* news biased who regularly watched it. The overwhelming majority (around 80%) of those right-wing voters who did not watch *m1* news thought it was politically unbiased. They were not affected by the opposition's criticisms related to the governmental occupation of PSB media. They simply evaded this question, as had been suggested by the right-wing parties themselves, who didn't explicitly address the problem of public TV at all. Meanwhile, the other half of the right-wing electorate, watching *m1* regularly, did recognize the programme's bias in a proportion close to left-wing viewers (46% versus 58%)! Again, these numbers are worth considering, for they come from an open-ended survey question which is able to measure only the most explicit and most reflected opinions. There are good reasons to presume that more detailed interview methods would have shown even higher proportions.

The above findings raise several questions. Do *m1* news viewers, recognizing the bias of the programme in large numbers, evade the effects of the programme? If not, how are they affected by *m1* news in the function of their political awareness? How can it be that right-wing viewers,

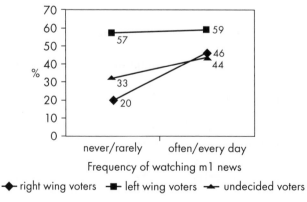

Percentage of those perceiving m1 news as biased towards government

Frequency of watching m1 news

◆ right wing voters　■ left wing voters　▲ undecided voters

Figure 1: Bias awareness by *m1* exposure and party preference (%)

supposedly selecting *m1* news for ideologically consonant contents which can be appreciated as 'real' and 'truthful', found the programme distorted in line with the government's political interests? Why, by contrast, are *m1* news exposure and bias recognition totally uncorrelated among left-wing voters? The above results suggest that the interplay of bias recognition, political expertise, media exposure and media effects may follow ultimately different patterns in the two voter segments. This is the main hypothesis to be examined below (for details of the empirical analysis and presentation of the variables used, see *Appendix 1., 2., 3.*).

For examining whether and how the patterns of media effects and political identity formation differed in the left-wing and the right-wing part of the electorate, we have kept the two electoral segments separate and constructed several OLS regression models in both of them. Three types of correspondences have been examined.

First, factors influencing people's opinions about the leading political issues of the campaign have been revealed. Opinions about the following four issues have been examined: the introduction of a state subsidized real estate credit; a referendum campaign for Hungary to be nominated for the organization of the 2012 Olympic Games; a special status of citizenship provided to Hungarian ethnic minorities living in surrounding countries; and the opening of the labour market to Romanian citizens (see *Appendix 1.*). These issues were initiated by the government and deliberately timed to the period of the electoral campaign. We have examined how favourably people judged them. The first block of regression models presented in table 3 reveals the factors influencing these issue judgements in both voter segments. Thus, the first block of table 3 presents eight regression models altogether: four models in each of the two voter segments.

In the second block, one regression model (constructed in each voter segment) will be presented, revealing what factors account for the recognition that *m1* news is politically biased. The regression model shows how political expertise, exposure to *m1* news and other media correspond to *m1* bias awareness. The third block of models explains the consumption of *m1* news and another programme, the talk show *Heti Hetes*, which runs each Saturday night on the private channel RTL Klub.[15] The infotainment political show, with popular journalists and actors commenting on politics, hit a point of extreme success in Hungary. The talk show was highly critical of the government and loyal to opposition. In 2002, among all other media programmes and outlets, *Heti Hetes* proved the only rival to *m1* news in terms of political mobilization. A total of 47 per cent of left-wing voters reported to watch it every week, while only 30 per cent of the right-wing did so. The significant, although not overwhelming, difference between the two segments parallels the one revealed in *m1* news exposure (obviously, in an opposite direction). Unfortunately, we do not have survey data about people's awareness of *Heti Hetes* bias; however, there is considerable focus group evidence that people did recognize the programme's critical and many times hostile tone against the government.

As presented in *Appendix 2.*, several independent variables have been entered into the above fourteen regression models: various measures of social status, political expertise and media consumption. In table 3 only those independent variables are presented which will be relevant for the following analysis.

Models in the first block have verified our previous suggestion that *m1* exposure and *m1* bias awareness affect people's political opinion differently in the two politically opposing segments.[16] There are good reasons to argue that the following correspondences may be read causally, as signifying media influence (see *Appendix 3.* on "estimating causality"). While *m1* news-viewing affected three opinions out of four in the right-wing segment (β-s are, respectively,

Table 3

	Dependent variables:	Voter segments:	Independent variables				Overall R²
			Political expertise	M1 news-watching	Heti Hetes-watching	M1 bias recognition	
First block of models	Real estate credit	**GOV**		**−0.26**			**0.10**
		OPP			.11°	0.17	**0.03**
	Status law	**GOV**	**−0.21**	**−0.15**	**0.15**		**0.18**
		OPP	−0.13	−0.14		0.12	**0.04**
	Employment	**GOV**	**−0.19**	**−0.13**			**0.13**
	pact	OPP				0.12°	**0.07**
	Olympic	**GOV**	**−0.20**				**0.07**
	Games	OPP	0.12°			0.21	**0.04**
Models 2.	Bias	**GOV**	**0.14**	**0.11°**	**−0.14**	–	**0.11**
	recognition	OPP	0.27		0.30	–	**0.26**
Models 3.	M1 news-	**GOV**	**0.16**	–		–	**0.32**
	watching	OPP		–		–	**0.12**
	Heti hetes-	**GOV**			–	–	**0.22**
	watching	OPP			–	–	**0.15**

The table presents the standardized regression coefficients (β) of fourteen OLS regression models, and the corresponding RÇ values representing the proportion of the total variance explained by the model. Only associations of r<0.05 significance are presented. (° : r<0.07.)

In the first block (the first eight models), negative signs represent pro-government opinion. In the second block, positive signs represent high m1 bias awareness.

The complete regression models are available from the author.

−.26, −.15, −.13, n.s.), it influenced only one opinion among left-wing voters (β-s are, respectively, n.s., −.14, n.s., n.s.). m1 exposure effected issue judgements only in the right-wing segment. By contrast, m1 bias awareness affected the opinions of left-wing voters only. Among left-wing voters, the bias-aware rejected the government's messages more sharply than the non-aware (β-s are, respectively, .17, .12, .12, .21). In the right-wing group, no such correspondence between bias awareness and issue judgements has emerged.

Political expertise has also brought different effects on political opinions in the two groups. The political expertise variable expresses a higher interest in politics, willingness of participation and higher factual knowledge on politics. In the right-wing group, the politically aware tended closely to follow the ideological cues offered by their parties. Expertise corresponded to political opinion in three issues out of four (β-s are, respectively, n.s., −.21, −.19, −.20). This pattern of the effects of political awareness underlies John Zaller's and the Uses and Effects model's presumptions about instrumental processing. The more politically aware the respondent was, the more he or she followed the cues his or her favourite party offered in the particular issues. Meanwhile, the effect of expertise on political opinions has proved highly ambivalent among the left-wing (β-s are, respectively, n.s., −.13, n.s., .12). This pattern evokes, if anything, the systematic processing model, assuming that the politically aware will negotiate each issue, instead of heuristically following party cues.

The second block consists of two models, explaining bias recognition in the two political segments. Here, also, rather different patterns have arisen. Among pro-government voters, bias recognition has proved slightly to correspond with political awareness, *Heti Hetes* watching and *m1* news watching. The considerable positive correlation (.24) revealed in Table 2 has proved significant even after entering various control variables: frequent *m1* news viewing has proved to increase, instead of decreasing, *m1* bias awareness.[17] Meanwhile, among left-wing voters, two salient correspondences have been revealed: political awareness (β= .27) and *Heti Hetes*-watching (β= .30) have strongly enhanced people's ability to recognize *m1* news bias.

Models in the third block have explained the consumption of *m1* news and the talk show *Heti Hetes*. *m1* news has proved to attract the political experts only among right-wing voters. Among left-wing voters, no such correspondence of political expertise and media exposure has been revealed.

5. Discussion

The data presented above reveal two divergent dynamics by which left-wing and right-wing viewers formed their political identities and knowledge. The two different patterns of political identity formation have evolved in accordance with political parties' communication strategies and the current general political context. The two different patterns are revealed in figures 2a and 2b, in path model-like schemes, based on the above presented regression models. The figures are illustrative, aimed to visualize the evidence presented in table 3.[18] The associations explored in the above regression models are symbolized here by abstract plus and minus signs.[19]

The complexity of the above results verifies the basic presumption of all the three theoretical models presented earlier: that media effects are mediated by the selectivity, competence and engagement of audiences.

Out of the three approaches, our findings harmonize the less with the systematic/heuristic processing model. Some evidence, however, underlies this latter approach as well. The finding

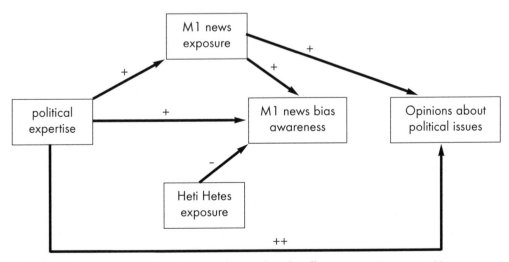

Figure 2a: Exposure, expertise, bias awareness and media effects among Government Voters

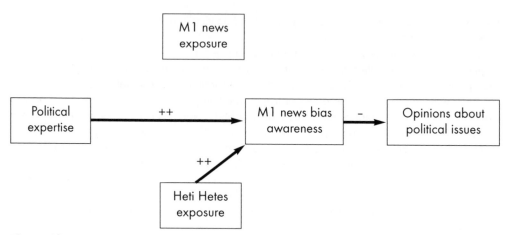

Figure 2b: Exposure, expertise, bias awareness and media effects among Opposition Voters

that political expertise has correlated positively with *m1* news bias awareness in both voter segments suggests that the more politically aware are more able to critically reflect on the veracity of media contents. However, as it will be argued, the higher bias awareness of political experts cannot be entirely equated with the critical stance implied by the idea of systematic processing. As for Rubin's Uses and Effects model, which presumes audience activity to catalyze cultivation effects: this model has been backed by the positive correspondences between political expertise, *m1* exposure and partisan issue judgements revealed in the right-wing segment. However, as we shall see, the patterns revealed in the left-wing segment counter the UE model. In the following, John Zaller's "tribal" approach will be applied to analysing right-wing and left-wing identity formation.

Among right-wing voters, almost all the factors examined constituted a rather stable and coherent system. The coherent positive correspondences between political expertise, *m1* exposure and political issue judgements evoke John Zaller's "tribal" approach and Alan Rubin's idea of instrumental processing. An "instrumental" pattern of information processing characterized right-wing voters: the politically involved chose a programme affirming their dispositions (*m1* news) and judged the political issues in a more partisan way than the non-involved. Beyond this direct association, political expertise had a more indirect ideological effect, as well: experts watched more *m1* news, which then sharpened their ideological engagement. *m1* news-viewing has been proven to make government voters even more engaged, judging political issues through ideologically coloured glasses. *m1* viewers trusted the programme, entered its world and appropriated its discourse. They became affected by the cultural power of the programme, which channelled and sharpened their basic sympathy towards the government.

This pattern is in accordance with right-wing parties' strategies, who tried to catch the electorate by an offensive campaign, making people engage with an ideologically coherent overall vision about the nation (based on symbols and promises, like national unity, "awaking" local communities, an individual entrepreneurial ethos, economic progress, surpassing the "old world", a sharp rupture with the communist past). Political expertise and exposure to *m1* have both amplified right-wing voters' engagement with this coherent and appealing political vision. These interrelations, evoking John Zaller's model, project a pattern of "blind tribalization".

However, one important thing diverts the above supposed pathway: the fact that political expertise and $m1$ exposure have not only sharpened ideological engagement, but also contributed to a higher level of bias recognition! A highly ambivalent fact: people recognized the bias of the programme they were effected by. Meanwhile, $m1$ bias awareness did not tender right-wing voters' ideological opinions with the four political issues examined. Why did bias awareness not trigger resistance or evasion?[20] To resolve the above ambiguities, the very conception of media effects will be reconsidered and re-theorized in terms of a dramaturgical "alliance".

Left-wing voters formed their identities and knowledge by completely different dynamics. The point is not merely that $m1$ news effects have been evaded: more important is the fact that in the left-wing segment, no positive correspondence has emerged between political expertise, exposure to left-wing media (*Heti Hetes*)[21] and the cultivation of partisan issue judgements. These findings counter the UE model's presumption that attitude-consistent programmes, perceived as "real", and political expertise would have a mobilizing effect and trigger "instrumental" processing. Neither has the other important UE presumption, that media perceived as "unreal" would trigger a passive, evasive stance, been backed by our data. In the left-wing segment, the perception of $m1$ news as distorted has triggered something more than passive avoidance. It had a real mobilizing, activating force: it has proved the only variable robustly corresponding with issue judgements, sharpening them, making them more partisan. In contrast to the UE model, $m1$-bias awareness did not merely disaffect left-wing viewers: it seems to have "activated" them and led to the cultivation of more partisan issue judgements. Moreover, $m1$-bias awareness was the only factor related to political expertise and *Heti Hetes* consumption. Political experts and *Heti Hetes* viewers found $m1$ news particularly biased, independently of whether they watched it or not.

The above co-existence of ideological engagement and a critical awareness about the bias of ideologically dissonant media evokes Zaller's theory. Zaller points to the fact that the "systematic", active criticism of ideologically dissonant content may be as much an important part of political engagement as the "instrumental", affirmative stance towards consonant contents. As Zaller has highlighted, the reflexive criticism of media distortion does not imply audience autonomy at all, if it is directed to ideologically dissonant media. For what such criticism implies is not reflexive distance, but an emotional "negative engagement" with repugnant political actors.

Awareness of $m1$ news bias was in line with opposition parties' rhetoric, accusing the governing party of occupying PSB television. In 2002, opposition parties were less determined than their competitors in creating an ideological unity of voters. Of course, they have presented mobilizing ideological visions (modernization, solidarity, anti-nationalism) and campaign promises (that of a widespread social programme). However, equally important was the strategy to gather together, by a negative campaign, all those people unsatisfied with the government's pursuits. In their negative campaign, parties in opposition presented the government menace in multiple ways (threatening democracy, the civil sphere, everyday life, the poor, the secular, the minorities, the media).

Left-wing voters treated the obvious occupation of PSB television as a symbol well representing the government's unscrupulousness and rallied against it. The high-bias awareness of politically knowledgeable left-wing voters (73% of them proved to be bias-aware) signifies their ideological closeness to parties in opposition. By contrast, many fewer of the less knowledgeable left-wing voters recognized *m1* bias (only 37%). Given the fact that this difference was independent of whether people did or did not watch *m1* news, it evokes Zaller's account on the tribal ideological attitude among the political "experts". This argument suggests, again, that *m1* news-bias awareness amplified partisan engagement, either directly, or in an indirect way, mediating the force of political expertise and of *Heti Hetes* to sharpen partisan issue judgements.

At the same time, as it was the case in the right-wing segment, the active, interested, knowledgeable part of the left-wing electorate (the "experts") kept more distance from their parties than presumed by Zaller's model. In the case of the four political issues examined, no signs of Zaller's "blind expert tribalism" have been revealed. Experts have not shown stronger ideological engagement than non-experts in judging these issues. As presented in table 3, expertise has related to the four issues in various ways. For example, in the case of the minority status law, the leading issue of the campaign, left-wing political experts have proved less, and not more, ideologically engaged than non-experts! They relied less, and not more, on partisan cues when judging this issue. Importantly, neither did experts watch more frequently the ideologically consonant, left-wing talk show *Heti Hetes*.

In the left-wing segment, motivated voters (be they political experts or viewers of a politically engaged talk show) did have a say about which issue or message to engage with. Active voters' engagement was oriented to the issue of government control over PSB media only, one element of the multi-faceted campaign rhetoric of left-wing political parties. Their engagement, similarly to that of right-wing experts, has proved partial and conditional, which evokes, again, the notion of "alliance" instead of Zaller's "blind tribalism". The final chapter offers a dramaturgical re-thinking of people's engagements as "alliances" between audience and performer.

6. Conclusions: the suspension of disbelief as a conditional engagement and the cultural politics of 'alliance'

The year of 2002 brought to Hungarian voters the first fully mediatized campaign of the country's democratic history. The spectacular campaign, triggering an unusually sharp symbolic polarization, figures as an ideal terrain for dramaturgical analysis. Political and media actors performed highly expressive, partisan utterances which triggered the audience to enact "attendance"-like reception practices: paying focused attention, investing mental and emotional energies into engagement, imagining a community "around" mediated experiences, attributing to particular performances a special, more-than-ordinary importance. In early 2002, political speeches, media events orchestrated to the campaign (Csigó 2006) and TV programmes like *m1* news or the talk show *Heti Hetes* did stand apart, for many people, from the ordinary flow of politics and media-as-usual. People related to them as performances to be "attended", and this attitude opened the way to the ambivalent play of engagement: the fusion of audience activity and dramaturgical power.

Audiences' "attendance"-like attitude may stand behind the main finding of our analysis: the fundamental asymmetry of right-wing and left-wing political identity-formation. As if voters, following their basic political attitudes, would have entered two separate aesthetic and ideological power fields, two distinct "theatres" of political spectacle. Turning their attention, selectively and deliberately, to those actors and programmes they found more reliable, they have exposed themselves to these latters' dramaturgical, rhetoric power.

In spite of their basic divergence, the two patterns of identity formation correspond to each other in several respects. These connections will be revealed below, in four consecutive points.

First, it will be argued that the critical recognition of m1 bias did in neither segment play a deconstructive, emancipating role (1). Instead, it made part of an "alliance" between audiences and their favourite political or media actors (2), an alliance based on the former's permissiveness and opportunistic stance – typical to the reception of artistic performances in general. Then, the empirically revealed media uses and effects will be re-interpreted in the terms of "alliance" (3). Finally (4), it will be argued that such a dramaturgical re-thinking of media effects and audience engagements is inevitable for understanding how audiences relate to the torrent of overly dramatized, expressive and increasingly partisan performances, sharply competing for audience loyalty.

1. The empirical evidence presented clearly warns that the mainstream opposition of bias awareness and political or media influence may be idealistic and unreal. Recognizing media bias does not at all guarantee independence from media and political effects. On the contrary, it is a knowledge which, like all other knowledge, relies on resources of trust and authority. As we have seen, awareness of m1-news bias did not lead right-wing voters to turn away from the programme or discount its ideology. On the contrary, it has proved to be embedded in the net of positive – "instrumental", or "tribal" – correspondences between political expertise, m1 exposure and partisan issue judgements. m1-bias awareness among left-wing viewers did neither embody a critical distance: it was closely related to left-wing parties' campaign messages and it was the only factor directly sharpening the judgements on political issues. These findings highlight an important shortcoming of mainstream research which, in the quest for the critical capacities of audiences (be it local resistance or self-governed individual action), tended to undertheorize the authority resources these practices require (cf. Condit 1989; Dayan 2002).[22] Zaller's "tribal" approach has been applied because it sensitively grasps how far audience activities, choices and reflections are nourished by authority attributed to trusted political and media actors/discourses.

However, the same "tribal" logic of Zaller's resonance model deserves criticism for omitting that the engagements explored were, by far, not mechanical, and people did keep a critical distance from the actor they engaged with. Political 'experts' did not crowd into ideologically homogeneous tribes chasing away any independent thought. They related to media with a stance more ambivalent and reflexive than a blindly tribal one. The fact that many right-wing voters recognized the bias of their favourite news programme reveals the contingency of engagement, as does the fact that in the left-wing segment political expertise did not sharpen the judgements of political issues in general, it increased only m1-bias awareness.

2. Following this line, I will argue for thinking of engagements as conditional, partial and opportunistic, having a provisory and limited scope, moved by the finer logic of "alliance" or "contract". Although Zaller's model sensitively shows how audience expertise and activity are saturated by media power, it does not grasp the conditional, "contractual" element in audience engagement. The "contractuality" of audience engagement implies that audiences' subordination to actors' power is willing and, importantly, partial and provisory. This understanding, inspired by theatrical experience, grasps audience engagement neither as a mere effect of propaganda, nor as a naive and illusory belief in the actor's "organic" leadership.

Many theories of theatre have pointed to audiences' active, cooperative stance towards the dramaturgical strategies of actors (Schechner 2003). The catharsis and faith triggered by performing arts have long been associated with audiences' will to identify. This will has been supposed to neutralize audiences' natural aversions to identifying with something they know they are not identical to (cf. Boulton 1960, ref. by Alexander 2006). In aesthetics, this mechanism is known as the "suspension of disbelief", a deliberate permissiveness from the part of the audience willing to reach "poetic faith", as Coleridge first declared two centuries ago. Suspending disbelief is an attitude traditionally attributed to audiences of artistic performances, especially imitative art, to listeners of stories in general, to players enjoying games and, finally, to fans who can belong to each of the above categories.

Highly important is the temporary and liminoid quality of this suspension. Theatre audiences, no matter how "enchanted" they may become, do not wish completely to dissolve their distance from actors: they only suspend it for the duration of the performance. Although they give the chance for a cathartic experience to arrive and to change their lives, in most cases they return to the social roles and habits they "left out in the lobby" for the time of the performance. In theatre, people's engagement with the performance is inherently "contractual": in fact, they paid for it at the cash desk. On the whole, audiences may get carried away by powerful feelings induced by performers, but this performative "fusion" (Alexander 2006) is temporary and conditioned by the actual mood of the audience.

Seen from a "dramaturgical" angle, the willing "suspension of disbelief" (for Goffman's similar arguments, see Burns [1992:304]; see, also, Galgut 2002) is an inevitable factor in the symbolic traffic between media and audiences. It works in those particular moments when people imaginarily de-activate the symbolic distance separating them from media or political actors, when they suspend their unfocused and unselective viewing habits for the sake of an intense emotional experience. Dayan and Katz's media events (1992) may serve as typical examples of such heightened and emotionally overloaded moments that make some viewers "surrender" (Katz 1996:16) for the period of the ritualized performance. In such moments, audience engagement is motivated by the wish to reach, provisorily, an intense emotional experience which gives meaning to the world and a sense of agency for coping with it. The idea that audiences' willingness for immersion is fundamental in ritual experience has been quite common in ritual theory, as well: "ritual only comes alive experientially, emotionally, subjunctively, when actively read by audiences/readerships who are prepared to 'participate' within it as symbolically meaningful to them, and who are prepared to accept the imagined solidarities it offer" (Cottle 2006:429).

The above moment of deliberate permissiveness, when audiences "get exposed" to a dramaturgical power they cannot fully control, is crucial in the establishment of "alliances" with actors of artistic — and, increasingly, media and political — performances. The act of "suspending disbelief" opens a way for media effects, but also guarantees a certain distance, a possibility for withdrawal, a break in the flow of influence. This ambiguity is what a "dramaturgical" approach points to, grasping TV audiences as "effect seekers" and media effects as "alliances" with media actors. Accordingly, the distance which is inscribed in the reception of theatre may saturate political engagements, as well as exemplified by the commonly known proneness of voters to justify their political decision by highly opportunistic arguments: "voting for her for lack of anything better" or "voting for anybody but him".

3. A dramaturgical interpretation of our empirical findings points to a similar opportunism in right-wing engagement: those right-wing $m1$ viewers who recognized that the programme was distorted might have decided to be loyal to it for lack of anything "better". Aware in considerable proportions of $m1$'s bias and still keeping to the programme for want of another programme they would have found more reliable, many of the right-wing viewers "allied" with $m1$ news. They devalued the significance of $m1$ news' bias and suspended the distance and

criticism which was – potentially – inscribed in their bias awareness. They "bracketed off" this problem and focused on the positive, ideologically consonant content of m1 news. This permissiveness enabled m1 news further to sharpen their ideological engagement. The same permissiveness may explain why the awareness of governmental control over public media did not moderate the "tribal" correspondence between political expertise and partisan issue judgements.

By contrast, in the left-wing segment, political experts and *Heti Hetes* viewers did not judge the political issues more sharply than the "average" left-wing voter. They were less keen on entering into a closed ideological universe than m1 viewers and political experts in the right-wing segment. They only rallied with the message that m1 news was biased, as an apparent, palpable proof of the government's unscrupulous appetite for power. Thus, left-wing audience "activity" comprised an increased political engagement only with the message that m1 news was biased. The significance of this bias was aggrandized – in sharp opposition to the above urge of right-wing voters' to "bracket it off". The prominent weight given to m1 bias had an ideological function and opened the door for influence. m1-bias awareness considerably sharpened political issue judgements and played a mediating role, enhancing a more heightened engagement of political experts and *Heti Hetes* viewers.

4. In the 2002 electoral campaign, not only m1 news and *Heti Hetes* played a strongly partisan role. High partisanship was typical to other media programmes as well (mostly linked to public service TV and radio and print media), contributing to the unprecedented fierceness of the electoral campaign. There is more in the above intense media partisanship than the heritage of Hungary's autocratic political past. Interestingly, the 2002 campaign equally resulted from the country's democratic deficit and mirrored the newest trends of political communication in western democracies. Intense media partisanship in Hungary emerged in line with the general takeover of western media by a torrent of highly moving, expressive, partisan media contents (Mazzoleni et al. 2003). Ever-intensifying media competition and the global mobility of international campaign experts (Hungarian parties in our case hired Berlusconi and Blair campaign experts) are only two factors in the process of cultural and economic globalization affecting national media and political systems.

By this transformation, an "external pluralism" of highly engaging and partisan programmes takes the place of the "internal pluralism" characterizing the factual programming of the previous, less competitive period. Media "supersaturation" (Gitlin 2001) implies not only the overflow of sounds and images, but also that of expressivity, partisanship, melodrama and tension-making in popular, post-factual and post-documentary media (Corner 2000). With the rise of a spectacular, "dramaturgically oversaturated" media environment (Csigó 2007), the relation of media users to political and media actors increasingly takes the shape of the actor-audience relation characterizing performing arts (Street 1998; Corner-Pels 2003 and van Zoonen 2005). People' engagements with highly partisan and moving media performances are of a "theatrical" character: they "fuse" media power, audience selectivity and, importantly, audiences' competence of keeping distance from the object of their own engagement. This is what is expressed by the notion of "alliance": a contractual relation allowing subordination and distance at the same time.

Certainly, there are audience engagements which are blind, which result more from the imposition of belief, rather than the suspension of disbelief. However, as the above study hopefully has demonstrated, engagements with dramaturgically powerful media performances may, and many times do, allow self-distanciation and an active search for authentic experience.

Understanding the fragile dynamics of audience engagement will be a prominent challenge equally for academia and business[23] in the new, hypercompetitive, media-saturated cultural landscape. The above "dramaturgical" approach to engagement may offer important signposts for understanding the new media landscape: not merely as a descriptive tool, but also as a potential theoretical basis for our hopes that intensifying excess and partisanship in popular television do not necessarily result in propagandistic effects, in blindly tribal mobilization.

Appendix: research design and applied variables

The following analysis makes part of wider research exploring the uses and effects of factual media in Hungary. The data were collected the early spring of 2002, during the middle period of the parliamentary election campaign. The research consisted of focus group research, content analysis and a one-wave representative survey research conducted three weeks before the election. Here, only data coming from the latter will be deployed.

1. Dependent variables: political opinions on the issues of the campaign

The political effects of TV news have been measured primarily as their influence on people's opinions, party preference-controlled, on the hottest issues of the campaign. Four issues have been selected for analysis, each being important in the campaign and each grasping audience attention.

- The first issue is a law introduced by the right-wing government. The law gave special status to Hungarian minorities living abroad, guaranteeing rights to health services, employment and voting for those settled in Hungary (hereinafter referred to as 'status law').
- The law triggered negative reactions in surrounding countries. At the insistence of the Romanian government, employment rights were extended to Romanian citizens of all ethnicities ('employment pact').
- Right-wing parties, as another element of their 'popular nationalist' campaign, launched a referendum campaign for Hungary to be nominated for the organization of the 2012 Olympic Games. They claimed to have collected more than one million votes ('Olympic Games').
- Finally, the right-wing government's politically most successful act will be examined: the introduction of state-subsidized real estate credit for young people ('real estate credit').

The following analysis will explain the variance of pro-government and pro-opposition opinions about these four issues. In three of the four issues, I have measured people's attitudes by a five-level scale, with one end representing an opinion favourable to the government, the other representing an opinion close to that of the opposition. In the fourth case, that of the Olympic Games, several questions have been asked and factor-analysed: one factor has emerged, contrasting favourable and disapproving opinions.

2. Variables both dependent and independent in various models

Media consumption

An ultimate question of the analysis addressed the potential effects of TV news on viewers. In addition to the PSB TV evening news programme (m1 news), the two leading commercial channels' evening news have also been examined (RTL Klub news, TV2 news).

Alongside the news programmes, the effects of *Heti Hetes*, a politics-centred infotainment talk show has been analysed.

The other media organs entered into the model were the two leading political newspapers (the left-wing *Népszabadság* and the right-wing *Magyar Nemzet*) and *Fókusz* (*Focus*), a human-interest infotainment magazine broadcast every day after the early evening news at RTL Klub.

Bias recognition

People were asked that out of the three news programmes available which one is biased in favour of the government. They could freely name any of the three evening news programmes. A total of 41 per cent of respondents have claimed $m1$ is biased. By contrast, far fewer respondents judged the two commercial TV news programmes to be pro-government or pro-opposition (around 10% only).

Independent variables:

Social status position

The first set of independent variables has expressed people's social status position. It has been measured by 'classical' status variables, like gender, income, level of education, age, residence, religion, labour-market activity.

Political affiliation

In the 2002 parliamentary elections, a right-wing coalition in government and its left-wing opposition struggled for power. The right-wing coalition was led by the populist Alliance of Young Democrats (FIDESZ), while the dominant force of the left-wing coalition was the post-communist Hungarian Socialist Party (MSZP). The left-right cleavage between parties was broadened ad infinitum in the campaign, which triggered an unprecedented ideological dissociation of the two political blocs' electorate. Hungarian society at that time was divided into three broad political segments of similar weight. One-third of the electorate sympathized with the government, parties in opposition had the sympathy of another third, while the remaining segment was mostly composed of undecided or uninterested citizens (and a narrow fraction of followers of marginal parties).

Political expertise

The political expertise index is a linear combination of the following variables: the overall knowledge of the names of party leaders; the overall number of 'don't know' answers to factual and attitudinal questions; the frequency by which the respondent discusses public issues in the family or at the workplace; interest in politics; willingness to vote. The five variables have been entered in Principal Component Analysis, the results of which are deployed as follows. The first principal component has accounted for 43 per cent of the total variance.

	political expertise
willing to vote	0.56
general level of knowledge	0.76
talks about news	0.53
knowledge of party leaders	0.72
interest in politics	0.69
variance explained	43%

3. Estimating causality

It is important to note, first, that no definitive estimation of causality is possible in a one-wave survey research project. As a first step, the association of TV news viewing and party preference has been estimated by the linear regression method (social status, political expertise and other media consumption controlled). This model has shown only one of the three news programmes to be efficient: $m1$ news (β=.19, r<.01). However, the direction of this association cannot be theoretically established: these raw data do not reveal whether pro-government voters chose $m1$ news, or $m1$ news influenced people to sympathize with the government. Since political identification is a rather stable attitude, it certainly orients media selection to a great extent.

Meanwhile, there are good reasons to presume that people have much less crystallized attitudes about the very concrete issues parties dispute in a given period. People do not follow automatically their favourite parties' instructions when making judgements – especially if the issues to be judged may have consequences for their everyday lives. Political identifications and everyday considerations may even clash in such cases. Moreover, given the complexities of political issues, people can be much less certain as for which news to turn to for 'reinforcing' their prior opinions on particular issues. Thus, it is highly improbable that people would, on the one hand, have stable and crystallized 'issue-specific' attitudes about all the issues arising in a given period and, on the other, have well-established knowledge and expectations about which news programmes are the most consonant with these attitudes. The positive correspondence between, say, the "status law" issue and $m1$ news-viewing – party preference-controlled – cannot be derived from viewers' self-controlled selectivity, by which they would have chosen $m1$ news following some previous expectations about $m1$ coverage of the specific issue of status law.

People choose some news programmes over others as a result of broad political and other dispositions and not concrete, issue-specific preferences. Thus, by keeping political identification under control, the associations demonstrated between media exposure and opinion on an issue can rightly be regarded as (mostly) products of media effects, beyond the intentional control of voters.

Notes

1. How does "uniqueness" affect the generalizability of my argument? Certainly, easy generalization would lead us astray: in late modern politics no campaign can be taken as "typical" and representing the overall logic of campaigning. On the contrary: all campaigns are unique to some extent, and various genres or formats of campaigning have to be distinguished. The 2002 electoral campaign in Hungary embodied the genre of campaigns with high emotions and sharp symbolic polarization, similar to the 2000 or 2004 USA campaign or the 2007 French presidential election. If my findings can be put into a more general frame of relevance, this is certainly the context of highly emotional, spectacular politics. This is consistent with the aim of my research: understanding the overall "spectacularization" of media discourse in late modern culture.

2. I am grateful to Daniel Dayan for suggesting this notion, which wittily captivates the nature of audience practices to be analysed in this article.

3. In the tradition of "media effects" research (McLeod et al. 2002), effects have been defined as operating independently of audiences' intentions, implying, thus, a factor of imposition and, also, a factor of passive subordination from the part of the audience. Media effects studies (the experimental analysis of attitude change or the exploration of macro-level processes of cultivation or agenda-setting) have mostly neglected to deal with audience intentions as integral, fundamental components

of the power mechanisms of media. As opposed to the above presumption of "message-driven" media effects, the U&G school and other forms of "active audience" research have grasped audiences as deliberately seeking in media what is "their own" and perceiving media content in highly selective ways. The general view about the "minimal consequences" of political campaigns (for a critique, see Iyengar-Simon 2000) and frequent references on the "value reinforcement" thesis (that media would "merely" gratify pre-existing preferences of receivers) express this 'effect-less' understanding of media use.

4. The spectator is in a structurally different position from that of the actor, meanwhile, they both engage in a common work of creating a moving and living experience.

5. Some researchers speculating about possible 'reciprocal' models of effects and selectivity have clearly recognized the gap mainstream research maintains between the two (Eveland et al. 2003: 362). This gap, they have argued, hampers scholars "from drawing a connection from consumption goals to exposure outcomes. They can measure the gratification people seek, and they can assess exposure effects, but methodologically, they have been unable to draw a casual connection between the two" (Tewksbury 1999:23).

6. I am referring to intense global-local cultural exchange (Pieterse 2000); new hybrid media genres ("infotainment", "advertainment", "factoid", "advertorial", "edutainment", "infomercial" and so on); the amalgamation of private and public spheres and issues (Silverstone 1994); the rise of "citizen-consumers" (Scammell 2000) and of popular media enabled "cultural citizenship" (Hermes 1998:158; Hermes 2005; Dahlgren 1995:146; Dahlgren 2003).

7. Moreover, the above model has been underlined mostly by experimental evidence, deserving the usual criticisms for producing unreliable results in highly artificial situations.

8. This contrast is consistent with our commonsensical understanding of ME and U&G schools as antagonistic. However, it is worth remembering that early U&G research intended less to deny media influence itself than to point to its necessary mediatedness by audience motivation. This lies behind Elihu Katz' long-standing warning: "even the most potent of the mass media content cannot ordinarily influence an individual who has 'no use' for it" (Katz 1959, ref. by Rubin 2002).

9. Meanwhile, they have presented impressive empirical evidence against the classical models of media effects! For example, Rubin and Perse have demonstrated that no cultivation effects exist if the classical questions of cultivation research (e.g., about violence) are asked 'positively' in terms of 'gratification'. Television, which has been claimed to 'increase distrust', has not been proven to 'decrease trust' and so on. The authors have also found that "ritualistic, heavy television exposure was not linked to negative effects" (Rubin-Perse 1987:125–126). These results have received unintended empirical backing from the proponents of the systematic/heuristic processing model, who sometimes found unanticipated correlations. Krosnick and Brannon, for example, have explored the way in which political expertise facilitates priming effects (1993) (for similar results, see Miller-Krosnick 2000; Tewksbury 1999).

10. The problem results probably from the too abstract level of analysis. Extremely broad attitudes have been examined; like attention, in general, or the perception of the medium itself (perceiving 'television' as real). Variables intended to represent the 'effects' of media have also been too broadly defined (e.g., the respondent's emotional attachment to soap operas, or his or her fear of victimization). The abstractness of these attitudes allows us only to presume but not to prove that they result from media exposure.

11. This pattern works only in cases where there is an ideological variation in media content. In a case in which 'one-sided' information dominates the field, Zaller has presumed a different pattern between expertise, ideology and media effects.

12. Much revelatory is the high number Google hits (in 2006 November) to the term "Hungarian state television" (1660 hits), compared to the rare hits of search items like "Hungarian public television" (243 hits) or "Hungarian public service television" (30 hits).

13. In addition to the hundreds of blog and forum participants calling public television 'royal', the term often appears in mainstream journalism as well, for example, in a leading news portal's interview with the press secretary. http://index.hu/velvet/celeb/boglar1118/.

14. In the following, the 'undecided' group will be left out of the analysis.

15. It is a franchised programme of the RTL company, which originally ran in Germany under the name of *Seven Days, Seven Heads.*

16. In opposition to *m1* news, the other relevant political programme, the left-wing talk show *Heti Hetes*, has not influenced political opinions in either of the two groups.

17. Interestingly, watching the highly opposition-biased talk show *Heti Hetes* has negatively corresponded to the awareness of *m1*'s bias. This finding would need further explanation.

18. In fact, the figures are only of illustrative nature; however, they follow a path-model-like scheme. Accordingly, the associations presented exist after controlling all the variables lying 'behind' (i.e., on the left of) a given variable and after controlling social status as well.

19. The ++ sign appearing three times in the two figures represents a correspondence I have qualified strong and prominent.

20. A possible explanation might suggest that right-wing viewers judged *m1* bias more positively than others. This is not the case: right-wing and left-wing viewers have equally seen *m1* bias as negative, opposed to objectivity and other positive attributes.

21. ...and other, less important left-wing media formats which are not analysed here in detail...

22. For a similar critique, see Daniel Dayan's (2002) comments on David Morley's *Nationwide* project, a classical example of mainstream media reception research. The same objection regarding Morley's work has been formulated by Michelle Condit (1989).

23. As a growing body of quasi-theoretical speculations in media business makes it clear (see the blog of Max Kalehoff, Nielsen Buzzmetrics Vice-President, about "engagement marketing" [Kalehoff 2006]).

References

Alexander, J. (2006). 'Cultural Pragmatics: Social Performance between Ritual and Strategy' in J. Alexander, B. Giesen and J. L. Mast (eds.) *Social Performance. Symbolic Action, Cultural Pragmatics and Ritual* (New York, Cambridge University Press), pp. 1–28.

Alexander, J., B. Giesen and J. L. Mast (eds.) (2006). *Social Performance. Symbolic Action, Cultural Pragmatics and Ritual,* New York, Cambridge University Press.

Alexander, J. C. (2003). *The Meanings of Social Life: a Cultural Sociology,* New York, Oxford University Press.

Allan, S. (1999). *News Culture,* Buckingham, Open University Press.

Altheide, D. L. and R. P. Snow (1979). *Media Logic,* Beverly Hills, Calif., Sage.

Argejó, É. (eds.) (1998). *Jelentések könyve* (*The book of reports*), Budapest, Új Mandátum.

Bajomi-Lázár, P. (2002). 'Közszolgálati televíziózás Közép-Kelet-Európában' (*Public service television in East Central Europe*), *Médiakutató*, 3:2, pp. 73–86.

Basil, M. D. (1996).'Identification as a Mediator of Celebrity Effects', *Journal of Broadcasting and Electronic Media*, 40:3, pp. 478–495.

Beck, L. (1998). 'Három március hírei a képernyőn' (*The March news in three years on the screen*) in É. Argejó (eds.) *Jelentések könyve* (*The book of reports*), (Budapest, Új Mandátum), pp. 100–115.

Bennett, S. (1997). *Theatre Audiences: a Theory of Production and Reception*, London, Routledge.

Blumler, J. G. (1970). 'The Political Effects of Television' in J. D. Halloran (eds.) *The Political Effects of Television* (London, Panther), pp. 68–104.

Boulton, M. (1960). *The Anatomy of Drama*, London.

Burns, T. (1992). *Erving Goffman*, London, Routledge.

Busselle, R. W. (2001). 'Television Exposure, Perceived Realism and Exemplar Accessibility in the Social Judgement Process', *Media Psychology*, 3:1, pp. 43–67.

Cappella, J. N. and K. H. Jamieson (1997). *The Spiral of Cynicism. The Press and the Public Good*, New York, Oxford University Press.

Chaffee, S. H. and J. Schleuder (1986). 'Measurement and Effects of Attention to Media', *Human Communication Reearch*, 13:1, pp. 76–103.

Condit, C.-M. (1989). 'The Rhetorical Limits of Polysemy', *Critical Studies in Mass Communication*, 6:2, pp. 103–122.

Corner, J. (2000). 'What Can We Say about Documentary', *Media, Culture & Society*, 22:5, pp. 811–818.

Corner, J. and D. Pels (2003). 'Introduction: The Re-styling of Politics' in J. Corner and D. Pels (eds.) *Media and the Restyling of Politics* (London, Sage), pp. 1–19.

Cottle, S. (2006). 'Mediatized Rituals: Beyond Manufacturing Consent', *Media, Culture, Society*, 28:3, pp. 411–432.

Couldry, N. (2000). *The Place of Media Power. Pilgrims and Witnesses of the Media Age*, London, Routledge.

Curran, J. (1996). 'The Future of Public Service Broadcasting', *Javnost*, 3:3, pp. 1–20.

Csigó, P. (2002). 'A televíziós hírműsorok a választási kampány időszakában' (*Television news programs during the election campaign*) in M. Sükösd and M. Vásárhelyi (eds.) *Hol a határ? (Where are the limits? Campaign strategies and ethics in the 2002 election campaign)*, (Budapest, Élet és Irodalom), pp. 329–344.

Csigó, P. (2006). 'Celebratory Politics in Hungary: a dramaturgical rethinking of promotionalism and mediatization', *CRESC Conference*, Oxford, UK.

Csigó, P. (2007). 'Downbreaking News – Toward a Dramaturgical Approach to Popular Media and Public Communication': Paper presented at the International Communication Association conference, San Francisco, USA.

Dahlgren, P. (1995). *Television and the Public Sphere*, London, Sage.

Dahlgren, P. (2003). 'Reconfiguring Civic Culture in the New Media Milieu' in J. Corner and D. Pels (eds.) *Media and the Restyling of Politics* (London, Sage), pp. 151–171.

Dayan, D. (2002). 'The peculiar public of television', *Media, Culture, Society*, 23:6, pp. 743–765.

Dayan, D. and E. Katz (1992). *Media Events: the Live Broadcasting of History*, Cambridge, Mass., Harvard University Press.

de Vreese, C. H. and H. G. Boomgarden (2006). 'Media Message Flows and Interpersonal Communication. The Conditional Nature of Effects on Public Opinion', *Communication Research*, 33:1, pp. 19–37.

Eveland, W. P., D. V. Shah and N. Kwak (2003). 'Assessing Causality in the Cognitive Mediation Model. A Panel Study of Motivations, Information Processing, and Learning During Campaign 2000', *Communication Research*, 30:4, pp. 359–386.

Fiske, J. (1992). 'The Cultural Economy of Fandom' in L. Lewis (eds.) *The Adoring Audience* (London, New York, Routledge), pp. 30–50.

Frith, S. (1996). 'Music and Identity' in S. Hall and P. du Gay (eds.) *Questions of Cultural Identity* (London, Sage), pp. 108–128.

Galgut, E. (2002). 'Poetic Faith and Prosaic Concerns. A Defense of Suspension of Disbelief', *South African Journal of Philosophy*, 21:3, pp. 190–199.

Gantz, W. (1978). 'How Uses and Gratifications Affect Recall of Television News', *Journalism Quarterly*, 55:Winter, pp. 664–672.

Gerbner, G. and L. Gross (1976). 'Living with Television: the Violence Profile', *Journal of Communication*, 26:2, pp. 173–199.

Gitlin, T. (2002). *Media Unlimited: How The Torrent of Images and Sounds Overwhelms Our Lives*, New York, Henry Holt and Co.

Goffman, E. (1974). *Frame Analysis: An Essay on the Organization of Experience*, New York, Harper & Row.

Goffman, E. (1990). *The Presentation of Self in Everyday Life*, London, Penguin Books [1959].

Grabe, M. E., A. Lang and X. Zhao (2003). 'News Content and Form. Implications for Memory and Audience Evaluations', *Communication Research*, 30:4, pp. 381–413.

Groenendyk, E. W. and N. A. Valentino (2002). 'Of Dark Clouds and Silver Linings. Effects of Exposure to Issue Versus Candidate Advertising on Persuasion, Information Retention, and Issue Salience', *Communication Research*, 29:3, pp. 295–319.

Grossberg, L. (1992). 'Is There a Fan in the House? The Affective Sensibility of Fandom' in L. Lewis (eds.) *The Adoring Audience* (London, New York, Routledge), pp. 50–69.

Grossberg, L. (1992). *We gotta get out of this place: popular conservatism and postmodern culture*, New York, Routledge.

Grossberg, L. (1996). 'History, politics and postmodernism: Stuart Hall and Cultural Studies' in D. Morley and K. H. Chen (eds.) *Stuart Hall. Critical Dialogues in Cultural Sudies* (London, Routledge), pp. 151–174.

Hall, S. (eds.) (1997). *Representation. Cultural Representations and Signifying Practices*, London, Sage.

Hawkins, R. P. and et al. (2001). 'Predicting Selection and Activity in Television Genre Viewing', *Media Psychology*, 3:3, pp. 237–263.

Hermes, J. (1998). 'Cultural citizenship and popular fiction' in K. Brants, J. Hermes and L. Van Zoonen (eds.) *The Media in Question* (London, Sage), pp. 157–167.

Hermes, J. (2005). *Re-Reading Popular Culture. Rethinking Gender, Television and Popular Media Audiences*, Oxford, Blackwell Publishing.

Holbrook, R. A. and T. G. Hill (2005). 'Agenda-Setting and Priming in Prime Time Television: Crime Dramas and Political Cues', *Political Communication*, 22:3, pp. 277–295.

Iyengar, S. and D. R. Kinder (1987). *News that Matters: Television and American Opinion*, Chicago, IL, University of Chicago Press.

Iyengar, S. and A. F. Simon (2000). 'New Perspectives and Evidence on Political Communication and Campaign Effects', *Annual Review of Psychology*, 51, pp. 149–169.

Jakubowicz, K., 'Poland' in D. Paletz, K. Jakubowicz and P. Novosel (eds.) (1995). *Glasnost and After. Media and Change in Central and Eastern Europe* (Cresskill, NJ, Hampton Press), pp. 129–148.

Kalehoff, M. (2006). 'Are Engagement Believers in Denial?' http://blogs.mediapost.com/ spin/?p=887, 2006 (last accessed: 20 May).

Katz, E. (1980). 'On Conceptualizing Media Effects', *Studies in Communications*, 1, pp. 119–141.

Katz, E. (1996). 'Viewers Work' in J. Hay, L. Grossberg and E. Wartella (eds.) *The Audience and its Landscape* (Oxford, Boulder, Westview Press), pp. 9–23.

Kellner, D. (2003). *Media Spectacle*. London, Routledge.

Kim, J. and A. M. Rubin (1997). 'The Variable Influence of Audience Activity on Media Effects', *Communication Research*, 24:2, pp. 104–135.

Kiousis, S. and M. McCombs (2004). 'Agenda Setting Effects and Attitude Strength. Political Figures during the 1996 Presidential Election', *Communication Research*, 31:1, pp. 36–57.

Knobloch, S. and et al. (2004). 'Affective News. Effects of Discourse Structure in Narratives in Suspense, Curiosity and Enjoyment While Reading News and Novels', *Communication Research*, 31:3, pp. 259–287.

Krosnick, J. A. and L. A. Brannon (1993). 'The Impact of the Gulf War on the Ingredients of Presidential Evaluations: Multidimensional Effects of Political Involvement', *American Political Science Review*, 87:4, pp. 947–512.

Lee, G. and J. H. Cappella (2001). 'The Effects of Political Talk Radio On Political Attitude Formation: Exposure Versus Knowledge', *Political Communication*, 18:4, pp. 369–394.

Liebes, T. (1995). 'Notes on the struggle to define involvement in television viewing' in J. Hay, L. Grossberg and E. Wartella (eds.) *The Audience and its Landscape* (Oxford, Boulder, Westview Press, pp. 177–186.

Livingstone, S. (1996). 'On the continuing problems of media effects research' in J. Curran and M. Gurevitch (eds.) *Mass Media and Society* (2nd ed.) (London, Edward Arnold), pp. 305–324.

Marshall, D. (1997). *Celebrity and Power: Fame in Contemporary Culture*, London, University of Minnesota Press.

Mazzoleni, G., J. Stewart and B. Horsfield (eds.) (2003). *The Media and Neo-Populism*, Westport, Praeger.

McGuire, W. J. (1986). 'The Myth of Massive Media Impact: Savagings and Salvagings' in G. Comstock (eds.) *Public Communication and Behavior* (Orlando, FL, Academic Press), pp. 173–257.

McLeod, D. M., G. M. Kosicki and J. M. McLeod (2002). 'Resurveying the Boundaries of Political Communications Effects' in J. Bryant and D. Zillmann (eds.) *Media Effects:Advances in Theory and Research* (2nd ed.) (Hillsdale, NJ, Lawrence Erlbaum), pp. 215–267.

McNair, B. (2003). *News and Journalism in the UK*, London, Routledge.

Miller, J. M. and J. A. Krosnick (2000). 'News Media Impact on the Ingredients of Presidential Evaluations: Politically Knowledgeable Citizens Are Guided by a Trusted Source', *American Journal of Political Science*, 44:2, pp. 301–315.

Moog, S. and J. Sluyter-Beltrao (2001). 'The Transformation of Political Communication?' in Axford, B. and R. Huggins (eds) *New Media and Politics* (London, Sage), pp. 30–63.

Morley, D. (1992). *Television, Audiences and Cultural Studies*, London, Routledge.

Mungiu-Pippidi, A. (2001). 'Államiból közszolgálati. A kelet-közép-kelet-európai televíziók sikertelen reformja' (From state to public service: the failed reform of television in East Central Europe), *Médiakutató*, 2:4

Perse, E. M. (1990). 'Audience Selectivity and Involvement in the Newer Media Environment', *Communication Research*, 17:5, pp. 675–697.

Perse, E. M. (1998). 'Implications of Cognitive and Affective Involvement for Channel Changing', *Journal of Communication*, 48:3, pp. 49–67.

Petty, R. E. and J. T. Cacioppo (1986). *Communication and Persuasion: Central and Peripheral Routes to Attitude Change*, New York, NY, Springer-Verlag.

Pieterse, J. N. (2000). 'Globalization as Hybridization' in F. Lechner and J. Boli (eds.) *The Globalization Reader* (Oxford, Blackwell), pp. 99–109.

Pinkleton, B. E. and E. W. Austin (2002). 'Individual Motivations, Perceived Media Importance, and Political Disaffection', *Political Communication*, 18:3, pp. 321–334.

Popescu, M. and G. Tóka (2002). 'Campaign Effects and Media Monopoly: the 1994 and 1998 Parliamentary elections in Hungary' in D. M. Farrell and R.Schmitt-Beck (eds.) *Do Political Campaigns Matter? Campaign Effects in Elections and Referendums* (London, Routledge), pp. 58–75.

Prior, M. (2005). 'News vs. Entertainment: How Increasing Media Choice Widens Gaps in Political Knowledge and Turnout', *American Journal of Political Science*, 49:3, pp. 577–592.

Richardson, J. D. (2005). 'Swifting Social Identities: The Influence of Editorial Framing on Reader Attitudes on Affirmative Action and African Americans', *Communication Research*, 32:4, pp. 503–528.

Roessler, P. (1999). 'The Individual Agenda-Designing Process', *Communication Research*, 26:6, pp. 666–700.

Romer, D., K. H. Jamieson and S. Aday (2003). 'Television News and the Cultivation of Fear of Crime', *Journal of Communication*, 53:1, pp. 88–104.

Rubin, A. M. (2002). 'The Uses-and-Gratifications Perspective of Media Effects' in J. Bryant and D. Zillmann (eds.) *Media Effects:Advances in Theory and Research* (2nd ed.) (Hillsdale, NJ, Lawrence Erlbaum), pp. 525–548.

Rubin, A. M. and E. Perse (1987). 'Audience Activity and Television News Gratifications', *Communication Research*, 14:1, pp. 58–84.

Rubin, A. M., E. Perse and D. S. Taylor (1988). 'A Methodological Examination of Cultivation', *Communication Research*, 15:2, pp. 107–134.

Ryan, M. L. (2001). *Narrative as Virtual Reality: Immersion and Interactivity in Literature and Electronic Media*, Baltimore, Johns Hopkins University Press.

Scammel, M. 2000. 'The Internet and Civic Engagement: The Age of the Citizen-Consumer', *Political Communication*, 17: 351–355.

Schechner, R. (2003). *Performance Theory*, New York, Routledge.

Schoenbach, K. and E. Lauf (2002). 'The "Trap" Effects of Television and Its Competitors', *Communication Research*, 29:5, pp. 564–583.

Schulz, W., R. Zeh and O. Quiring (2005). 'Voters in a Changing Media Environment: A Data-Based Retrospective on Consequences of Media Change in Germany', *European Journal of Communication*, 20:1, pp. 55–88.

Shrum, L. J. (1995). 'Assessing the Social Influence of Television. A Social Cognition Perspective on Cultivation Research', *Communication Research*, 22:4, pp. 402–429.

Shrum, L. J., R. S. Wyer and T. C. O'Guinn (1998). 'The Effects of Television Consumption on Social Perceptions. The Use of Priming Procedures to Investigate Psychological Processes', *Journal of Consumer Research*, 24:4, pp. 447–458.

Silverstone, R. (1994). *Television and Everyday Life*, London, Sage.

Street, J. (1998). *Politics and Popular Culture*, Philadelphia, Temple University Press.

Sükösd, M. and P. Bajomi-Lázár (eds.) (2003). *Reinventing media: media policy reform in East-Central Europe*, Budapest, CEU Press.

Tewksbury, D. (1999). 'Differences in How We Watch the News', *Communication Research*, 26:1, pp. 4–29.

Tsafti, Y. and J. H. Cappella (2003). 'Do People Watch What They Do Not Trust? Exploring The Association Between News Media Scepticism and Exposure', *Communication Research*, 30:5, pp. 504–529.

van Zoonen, L. (2005). *Entertaining the Citizen: When Politics and Popular Culture Converge*, Lanham, MD, Rowman & Littlefield Publishers.

Zaller, J. R. (1992). *The Nature and Origins of Mass Opinion*, New York, NY, Cambridge Univerity Press.

Zaller, J. R. (1996). 'The Myth of Massive Media Impact Revived: New Support for a Discredited Idea' in D. C. Mutz, P. M. Sniderman and R. A. Brody (eds.) *Political Persuasion and Attitude Change* (Ann Arbor, University of Michigan Press), pp. 17–78.

Zaller, J. R. (2001). 'Monica Lewinsky and the Mainsprings of American Politics' in W. L. Bennett and R. M. Entman (eds.) *Mediated Politics. Communication in the Future of Democracy* (Cambridge, Cambridge University Press), pp. 252–279.

Zillmann, D. and J. Bryant (1985). 'Selective-Exposure Phenomena' in D. Zillmann and J. Bryant (eds.) *Selective Exposure to Communication* (Hillsdale, NJ, Lawrence Erlbaum), pp. 1–10.

Zillmann, D. and et al. (2004). 'Effects of Lead Framing on Selective Exposure to Internet Reports', *Communication Research*, 31:1, pp. 58–81.

The Disadvantaged in Infotainment Television: From Representation to Policy

Ferenc Hammer

1. Introduction

In this article, I highlight certain latest forms and trends in the ways contemporary media cultures discuss the life of socially disadvantaged groups. I also offer a few normative considerations to address the justice related and ethical issues connected to the making of meanings associated with the life of the poor and excluded. These normative accounts include communication regulation (particularly of television-related) and democratic theory (mainly concerning citizenship and legitimacy) questions. The chief empirical focus of my inquiry is television, particularly non-fiction entertainment programmes, such as light current affairs magazines, makeover shows, chat shows and reality television programmes. My empirical research has taken a closer scrutiny of *Fókusz*, a Hungarian daily light current affairs programme and, also, when applicable, I cite relevant observations from US and British media research regarding the subject.

I argue in this paper that the way individuals, institutions and texts perform classifications in the narrower field of the work of representation[1] (in various media genres as media professionals, communication regulators, media business people, audiences, media consumers, talk show participants etc.) about the vocabulary, and reasons and consequences of poverty, these classifications are connected to the social spheres of work, competition, consumption, social stratification, wording and content of policy, and even to social research in numerous indirect but empirically observable ways. My argument aims to step further of Bourdieu's accounts regarding this subject. My mapping of the texts and acts/facts of social inequality isn't a sheer teleological fact-hunting to unmask hidden forces of sublimed oppression. I argue instead that the ways texts regarding the life of the poor (and of the middle strata) are connected to facts of poverty (and of decent life) is dependent on the ways the society discusses issues of justice, that is, the nature, origin and acceptable levels of inequality in society (in everyday talks, sociology books, media criticism, evening news, makeover shows or current affairs programmes). Therefore, my argument regarding performances of contemporary western societies in making social justice is inherently entwined by an assertion of the democratic, that is, self-governing role of the media in our lives.

2. Down and out in media cultures in neoliberalism

The discussion of the life of the not-well-to-do has never been only an expression of a mere anthropological interest in the West. Descriptions and justifications regarding social inequalities – as expressions of godly order or of the competition of the social agents – have been central in earthly practices of power exercise and in the processes of reproduction and change of the rules of the society. Carefully crafted descriptions of the poor, or of "the creditable" (Adam Smith), for that matter, have always presented – often contested – arguments about the origin and justification of social inequalities. The proper context of Orwell's social excursions in London, Paris and Wigan is the Victorian tradition of portraying the vagrant, a firmly established character in English humour: "fat, drink-sodden and bearing no relation to his real-life equivalent" (Taylor 2003: 93). Somewhat earlier, Van Gogh when trying to define his artistic ends and means concerning painting the life of those at the low end had to consider that "the *banlieue* was to be meant to be melancholy, and that by 1886 there were even specialists – poets and painters – in the new commodity."[2] As the 2005 French violent upheavals, and particularly their media coverage have suggested, the banlieue has not lost its function and relevance to express fundamental meanings about nation, class and politics in France.

The minstrel boy, Sambo or Punch and Judy have not made their ways into television. Contemporary popular cultures discuss the life of the disadvantaged in not a singular or homogeneous way. Charity ads, *old school* documentary films, Jerry Springer or lifestyle makeover shows depict those in need all differently. It's worth taking a closer look at an ad for Christian O'Connell's morning show at Xfm.[3]

The small white letters under the table read: "Right: Derek wears vest and underpants, all model's own. Hair by himself. Furniture courtesy of his nan. He listens to Xfm." We can learn from this ironic ad that the centrepiece of the vocabulary of Derek's "bleak existence" is his body: Fat, undressed, uncomfortably presented (see his hands). A short look at the picture and the description of his apparel reveals he's deprived of consumption pleasures (the text's allusion to the donor of the furniture casts a dark cloud over his presumable emotional life) that his really grim glance seems to attest. Derek doesn't seem to present a really remarkable past, but at least he has future: Xfm. One more thing needs to be added. A closer look at the left side of the radio tells the viewer that could have been difficult to experience only from a sheer picture. An age-old tradition has gained an expression here. Yes, probably poor Derek stinks too. The wretched smell, and smell, as a visually and spatially uncontrollable entity, is a par excellence danger: a revolt against deocracy, that is, the rule of the good-smelling.

The second example is also an ad[4] but pursuing a completely different goal than just having a fancy look at uncool losers. This picture marshals Missingpersons.org's mission, that is, to find disappeared people in order make their families happy again. Being not an Englishman, I find it not easy to locate this family on the British social map, but a few things seem certain. They are sad as Derek (though for a different reason), two out of three seem to be positively plump also, their apartment looks not too spacey,[5] and the sight of the radiator at the centre of this ceremonially constructed picture suggests certain vulnerability too. The real puzzle is the framed photograph. If it was not there, the obvious missing person would be the father probably, but the picture shows a boy. In families waiting for a disappeared boy seems quite of a natural act to exhibit the photo of him,[6] but the appearance of the missing boy on the cupboard instantly points to another person missing from this picture, that is, from this family: the father. Though much subtler than in the case of Derek, a certain conclusion might apply to the mini-drama suggested by the ad. That is, it is always difficult to find missing people, but with the help of Missingpersons.org's ad, one needs less effort to spot the likely place where disappeared people are missing from: disintegrating lower middle-class families. The older daughter's chequered-patterned stockings lead us to another space of social categorizing.

Chavs[7] and chavettes are a source of contemporary grass-roots entertainment among — suspectibly mostly — the young in the UK.[8] The numerous websites — devoted to the thick descriptions of the outfit, presumed behaviour and mental state, morals and cultural preferences of young people living in the cheapest neighbourhoods — consider the wearing of Burberry (caps and other outfit) as the clearest visible evidence of someone being a chav.[9] The central position of the chequered outfit in contemporary cultural warfare among the youth may even suggest that the boy from the pervious picture is missing from a chav family, in fact. The following meticulous descriptions of the chav world leave no doubt about that the sartorial crimes of the chav are of just minor misdemeanour compared to other forms of sin.[10]

The choice of trainspotting to paraphrase for the goals of today youth's anger tells a lot about contemporary society. Trainspotting, the original activity, the proverbially pointless wasting of time in industrial capitalism through waiting to see rushing metal juggernauts employed characteristically by the modern state, has turned into something else. One group among the youth[11] has taken the role of making an order they like. They don't wait for the state. They do it themselves. The making of the order inherently involves the patrolling gaze over the outfit of the young (chavspotting). Though in my view any analysis would just blur the clarity outlined by this young conservative manifesto, I would still highlight a few novel elements in this upgraded "undeserving poor" memorandum. Yes, again, it is centred around the body. The ancient bodily sin (boozing) has been completed by newer ones. High cholesterol intake and smoking, while improper consumption (wearing only 9ct gold, smoking cheap cigarettes, living in council flats, listening to bad music etc.) has seemed to gain higher importance than it did with older experiences of dismissing the parasite poor. This chav-bashing sign of hygiene-politics exemplifies promptly the idea of the vicious waste of Britain.[12]

High cholesterol intake and the British future is also a central concern in a BBC makeover show titled *Honey, we're killing the kids!* In a 2006 spring episode, the production crew found a lower middle-class family with two children. They followed the family's everyday life for several days and with the help of physicians and dietary experts they recorded and analyzed what they saw. The point of the show was the final presentation of the research results for the family. It has revealed that the children watch too much TV, they do too little outdoor exercise and eat too much junk food. The pitch of the presentation has strangely echoed the final conclusion of the Chavspotting manifesto: "Choose rotting away at the age of 30, etc." The host of the show met the parents in a large spooky black room, suggesting some kind of unearthly, out of space and time experience. She explained to the parents that the research results about the children's unhealthy way of life could be displayed visually with the help of cutting-edge state-of-the-art visual editing technology. Science and technology can show how the children would look at the age of 40. The two pictures showed a burnt-out, middle-aged man with greyish hair and a bleak glance and a fat, stupid-faced woman, both digital transformations of the children's recent photos. But if children — with the help of their parents, of course – happen to play more outdoors, eat more fruits and vegetables etc., their picture would be this at the age of 40, said the show's host. The two pictures have shown two energetic-looking, young-faced, gently smiling upper-class Bohemians (quite interestingly, in the second case the man's scalp was significantly more haired than on the first picture, as balding would not been a genetically determined process). Moreover, she added, the children would live an average fifteen years longer as it was anticipated in the gloomy scenario. The dark unearthly studio room has revealed its meaning, a godly business. Indeed, fate has been given to the hands of humans: their children's fate.

This lifestyle makeover show has numerous implications for further discussion. As a show format rule, no one would question how and why a television crew would follow the family's daily life in their home. The future of the children (determined visually by digital technologies) is the function of how, first, their parents and then they treat their body. The social as such has melted into the air here or, rather, closed into the body of the future eco-zen, while in return, the seriously regulated and thoroughly patrolled body becomes the social. It is a signpost placing its owners at a certain social place, it is a historical entity as well, because it shows the true history of its making. The popularity of this show and the fact that the participating family has learnt something from this lesson leads us to another example where personal interest in participating in the show, matching with particular narrative and visual treatments produce unexpectedly interesting results for our analysis.

A young couple's medical mistreatment case was covered by *Fókusz*, a Hungarian light current affairs magazine.[13] They had three children and after the women underwent a

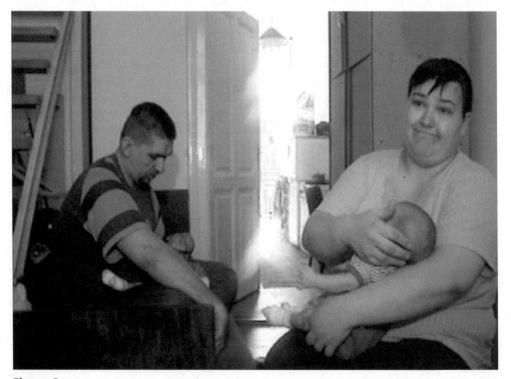

Figure 1

sterilization operation, she had become pregnant again and delivered twins.[14] The father, unemployed, living in a 28-square-metre apartment, now seven of them, their situation seemed severe, indeed (Figure 1). The mother described her case the following way:

> [After sterilization] in theory I couldn't have become pregnant, it would have been useless to do any kind of contraception, and because we trust each other, we didn't use condom, I cannot really take pills because once I had pancreatitis and the use of spiral was highly unrecommended for me, and that's why I wanted the sterilization.

She tells these intimate details about her medical record and their contraceptive dilemmas in prime time for about 800,000 viewers. The mother noted too that as a medically mistreated patient, she could have been entitled for compensation from the hospital (that would be of great help in their financial situation). During the interview the camera strolls around the apartment and then peeps into the bathroom (Figure 2).

It is a crucial point for my analysis. The family, probably motivated by expected gains to be yielded through the public exposure of their private matters, allows the TV crew to their private sphere, including their contraceptive habits. The camera finds it natural to peep into the bathroom. Why? Why not? If the couple was willing to tell all these things, why would an insert on the bathroom be extraordinary? The extraordinary feature of this bathroom-peeping can be revealed if one compares this report with other reports when the protagonist, let's say, is a famous hunter who shot a huge leopard in Africa. Would the camera peep into the bathroom

Figure 2

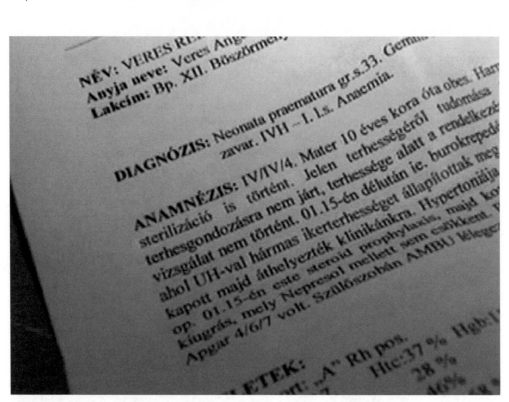

Figure 3

Figure 4

of the hunter? Why would it? It would make no sense at all. Here, I think, we have spotted something important in the real-life current affairs reports.

First, the less well-to-do someone, the more material[15] (or other kind of crisis-resolving) incentive is there for the participation in the programme. Indeed, *Fókusz* production office receives dozens of "last straw" (last chance) letters per day from people around the country who think that public exposure of their problem can be of help.[16] It is just a speculation, but my hunch is that if the family above had lived in decent middle-class circumstances, they would have called their lawyer instead of *Fókusz*.

Second, it seems also, that the less well-to-do the report's subject, the more the narrative and the camera feels encouraged to reveal the subjects private matters (for example, the reaction of the subject's pancreas to contraceptive pills or their bathroom). In another insert — illustrating the "just-the-facts" poetic signature of *Fókusz* — the camera peeps into the medical documents of the unfortunate mother. This probably helps to convey a "real-

Figures 5–7: From top to toe

Figures 8–10: From top to toe

life" image, but probably it helps less the mother that her name, her mother's maiden name and address is exposed in prime time television (Figure 3). But, as we will see, the sheer exposure of a body can be motivated by various things. Further specifications can be drawn from the comparison of two other *Fókusz* reports.

The two reports, about a homeless woman in a country town who was thrown out from her council flat among obscure circumstances,[17] and about a female dentist who won a mothers' beauty contest,[18] follow the usual *Fókusz* format. The usually 4–6-minute reports are based on the "God's voice" background narration, and the parallel flow of visual material consisting of a relatively large number of shots that give the reports a dynamic, sometimes music video, kind of image. Report subjects speak two or three times altogether no more than five sentences. This sound-bite-ish format implies, first, that report subjects act mainly as authenticating figures for the report.[19] Second, since they are not allowed to talk too much, but still they are the protagonists, an average report contains relatively large amounts of inserts that show the subject doing certain "relevant" or "typical" skits (the homeless woman walking in the street, a lawyer reading business papers). It means that a prime-time current affairs magazine (that cannot contain long talks, long inserts and long reports without taking the risk of falling ratings) is almost deemed to mould all of its reports into a "music clip" format that (again based on the constraint of the necessity of showing the report subject) is also deemed to concentrate on the subject's body (instead of primarily their words). The two women appearing in the two reports received completely the same treatment from the production. The report's length, their opportunity to talk, their talk/skit ratio, the narration/own words ratio in the reports were close to equal. The anchor, Anikó Marsi, showed certain sympathy towards both subjects, and both women's body were scanned carefully by the camera. In the case of the dentist, it was easy because the production team joined her when new bath-suit pictures were made for her beauty portfolio in a photo studio.

In the case of the homeless woman, the camera simply scanned her from top to toe and then later the other way around.

The striking similarity in the portrayals of these two women can be a novel momentum when considering the widespread opinion in media studies (probably going back to Susan Sontag's (1977) analysis in *On Photography* of August Sander's catalogue of the German people) that the camera treats differently the middle class and the poor. Suffice to say, the very strictly observed technical-editorial rules at the current affairs programme I examined give little space for "class-based" visual distinctions. The key differences lay somewhere else.

3. Double standards in representing class

The striking similarity in portraying a homeless woman and a beauty queen/successful professional/mother in terms of all the observable features of the current affairs reports suggests that, in fact, the similarities are the very acts that show where the differences are. We have seen pleasures of decent life vs suffering, attractiveness vs ugliness, success vs failure, socially embedded situation (family, work) vs disembeddedness (sleeping in a ditch) and story transparency vs narrative misgivings (about the council flat affair). These narrative differences have been structured around two sets of visual representations (both centred around the subject's body), and it suffices to say that this current affairs format connects narrative information (about the subjects) to the bodily appearance of the subject with a rampant capacity. To identify the exact structure of the differences of portraying different social situations, the analysis should involve an account of the report topics, for which I have analyzed 312 reports with particular attention to portrayals of poverty.

Though methodological nit-picking is rarely discussed in a chapter-size study, the identification of poverty reports in my analysis has to be addressed here, because the issue at stake in the whole study is about the nature and politics of classification of signs of social differences. In this research, I analyzed television report texts with the help of sociological categories used by sociology and social policy research. The "poverty test means" of the texts — taken from mainstream sociology and social policy research — were the following:

- Absolute poverty: homeless, starving, nothing to wear;
- The protagonist or, if s/he's a child, all of the adults in the family (1 or 2 persons) are long-time unemployed;
- Some sort of social assistance is the main income source of the protagonist (or of the family);
- Public utility (water, electricity, gas) turned off by the provider;
- The protagonist's personal environment suggests deep poverty;
- The protagonist lives (used to live) in a state orphanage.

This methodology — classifying television report texts with conventional sociological means — presents a junction where methods of two classification regimes — empirical sociology and editorial practices of commercial television — meet. With the help of this tool, I could identify about one-tenth of the reports (30 out of 312) as "poverty reports", while exactly half of the reports (156) could be classified as "middle-class reports". Taking common sense differences between the life of the disadvantaged and the middle strata, it is not surprising that reports covering their life follow somewhat different patterns. But a closer scrutiny of the themes of and certain motifs in the reports can reveal a somewhat worrisome system of differentiation. As the textual analysis of the reports revealed, the portrayal of the poor (or, more accurately, "the-poor-as-defined-by-*Fókusz*") in the reports differs from the programme's "middle-class reports" the following ways:

- In middle-class reports the protagonist can do something that most of us cannot do (being a Robert de Niro look-alike or scuba diving in a sunken battle ship), while in poverty reports the protagonist is unable to do what most of us can do. Due to this double standard, the "uniqueness" in poverty reports implies that the viewer will be neither informed about others who also share the problem, nor what might cause that suffering. The reports lack any social context.
- Fear and risk in poverty reports appear in the contexts of suffering, loss and uncertainty, while in middle-class reports fear and risk is more about thrill, pleasure, gain, exceptionality, consumption ("challenge", "adrenaline" etc.).
- In each of the thirteen body reports of the 30 poverty reports, the body was presented in the context of suffering, illness or disability. In the 82 "middle-class body reports" (out of 156), 39 are also about suffering, illness or disability, while 43 reports discuss the middle-class body as a source of pleasure, passion, hobby or a tool for finding new roles or identities, or a source of success, or the object of work or effort to make it perfect.

In summary, Fókusz, the light current affairs programme in Hungary, discusses poverty in an essentializing manner because:

- The given problem in the report is discussed solely in the context of the life of the given person;
- Reasonable causes and expected consequences of the problem are not discussed;

- The presented problem stems from the person's personal ill-fortune or failure;
- The viewer can learn nothing about the poor person but details of the problem.

No doubt, this essentializing framing stems much more from the human interest report format than from actual editorial decisions of *Fókusz* staff. Most likely, this editorial frame is perfect to cover a *Guinness Book* record attempt. But it is questionable whether this format is appropriate to cover topics that seriously address issues of social justice. Apart from the hunch that a homeless woman's story may require a different editorial treatment than a story of a cat which is addicted to cigarette butts, representational features of late modern status formation and social structure may add a few further considerations to evaluate treatments of poverty in light human interest genres.

4. Poverty and exclusion in late capitalism

Social exclusion – especially its elements associated with symbols and meanings – operate mainly in a field that falls beyond the terrain of traditional citizenship (civil rights, political rights and social rights). Power-related differences in modern democracies cannot be described along different levels of access to these three types of rights, because these are protected by law and constitution. The tendency of human beings to compete and to gain the possible largest control over the social world has found an appropriate field in culture, and, indeed, the cultural principle is the main dimension that explains social mobility, status or stratification. Power in contemporary democratic societies is a function of wealth one accumulates in various currencies of cultural citizenship (knowledge, habitus, network, attitude, meanings, ability to make others accept our meanings, representations, position in the equity discourse etc.). A successful performance in the field of cultural citizenship is, nevertheless, a predominantly middle-class privilege, especially because of the strong connection between the notions of socially constructed meanings and consumption. While the dynamic of construction of cultural differences can be praised in the context of the middle class as an unprecedented opportunity to freedom to pursue choices and seek bonding, the same cultural principle has turned out as nearly catastrophic with relation to disadvantaged groups in the society. Their exclusion is no longer based on lack of access to civil, political or basic social rights, but rather on their performance along a web of culturally defined norms. Paraphrasing Charles Taylor, one could claim that the equality of civic, political and social rights is, in fact, the politics of exclusion.

Eurostat, the statistical office of the European Commission, commissioned research in 1995 focusing on the nature of determinants of exclusion and poverty that "cannot be translated into monetary terms". The process of reflecting on basic questions regarding exclusion (its definition, causes, what people are excluded from etc.) has resulted in a genuine statistical measurement instrument which serves as a complementary method to income- and wealth-based survey methods. The document (Eurostat 1995) defines exclusion as a process and identifies five social systems performing exclusionary dynamics. One of these fields is labelled as a "system of symbolic references", associated with concepts such as "identity, social visibility, self-esteem, basic abilities, interests and motivations, and future prospects". The "breakdown of the images and representations attached to the [social] activities [of the excluded] and which are important elements of social identification and integration" serve as central processes in the system of symbolic references. The document outlines an overview of fourteen fields of new indicators.[20]

Two of them require particular attention. First, the field of "Social representations" includes a set of indicators referring to images and representations regarding the capacity of the people to act (or not) in order to improve their situation, and "the identification of negative expectations concerning some key vulnerability factors (racism, precarious housing, unemployment, isolation, health problems, family breakdown, social isolation and others)". If one compares this list of "key vulnerability factors" with key themes in poverty-related reports in *Fókusz*, the similarity is truly striking. What follows from this is that poverty portrayal in this current affairs magazine reinforces certain cultural patterns week by week, which – both as distancing mechanisms between the poor and the rest, and a self-fulfilling image for the excluded – contribute to the reproduction of social exclusion – as the methodology of Eurostat suggests. Another important indicator domain of exclusion is called "Symbolic references". This domain contains references (among others) to question items regarding self-esteem, social identity and cognitive and behavioural abilities. Comparing this set of variables to current affairs reports portraying sad, crying, trembling-handed poor people who have nothing to wait for and nothing to miss, who struggle with problems which are sometimes unclear even for the reporter, one might have an impression that the vast majority of poverty portrayals in *Fókusz* would qualify as an audio-visual record of the ideal typical poor and excluded person. As it has been in the case of the previous set of indicators (symbolic references), poverty-related (otherwise correct and sometimes even emphatic) television programmes describe exclusion in such a way that in the course of the portrayal a distant and closed world "outside" might induce feelings of sympathy but not so much responsibility.

Summarizing this last section, we have found that Eurostat (the statistical apparatus of the European Commission) considers images and symbolic representations of the poor (or of poverty) as active and measurable factors in the process of exclusion producing poverty. With this, the notion of culturally constructed meanings (and concerns associated with it) has now occupied a mainstream position in the policy discussion. If the symbolic *per se* (image, mode of representation of the image and modalities of media consumption of the image of the poor) do contribute to matter-of-fact, real-life and substantial exclusion of groups and individuals, one might argue that media policy has to consider poverty representation concerns (associated with content and production) appropriate to be regulated in a public interest context.

What follows from this are the following:

- The justifiedness (and the performance) of media portrayals of the poor cannot be regarded as sufficiently regulated through mere consent between the portrayed and the producer.
- The public interest is not damaged only if freedoms of the producer to free expression; interviewee to free speech; viewer to access to information and entertainment are all amended by an argument explaining how that particular act would compensate the harm caused by the symbolic representation (therefore matter-of-fact perpetuation) of personal suffering.
- Particular care is needed if the image of social exclusion (therefore, real-life reinforcement of exclusion) is a commodity, which can be sold, "refined" or consumed.
- The notion of exclusion (social, economic, geographical, age-related, ethnic, cultural etc.) per definition implies lower social visibility of the excluded. Therefore, their television representations serve as a source of primary information for a large portion of the society These representations possess a large capacity to establish the "standard social distance" between the excluded and the rest of the people. This "standard gap" is a key element in terms of norms of social justice, because it contains

- Descriptions and qualifications for being "inside" or "outside";
- Definitions, explanations and justifications for social differences;
- A choice of norms evaluated as relevant regarding the responsibility of the excluded for their situation, responsibility of the rest of the society towards the excluded.

In summary, I argue that the performance of media portrayal of the poor has to be evaluated in the context of public interest justifications, because the images and representations in question constitute elements belonging to the cultural citizenship of the excluded. Beyond rights – I would define cultural citizenship as (1) a lexicon; that is, a set of meanings associated with life of groups and individuals, (2) access; that is, people's ability to make others accept meanings they prefer representing, as well as access of people to others' image and representations whose cultural citizenship is being acknowledged and protected, (3) representation; that is, the mechanisms through which meanings associated with life of groups or individuals are being produced, reproduced or changed, and, finally, (4) protection; that is, the nature and extent of attention of communication regulation to text- and access-related concerns of groups or individuals and, more generally, the extent policy and politics are ready to integrate the process when groups and individuals want others to recognize particular meanings chosen by them to represent their life.[21]

5. Words and policies

Urban studies scholars and housing policy experts were among the first ones who have provided a comprehensive analysis of the relationship between wording of social problems (choice of words, metaphors, lines of argument) and particular policies supported by the world-view (implied by that wording).[22] Poverty policies have been also scrutinized in terms of their discursive context; most influential among these accounts is Herbert Gans' (1995) analysis of the relationship between a linguistic innovation (underclass) and the changing preferences in US anti-poverty policies.

Although it would seem as a "semiotic zeal" to point out the direct influence of words on government policies, the spread of this expression (together its twin concept, the undeserving poor) as a result of the work of journalists, researchers and funding agencies has nevertheless contributed to the legitimizing of the welfare cuts in the 1980s in the US.[23] Loïc Wacquant (2001) presents an evidence in his illuminating *Prisons of Misery* how the rapid emergence of the *zero tolerance* penal philosophy and practice in the US (and elsewhere) was accompanied by the portrayal of the poor in the context of deviance by the mass media. Finally, Zygmunt Bauman suggests in his seminal piece on the "new poor" that attempts to welfare-dismantling practices (as the turn from universal service provision to means testing) could have never been as successful as they were if they had not been supported by popular media depictions of the "deviant poor". In Bauman's (2001: 71) words:

... the abnormality of the underclass phenomenon 'normalizes' the issue of poverty. It is the underclass, which is placed outside the accepted boundaries of society, but the underclass constitutes, as we remember, only a fraction of the 'officially poor'. It is precisely because the underclass is such a big and urgent problem that the bulk of people living in poverty are not a great issue that needs to be urgently tackled. Against the background of the uniformly ugly and repulsive landscape of the underclass, the 'merely poor' shine as temporarily unlucky but essentially decent people who – unlike the underclassers – will make all the right choices and eventually find their way back into the accepted boundaries of society. Just as falling into the underclass and staying there is a matter of choice, so the rehabilitation from the state of poverty is also a matter of choice – the right choice this time.

These examples of reflection on the relationship between media texts and public policy, and our findings of poverty portrayals in television infotainment, suggest that the portrayal of the poor in Hungary's most popular factual entertainment programme deserves policy attention, because they do contribute to the nature of prevailing notions of solidarity, let these notions be formulated by television programmes, social policy agendas, public opinion changes or individual viewer reactions. Reformulating this statement to the language of media regulation, I claim that television portrayal of the poor, as an important factor in the formation of norms of solidarity and exclusion, represents a public interest concern sufficient enough to consider its protection from sheer market forces.

6. Conclusions: communication policy

Although the notion of stereotype is a rather outdated concept in cultural analysis, and as recent Ofcom regulations suggest, in media policy too, I have chosen this term to address problems of poverty portrayals in infotainment television. I argue that stereotyped and essentialized portrayal of the poor requires regulatory attention for the following reasons:

- Stereotyping is a *human dignity* concern. Human dignity possessed by individuals is the function of their ability to control meanings associated with their life. Stereotyping people is therefore an act of deprivation of their human dignity.
- Stereotyping is a *democratic participation* concern. The conceptual added value of the notion of exclusion, compared with poverty, is that – apart from material hardships – it reflects a deprivation from participation in the community. In contemporary modern societies "participation" is more often media portrayal than individual participation, while "community", in concrete terms, resembles media audiences. Therefore, exclusion of a group is a function of the nature of their portrayal in the media. The rationale for free expression as a public interest value lies in its capacity to create dialogue and a forum for managing public issues. Therefore, particular care is needed when, in the name of public interest, free expression is protected at the expense of depriving groups or individuals from entering into the public dialogue, because as subjects of stereotypes they are deprived from controlling meanings about their life and, therefore, excluded from rational deliberation.
- Stereotyping is an *access* concern. Stereotyped portrayal can affect viewers' access (as a communication right) to undistorted information. This fundamental right is an essential element of the set of instruments protecting public debate as a means of democratic self-government.
- Stereotyping is a *cultural citizenship* concern. Social exclusion in modern democracies is strongly connected to socially constructed meanings people hold with or without their will and intention. These meanings serve as guidelines for others (and for the individuals themselves) in the process of their recognition as members of their communities (possessing particular notions of cultural citizenship).
- Policy acknowledges representation as a means of exclusion. Eurostat, the statistical office of the EC, has developed a set of measurable non-monetary indicators of poverty and exclusion – supplementing income and wealth-based indicators – such as symbolic references, images

and representations. Eurostat (1998) argues: "Social exclusion can be identified not only through objective aspects of people's lives, but also by images related with their social positioning and their ability to make choices to act."

■ Empirical research on framing effects proves that the main portrayal genres that infotainment programmes employ may induce victim-blaming and scapegoating sentiments in the viewer (Iyengar 1991).

■ Social stratification research shows that cultural variables constitute key factors in status formation. Exclusionary television contents, patterns of media consumption, levels of trust in the media and other people, patterns of self-perceptions and perceptions of other groups as strongly correlating factors contribute to the widening of the gap between the excluded and the rest of the society.

■ Social policy studies suggest that exclusionary public rhetoric often paves the way for exclusionary social policies; the career of the concept of underclass under the Reagan administration is a notable example.

Rather contrary to this normative analysis, neither Hungarian nor community communication regulation instruments in the European Union address questions of portrayals of the disadvantaged in the media. In these instruments, the main subject of communication rights is the individual. Therefore, they cannot address cases when infotainment television pays for disadvantaged people to show something sensational in television chat shows (á la *Jerry Springer*). Poverty is not an identity politics issue; therefore, instruments that protect men and women, ethnic or language minorities don't apply either. Media self-regulation exists mostly in countries and industries where it is least needed, while in the area of poverty representation in commercial television it is virtually unknown. We can argue, therefore, that communication regulation contributes to the naturalization of social exclusion in contemporary Europe.

Solidarity in a society is a peculiar public good. If it increases, it is beneficial for all. If people abuse or destroy it, they take away trust and solidarity from everyone's life, especially from those people's life who really need solidarity and trust. What follows from it is this: if a society cannot regulate itself in a way to ensure that a loss of a public good (solidarity) would be distributed in an equal manner to everyone, the least the society should do (as a second-best option or compensation) is to acknowledge the protection of solidarity in the name of the public interest.

Notes

1. See du Gay's "circuit of culture" model in Hall (1997).
2. Clark's (1985: 26) description follows: "The banlieue was the place where autumn was always ending on an empty boulevard, and the lost traces of Hausmann's city — a kiosk, a lamppost, a cast-iron pissotière — petered out in the snow. It was the territory of ragpickers, gypsies, and gasometers, the property of painters like Jean-François Raffaëlli and Luigi Loir."
3. A popular radio station in London. The photo is a courtesy of Xfm that I'm grateful for.
4. Source: http://www.missingpersons.org.
5. Their arrangement suggests that the viewer watches them from a TV set that cannot be in the middle of the room. Also, see the cupboard stuffed behind the sofa.
6. If it was the father, probably they would have put a more recent picture of him in the frame.
7. Interestingly, the term comes from the Romani chavo (young lad).

8. Nayak's (2006) account of the chav/ette discourse suggest a youth class warfare. Though lifestyle differences are particularly appropriate means for everyday social classifications, the chav discourse does not always dovetail neatly with a presumed logic of a class conflict.

9. The unanimous popular fury over the appropriation of Burberry by the young of the poor British suburbs seems a bit unclear for me. Is it because a cultural icon of the British belle epoque is in the wrong hands (or on wrong heads)?

10. The source of the texts is http://www.chavscum.co.uk, a chav-bashing site, also selling antichav merchandise such as T-shirts with the paraphrased *Trainspotting* text.

11. Some of the items from their list of lament would have sounded so helplessly of an adult whinny a generation ago: "Spitting at the bus stop"!

12. The sign man throws a Burberry baseball cap to the bin.

13. Full-blown reality entertainment started in 1997 with the appearance of commercial channels of terrestrial broadcast. These days Hungarian audience (of about 10 million people) has an access to three national channels of ground transmission (a public service station, MTV1 and two commercial ones: TV2 and RTL Klub), to a public service channel of satellite transmission (Duna TV) with the mission of serving Hungarians abroad, and to numerous local, cable and satellite channels. In 2007, M1, TV2 and RTL Klub and a few smaller channels have daily and/or weekly programmes that can be characterized as reality entertainment, including light human interest magazines, police magazines, confessional chat shows, reality shows, makeover shows etc. Reality programming has had certain early forms before 1989, such as the high-quality documentary film tradition, "serious" talk shows of highly respected senior TV personalities and the ill-famous *Blue Light* (*Kék fény*), a police magazine exposing good citizens of the People's Republic of Hungary to horrendous examples (and consequences) of anti-social behaviour. However, reality TV as a full-blown entertainment genre can be associated now mainly with the two foreign-owned commercial stations, RTL Klub and TV2. The appearance of a new reality entertainment genre has made a remarkable stir-up among the audience. These programmes have been very popular, as prime-time programmes they contribute significantly to the overall ratings of their channel, and, also, they have produced sharp dividing lines in the audience. Reality programming has had an interesting neighbour-scene outside of television as well; independent Hungarian fiction cinema and literature have often employed recently topics and characters resembling remarkably to human interest reports of reality TV programmes, all navigating on the troubled waters between fiction and reality. The relatively short history of Hungarian factual entertainment programming can be regarded as a fast-moving and bloody evolution scene, about 95 per cent of the overall number of reality productions now belong to the extinct species category. Though probably the most memorable accounts of reality entertainment in the past years are connected to the craze around reality shows of the *Big Brother* kind, but *Fókusz*, a daily prime-time human interest magazine of RTL Klub, is the oldest one among them. It was launched in 1997 as a daily tabloid magazine with a strong human interest feature, designed straightforwardly after the German *Explosive* and the US *Insider's View*. From its very beginning, it has been a prime-time programme starting around 7:00 PM, right after the evening news, and now preceding RTL Klub's own produced daily soap called *Barátok közt* (*Among Friends*). Its length is about 30 minutes, including commercials, and it is usually comprised of four or five reports (divided by commercials). In terms of its topics, style, genre, narrative, visual rhetoric and, most important, its anchors, *Fókusz* was designed to present a dynamic youth appeal. Its young anchors are celebrities themselves, appearing on magazine covers. About 80 per cent of its reports have been produced by the *Fókusz* staff itself, and the remaining 20 per cent are foreign productions. Some reports (especially about missing people, medical problems and certain conflicts) can be characterized as "last chance" attempts of

those appearing in those reports. In an average day, the four or five reports of one day's *Fókusz* programme represent a wide variety of the types above, producing a rather heterogeneous set of people, topics, problems, genres and narrative standpoints represented in one day's programme. The anchor leads, preceding the reports in which they describe the upcoming story, play important pedagogical roles offering preferred readings for the audience about the story in a cognitive and, perhaps, more importantly, in an emotional-attitudinal context as well.

14. *Fókusz*, 15 May 2000.

15. Neither Hungarian television regulation nor RTV Klub's code of conduct addresses the issue of payment for report subjects. An informer working at one of the big confession chat shows told me (and, therefore, I do not disclose the name of this person) that the manager of the given part receives a fixed sum of money for the show from which he has to cover the fees associated with finding confessing people, and the leftover is his payment for the show. This way of cutting costs suggests that confessing people can be often those asking only pennies for their performance.

16. Interview with Péter Kolosi, Program Director at RTL KLUB, 22 June 2002.

17. *Fókusz*, 12 May 2000.

18. *Fókusz*, 29 December 2000.

19. Once in a while, when using these kinds of reports at university classes in teaching, sometimes I show only the utterances of the report subjects, and the students are to guess what the reports are about. They are not always successful.

20. They are the following: Attributes of each member of household. Relation of each member of household with the economy, the labour market and the social security system. Economic situation of the household. Family of origin. Consumption patterns and living conditions of the household. Housing and the neighbourhood. Citizenship and participation in society. Social representations. Health and welfare. Social links. Economic area. Institutional. Territorial. Symbolic references.

21. If one finds this point somewhat odd, I would call attention to the fact that while people in need bombard editorial offices of TV current affairs magazines via phone and letters with their personal stories, the term *paparazzo* was coined to describe another strategy of these magazines towards the rich and famous. While in the first case no particular regulation has been regarded as important, in the second case media regulation pays detailed attention to such details as the use of high-focus camera lenses. This element of cultural citizenship refers to inequalities in the competition of recognition of differences, for example, gendered stereotyping has been addressed by communication, while the notion of stereotyping the poor has been largely overlooked by regulatory attention.

22. Jim Kemeny (2001) points out that the main metanarrative of housing policy and policy research is the dichotomous treatment of society/market (as "natural") and the state (as "artificial"), which treatment of social reality favors certain issues, problems, policies, solutions and particular groups of people, in the expense of other issues, policies and people. Robert Furbey (1999) discusses eloquently how such terms as *reconstruction*, *renewal*, *redevelopment*, *revitalization* and, finally, *regeneration* as catchwords for urban policy in the UK since World War II have paved the ways for different policy strategies.

23. Discussed in particular aspects by Reynolds Eblacas (1999) and Sotirovic (1999).

References

Bauman, Z. (2001/1998). *Work, consumerism and the new poor*. Buckingham and Philadelphia: Open University Press.

Clark, T. J. (1985). *The Painting of Modern Life: Paris in the Art of Manet and his Followers*. New York: Knopf.

EUROSTAT (1998). 'Non-Monetary Indicators of Poverty and Social Exclusion'. http://www.cerc.gouv.fr/sitedoc/poor/poora4.html.

Furbey, R. (1999). 'Urban 'Regeneration': Reflections On a Metaphor'. *Critical Social Policy*. Vol. 19(4), pp. 419–445.

Gans, H. J. (1995). *The War Against the Poor*. New York: Basic Books.

Hall, S. (1997). 'The Work of Representation' in Hall, S. (ed.) *Representation: Cultural Representations and Signifying Practices*. (London: Open University Press/SAGE), pp. 1–12.

Iyengar, S. (1991). *Is Anyone Responsible? How Television Frames Political Issues*. Chicago: University of Chicago Press.

Kemeny, J. (2001). 'Society versus the State. The social construction of explanatory stories in social policy research.' http://www.cf.ac.uk/cplan/conferences/hsa_sept01/kemeny-j.pdf.

Nayak, A. (2006). 'Displaced Masculinities: Chavs, Youth and Class in the Post-Industrial City'. *Sociology*, 40:5, pp. 813–831.

Reynolds Eblacas, Paula (1999). 'American Journalism vs. the Poor. A research review and analysis'. http://list.msu.edu/cgi-bin/wa?A2=ind9909e&L=aejmc&F=&S=&P=2695#TOP.

Sontag, S. (1977). *On Photography*. New York: Picador.

Sotirovic, Mira (1999). 'Media Use and Perceptions of Welfare'. http://list.msu.edu/cgi-bin/wa?A2=ind9910a&L=aejmc&F=&S=&P=11686#TOP.

Taylor, D.J. (2003). *Orwell: The Life*. London: Chatto & Windus.

Wacquant, L. (2001). *A nyomor börtönei* [Misery]. Budapest: Helikon Kiadó.

Radicals Online: The Hungarian Street Protests of 2006 and the Internet

Mónika Mátay and Ildikó Kaposi

Introduction

In autumn 2006, at the time of the 50th anniversary of the Hungarian uprising against Soviet rule, Hungarian politics made international headlines following a series of events that saw more street protests, rioting and violence than during or since the country's transition to democracy in 1989 and 1990. Triggered by a leaked recording of the Socialist prime minister's admission that he and his government had consciously misled the public through a series of lies in order to win re-election, demonstrations began outside Parliament and elsewhere in the country. This study explores the question of what role the Internet played in the street protests and how the protests were played out online.

The link between political mobilization and communication technologies is often stated to be powerful (Jones 1994). Satellite television has been credited with playing a role in the political transformation of Hungary in 1989 (Chadwick 2006), while the Internet played an important part in autumn 2006. Research on political activism and social movements on the Internet shows that organizations outside mainstream institutional politics are making use of the Internet-enabled exchange of information for coordinating political activity (Ayers 1999; Kahn and Kellner 2004; McCaughey and Ayers 2003). Environmental activists (Pickerill 2001; Tsaliki 2003), practitioners of independent, non-mainstream journalism (Hyde 2002; Pickard 2006) and anti-globalization protesters have relied on the Internet for grass-roots activist mobilization. Non-mainstream groups using the Internet for campaigning and recruitment also include racist, anti-Semitic, revisionist organizations as well as terrorist groups (Campbell 2006; Conway 2006; Reilly 2006), although the activities of these online groups are less widely researched.

Political symbols and rhetoric used in the Hungarian protests suggested that extreme right-wing activists or their sympathizers were active participants in the events.[1] Our analysis was therefore focused on the content of the major sites, news portals, mailing lists, discussion forums and online media of the radical Right in the period between 17 September and 4 November 2006. The combined analysis of these portals and sources may help in gaining an extensive picture about the representation of the events among radical and extreme right-wing political groups in Hungary. The focus on these sites also helps further the research agenda proposed by Silver (2003), who highlighted the importance of extending research on online activism to right-wing forces.

Sources and method of analysis

The online sources we analysed are heterogeneous in terms of their function, institutional, technical and financial background, the tone of their articles and materials, and even their political convictions. Some are party websites, some were set up specifically for the demonstrations, while others are online news media outlets.

The portal kossuthter[Kossuth Square].com was created after the beginning of the street protests with the aim of becoming "the official online forum for the demonstrations in Kossuth tér", providing a "credible source" of information for the public about "the goals and means of the demonstrations, the speeches, and the series of abuses by the authorities" (*Rólunk* in Kossuthter.com). The timeliness of the site prompted its registrations as a .com domain, for this only takes two days to accomplish.

According to its self-definition, Kuruc.info is "one of the most visited Conservative-Christian online political portals" in Hungary (*A Kuruc.info lényege* in Kuruc.info). Launched after 2004, the portal operates under a domain name registered abroad, and it is hosted on an international server.

Founded in 2006, the portal Falanx.[phalanx].hu displays the motto: "Public battles with open helmets". It is maintained by a foundation with the primary aim of "publishing national political events that other media ignore or keep silent about", as well as "gathering and publishing background materials on current affairs with the participation of our readers" (*Projektjeink* in mha.hu).

Szent Korona [Sacred Crown] Radio defines itself as "the pure Hungarian voice". Unlike the news portals, their profile features a lot of music, but the repertoire, which ranges from folk music to 'national rock', includes Hungarian performers exclusively.

Hunhír[Hunnews].hu has been operating since 2002. They define themselves as an "independent national news portal" focusing on "music, history, politics, tradition". According to a November 2006 call posted on the portal, they are struggling with severe financial and technical problems that threaten the survival of the site. This may be one of the reasons why Hunhír was far less prominent in providing news and accounts of the events.

The Jobbik Magyarországért Mozgalom [Movement for the Better Hungary] registered the discussion forum Jobbik szoba [Jobbik room] in January 2004 to be a medium for youth (ages 14–30). Apart from online discussions, they get together monthly and also go to football games. "Members of Jobbik szoba constitute none other than an ancient, yet new community brought together not by money, not by interest, but faith, awareness, and love" (*Magunkról* in Jobbik szoba).

Only limited data about the popularity of the sites are available. This confirms the non-mainstream character of the sites, and at the same time makes it difficult to estimate the potential public appeal of their content. Information can be gained mostly from self-reported figures, often made public in cases of difficulties with the servers. Thus, for instance, Kuruc.info posted an announcement on 12 October 2006 about the difficulties their server was having in coping with the increased readership that had "grown to 40–50 thousand (meaning unique IP address visitors, not page views, the second is many times this number" (*A Kuruc.info bekeményít, de segítséget is kér*). On the other hand, Kossuthter.com warned its visitors on 23 October that their server may break down as "currently we have ten times the usual number of visitors" (*Túlterhelt a kossuthter.com 23.10.06.*), albeit the actual number was not published. Among the portals we analysed, Falanx.hu represents an exception from this perspective. Falanx.hu also carries advertising, and their opening page features a statistics link pointing to data on the visits to the site. Visits were recorded from September 2006, and it is clear from the numbers that there was a considerable growth in interest in Falanx.hu in October and November, presumably as a result of the events: the number of average monthly visits was 39,046 in September; 98,311 in October; and 84,895 in November.[2] According to the site, Jobbik szoba attracted 30,271 visitors from June 2005.

We conducted a directed qualitative content analysis of the sources in order to examine the validity of our theoretical assumptions. Initial coding categories were formed based on theories of political activism and social movements. Textual elements collected from the websites were coded according to the categories. During the course of the analysis, we kept returning to the original categories, modifying them in the light of the textual data where that became necessary.[3]

Our primary aim was to explore the themes related to the demonstrations. How extensive is the coverage of these events, and what position does it take among other topics? The most frequently declared demand of the demonstrations was the resignation of the government. Were there also other goals motivating the demonstrators and, if so, how much consensus was there about these? The research also explored the main elements of the political ideologies that could be reconstructed from the online contents. Marking historical, cultural and political references is fundamental to creating identities. What were these references, and what function did they have in the different texts?

News items, opinion pieces and discussion forum postings also make possible analysis of values reflected on the sites. What are the negative and positive values, and in what context do they appear? One of the important elements of the rhetoric used by the demonstrators is the precise and clear differentiation between "ingroup" and "outgroup": the creation and constant evocation of the enemy's image. The content analysis explores the people and groups that the authors of online content regarded as the enemy.

Prime Minister Gyurcsány became a central figure of the events. His speech that was leaked on 17 September 2006, played a direct part in provoking the political crisis. The analysis explores the representations of the prime minister online, including the characteristics and actions attributed to him, together with the issues of political responsibility or accountability.

One of the most important and most interesting questions the content analysis may help answer is whether the demonstrators used the Internet for political organization. Are there direct calls for mobilization in the online materials, and, if so, what kinds of action do they urge and how? What buzzwords do authors use in addressing their audience, and how do they justify the necessity of participation?

The sources used in the research are highly heterogeneous. Texts are widely borrowed, copied, linked and cross-referenced from other portals or offline publications. Nevertheless, we considered all content as a "single text" and did not differentiate between speakers. This may occasionally work against the subtlety of interpretations, but we believe it does not undermine the accuracy of our interpretations.

News Agenda

From 17 September, the day when Prime Minister Gyurcsány's speech was leaked, news and information about the political crisis and the demonstrations dominated the online media pages and discussion forums. The situation remained unchanged during the ten to twelve days following the eruption of the crisis. The "revolutionary" themes included:

- Developments as the protests unfolded in the capital and the country;
- Police reaction and later accounts of trials;
- Advice and information specifically targeted at the demonstrators;
- Comments by foreign politicians and international news media;
- Reports on international actions of solidarity;
- Positions taken by Hungarian parties and public figures about the protests;
- News about the leaders and outstanding activists; and
- Information about legal aid provided for the victims of the events.

The political news structure began to change in the last days of September, but even then stories other than covering the "revolution" were rare. Kuruc.info assigned top importance to the demonstrations, starting a new section under the heading of "Revolution". The editors compiled a chronology of the critical, street-fighting days (and nights), based on information gathered from reporters on the scene, participants and eyewitnesses, occasionally offering minute-by-minute updates on the events. The majority of the coverage, however, relied on other news sources, often citing stories by mainstream media outlets known for their right-wing political leanings (e.g., *Hír TV* or the right-wing daily *Magyar Nemzet*). The sites also regularly quoted each other.

Us and Them: Representations of the Self and the Enemy

Who is with us, and who are we fighting? These simple but crucial questions constantly preoccupied the authors of online content. The materials reflect the complexities of self-identification and reveal that – as can be expected in critical political situations – establishing a definition of the self is more difficult than marking the enemy. Producers and users of extreme right-wing sites were characterized by divisions and splits. Their views diverged significantly about who could be considered authentic figures. The ingroup was amorphous and shifting constantly in reaction to the fast-paced changes of the events.

The activists, participants in the events and the news editors were suggesting that the scandal engulfing the prime minister had evoked unprecedented solidarity in the nation.[4] Thus, in theory the broadest "Us" group included all 15 million Hungarians, with the proviso that this concerned only "real" Hungarians. However, there was no consensus among the speakers about who exactly these may be. The most frequently mentioned categories included "revolutionaries" ("demonstrators", "heroes") or "the young". In one of his messages, one of the particularly radical leaders of the protests listed the groups the revolution could count on as follows: "Hungarian cool goons, bikers, skinheads, headbangers from patriotic concerts" (*Budaházy üzen a föld alól is - Gyurcsányt még nem fogták el* in Kuruc.info 26.09.)

The creation of the enemy, and the constant emphasizing of its presence is one of the pillars of revolutionary rhetoric. This marks all historical situations when a politician, a leader or a group wants to hammer out a new community and tries to awaken solidarity among the people belonging together.[5] This is especially true about critical periods like revolutions or civil wars when possession of power becomes questionable. Marking out the enemy, emphasizing the potential danger for the ingroup are also capable of diverting attention from the concrete political actions and debates, diminishing the differences and conflicts within the ingroup and awakening the members of even politically and culturally heterogeneous groups to their shared interests.

The materials we analysed feature many varieties of the enemy. The primary opponent is the prime minister and his Hungarian Socialist Party, but we are going to discuss this theme in more detail later. For the authors of the sites, the vilest brand of the enemy is the hidden kind: the snitch and the provocateur. When interviewed as an eyewitness to the 23 October events, one of the alleged leaders of the demonstrators said, "My guess is that one third of this whole event, the leadership...I don't know how large a part, but I certainly sense an awful lot of snitches who collaborate with the authorities in the background." (A kezdet – okt. 23. hajnaláról in Kossuthter.com 10.31.) The presence of undercover agents, provocateurs is repeatedly mentioned in the news, as well as among the protesters in the street. Provocateurs are sometimes faceless figures: "There is an SMS sent around among the Kossuth Square demonstrators about provocateurs hidden in the crowd, wearing hoods, masks, and armed. The organisers believe the demonstrators should try to pick out these elements and unmask them." (Provokátorok a tömegben? Drámai a kép Budapesten in Falanx.hu 09.18. 22:19.) In a gesture of self-reflection, the editors refute such scaremongering as false: "...news spread among the crowd that hooded provocateurs are arriving from [the west].... That bit of news, too, proved to be a false alarm..." (Kuruc.info 09. 21.) Other times, however, specific individuals are named as provocateurs. Two men who gave speeches at the Kossuth Square demonstrations were revealed by Kuruc.info to have been union leaders and secret agents in the communist regime. According to the portal, both men spoke to the demonstrators with the intent of confusing them and undermining the protests. (Kossuth tér: Kőrösi Imre verőemberekkel foglalta el a színpadot In Kuruc.info 10.02.) Yet charges of provocation were also levelled at the man thrown into the limelight for his role in the siege of the national television building. The man later complained that "some right-wing politicians and media accuse him of organising the street riots as a paid political provocateur" (Toroczkai László lemond in Falanx.hu 10.07.).

Apart from provocateurs, online authors also constantly evoked the "enemy of the nation". Suggestions that these were shady, faceless persons or groups served to render them more universal and frightening than some specific individuals who could be challenged directly. A way of connecting the unidentified, obscure enemy and the government and the authorities was through the secret service agencies. News stories made it clear that the National Security Office kept the radical persons and groups who also appeared among the demonstrators under surveillance. Furthermore, the secret services were said to publish messages designed to be threatening, like when they 'threatened peaceful demonstrators with imprisonment for sedition'. (Megdöbbentő: A tüntetőket fenyegeti az NBH in Kossuthter.com 10.09.)

Among the clearly identified enemy, the police were the most reviled and also physically threatening group. The authors relied on a rich, slang-ridden vocabulary to refer to the police (cops, pigs, nigs, five-os). The police sometimes appeared as a fumbling congregation of ridiculous, dumb, helpless figures.[6] However, they were mostly represented as the frightful successor to the communist police, an armed force servicing the dictatorship that suppressed citizens' rights, beating up children, attacking women, the young and the elderly: [7] "...numerous dubious characters of the police, their abuses should be written up in a book...There are sadistic psychos among them who gratify their sick needs with unarmed victims...the troopers who stomped on the Hungarian flag are still among them today, one can expect no sympathy, understanding from them." (Gábor Szakács, rune carver: Elég volt a szadista rendőrök dicséretéből! in Kuruc.info 09.22.)

The alleged atrocities and abuses perpetrated by the police were leading news items in the online texts. Some of the news emphasized that the conduct of the police was incompatible with the law and democratic legal norms.[8] The editors and the discussion participants published detailed reports, eyewitness accounts about the police brutality seen in the street clashes.[9] These depicted the police as not just antidemocratic, but also brutishly ruthless, occasionally psychotic beings. The unprecedented vandalism of the police acts was coupled with obscene language that degrades citizens: "The height of the day was when one of the police said to a desperate, crying mother, 'What stinking bitch could give birth to such a sodding shit of a son?!'" (Kuruc.info 09.22).[10]

The texts regularly use expressions like "police hooligans", "police criminals", "police riff-raff", which suggests a reversal of roles; online authors sought to indicate that the rhetoric branding the demonstrators as a chaotic mob was, in fact, more applicable to those who attacked protesters ostensibly in the name of maintaining order. The mistakes, atrocities and possible unlawful acts committed by the police provoked outrage in a much wider strata of society than the supporters of the extreme Right, particularly in the wake of the events of 23 October.[11] However, radical right-wingers maintained throughout that a crisis of political legitimacy produced two interpretations of order. One approach claims that order is represented by the police acting to uphold the law. Some groups of the demonstrators on the other hand believe that if the police represents a government that has lost its legitimacy, then it itself illegitimate. A new order must therefore be created, and this task is to be performed by the revolutionary protectors of the nation.

Apart from the radical critiques addressed to the armed units controlled by the government, the sites also agreed that the demonstrations took place in a hostile media environment. Hungarian media were seen as wielding significant symbolic power dedicated to maintaining the rule of the government. The media were presented as manipulating the masses, distorting reality and uncritically serving the governing parties. One of the leaders of the protesters talked about the ?misleading, false information coming from the media and the secret services" (Sikerrel zárult az akaratnyilvánító Népgyılés in Kossuthter.com 10.29). Another leader of the rioters declared that "the only entities blocking the way of change are the court media and the police who protect the gang of liars" (Ne féljen senki! – üzeni a bujkáló Budaházy György in Kossuthter.com 09.29). Kossuthter.com considers it one of its missions to counterbalance this: "This website stands up against the distortions and lies of mainstream[12] media" (Rólunk). The immorality of the pro-government media is highlighted by the harrassement of the media that report the events truthfully (Médiaterror: a kormány betiltaná a HírTV-t! in Falanx.hu 09.27). Their reporters fell victim to tear gas attacks and police brutality on the scene. By implication, the right-wing online sites became the only reliable and authentic sources of information, providing a counter-balance to the dominance of pro-establishment mainstream media.

Representation of the Prime Minister

Ferenc Gyurcsány plays a central role in the online texts; he is the main political target of the demonstrators.[13] He gets the most attacks, since the main task is to get rid of the post-communist regime hallmarked by his name. All the comments about Gyurcsány are extremely derogatory, aimed at discrediting him morally, politically and psychologically. The intent of derogation appears in the use of sobriquets or the informal way of addressing him – although the authors on the sites believe that the latter is in fact encouraged by the prime minister himself when he addresses his compatriots in an informal, colloquial tone.[14]

The most often repeated accusation is that the prime minister lied in the election campaign, he tricked the nation: "Although as an old KISZ [Communist Youth Alliance] leader, Ferenc Gyurcsány must have remembered the old Pioneer maxim 'pioneers always tell the truth'" (Budaházy ismét üzen: Budapest köré blokádot! in Kuruc.info 09.28). Evidence for the claim that Gyurcsány lied is provided by the prime minister himself in the speech that was leaked and widely circulated on the Internet. The deliberate use of lies, the "tricks" he mentioned in the speech amount to election fraud, they are incompatible with the principles of parliamentary democracy and constitutionalism: "In a parliamentary democracy, the people exercise their power through their elected representatives. It is an important condition of free and democratic elections that voters have free access to all information needed to make a responsible choice." (*Rólunk* in Kossuthter.com.) Lying creates a bad precedent, and it undermines the moral basis for the prime minister's expectation that citizens should observe legal norms.[15] The reactions of the prime minister are considered to be arrogant and conceited, raising the issue of his personal responsibility for the street riots that got out of hand.[16]

An even more serious accusation states that since Ferenc Gyurcsány won the 2006 elections fraudulently, he is a common criminal: "A common criminal continues to be the prime minister of the country for a while yet. The police should restrain him." (Kuruc.info 09.20.) Election fraud, furthermore, also qualifies as political violence: opposition to it is a constitutional right and duty of the citizen.[17] According to the arguments, there is a direct connection between lying and fraud and dictatorship: "Cheaters, liars have no place in public life in a healthy democracy, because lying leads to dictatorship and causes grievous harm to Hungary." (*Rólunk* in Kossuthter.com.)

In a dictatorship, power-holders ignore the will of the people.[18] At the same time, vivid memories of dictatorship in Hungary cast their shadow over the premier and his party: 'The communists' successor party and its leadership are supportive of Ferenc Gyurcsány, a lying, illegitimate embodiment of dictatorial leanings." (*Kommunista időket idéző rendőrterror a fővárosban – A Magyar Nemzeti Bizottság 2006 Közleménye* in Kossuthter.com 10.23). One of the prominent accusations against Gyurcsány is his communist past, the role he played as secretary of KISZ. His career also attracts mockery. The deficient socialization of the parvenue former communist youth leader is highlighted by critics: "How could a former KISZ leader know about [civic/bourgeois culture], even if he has by now managed to buy the trappings of bourgeois life for himself?" (*A köz szolgálatát mindenki máshogy értelmezi* in Falanx.hu 10.15.)

As events unfolded, criticism of the prime minister became more pronouced. One of the leaders of the protests said: "Nothing has been the same since the apocalyptic siege of Hungarian Television. (...) Since then Ferenc Gyurcsány has severely discredited himself in front of the international media that, unlike his pet home-grown journalists, ask him serious questions. And he has grown into an increasingly spectacular tyrant..." (*Tudósításunk a Kossuth térről - Toroczkai visszatért!* in Kuruc.info 09. 26.)

It was asserted that the prime minister had not only been discredited politically and morally, but he also revealed his psychological flaws, proving to be a person unfit to fulfill his duties. He was said to be a "demented criminal" (*Budaházy üzen a föld alól is – Gyurcsányt még nem fogták el* in Kuruc.info 09.26), a "schizophrenic person, a clinical case, his mum's retarded sonny" (*"édesanyád"* In Falanx.hu 09.18). An expert psychologist confirmed the diagnosis of mental disturbance, citing Gyurcsány's lack of embarrassment when grilled about his lies in a CNN interview (*A pszichológus szerint Gyurcsány lényegében elmebeteg* in Kuruc.info 09. 22). According to the demonstrators, the prime minister is psychotic, cynical, and running amok until the final ruin of Hungary.

Political goals, programmes, mobilization

Divisions among the activists and sympathizers of the demonstrations were most clearly revealed when it came to provide a precise definition of their political goals and to provide an interpretations of the events. Some saw the siege of MTV as a heroic act that marked the beginning of the revolution, a foundation for the new, "revolutionary" calendar. Others, also vehemently demanding the resignation of the government, nevertheless, saw the siege as mere provocation or hooliganism.[19]

The only question all voices appear to agree on is the need to be rid of the Gyurcsány administration. Another, widely supported, goal is "real regime change"; however, details of what was meant were less clear.

The goal of removing post-communist forces from public life[20] was widely shared, but opinions were divided on how this should be achieved, and what would follow. Differences as to the goals to be pursued emerged as different groups of the Kossuth Square demonstrators submitted parallel petitions to Parliament, prompting the President of Parliament to talk about "a sort of petitioning contest" (Átadták a petíciót a Kossuth téri tüntetők in Falanx.hu 09.25). The authors of the different calls, appeals and declarations were united only in calling for the removal of the government, perhaps also describing the most adequate means of doing that. However, they failed to discuss the future, or did not go beyond very general and vague demands.[21] While the petitioners considered the current parliament a potential partner for negotiations, advocates of a more radical vision viewed the "cowardly and impotent" parliamentary opposition parties as unfit to govern and demanded new elections.[22]

Yet others went even further. Some groups of the Kossuth Square demonstrators argued that new elections by themselves were insufficient, because electoral law would only favour and return into power the four parties already in Parliament. The Revolutionary National Committee (Forradalmi Nemzeti Bizottmány) of Kossuth Square envisioned the revolution in three phases: "getting rid of the government, changing the constitution, changing the regime" (A Magyar Nemzeti Bizottság, a Forradalmi Nemzeti Bizottmány és az általuk létrehozott testületek in Kossuthter.com 09.28. 21:42). The radicals called for the convocation of a constitution-making national assembly, as only that could create a new, legitimate foundation for government.[23] The well-known blogger Tomcat stated clearly: the current government is illegitimate.[24] He summarized political demands on behalf of the demonstrators: 1. The government should resign; 2. A Constitution-Making National Assembly should be called; 3. The "political prisoners" who were taken into custody should be granted amnesty; 4. The demolished historical statues should be restored on Szabadság Square; 5. A new electoral law should be drafted that does not include the 5 per cent threshold for Parliament; 6. Independent experts should examine the state of the economy; and 7. Every Hungarian person should be granted Hungarian citizenship.[25] László Toroczkai went even further at the demonstration held on 28 October in the Castle area when he urged the demonstrators to set up alternative, shadow institutions parallel to the state institutions.[26]

Numerous other political demands appeared in the online texts we analysed; in order to realize these, it seemed necessary to keep up the continual flow of information and organizing; that is, mobilization.[27] Although some actors embarked on a tour of the country to promote this goal directly,[28] the geographical distances and the size of the crowds that were potentially interested in the protests made it necessary to also find more efficient tools. One of the our main research questions was whether the activists of the demonstrations used the online content resources for purposes of mobilization and organizing. The answer is clearly affirmative. Furthermore, the online sources reveal that communication channels used for information and mobilization were also extended to mobile phones. Apart from the SMS messages circulated among demonstrators, the online sources also make reference to at least one initiative where the information published on Kossuthter.com was distributed on mobile phones through WAP technology (WAP verzió in Kossuthter.com 10.03). However, we have no data on the reception of the messages of mobilization among users, or the number of people who may have been galvanized into some political action by the online messages.

During the first days of the demonstrations, site editors concentrated mostly on publishing news reports with quotes from the speeches made on Kossuth Square or at other scenes. Later on, however, the demonstrators themselves started using the Internet as a communication tool for organization and mobilization, publishing their declarations, calls, messages and advice on Internet forums and a mailing list set up specifically for this purpose.[29] Kuruc.info recommended online telephony for purposes of communication, because unlike with calls placed on mobile phones, the Hungarian authorities cannot eavesdrop on Internet conversations for technological reasons (*Nem tudják lehallgatni az Internetes beszélgetést* in Kuruc.info 10.10). The protesters also began using the main Hungarian social networking site, iwiw. In an effort to build their identity and image, they started registering on the site under the username "riffraff",[30] thus appropriating and subverting the offensive label attached to them by pro-establishment forces. A "Resistance Manual" was published on the Internet, containing tactical advice on "revolutionary activities" including demonstrations, battles with the police and being arrested (in Kuruc.info 10. 30).

György Budaházy, a leader of the protests who was wanted by the police and stayed in hiding, was one of the most determined users of the Internet. As a "revolutionary" on the run, he keeps distributing letters containing his messages through the Internet, or at least through online news portals. He articulated concrete programmes, called for action and also indicated the necessary steps. In the speech he gave on 21 September on Kossuth Square, he emphasized that the government could not be overturned by peaceful means and told the crowd what needed to be done: "At the end of his speech that drew thunderous applause, Budaházy sent a message to farmers: after thanking them for the food they had sent, he asked them to move not towards Budapest but towards the borders so that the MSZP criminals could not escape". (*Hazamennek pihenni a tüntetők* in Kuruc.info 09.22.) A few days later, on 26 September, he demanded much more radical action in a message of mobilization he sent "from underground" to several newsrooms, including Kuruc.info.[31]

Throughout the period covered in the research, Budaházy continued sending his messages. His letters interpreted the events and urged his followers and the sympathizers of the protests to political action. He called on the demonstrators to launch a counter-attack against the increasingly dictatorial regime, to publish the abuses of rights, and he recommended the Internet for this as an adequate and efficient medium that also has more credibility than television.[32] In another "message" he demanded a blocade around Budapest, and he also suggested that the Internet should be used to organize it.[33] As time went by, his messages became increasingly radical and, by the end of October, he was calling on his "Hungarian brothers" to take up arms.

Revolutionary rhetoric

The analysis of the texts shows that the speakers at the demonstrations, as well as the online authors and discussion forum participants, created a peculiar, revolutionary rhetoric. Since they failed to gain real political power, rally big crowds in their support, or even come to an agreement on a common programme, words provided the only ground for action apart from the weeks of demonstration on Kossuth Square and the occasional street riots. Thus, the language used in the period of the demonstrations acquired special significance.

The overwhelming majority of radical participants viewed the events of September-October as a revolution, and defined themselves as revolutionaries. "Revolution" was the most frequently used key term — although once again it needs to be emphasized that it is far from clear which events should be considered "revolutionary".[34] The vocabulary also contains other sacred expressions like "nation", "homeland", "Hungarian", "real Hungarian", "constitution", "the law". In a certain context, used ritually, these terms express an attachment to the revolution, that is, their function is to arouse solidarity.

One of the most important characteristics of the revolutionary rhetoric is the expression of the decisive break from the political elite that seized power after the fraudulent transition from the communist system, as well as the declaration of the rebirth of the nation. In a somewhat simplified way we can say that the past is of dictatorship, the future is of a free Hungary whose construction the revolutionaries are engaged in. In this sense, language is not a mere reflection on the political events, rather it represents a formative force by itself. It elevates the present from everyday chronology, treating it as extraordinary, mythical, a period with special meaning that will result in real change. In the mythical present, the new, morally impeccable heroes are born, they are exemplary and the guarantees of victory.

One of the fundamental functions of words is to create certainty for the community of revolutionaries in the midst of chaotic and ambiguous political events. Certainty is provided primarily through the constant emphasis on the importance of the cause and the widespread support it enjoys. This is why the editors report on the messages sent by demonstrators to international organizations, the reactions of foreign politicians, as well as on different solidarity events. It is for the same purpose that the demonstrations from the country are reported on in detail, elevating these events into the revolutionary chronology.[35]

Within the revolutionary rhetoric, there is a reversal of roles; the demonstrators turn the accusations levelled at them back on Ferenc Gyurcsány, on what they call his oppressive political regime and on the organizations and institutions serving what they consider as dictatorship. The revolutionaries declared that, in fact, they represented the rule of law and order, and when the power-holders call them riff-raff, it is no more than a false trick to cover up the fact that they are the real riff-raff.

Throughout the process, the Internet continued to serve as the medium for a collectively produced chronicle, a repository of textual (and audio, video) mementoes of the events. In a sense, the Internet is performing a "bardic function" (Fiske and Hartley 1978) for the 'revolution', albeit the sites we analysed attempted to elevate the oppositional and marginal into the centre of the social-political world, marking the mainstream as 'deviant'.

Political ideology and values

The websites analysed in the research show that the political views of their producers are rather heterogeneous. Instead of presenting a unified, considered political ideology, the positions presented online were occasionally incompatible even with each other, and sometimes – partly because they were expressed in generalities – they are difficult to interpret.[36] The online texts indicate that during the critical autumn period it was not primarily a shared political ideology or programme that brought together the different groups of demonstrators or their sympathizers under one banner. Apart from the outrage provoked by the prime minister's leaked speech and the desire to protest against it, the demonstrators were connected by some shared feelings, a sort of subcultural mode (see below for a more detailed discussion under "Political symbols, historical and cultural references").

Based on the reconstruction of the political arguments, the ideology presented on the sites shares many elements with other European radical and extreme right-wing movements, but at the same time it is specifically Hungarian in several respects. This duality can be explained by country-specific circumstances demanding similarly country-specific political answers, while some of the challenges, like globalization or neo-liberal economic policy, are the same in Hungary as in other parts of the world.

The primary ideology that appears in the online texts could be called "holistic nationalism" (Eatwell 2000). Unlike liberalism that is rational, individualistic and dedicated to pluralism and tolerance, this usually approaches the nation on an ethnic basis, or ties membership in the nation to assimilation to the national culture. The ideology of holistic nationalism is co-determined by the demonization of other groups and the definition of the sacred homeland. Apart from cultural assimilation, the conditions for belonging to the nation include long-term membership in the community, and the condition that only those should benefit from social provisions who significantly contribute to them. Furthermore, it is important that the beneficiaries of the national economy should be the members of the national community themselves. Apart from nationalism, the self-definition of radical right-wing forces includes opposition to the system, the fossilized, clientelistic partocracy. These political forces often define themselves as the representatives of the true interests of the people and the nation, unlike the regime of the establishment.

In a majority of online sources, elements of holistic nationalism appear mixed with the notions originating from specifically Hungarian circumstances. The common denominator of the diverse values appearing on the sites is the "national" character, a comprehensive category that encompasses a highly heterogeneous political field. It helps the handling of the differences of opinion that the speakers tend to define themselves in negative ways, i.e., they talk about what they cannot identify with. Communism and its legacy feature prominently among the rejected values and ideas. The producers of the contents are generally hostile to the Left, although this is manifest mainly in an "antibolshevic" rhetoric, the vilification of the current government and the Socialist Party.[37]

Anti-communism can still be relevant sixteen years after the collapse of the communist system because – the authors claim – the current parliamentary system that calls itself democratic is, in fact, based on the remnants of state socialism. There was no real regime change in 1989: the communist political elite managed to preserve its positions. What is more, the Socialist Party has built an even more totalitarian, Stalinist dictatorship, whose survival is guaranteed by the courts that have no independence from state authorities, the police that acts as the reincarnation of the communist secret police, and the corrupt left-liberal media.

Furthermore, the current system is built on an illegitimate constitution, because the 1949 communist constitution was given a mere "makeover" in the regime change.[38] The new constitution would be a symbol of national survival: "Without a constitution, the Hungarians have no future in the Carpathian basin in the middle of Europe. Without it, there can be no social justice, no solidarity and prosperity, no freedom, no feeling of being at home, and no equality in European participation", said a speaker on Kossuth Square (Kossuthter.com 10.18. 14:11). The primary goal, thus, is the creation of a new constitution, but none of the parties in Parliament are capable of delivering that.

The rejection of partocracy is manifest in the criticisms addressed to the government coalition, including contempt for the Socialist Party or fierce hostility towards the liberals. The "anti-liberal" sentiments are intertwined with diatribes against liberal politicians and some issues advocated by the liberal party: the demonized groups include Jews (often in the shape of anti-Zionist or pro-Palestinian views), Gypsies and homosexuals.[39] However, besides the government coalition the third most often attacked entity is the right-of-centre opposition party Fidesz; the authors of these online texts tend to reject the 'moderate' conservatism this party represents. The authors also believe NATO and EU memberships are harmful for the country.

Since the current order is illegitimate historically, legally and in terms of how power is exercised, a new legitimacy needs to be created – and that can be done only by a radical movement that enjoys the support of a broad social base. The efforts of the online authors are aimed at setting up and organizing this movement.

Among the values that can support them in their mission is religion, which had been persecuted under communism. The emphatically Christian faith often appears linked to the concepts of the nation and right-wing political identity. The ideology of Kuruc.info, for one, is defined by the editor in the following way: "Kuruc.info is a Christian-conservative, antiliberal online periodical. It is Christian but not bigotted, conservative but not obsolete, rather it is characterised by youthful energy. (...) its tone is highly critical **towards all political strands**" [highlighted in the original text].[40] A party since October 2003, Jobbik registered its discussion forum 'Jobbik room' in January 2004. The party defines itself as the authentic representatives of Christian-national ideas.[41] The authors of the 18 September Kossuth Square petition also address the "national, Christian" political forces with their request for help to bring down the government (in Kossuthter.com); alongside the national anthem, ecumenical Christian prayers were also part of the programme of the "first people's assemblies preparing the Constitution-Making National Assembly" (Felhívás rendszerváltó népgyűlésre in Kossuthter.com 11.22. 07:07); a prayer tent was set up on Kossuth Square; and a call was issued for a nine-day fast and common prayers "for settling the fate of Hungary" (Ima és böjt hazánkért in Kossuthter.com 09.28 16:23).

At the same time, Christianity can pose a problem for those right-wingers who seek national identity in ancient Hungarian traditions and culture. For, unlike cultural traditions that can be revived, the ancient Hungarian faith was alien to Christianity. Thus, a consistently developed Hungarian identity might even potentially lead to a rejection of Christianity: György Budaházy, for example, claims that he is no Christian: "...I do not profess the principle of Christian forgiveness. My faith is pagan, and I do not forget!" (Budaházy válasza Csurkának in Kuruc.info 10.12. 16:55.) This conflict is resolved in the Sacred Crown doctrine and the belief system surrounding it. These offer a synthesis of religion and nation, as well as democratic autonomy – this is why they can play a role in the preparations of constitution-making (A Magyar Nemzeti Bizottság, a Forradalmi Nemzeti Bizottmány és az általuk létrehozott testületek in Kossuthter.com 09.28. 21:42).

The Sacred Crown doctrine is "the ancient, unwritten historical constitution of Hungary", according to which the Sacred Crown "unites all of the Hungarian political nation"[42] (A Szentkorona-tan lényegéről röviden in Szent Korona Rádió 2006. május 10. 21:42). According to the beliefs surrounding the doctrine, Christianity does not contradict ancient Hungarian traditions; in fact, Hungarians were never pagans, they belonged to Christianity as early as the fourth and fifth centuries. Within Christianity, they followed the line of neither Rome nor Byzantium, "our ancestors were of the Jesus faith" – and Jesus himself was "never a Jew". (Comments posted by Honvéd to the article A Szentkorona-tan lényegéről röviden in Szent Korona Rádió 05.10. 21:23 és 21:01.)

The crown creates a mystic connection between the nation, its leader and the territory of the homeland. Territorial issues feature prominently on extreme right-wing sites; on this issue nationalism is often associated with revisionistic views, as Hungarians living as ethnic minorities in the territories Hungary lost after WWII are part of the unity of the nation.[43]

The desire for a unified nation is central to national themes and holistic nationalism. The different online voices are united in claiming that they are standing up to the government in the defense of the "national side". They believe that the politics of the treasonous government and the collaborator opposition lead Hungarians to grave danger, threatening destruction that only full national unity and a national revival can prevent.[44]

Political symbols, historical and cultural references

Besides language and rhetoric, the demonstrators calling themselves revolutionaries could also draw on political symbols, cultural references and references to the events of the past to create their identity. Similar to the programmes and political opinions, the world of symbols, too, is heterogeneous, contradictory, occasionally obscure.

The activists of autumn 2006 clearly identified with the heritage of 1956, presenting themselves as the successors to the revolution of 50 years ago — all the more so because the revolution then failed, and the arch-enemy of communism has not been defeated ever since. In order to emphasize the succession, they are continually searching for analogies between the events, actors and scenes of then and now (the siege of Hungarian Radio — Hungarian Television; the "boys of Pest" took to the streets then and now, and red blood flowed in the streets; Kossuth Square as a centre of the revolution).[45] Most historical references are made to the 1956 revolution. This can be explained partly by the 50th anniversary of the events, but theories of revolution also claim that revolutionaries prefer to choose a sequence of events (another revolution) they can identify with and they can consider as a script — the French Revolution served as a model for both Europe in 1848 and Russia in 1917.

However, the revolutionary tradition allows the demonstrators to identify not only with 1956, but also earlier revolutions and freedom struggles. The majority of the authors are characterized by freedom-fighter ways of thinking and rhetoric. Above all, they identify with 1848 (the year of the Hungarian uprising against Habsburg rule) and the eighteenth-century *kuruc* struggles for freedom from Habsburg rule, as indicated by the name of one of the most widely read portals.

The sites display an amalgam of different historical traditions. Extreme-radical groups are known to pay close attention to ancient Hungarian traditions, and the online materials confirm this. Among the links posted to Kuruc.info there are ones pointing to the 'Forrai Sándor Rune Writing Circle' and the '*Táltos* [shaman] Hub'. The editors constructed a separate website for those who are interested in ancient Hungarian culture, and they uploaded the biography of legendary Hungarian tribal leader Árpád to the portal. Visual references to ancient Hungarian religion, writing, culture and history also abound on the sites. The sympathizers have created an ancient Hungarian subculture (Hebdige 1979), offering not just a symbol but also a way of living and feeling. It is part of the self-definition of members of a subculture that they are in opposition to the dominant culture. The most visible aspect of their opposition is style: radical right-wing groups turn to ancient Hungarian culture (or its imagined versions), historical iconography (e.g., the map of historical Hungary) in their choice of clothing, decoration, music. The stylistic elements offer tools for symbolic politics, they help express resistance to global consumer culture and the neo-liberal policies encouraging it.[46]

Apart from the above, the cult of monarchy also appeared, especially in the form of reverence for the kings of the House of Árpád, as also shown by the elevation of the Árpád-striped flag into the symbol of the demonstrations.[47] The flag itself became the subject of heated political debate, with critics arguing that its use recalled Hungarian fascist terror (Hungarian Nazis used the historical flag pasting their symbol over it). Eventually, Jobbik launched the website arpadsavos.hu in defense of the flag, and they chose the red-and-white stripes as the symbol of their party. Medieval references the Sacred Crown is another primary cultural symbol, attesting to the glorious past and Hungarian excellence, while at the same time serving as a key to the survival of the nation.[48] In the cases of both the Árpád-striped flag and the crown, online articles are engaged in a struggle over the interpretation of historical symbols with "official" historians, opening another front of possible resistance for extreme right-wing, radical groups.

Finally, news reports and discussion materials featured numerous revisionist references and opinions. Apart from references to the losses suffered from the Trianon peace treaty, the politicians of the Horthy era and Governor Horthy himself appear as ideals. In the eyes of the authors and the editors, they are people who were the last representatives of legitimacy in Hungary. They are immediate predecessors, their heritage needs to be renewed, the road indicated by them needs to be followed.

Conclusion

The political crisis of autumn 2006 brought together radical political-cultural groups, but the shared identity they discovered following the siege of the Hungarian Television headquarters proved short-lived. The reason why this alliance could not last can be reconstructed from the online content of radical right-wing websites. These peripheral associations are pulled apart by forces far greater than the ones that could unite them. The government was temporarily shaken and could not respond to the crisis in a convincing way. For a time, that raised the visibility of political and ideological radicals, but not because they presented an attractive alternative for wide layers of society, rather because of the temporary undermining of central authority. These groups exploited the spontaneous outrage that drove people to Kossuth Square, and they undoubtedly had some experience in directing political performances. Their revolution, however, remained theatrical as they staged a play anachronistically, 50 (160, 300) years after the real freedom struggles, with those periods' costumes and sets, but in a twenty-first-century context. And the play had too many authors. Since the revolution eventually failed to materialize, the boundaries between the narratives unfolding in the streets and in virtual space became increasingly blurred. The bogeymen the activists relied on failed to scare anyone; similarly, they themselves failed to be really scary as bogeymen. Nonetheless, this does not mean that the questions asked by the radicals are not relevant. And we need to face the fact that while there are relevant questions, no adequate answers are forthcoming for now.

Our analysis shows that the Internet was used by the radical right-wing actors in the political events to exchange information, organize and coordinate action and mobilize support. Despite sophisticated and often effective uses of communication technology to further political goals, however, no radical political transformation occurred as a result in 2006. In this sense, communication technology failed to make a major impact on society on this occasion. However, the Internet served – and continues to serve – as a medium for sustaining an alternative, anti-establishment political narrative for marginal political groups, enabling them to write their own version of contemporary events and history. In the absence of a revolution, the Internet-enabled presence of radical right-wing voices in the public domain continues to be their most significant, symbolic achievement.

Notes

1. Further suggestions of the connection include the fact that one of the main organizers of the demonstrations was a member of the radical right-wing party Jobbik until 17 September 2006; while technical support for the website created for disseminating information about the demonstrations was provided by a company associated with online radical right-wing media outlets.

2. In September 2006, the online edition of the Socialist-affiliated daily Népszava.hu attracted 49,106 visitors; the Socialist portal amőba.hu, which is also the home of the prime minister's blog, had 151,629 visitors; the pages of the 24-hour, right-wing cable news channel, Hír TV, had 382,730 visitors; while one of the leading news portals, Index, had 1,438,572 visitors (source: Medián Webaudit). Compared to the previous month's data, this meant a 70 per cent increase for Hír TV and a 412 per cent increase for amőba.hu.

3. Based on Mayring, Philipp (2000). Qualitative Content Analysis. *Forum Qualitative Sozialforschung/Forum: Qualitative Social Research*, 1(2). http://qualitative-research.net/fqs/ fqs-e/2-00inhalt-e.htm (last accessed: 06.12.06), and Hsieh, Hsiu-Fang & Shannon, Sarah E. (2005). Three Approaches to Qualitative Content Analysis. *Qualitative Health Research*, 15(9).

4. Solidarity in this case encompassed also Hungarians living outside Hungary, their demonstrations and supportive declarations were constantly referred to by the editors.

5. Luther declared the Pope the Antichrist in the hope of seducing masses away from the Church. The French revolutionaries also indicated their enemies clearly, although these underwent changes with the progress of the events.

6. "They were brave. Gyurcsány Hussars. They weren't so heroic outside the national television headquarters, I saw that with my own eyes. But they executed a very heroic attack on an apolitical bartender." (Krisztián Vass: *Most jöttem a az MSZP székháza előtti csatából* in Falanx.hu 09.20.) The image of a bewildered, incompetent police is strengthened by a sound recording in which, allegedly, a commander of the police units, sent to defend the television building, speaks with headquarters. The recording is of a male voice saying he feels himself and his people to be in mortal danger, and he declares he is withdrawing his men from the building against his orders. (*A TV-székházat védő rendőrök kétségbeesett rádóbeszélgetése itt letölthető! – SOUND RECORDING* in Falanx.hu 09.26.)

7. See, for example, "23:19 The police launch a counterattack! The police used water cannons against the attackers, a part of Szabadság Square was taken back. The crowd are chanting slogans of 'ÁVH! ÁVH!' [State Protection Authority under the Communist regime]" (*Drámai a kép Budapesten (folyamatos frissítéssel)* in Falanx.hu 09.18.

8. "The EU legal experts consulted by the lawyers of the Kossuth Square demonstrators and our newsroom unanimously agree that should the police disperse the crowd in a similar, legally partially unregulated area, they would break several passages of international law, because in a democracy the right to free assembly cannot be curtailed in a manner devised by the currently reigning authorities." (*Aggályos a Kossuth tér kiürítésének terve* in Falanx.hu 10.19.)

9. See, for example, *Túlkapások: "Megvallattak, hogy vérzett a húsunk..."* (taken from mno.hu by Kuruc.info and by Szent Korona Rádió on 10.05.); *Brutális megtorlás a Markó utcában is* (Falanx.hu 10.05.); *Üzenet egy rendbontótól* (Kossuthter.com 10.29. 09:44).

10. The girlfriend of the radical blogger Tomcat told a similar story about her interrogation by the police: "There they kept interrogating me for hours, using psychological and spiritual terror. They threw disgusting criticisms at me about my appearance, my boyfriend, my religion, the credibility of my words, and me as a person. It was clear to me they were trying to prepare me (yes, I mean to fray my nerves) so that I would make a confession against Tomcat." (Kuruc.info 09. 20.)

11. Kossuthter.com posted an article from the left-liberal weekly *Élet és Irodalom* as a model of the truth, "currently a scarce good". The article offers criticism of police procedures on 23 October from a liberal perspective (*Igazságmorzsák az "élet és irodalom"-ból* 11.12).

12. Mainstream media are capable of credible reporting only if they are international. The reports of the BBC and CNN's interview with the prime minister also became important points of reference on the radical right-wing portals.

13. Falanx.hu dedicates a separate column to the analysis of the postings on the prime minister's blog.
14. See, e.g., "Feri – why shouldn't I call him that, after all he's my friend, he believes himself to be friend to all Hungarian citizens" (Blog: Elvették tőlünk 56'-ot In Falanx.hu 10.29).
15. "If the Prime Minister can get away with cheating, lying, then all the students who cheat have the right to lie without punishment, then everybody has the right to drive on the roads as they like, and unfortunately people will have the right to break windows, hit policemen, put buildings on fire." (Böjte Csaba levele a történtekről in Falanx.hu 09.22).
16. "Why did this have to happen? Because in his infamous speech Ferenc Gyurcsány said in advance that he was going to ignore the protests. ('let them demonstrate, they'll grow tired of it!')" (Az egyik Kossuth téri szónok nyilatkozata Budapesten in Falanx.hu 09.18 23:34).
17. The petition that was approved by the Kossuth Square demonstrators on 18 September states: "It is the duty of self-respecting citizens who care about the values of democracy to take action against political violence realized as fraud. The second section, third paragraph of our Constitution gives us the right by stating: 'The actions of any organization of society, any state body or citizen must not be directed at the forceful acquisition or exercising of power. Everybody is entitled and simultaneously obliged to take action against such attempts.'" (In Kossuthter.com.)
18. The commentaries Falanx.hu dedicates to Gyurcsány's blog are clear: "Pitiful. For unlike somone, the people would in fact know what their job is. And they would do it too, if only you let them, Mr. Dictator." (Blog: Elvették tőlünk '56-ot 10.29. 14:53.)
19. György Budaházy: "The September 18 events in front of the MTV headquarters replicated the events at Hungarian Radio in 1956. The 'public service' broadcaster refused to air the demands of the outraged crowds, arrogantly rejecting them, so the crowd besieged it." (Budaházy György levele Kuruc.info 09. 28.) Public Affairs Club of Szabolcs-Szatmár-Bereg County: "We have no doubt that a communist provocation occurred outside the MTV building, giving an excuse for Ferenc Gyurcsány and his thugs to retaliate with the methods of open dictatorship..." (Kilenc pontos büntetőfeljelentés a kormány ellen in Kuruc.info 09. 29.) Gábor Vona, vice-president of Jobbik: "Jobbik feels it important to state that its members took no part in the hooliganism and the street clashes.... Just because a few hundred people clash with the police, damage listed buildings and cars, the government will not change, they merely scare away the cautious majority." (gportal.hu 09.19.)
20. For example: "We cannot allow the return of left-wing dictatorship in Hungary under the shadow of police terror! We must finally complete the regime change!" (Kommunista időket idéző rendőrterror a fővárosban – A Magyar Nemzeti Bizottság 2006 Közleménye in Kossuthter.com 10.23.) "This event is peaceful, self-defensive in character, and unaffiliated with parties; at the same time it wishes to realise decisive support for a real regime change and Hungarian solidarity, protecting the national interests and values." (Szegeden készülnek – Felhívás rendszerváltó népgyűlésre in Kossuthter.com 11.22.)
21. See, for example, "Hungary should belong to the Hungarians, not capitalist interest groups" in gportal.hu 09.10.
22. See, for example, the 28 September declaration of the Public Affairs Club of Szabolcs-Szatmár-Bereg County. (Kilenc pontos büntetőfeljelentés a kormány ellen in Kuruc.info 09. 29.) Actor Mátyás Usztics also demanded early elections in his speech on Kossuth Square (Orbánt bírálta puhaságáért in Kuruc.info 10. 09.)
23. The rebel Budaházy states this position the most clearly: "We must achieve the disbanding of the illegitimate parliament, but not in a way where they quickly call new elections and we can once again choose from the same bunch like it happened on Sunday. No, we must reach a constitution-making assembly where we rethink everything, and where we get rid of this 'partocracy' and lay the foundations

for true popular representation. The time has come to end the picnic-like, singing, 'let's love each other', 'let's forgive our enemies' type of happening demonstrations and gear into attack again. Without the show of force, it would be impossible to overcome even a more democratic power, let alone this dictatorship." (*Budaházy: Gyurcsány leváltása még nem old meg semmit!* in Kuruc.info 10. 01.) Some speakers believe the new constitution is, in fact, the old one, for we need to return to the constitution "built on the foundations of the Sacred Crown" (*Kossuth tér: új alkotmány* in Kuruc.info 10.15).

24. Tomcat: *Forradalmi Kiskáté és csócselék-határozó + fotók* in Kuruc.info 10. 03.

25. Ibid. It is unclear whether the programme was authored by Tomcat or with the contributions of others.

26. "Among other things, László Toroczkai talks about the construction of the old-new system of institutions on the Sacred Crown. He also mentions the necessity of introducing a voluntary and small revolutionary tax (HUF 1,000 per month), for it is more useful to donate to the struggle, the perhaps drawn-out freedom fight than subsidise the thieving state.... Gyurcsány's ÁVH was there in force – 300 pribék –, there were police helicopters circling in the sky. Apart from the revolutionary tax mentioned above, Laci [Toroczkai] emphasised the beginning of the construction of our own parliament, media, and education system..." (*Több ezren a Várban: Budaházy felszólalt, Toroczkai: párhuzamos magyar intézményrendszer* in Kuruc.info 10. 28.)

27. A man published his prison diaries on Kuruc.info, and in the diary he claims the news portal had also engaged in direct mobilization. He says that within a year, 800 people volunteered for the Action group of Jobbik. Activists were notified about what to do through an SMS-sending system financed by Kuruc.info (*Tankvezető a cellatársam – Novák Előd börtönnaplója. Mozgósítunk* in Kuruc.info 11.03).

28. "As he stated days before, László Toroczkai – a member of the Hungarian National Committee 2006 – embarked on a tour of the country for the sake of thinking together and better organising. He is trying to construct bridges through his person between the demonstrators scattered around Hungary, on the one hand spreading motivation, on the other gaining and forwarding strength between the crowds, groups that are demonstrating in isolation from one another." (*Toroczkai László járja az országot* in Kossuthter.com 09.29.)

29. The organizers of the 22 September support demonstration in Csíkszereda, Transylvania, were rallying supporters specifically through the Internet (Kuruc.info 09.22). News of the mailing list was reported by Kossuthter.com: "A mailing list was created so that the organisers of the demonstrations in individual towns/settlements could be in touch with each other. It is important that they could cooperate and coordinate their actions, this way the demonstrations can become much stronger and united. (...) The essence of the mailing list is that one sends a single message to the central address, but all list members receive it. Through this the events of the demonstrations can be concerted much faster and more efficiently." (*Levelezőlista a tüntetések szervezőinek!* in Kossuthter.com 10.09.)

30. *Csócselék" mozgalom az iwiw-en* in Kuruc.info 10.30.

31. "Patriots! What's this inactivity? They'll never get scared by this picnic demonstration... Fortunately, the film footage showing the mindless police brutality is already on the net, this is what needs to be told to the world." (*Budaházy üzen a föld alól is – Gyurcsányt még nem fogták el* in Kuruc.info 09. 26. 02:15.)

32. "Demonstrators, organisers! News of police brutality and unfairness at the courts keep coming. This is what needs to be made the most important issue for now. Every speaker should attack the authorities for their Communist ÁVÓ methods! Protest demonstrations must be taken to the police and the courts, I hear Toroczkai is already agitating for this, this is the right path. We must launch a total attack against them on the issue of abusing rights. The population of the country must be enlightened about these cases, the addresses of the websites where these can be found on the Internet must be announced, because most people have no idea these are occurring. Unfortunately, even those who have Internet access only watch TV." *Budaházy újra üzent – Gyurcsány villájához megy?* in Kuruc.info 09.27. 17:38.

33. For the blockade, he is counting on farmers previously involved in road block demonstrations, and he urges those who have the telephone numbers made available on the Internet on the previous occasion to publish them (*Budaházy ismét üzen: Budapest köré blokádot* in Kuruc.info 09.28. 19:33).

34. See, for example, Dr Koncsek Krisztián: *Most forradalom, vagy sem?* in Falanx.hu 09.20 15:52.

35. Mobilization and the creation of the enemy are also important elements of the rhetoric. Both are discussed in detail above.

36. The difficulties of interpretation are illustrated by one of the speeches from Kossuth Square: "Let us first clarify what the ideological background of the Kossuth Square movement is like. I see it as basically conservative, democratic, and nationalistic in character. (I would add that traditionally, right-wing ideologies are conservative, authoritarian, and nationalistic, therefore we could say that this ideological mixture, independent of parties, is based fundamentally on right-wing foundations, and also contains values from the left.) In the current situation, this is understandable and justified, some kind of a reaction to today's world. But. Does conservativism, democratism or nationalism mean any sort of ideological novelty? No, for these ideas and ideologies were shaped in the 18–19th centuries, in an era of the bourgeois movements aimed at realising democracy and the birth of nation-states." (*Horváth Tibor beszéde* in Kossuthter.com 10.18. 13:21.)

37. It is worth noting that the demonization of communism is not a Hungarian invention: it was also a defining feature of the political self-image of western liberal democracies during the decades of the Cold War.

38. As the blogger Tomcat states: "What is wrong with the constitution? It's illegitimate. The thousand-year Hungarian constitution was suspended in 1944 with the German occupation. We had no constitution until 1949. In 1949, the Rákosi government created the current constitution in the shadow of Russian tanks. (...) In 1989, this constitution was updated by the still-reigning Communists under the guise of ‚reform', for example changing the word ‚people' to ‚nation', and renaming the country a republic, but no substantive change occurred. Power is currently divided between several parties, but only the most naive would believe there is a difference among these. The Gyurcsány government completed the rearrangement of power called regime change, through such severely antidemocratic moves as the merging of the Ministries of Interior and Justice...There is no point in merely changing the government, we must reinstitute the Sacred Crown constitution that had supported the nation for a thousand years. This does not necessarily imply a monarchy, although we were doing fine with that for a few decades..." *Forradalmi kiskáté és csócselék határozó + fotók* in Kuruc.info 10.03. 01:34. A member of the Hungarian National Committee articulates similar demands: "We can, we must leave behind the current, debilitating constitutional ties! We must discard the botched Stalinist constitution! Together we must declare the fourth Republic!" *Kossuth téri kiáltvány* in Kuruc.info 09.20. 07:57.

39. For example, Kuruc.info's article about the liberals' campaign refers to it as a 'liberal flow of sewage' (*Tamás Molnár: Liberális szennyáradat – megkezdte kampányát az SZDSZ* 09.11. 00:21; Falanx.hu recommends a documentary about Hamas on its opening page; a user on Jobbik chat says, "...a party wants to ensure allowances for fags (and I refuse to call them gays), dilettantes, deviants and those who don't want to work." (*Ami közös bennem és Gyurcsányban* in Jobbik szoba 09.06.08:25.)

40. The text continues as: "Its journalists believe it is also our job to cover issues deemed taboo by other publications, the left- and right-wing party fanfares disguised as media outlets.... Besides being strongly antiliberal, Kuruc.info also wishes to mercilessly point out the actions of the right-wingers who have for 16 years collaborated in the maintenance of left-liberal dominance. The journal is exceptional also in the sense that apart from news reporting, it also relies on the tools of performance in presenting phenomena that endanger Hungarians." *A Kuruc.info lényege* in Kuruc.info 04.10. 03:24.

41. *Magunkról* in Jobbik szoba. The party is working towards the creation of a nation that "knows itself and wants to explore itself". Furthermore, they would like to "save a heritage, and re-create it".

42. Thus, its members are "all individuals of the political Hungarian nation (including the nationalities or Hungaruses), the territory of the Sacred Crown, that is the land of the country, and the ruler." (*A Szentkorona-tan lényegéről röviden* in Szent Korona Rádió 2006. május 10. 21:42.)

43. The banner of Hunhír.hu features the pre-WWII historical map of Hungary, and one of their columns is titled 'Down with Trianon'. Instead of similar obvious declarations, the other sites rather prefer to include the issues of Trianon in different materials, e.g., in their coverage of commemorative meetings, marches. The revisionist idea also appears in some of the speeches on Kossuth Square: "Let Europe hear, let the whole world hear that the Hungarian nation wishes no more to live as slaves to multinational capital and the neobolshevism budding in its wake! A return to the Ancient Virtues! I believe in one God, I believe in one Homeland, I believe in the one Eternal Divine Truth, I believe, I BELIEVE in the resurrection of Hungary!" (Gábor Kistót: *Igazságot Magyarországnak! Nem hazugságot!!!* in Kossuthter.com 10.12. 11:58.)

44. "To obey the call of my country, to give my life so that other Hungarians can live. I believe that be it Fidesz, be it MSZP, be it whomever, in a few years' time 'anyone may come, for the last Hungarian has died'. Now this is what needs to be realised and do something about it." (*Az utolsó magyar* in Jobbik szoba 09.11 11:15.)

45. The continuity between 1956 and 2006 is sanctified by the 1956 veterans who also marched to the streets in 2006: e.g., "According to unconfirmed reports, [1956 veteran] Mária Wittner has led tractors to block the boulevard. (*Drámai a kép Budapesten* in Falanx.hu 09.18). An earlier advertising campaign by Hungarian Television also helps develop the parallels: "If you were a revolutionary, which television would You besiege?, a recent billboard advertisement for the public service broadcaster asked. It seems like the message has acquired a new meaning." (*Ön melyik TV-t foglalná el?* in Falanx.hu 09.19. 06:36.) The latest marching of the "boys of Pest" inspires Italian football fans to write a song: "Fans of Inter sent their message over the weekend from the San Siro match against Milan. The sign saying 'Avanti Ragazzi di Budapest' was already displayed on October 25 by Roma fans, referring to the parallel between the events of '56 and today." (*Az Inter szurkolók üzenete* in Kossuthter.com 11.01 18:16.) Furthermore, shocking pictures of the victims of police brutality were published on Kossuthter.com (10.24. 22:13) under the heading "Blood is red in the streets of Budapest", a direct quote from a poem written to commemorate the events of 1956.

46. Perhaps the best examples of culturally expressed politics are the songs that were inspired by the events. Musician Waszlavik László Gazember composed a recruitment song for the Kossuth Square demonstrators (*Kossuth tér induló* in Kossuthter.com). The leaked recording of the prime minister's speech was used with creative diversity, remixed by DJs in different styles (e.g., dance, Depeche Mode, Latin mix). The DJs attributed explicitly political significance to the success of the songs: "2006. 10. 05.: The mix titled 'Elqrtad' was downloaded 301,000 (!!!) times in 5 days. Thank you! And they say people are turned off politics. Right..." (Pilu in www.stonebridge.hu/pilu/ver_flash.html.)

47. "But in the meantime the Árpád-striped flag rises high. For let us realise this is the symbol of the revolution. Like the flag with the hole was in '56." (Budaházy György: *Suttyó-diktatúra készül* in Kuruc.info 10.27. 11:28.) The blogger Tomcat also defends the árpád-striped flag: "...what's wrong with historical Hungarian symbols? Where have you seen e.g. Americans scorning the eagle, or the French the Gallic rooster? Or even the Germans the German eagle and iron cross? Or the Russians the red star? These are our national symbols. And symbols are not for themselves, there are common values attached to them. By displaying them, the crowd expresses their shared acceptance of these values." (*Forradalmi kiskáté és csócselék-határozó* in Kuruc.info 10.03. 01:34.) Hungarian National Committee member Tamás Molnár expressed similar thoughts: "The organising committee of the moral revolution of Kossuth Square was astonished to find out about the latest attack launched by

the anti-Hungarian internationalists against the historical Árpád flags and national symbols. In the name of the organisers of the demonstrations we declare that these traditional Hungarian symbols create unity, community, and solidarity. They announce inclusion, not exclusion.... they embody a successful Hungarian future. The red-and-white striped flags symbolise a strong, proud, and independent Hungarian constitutional state, the power of the majority." (*Nemzeti összefogást a szélsőbaloldali visszarendeződés ellen!* in Kossuthter.com 10.16. 13:05.)

48. "Have faith in the power of the Sacred Crown, observe its teachings, let yourselves be guided by the Sacred Crown!" (*A délvidéki szolidaritási nagygyűlés üzenete a budapesti tüntetőkhöz* in Kuruc.info 09.21. 20:45.) The blogger Carpathia gives a "lesson in history" to his readers: a liberal politician called the Árpád-striped flag a Nazi symbol, but he is mistaken, because it is, in fact, the flag of the ancient Hungarians (Jobbik szoba 10.18. 09:53).

References

Ayers, J. (1999). 'From the Streets to the Internet: The Cyber-Diffusion of Contention'. *Annals of the American Academy of Political and Social Science 566*, 132–143.

Campbell, A. (2006). 'The search for authenticity: An exploration of an online skinhead newsgroup' *New Media & Society* 8 (2), 269–294.

Chadwick, A. (2006). *Internet Politics. States, Citizens, and New Communication Technologies*. Oxford, Oxford University Press.

Conway, M. (2006). Cybercortical warfare: Hizbollah's Internet strategy. In *The Internet and Politics. Citizens, voters and activists*, Oates, S., Owen, D. and Gibson, R. (eds.), London and New York, Routledge.

Eatwell, R. (2000). 'The Rebirth of the 'Extreme Right' in Western Europe?' *Parliamentary Affairs*, vol. 53, 407–425.

Fiske, J. and Hartley, J. (1978). *Reading Television*. London, Methuen.

Hebdige, D. (1979). *Subculture: The Meaning of Style*. London, Routledge.

Hyde, G. (2002). 'Independent Media Centers: Cyber-Subversion and the Alternative Press.' *First Monday* 7(4).

Jones, A. (1994). 'Wired World: Communications Technology, Governance and the Democratic Uprising'. In Comor, E. (ed.), *The Global Political Economy of Communication: Hegemony, Telecommunication and the Information Economy*. Basingstoke, Macmillan.

Kahn, R. and Kellner, D. (2004). 'New media and Internet activism: from the 'Battle of Seattle' to blogging' *New Media & Society* 6 (1), 87–95.

McCaughey, M. and Ayers, J. eds. (2003). *Cyberactivism. Online Activism in Theory and Practice*. New York, Routledge.

Pickerill, J. (2001). 'Weaving a green web: Environmental protest and computer mediated communication in Britain.' In *Culture and Politics in the Information Age: A New Politics?*, Webster, F. (ed.). London and New York, Routledge.

Pickard, V. W. (2006). 'United yet autonomous: Indymedia and the struggle to sustain a radical democratic network.' *Media, Culture & Society*, 28(3): 315–336.

Reilly, P. (2006). 'Civil society, the Internet and terrorism: case studies from Northern Ireland.' In *The Internet and Politics. Citizens, voters and activists*, Oates, S., Owen, D. and Gibson, R. (eds.), London and New York, Routledge.

Silver, David. 2003. 'Current Directions and Future Questions. In Cyberactivism.' In McCaughey M. and M. D. Ayers (eds), *Online Activism in Theory and Practice*. London – New York: Routledge.

Tsaliki, L. (2003). 'Electronic citizenship and global social movements'. *First Monday* 8 (2).

AUTHORS BIOGRAPHIES

Auksò Balãytienò is associate professor of journalism at Vytautas Magnus University in Kaunas, Lithuania. She had been Head of the Department of Journalism for eight years and in 2006 she assumed the position of the Secretary of the University with responsibilities in information management and communication. Her research and teaching activities focus on comparison of media structures and journalism cultures, media policy and journalism online. She is interested in the role of the media in development of European public sphere. She has been teaching as a visiting professor at universities of Dortmund, Madrid, Ulster, Tampere, Copenhagen, Valencia and Tartu. In 2001/2002, she held Erich-Brost Professorship in International Journalism at the University of Dortmund. She has extensive experience in project administration and coordination and has been actively involved in a number of international projects funded through European Commission, European Science Foundation, Nordic Council of Ministers, Lithuanian State Science and Studies Foundation. She provides scientific consultancy to the media on the impact of the Internet on journalism. Her scientific publications include 3 books and over 70 articles.

Péter Bajomi-Lázár is the editor of the Hungarian media research quarterly *Médiakutató* [Media Researcher], director of research at King Sigismund College and associate professor of communication at the Budapest School of Economics. He earned a Ph.D. at the Central European University's Department of Political Science in Budapest, Hungary in 2004. His book *A magyarországi médiaháború* ("Media War in Hungary") was granted the Pulitzer Memorial Award in 2002. His major publications in English include *Reinventing Media. Media Policy Reform in East Central Europe* (co-edited with Miklós Sükösd, Budapest: Central European University Press, 2003); *Media & Politics* (co-edited with István Hegedıs, Budapest: Új Mandátum Publishing House, 2001).

Péter Csigó is assistant lecturer at Budapest University of Technology and Ph.D. canditate at EHESS, Paris. His research interests include popular media and politics, media commercialization, media reception analysis, popular culture and citizenship, and everyday uses of new media. He is author of several publications in media and political communication studies. One of Csigó's recent articles explores the process of "Late modern individualization and the uses of new media in Hungary" (Napvilág Kiadó, in Hungarian), another one examines TV news' loss of power in the new media environment (Downbreaking News [in English: ICA Conference paper, 2007; in Hungarian: *Médiakutató*, 2005/4]). He is editor in chief of *EastBound*, an electronic journal in media and cultural studies, and has offered courses in media sociology, television and convergence studies, and media reception studies at BUTE, ELTE University and Budapest Corvinus University.

Peter Gross is director of the School of Journalism and Electronic Media at the University of Tennessee. Since 1989, he has directed journalism workshops and lectured in a number of Western and East/Central European countries and former Soviet republics. In 1996, he was a research fellow at the Woodrow Wilson International Center for Scholars in Washington, D.C. He is the author of *Entangled Evolutions. Media and Democratization in Eastern Europe* (Johns Hopkins University Press/ Woodrow Wilson Center Press, 2002) and *Mass Media in Revolution and National Development: The Romanian Laboratory* (Iowa State University Press, 1996), for which he received the 1996 American-Romanian Academy of Arts and Sciences Book Award. He is co-author of *Eastern European Journalism. Before, During and After Communism* (Hampton Press, 1999). He also published several books in Romania, including *Mass Media and Democracy* (Polirom, 2004), *Introduction to Newswriting and Newsgathering* (Editura de Vest, 1993), and *Giants With Feet of Clay. The Post-Communist Romanian Press* (Polirom, 1999). His latest book, *Media and Journalism in Romania* (co-authored with Mihai Coman) was published in Germany in 2006.

Ferenc Hammer is assistant professor at the Institute for Art Theory and Media Studies at the Eötvös Loránd University in Budapest. He teaches and conducts research in the fields of media representations of inequalities and conflict, and in cultural history, including fashion under communism or social histories of colours. In 2006 he was a research fellow at Birkbeck College in the Cultures of Consumption Programme, funded jointly by the Economic and Social Research Council and Arts and Humanities Research Council in the UK. In 2002/3 he was a fellow at the International Policy Fellowship of the Center for Policy Studies at Central European University and the Open Society Institute in Budapest, conducting research on policy implications of media portrayals of social inequalities. His most recent publication is "Sartorial Manoeuvres in the Dusk: Blue Jeans in Socialist Hungary" In F. Trentmann & K. Soper (eds.) *Citizenship and Consumption*. London: Palgrave Macmillan, 2008 (in print).

Aida A. Hozic is associate professor in the Department of Political Science at the University of Florida. She is a graduate of the University of Sarajevo, Bosnia and Herzegovina (B.A.), The Johns Hopkins University - School of Advanced International Studies (M.A.) and the University of Virginia (Ph.D.). Hozic has also taught at Central European University in Budapest and Bogazici University in Istanbul. A recepient of MacArthur, Fulbright, Soros and IREX fellowships and grants, she is the author of *Hollyworld: Space, Power and Fantasy in the American Economy* (Cornell University Press, Ithaca, NY, 2001) and a number of articles on politics, economy and representation of the Balkans.

Karol Jakubowicz is Chairman, Intergovernmental Council of the UNESCO Information for All Programme, and a member of the Council of the Independent Media Commission in Kosovo. He also heads Working Group 2 of the COST A30 ACTION "Eastmember of the Council of the Independent Media Commission in Kosovo. He also heads Working Group 2 of the COST

A30 ACTION "East of West: Setting a New Central and Eastern European Media Research Agenda" of the European Science Foundation He has taught at the Institute of Journalism, University of Warsaw (1997-2002) and has been Visiting Professor at the Institute of Journalism, University of Dortmund, and at the Amsterdam School of Communications Research, University of Amsterdam. He has extensive experience working as a journalist and executive in the Polish press, radio and television, as well as for the National Broadcasting Council of Poland. He has been active in the Council of Europe, in part as Chairman of the Steering Committee on the Media and New Communication Services (2005-2006). He has been a member of the Digital Strategy Group of the European Broadcasting Union, and is an expert working with the Council of Europe, UNESCO, European Union and OSCE. His scholarly and other publications have been published widely in Poland and internationally. His most recent publications include *Rude Awakening. Social and Media Change in Central and Eastern Europe* (Hampton Press, U.S., 2007), and *Public Service Broadcasting: The Beginning of the End, or a New Beginning?* (WAIP, Poland, 2007; in Polish).

Ildikó Kaposi is assistant professor of communications at the American University of Kuwait. She got her Ph.D. in 2006 from the Department of Political Science at Central European University, Budapest. Her research interests include e-democracy, ICTs and politics, political communication, media and democracy, and the political economy of mass media. Her doctoral thesis "Virtual Deliberation" was based on an ethnographic research of an online political discussion forum in Hungary. She worked with Stephen Coleman on a research on e-democracy in emerging democracies, published in 2006 as "New Democracies, New Media: What's New?" by the University of Leeds and the e-Governance Academy. Currently she is co-investigator on the "Kuwait Oral History" project funded by the Kuwaiti Council for Private Universities Executive Committee for Research and Development. Her publications include "Between State Control and Bottom Line: Journalism and Journalism Ethics in Hungary" (with Éva Vajda), in J. Atkins (ed.), *The Mission. Journalism, Ethics, and the World,* 2002. She published articles in Hungarian about the public service media, the rise of commercial television in Hungary, press subsidies, and the transformations of the Hungarian press. She was co-founder and editor of the Hungarian academic journal *Médiakutató* [Media Researcher].

Epp Lauk is professor of journalism at the Department of Journalism and Communication, Univeristy of Tartu, Estonia. She was also head of the Estonian Press Council and vice president of the Baltic Association for Media Research. In 2004, Lauk taught at the University of Oslo's Department of Media and Communication, where she held Master's seminars on the historical development of the methods and forms of media censorship in different political regimes in Europe during the communist and post-communist periods. She has been teaching, conducting research and publishing in the fields of journalism history, society and media in transition, media literacy; freedom of speech and censorship. Selected publications include: "Historical and Sociological Perspectives on the Development of Estonian Journalism" (1997); "A Landscape After the Storm: Development of the Estonian Media in the 1990s." (2003); "Some Reflections on the Comparability of Newspaper Markets" (2004).

Mónika Mátay is associate professor of history at the Economic and Social History Department at Eötvös Lóránd University in Budapest, Hungary. In addition to her home institution, she taught the history of the media, cultural history, historiography, and other subjects as visiting scholar at Rutgers University, Central European University, University of Triest, Montclair State University, University of Debrecen, the California Education Abroad Program, Institute for Social and European Studies (Koszeg), Mathias Corvinus College (Budapest), and Historical Anthropology Program (Budapest). Her research focuses on the history of the European public sphere, mentality, everyday and private life, and private conflicts such as divorce and inheritance skirmishes. She is on the editorial board of a Hungarian academic journal, *Médiakutató* [Media Researcher]. She is the co-editor of several books and journals including a collection of essays *Fin-de-siècle Budapest, the sinful city* (Budapest, 2005). Her book, *Games at the Court: Divorce in Debrecen 1793–1848* was published in 2006 (Debrecen). Currently she is working on her next book where she analyses the media representation of the scandalous murder of a prostitute in Budapest, 1885.

Alina Mungiu-Pippidi is professor of democracy studies at the Hertie School of Governance in Berlin. She was a researcher in political communication at Harvard University after completing a Ph.D. in Social Psychology in 1995 at the University of Iasi in Romania. She was a Visiting Scholar at Stanford, Harvard, the European University Institute and the St. Antony's College at Oxford University, among others. She is a board member of the *International Forum of Democracy Studies* and the *Journal of Democracy*. She has consulted for Freedom House, UNDP and World Bank on issues of state building in the Balkans and former Soviet Union. She founded in 1996 the think tank Romanian Academic Society, which has since played an important role in promoting good governance in Romania. She is the co-editor of *Nationalism after Communism* (CEU Press, 2005) and the author of *Deux Villages*.(l'Harmattan, Paris, 2005), as well as of numerous journal articles and book chapters on the postcommunist transition and the European Union.

Zrinjka Peruško is associate professor of media studies at the Department of Journalism, founder and Chair of the Centre for Media and Communication Research (CIM) of the Faculty of Political Science, University of Zagreb. She was Head of the Department for Culture and Communication at the Institute for International Relations (IMO), Zagreb, until May 2006. She holds a PhD (1998) and B.A. (1985) in sociology and M.A. (1990) in communication studies from the University of Zagreb. She was Fulbright Visiting Professor at the Department for Communication and Culture, Indiana University, Bloomington, USA (2001–2002). Her academic interests are media policy and system changes in democratic transition, especially regarding media concentration, diversity and pluralism in Croatia and Central and Eastern Europe. Her most recent texts include the Croatian chapter in *Television Across Europe: Regulation, Policy and Independence*. EUMAP & NMP: Budapest, 2005; "Media and Civic Values" in Ramet, S. and. Matiç, D, (eds) *Democratic transition in Croatia*. Texas A&M University Press, 2007; Her book on media and democracy (*Demokracija i mediji*, Barbat) was published in Zagreb in 1999. Peru‰oko is member of the Group of Specialists on Media Diversity of the Council of Europe which she chaired in 2006 and 2007, UNESCO International Program for Development of Communication (IPDC, 2000–2003, 2005–2008), Croatian National Commission for UNESCO (2004-2008), and was member of the Council of Europe Advisory Panel on Media Diversity (AP-MD).

Helena Popoviç graduated from the Faculty of Philosophy, Department of Sociology in Zagreb (2004), and holds an MA in Sociology and Social Anthropology from the Central

European University in Budapest (2005). She also completed a one-year programme at the Centre for Women's Studies in Zagreb (2003). Popović is currently employed at the Department for Culture and Communication, working as research fellow on the project Media, Communication and Cultural Aspects of Civil Society. In 2004 she participated in the international research project "The Information Wars surrounding the Balkans since 1991" (organized by the KomTech-Institute for Communication and Technology Research, Solingen, the Institute for Political Science, University of Innsbruck, and the Institute of Design and Assessment of Technology, Vienna University). Her research interests include media anthropology, visual communication, political communication, civic activism in the context of new media, and gender representation in the media. Popović is member of the CEU Alumni Association and the Croatian Sociological Association.

Colin Sparks is professor of media studies and director of the Communication and Media Research Institute (CAMRI) at the University of Westminster in London, UK, where he has spent almost his entire professional career. He holds a BA in English Literature from the University of Sussex and a PhD in Cultural Studies from the Centre for Contemporary Cultural Studies at the University of Birmingham. His research interests, however, lie more in the political economy of the media than in cultural studies. He has published widely on tabloid media, media in transitional societies, and on media and globalization. His most recent book is *Globalization, Development and the Mass Media* (Sage, 2007). He is on the editorial boards of a number of scholarly journals, including *Javnost/The Public*, *Westminster Papers in Communication and Culture*, and *Media, Culture and Society*, of which he was a founding member and is at present Managing Editor. His current research interest is in extending the study of media in transition beyond cases of post-communism to try to account for developments in other kinds of societies that have also experienced recent major changes.

Miklós Sükösd is associate professor at the Department of Political Science, and academic director of the Center for Media and Communication Studies at Central European University in Budapest. (B.A./M.A. in Sociology and Cultural Studies, Institute of Sociology, Eötvös Lóránd University, 1985; M.A. in Sociology, Department of Sociology, Harvard University, 1994; Ph.D. in Political Science, Hungarian Academy of Sciences 1992.) His research, teaching and consultancy concerns political communication, media policy, and environmental politics, especially in Central and Eastern Europe. Sükösd also serves as Chair of COST Action A30 "East of West: Setting a New Central and Eastern European Research Agenda", a European media research network that produced the present book. He has published 20 books, several book chapters and articles including, *Public Service Television in the Digital Age: Strategies and Opportunities in Five South-East European Countries* (with A. Isanović, Sarajevo: Mediacentar, 2008)**;** *Anarchism in Hungary: Theory, History, Legacies* (with A. Bozóki, Boulder, Colorado: Social Science Monographs, 2006); *Reinventing Media: Media Policy Reform in East Central Europe* (with P. Bajomi-Lázár, Budapest: Central European University Press, 2003); "Democratic Transformation and the Mass Media in Hungary: from Stalinism to Democratic Consolidation in Hungary" in R. Gunther and A. Moughan (eds.), *Democracy and the Media: A Comparative Perspective* (Cambridge: Cambridge University Press, 2000).

European Cooperation in
Science and Technology

COST – the acronym for European **CO**operation in the field of **S**cientific and **T**echnical Research – is the oldest and widest European intergovernmental network for cooperation in research. Established by the Ministerial Conference in November 1971, COST is presently used by the scientific communities of 35 European countries to cooperate in common research projects supported by national funds.

Web: www.cost.esf.org

The COST A30 Action "*East of West: Setting a New Central and Eastern European Media Research Agenda*" is a 4 year long (2005–2009) COST research project that has established an outstanding network, bringing together approximately 70 distinguished media and communications researchers from 27 countries in Western and Eastern Europe. The main objective of the Action is to increase the knowledge concerning media production, media reception and use, and the political implications of the transformation of the media landscape in the Eastern and Central European context. The Action aims at organizing a European social science research network with a clear focus on emerging problems of Central and Eastern European media in a comparative perspective. The Action is also building a network of media studies and communication research centers, higher education programs and departments in Western and Eastern Europe.

Web: www.costa30.eu

SETTING SCIENCE AGENDAS FOR EUROPE

ESF provides the COST Office through an EC contract.

COST is supported by the EU RTD Framework programme.